STARCK'S PRAYER BOOK

Revised Concordia Edition

From the German Edition
of Dr. F. Pieper

Translated and edited by W. H. T. Dau;
Revised by William C. Weedon

CONCORDIA PUBLISHING HOUSE • SAINT LOUIS

Cataloging-in-Publication Data

Starck, Johann Friedrich, 1680-1756.
  [Taegliches hand-buch in guten und boesen tagen. English] Starck's prayer book : from the German edition of Dr. F. Pieper / translated and edited by W.H.T. Dau ; revised by William Weedon. — Rev. Concordia ed.
      p. cm.
  Includes index.
  ISBN-13: 978-0-7586-1421-6
  ISBN-10: 0-7586-1421-7
  1. Devotional exercises. 2. Lutheran Church—Prayers and devotions.
      I. Dau, W. H. T. (William Herman Theodore), b. 1864. II. Weedon, William. III. Title.
  BV4834.S713 2009
    242—dc22
  2009011456

1 2 3 4 5 6 7 8 9 10   18 17 16 15 14 13 12 11 10 09

CONTENTS

Part 3: Prayers for Various Spiritual and Bodily Blessings

Book 2: For the Use of Those Afflicted

Book 3: For the Use of the Sick

Book 4: For the Use of the Dying and Those Attending Them

Book 5: Prayers for Special Occasions

PREFACE TO THE NEW EDITION

I didn't like it. Not at first. I do not think I am all that unusual in my opinion either. Starck's prayers are meat for the soul in an age accustomed to devotional cotton candy. They challenge the Christian on all sorts of levels. Yet the longer I lived with these prayers, the more I realized how great this work truly is. It is a treasury of prayers that ultimately will not wear out because the foundation common to all the prayers in this book is simply the Word of God, praying back to God the very things He has said to us.

The fluidity with which Starck moves in and out of scriptural language and allusion draws the person who faithfully uses this book into the eternal conversation between God and humanity. Bonhoeffer once observed that not knowing how to pray is a most painful situation. Yet that painful situation is not at all uncommon today. How does one offer petition? Thanksgiving? Confession? Adoration? How can we speak to God in a way that is pleasing and acceptable to Him?

The answer Starck gives is only in and through and with our blessed Lord Jesus Christ. He leads us in our prayers, and they are offered, then, in confidence and joy. Because we pray in and through and with our Lord Jesus Christ, Starck's prayers are brazenly Trinitarian. No "Christo-monism" here. Here is the richness of speaking to our heavenly Father, to our only Savior Jesus Christ, and to the Holy Spirit, our comforter. Starck's prayers do what all genuine prayers do: they draw the reader into the internal life of the Blessed Trinity and teach the joy of living in His presence throughout the day, throughout the week, throughout the year, throughout the good times and the bad. In the great faith that can come only by the working of the Holy Spirit through the saving Gospel, Starck pulls us in the joy of receiving from God's loving hand both adversity and joy.

This book is offered in slightly updated garb, to Christians of the twenty-first century who live in a world very different from that inhabited by a Lutheran clergyman of the seventeenth century, in the hope that those who use it will discover, in the vibrant faith that rings through and shapes these prayers from another era, the voice of the faith once delivered to the saints.

Soli Deo Gloria!
William Weedon
Editor

PREFACE TO THE 1921 EDITION

Johann Friedrich Starck, a favorite author of evangelical Germany in the era of Pietism, has more than any other writer of devotional literature maintained his hold on the hearts of practicing (not merely professing!) Christians. Even Arnd's *True Christianity*, booksellers assert, does not equal the influence that Starck still exerts on thousands of Christians by his *Prayer Book*.

The leading facts of Starck's life are these: He was born October 10, 1680, at Hildesheim in Hanover. His father had formerly been a citizen of the old imperial city of Frankfurt-on-the-Main. After completing the regular course of studies at the *Gymnasium* at Hildesheim, young Starck entered the University of Giessen, where his inner life received permanent impressions in the devotional exercises *(Erbauungsstunden)*, which his theological teachers May and Lange conducted with a select company of students. After his graduation from the university, Starck had to wait a considerable time before he was called to a pastorate. This time he spent partly as assistant in the evangelical church at Geneva, where Reformed influence was dominant, partly as instructor in his ancestral home city of Frankfurt. In 1715, he was called to the pastorate of Sachsenhausen, and in 1723 he became pastor, first of the Barfuesserkirche, then of the Spitalkirche at Frankfurt. In 1742, he became a member of the Consistory, and labored with unbroken strength as preacher, pastor, and author till a great age; he died July 17, 1756.

Starck's predecessor in Frankfurt had been Philip Spener, "the father of Pietism," and it fell to Starck's lot to water what Spener had sowed. For thirty years he conducted "private" devotional exercises on Sunday afternoons. These exercises, which were attended by a number of earnest souls, were private only in as far as they were distinct from the regular public services at the church. At these exercises Starck endeavored to impress the evangelical truths of Christianity, the priceless privileges of the grace of Christ and the Christian ordinances, and the practical duties of a consistent Christian life on his individual hearers with true pastoral tact, and became to many a spiritual pedagogue and guide of great wisdom and power. Starck had a Savior's eye and heart for the lowly and forsaken, and sought them out for special instructions. For servants who could not attend the public services he wrote many an edifying tract; the poor and needy found in him not only a sympathetic advisor but also a ready, unwearied, and generous helper.

Starck loved nothing sensational, nothing that was for mere display in matters of religion. Christian life, to him, was real and earnest, to be conducted in a sober mind. He was always bent on its practical applications to every pursuit and action, and on enlisting really the whole of a person in the service of the Master. While he maintained the confessional position of the Evangelical Lutheran Church, and rejoiced to be a member of it, his teaching was tinged with the peculiarities of the Pietistic tendency. To mention only one of these, the sharp line of demarcation between justification and sanctification that is seen in the writings of the apostle—the line that divides the gracious forgiveness of sin for Christ, an act exclusively of God, from the godly life which follows wherever the absolution of the Gospel has been accepted by a penitent and believing heart—sometimes becomes faint in Starck's writings. Thus what God alone does, and what the regenerate child of God does by the prompting of the Holy Spirit, are not always kept strictly apart. However, this defect occurs only occasionally, perhaps least in the *Prayer Book*, and there are so many sections in Starck's writings that are entirely free from error that Starck himself supplies the needed correction for his occasional deviations from the straight path of the sound doctrine.

When Dr. F. Pieper, years ago, examined the *Prayer Book* with a view to applying, wherever needed, this self-correction of Starck, this was done with no sacrilegious hand, but really to secure for Starck a fuller reward of his faithful labors for a sincere and zealous Christian life. The revision really helped Starck to speak his full Christian mind everywhere, and to discard what was of inferior value or even misleading in his presentation of Christian truths. The chief object, of course, was to secure the minds of less trained Christian readers against false impressions that they might receive from a misstatement in their favorite. The same reasons have prompted the present translation of the *Prayer Book* into English. It was begun ten years ago, but was interrupted for quite a number of years at the end of the First Division, partly because the translator lost the aid of his stenographer, partly because the work at Concordia Seminary grew to unusual dimensions. That he was at all enabled to complete it is due in no small measure to the help of the Seminary Board, which during the last two years has engaged a stenographer, who is at the service of members of the faculty. Grateful acknowledgment for this aid is herewith made.

The translation is made from the German edition of Dr. Pieper of 1900. Comparison was possible to the translator only with the editions published by Kohler and the German Literary Board. Each of these editions has its distinct merit, the latter excelling by its faithful adherence to the original, its apt renderings, and happy paraphrases. Both renderings have proved helpful to the translator, though he decided to prepare an entirely new translation from the original, and even at the risk of being faulted with Germanisms permitted the peculiar style and thought connection of the original to be reflected in the translation. At times, too, the exact thought of the original required a return to Luther's translation of the Bible. Nor has the use of texts from apocryphal books, which Starck has used with power, been altogether avoided. To guard against a misconception, the translator would state here that he does not regard these books as inspired, but, with Luther, considers some of the apocryphal books instructive reading matter. Nor does he feel any Puritanic qualm in such use.

The reproduction of Starck's poetry has been attempted, so far as the present translator is aware, in only one instance, and that with indifferent effect, as was to be expected. The poetry for the present edition has been gathered from many sources, not a few of them at the present time unknown to the editor; and though it lacks that direct connection with the meditational portions preceding which is seen in Starck's poetry, it is hoped that it may be found to possess value also independently of the particular sections to which it is found attached.

The four last divisions or "books" of the *Prayer Book* were prepared during the distressing years of the late European war. This work proved to the editor a great mental and spiritual relief. It was a luxury to spend many an hour in the company of a person on whom the spirit of prayer has been poured out in such abundant measure as on Starck. It was faith-confirming and inspiring work that the translator was permitted to do. He can offer no better wish to the readers of this book, now that it starts on its voyage to the increasing English homes and hearts in our church community, than this, that the light and strength, the cheer and comfort that has come to him out of the pages of this book in many a weary and despondent day may stream into the hearts of the readers, even though they be free, as the editor hopes they are, from all weariness and despondency.

W. H. T. DAU

Book I

For Use in Health

Part One: Morning, Noon,
and Evening Devotions

PREPARATION FOR THE DIVINE SERVICE

EXHORTATION

*One thing have I asked of the LORD, that will I seek after: that
I may dwell in the house of the LORD all the days of my life, to gaze
upon the beauty of the LORD and to inquire in His temple.* Psalm 27:4

Immediately after the fall, God, in His wisdom, directed Adam, the
first man, to offer sacrifices. Adam's children, Cain and Abel, were, in
turn, directed by their father to do the same. (Their sacrifice is expressly
mentioned in Genesis 4:3–4.) These sacrifices were not offered in silence!
In fact, at such sacrifices they praised God for the benefits received from
Him, and also proclaimed the name of the Lord. Those offering the sacrifices confessed their sins, prayed to God for forgiveness, and declared
their faith in the coming Messiah, Jesus Christ, who was to shed His
blood for humanity like the animals offered in sacrifice. The patriarchs
retained this form of worship until in the wilderness God commanded
the ark of the covenant to be erected, which afterward furnished the pat-
tern for Solomon's temple.

Further, in the Old Testament, God singled out the seventh day as a day of rest and commanded that day to be kept holy. In its external meaning this commandment does not apply to Christians. Just like other laws in the Old Testament having to do with particular practices, persons, seasons, and locations, this, too, is an entirely external affair; in the New Testament, Christians have been given freedom by Christ regarding all such matters. Still, in the exercise of our Christian freedom, we Christians in the New Testament also keep festival days and days of rest, especially Sunday, so we have time and opportunity to attend the Divine Service, to gather with fellow Christians to hear and study God's Word, to receive the Sacraments, and to praise God with our hymns and prayers.

On the arrival of a day of this kind, a believing Christian should free the mind from earthly matters and stop working, prepare by prayer for the coming Sunday or holy day, praise God for the many blessings received during the past week, and look up in the Bible or hymnal the assigned readings for the Feast or Sunday and meditate on them, thus being prepared for reverently hearing the Word.

PRAYER

Gracious and merciful God, I come before Your holy face today with praise and thanksgiving. You have graciously kept me during the past week and bountifully blessed the work of my hands. You have preserved my going out and my coming in. You have kept me in all my ways and have shown me so much kindness in body and soul. For all of this I praise and magnify You with my whole heart! I will forget what is past, lay down the burden of all my labors and callings, turn my mind to heaven alone, to my God, that I may rejoice in You.

O gracious God, grant that I may spend the coming Sunday [or Feast] in Your fear and grace. Keep me from evil company, lest Satan by his wicked attacks keep me from attending the Divine Service. Help me refuse to follow his enticements. Guard me, lest I spend this day in idleness, wastefulness, immorality, or sinful amusements, and thus inflict great harm on my soul. Grant me Your Holy Spirit that I may gladly hear and learn Your Word this day. When Your Word is being preached, open my heart that I may listen to it and receive it within me as a precious treasure. Help me to build myself up in my Christian faith and to grow in the knowledge of the truth. Grant that the Word I hear at church may change and sanctify me. As I grow in years, grant that I may also grow inwardly, in faith and piety. Grant me grace to become a new creature and to be and remain a living member in the Body of my Lord Jesus. Grant that I may reverently close my worship and carefully treasure up what I have learned. Grant me grace to be constantly mindful of the Word that I have heard, so that I may walk, speak, live, and act according to it, and thus prove not to be a forgetful hearer, but a doer of the Word. Grant me to keep the Sabbath always in this manner until You bring me to the unending joys of heaven, to the Sabbath that never ends, through Jesus Christ, my only Redeemer and Savior. Amen.

HYMN

Lord, open now my heart to hear,
And through Your Word to me draw near;
Let me Your Word e'er pure retain;
Let me Your child and heir remain.

Your Word inspires my heart within;
Your Word grants healing from my sin;
Your Word has pow'r to guide and bless;
Your Word brings peace and happiness.

To God the Father, God the Son,
And God the Spirit, Three in One,
Shall glory, praise, and honor be
Now and throughout eternity. LSB 908:1–3

EXHORTATION TO MORNING PRAYER ON SUNDAY

Give ear to my words, O LORD; consider my groaning. Give
attention to the sound of my cry, my King and my God, for to You
do I pray. Psalm 5:1–2

Our whole life should be spent in nothing else than prayer and thanksgiving. Every day we should call upon God in prayer for His blessing, aid, assistance, and grace. When we have obtained our requests, we should return heartfelt thanks. Accordingly, when you awake from sleep in the morning, first of all, raise your eyes to heaven. Do not start thinking about your business and work; do not immediately hurry after some gain. First, kneel down, return thanks to God, and commend yourself to His gracious protection. Do not fear that you lose too much time by devoting a brief half hour in the morning to prayer, to reading a chapter of the Bible or some devotional book. No. The time you spend in prayer will bring you thousandfold blessing in your work, and what you have read will be like honey in your mouth all day long.

So, when you awake and arise in good health in the morning, consider first how many good Christians, who are probably more pious than you, have spent the past night in anguish and sorrow, in pain and sickness, in terror and great unrest, while you experienced none of this. Next, consider that others during the night suffered misfortune, damage, danger, and tribulation, while you lacked nothing. Thank God for His protection! Then pray to God at the break of day to keep you in His grace during the day, that you may commit no sin either against Him or your neighbor. Pray God to be at your side during the day, to keep and bless you as you go about the callings you have received. Then, surrender yourself to God that you may remain in His love, have Him in your thoughts, and not offend Him knowingly or willingly. Finally, do not doubt that the Lord will graciously hear your groaning and your prayer, and will give and grant you whatever is profitable to the salvation of your body and soul throughout the day.

MORNING PRAYER ON SUNDAY

Lord, be pleased to hear my voice in this early hour. Early will I come into Your presence and will give heed to You, O gracious God. You are worthy to receive praise and glory and honor. Who would not fear You, O King of the nations? Who would not honor You, O loving Father? I come before You in this morning hour and give You humble thanks because during this night You have been a fortress around me and mine. You have again renewed to me Your goodness and faithfulness. Be with me and protect me this day also in all my ways. Grant that this day in particular may be a day for building up and refreshing my soul. According to Your compassionate love, You have given to us Your precious Word, and you have ordered that it should be publicly proclaimed. Enlighten, sanctify, and instruct my soul, that I may gather treasures from Your Word that will comfort me in danger and death, in crosses and trials, and which neither moth nor rust can corrupt and no thief can break in and steal.

I am glad because I have Your promise that we shall go into the house of the Lord and that our feet will stand inside your gates, O Jerusalem. One thing have I desired of the Lord that I will seek after: that I may dwell in the house of the Lord all the days of my life to behold the beauty of the Lord and to inquire in His holy temple. My God, let it be my delight today to hear Your Word, to be built up in You, to sing hymns of praise and thanks to Your glory, to pray fervently, and to make my heart an offering to You. How lovely is Your dwelling place, O Lord of hosts! My heart sings for joy to the living God.

Grant that I may not be a forgetful hearer, but may become a doer of the Word. Open my heart, as You once opened Lydia's, that I may receive the seed of Your Word with joy. Then seal my heart, that Satan may not rob me of Your Word. Grant that I may today lay a firm foundation for my Christian faith, for the knowledge of Jesus Christ, for my trust, for my charity, for my self-denial, and for my becoming dead to the world. Grant that I may ponder Your Word during the entire week, that I may live according to it and bring forth a crop of good fruits. Guard me against temptations, lest Satan attack me by his instruments and I be drawn into the sinful practice of the world, and thus bring a grievous curse upon me. Be pleased, O Lord, to accept my worship at church and at home, my praying, my hearing, my reading, and my singing. Be Yourself, O my Jesus, my teacher, that I may grow in the inner man. Yes, dwell in me by faith until I shall be inseparably united to You in heaven above.

O Holy Spirit, enter in, And in our hearts Your work begin, Your dwelling place now make us. Sun of the soul, O Light divine, Around and in us brightly shine, To joy and gladness wake us That we may be Truly living, To You giving Prayer unceasing And in love be still increasing. Amen.   *LSB 913:1*

BELIEVING CHRISTIANS GLADLY HEAR AND LEARN GOD'S WORD ON SUNDAYS

EXHORTATION

How lovely is Your dwelling place, O LORD of hosts! My soul longs, yes, faints for the courts of the LORD; my heart and my flesh sing for joy to the living God. Psalm 84:1–2

The Word of God is the greatest treasure that He has given to us, for His Word is to lost sinners the Word of life! It brings us out of sin into righteousness, out of death into life. Besides, God has shown us a special favor in establishing the holy preaching office so His Word may be proclaimed and explained publicly to all who gather to hear it. God has promised to give a special blessing to the public preaching of His Word. All those who reverently hear the Word will share in this blessing.

When the day arrives that the Christian Church has appointed for the public preaching of the Word, Christians should not just stop work and be idle. People who are not Christians do that well enough! No, Christians should let this be the chief concern: to hear and learn God's Word. Whenever people are busy hearing and learning the Word of God, a true Sabbath is being observed. Without this happening, the day cannot be considered a Sabbath in any Christian sense.

Because of these things, a true Christian should be careful not to waste the day in laziness and idleness. Nor should the day be spent in partying and eating and getting drunk. Nor should the true Christian miss hearing God's Word because of greed or frivolous activity. Rest assured that much depends on the proper manner of keeping Sunday. A great blessing is attached to it. Who knows the reason why so many people live under a curse, devoid of God's blessing? Our ancestors used to say: "As the Word of God *you* treat, so *God* will treat your bread and meat." In conclusion, having heard God's Word, we should keep it in a good and honest heart; we should live according to it; we should at once reduce its rules of life to practice. At the same time, we should gather a supply of comforting, instructive, and powerful Scripture passages to use in times of tribulation and death.

PRAYER

This is the day that the Lord has made, let us rejoice and be glad in it! I thank You, O God, for the countless blessings You have showered on me today. On a Sunday, Jesus, my Savior, rose from the grave. On a Sunday, the Holy Spirit was poured out on the apostles. So it is proper that on this day I call to mind my redemption through Jesus Christ and the gift of the Holy Spirit, who was poured on me abundantly in Holy Baptism.

I thank You for Your holy and pure Word, which was preached to me this day as You have ordained for the salvation of my soul. I thank You for all the bodily and spiritual blessings received from Your fatherly hand throughout my life. I thank You because You have guided, led, preserved me from my youth, and shown me so many favors in body and soul. Who could ever recount all Your blessings?

However, this day will be not only a day of thanksgiving but also a day of prayer. I beg You, my God and Father, grant me to spend this day in Your fear. Keep me from temptations, vain thoughts, and evil company. How I wish that every artery in me were a tongue and every drop of blood a voice to praise and glorify You, O Blessed Trinity, Father, Son, and Holy Spirit! I pray that not a single hour would go by in which I do not show forth Your praise!

Seal the Word that I have heard in my heart. Grant that I may diligently ponder it, let it govern my life, and that I may walk accordingly. As I have now grown to be a week older, grant that I may increase in Your knowledge, in love and piety, and that I may grow in the inward self. I pray for the gift of Your Holy Spirit. May He put me in mind of Your Word during this week and throughout my life. May He guide, govern, and lead me. Bless my labor and employment, and grant me to continue to live in Your grace for the rest of my days and years, until at last I reach heaven, where I may, with thanksgiving, keep the eternal Sabbath.

This is the day the Lord has made; He calls the hours His own. Let heav'n rejoice, let earth be glad And praise surround the throne. Amen.

LSB 903:1

SUNDAY HYMN

O day of rest and gladness,
O day of joy and light,
O balm of care and sadness,
Most beautiful, most bright;
This day the high and lowly,
Through ages joined to bless,
Sing "Holy, holy, holy,"
The triune God confess.

This day at earth's creation
The light first had its birth;
This day for our salvation
Christ rose from depths of earth;
This day our Lord victorious
The Spirit sent from heav'n,
And thus this day most glorious
A threefold light was giv'n. LSB 906:1–2

BELIEVING CHRISTIANS CONSIDER THE DAILY AND ETERNAL SABBATH

EXHORTATION

So, then, there remains a Sabbath rest for the people of
God. . . . Let us therefore strive to enter that rest. Hebrews 4:9, 11

God had strictly prohibited the Jews from doing any work on the Sabbath day. So strictly and rigidly did God maintain the Sabbath in the Old Testament that He caused a person who was gathering wood on the Sabbath to be stoned, as we read in Numbers 15. This commandment does not concern us Christians in the New Testament, as St. Paul shows in Colossians 2.

However, the Sabbath of the Jews was a shadow, a type, of the true, spiritual Sabbath that Christians keep every day. It does not consist in ceasing from work and giving one's self over to idleness, but it is rather a person's ceasing from sin. This means that, as the Jews by God's commandment rested from their manual labor, so a Christian by God's command ceases every day from impiety and malice. A Christian is careful not to speak evil against God or neighbor, not to do evil either alone or in others' company, not to be misled by others, but to keep the soul unspotted from the world.

While, on the one hand, Christians avoid these things, Christians are also zealous, on the other hand, to remember God frequently as they go about their vocations. They earnestly beg God to grant them His Holy Spirit to govern and comfort them. That is the spiritual and daily Sabbath the children of God keep all the time.

Those who are eager to keep this daily Sabbath can rest assured that they will keep the eternal Sabbath in the life everlasting, which consists in this: that the believers and the chosen children of God are delivered from all bodily labor, from all crosses, tribulations, and from all sins; that they behold God face-to-face, are occupied with Him and praise and worship Him without end. Oh, what a holy and glorious Sabbath! This Sabbath will never be disturbed. However, it will only be obtained by those who continue in faith and in the love of Jesus unto death.

PRAYER

Holy and merciful God, I hear Your Holy Word, by which You made me Your beloved child and delivered me from the dominion of the devil. Therefore, I remember on this day the spiritual Sabbath. I call to mind that I must cease from sin and consecrate my body and soul, indeed, my whole life to You. From now on, my God, my daily labor will by grace consist in doing Your will, not mine. It will consist in expelling, by Your power, evil desires and thoughts, so that You alone may rest in me, enlighten me, and sanctify me more and more. O God, grant that this spiritual Sabbath celebrated in my heart may never be disturbed. You, O Lord, pray within my heart, sing within my heart, and teach within my heart. In that way my heart will be a temple consecrated to You. And when I have finished the days of my life according to Your counsel, and at the same time have finished the spiritual Sabbath, O God, then let me enter the heavenly, unending Sabbath. There Your saints in everlasting rest and blessed heavenly joy praise You in the temple of glory. There I shall join with angels and cherubim in singing to You: Holy, holy, holy. O my God, grant that I may obtain such happiness. Amen.

HYMN

Oh, what their joy and their glory must be,
Those endless Sabbaths the blessed ones see!
Crowns for the valiant, to weary ones rest;
God shall be all, and in all ever blest.

In new Jerusalem joy shall be found,
Blessings of peace shall forever abound;
Wish and fulfillment are not severed there,
Nor the things prayed for come short of the prayer.

We, where no trouble distraction can bring,
Safely the anthems of Zion shall sing;
While for Your grace, Lord, their voices of praise
Your blessed people shall evermore raise.

Now let us worship our Lord and our King,
Joyfully raising our voices to sing:
Praise to the Father, and praise to the Son,
Praise to the Spirit, to God, Three in One. LSB 675:1–4

EVENING PRAYER FOR SUNDAY

Lord, abide with me; for it is toward evening and the day is now far spent. O living and almighty God, Your works are past knowing, and the goodness You show our human race is beyond all telling! I will tell of Your grace and truth, of Your love and mercy, for You have me shown me today much kindness in body and soul. You have fed my soul with the bread of life. You have let me drink from the living fountain. Your Word has been sweeter than honey to my mouth. Let Your Word always be a light to my way all my days, that I may order my walk according to it; then I will not stumble or fall from Your grace.

You have also been my deliverer, my comforter. In temporal matters, You have allowed me to live in good health until this evening. I am not worthy of all the mercies Your love has showered on me. Come to my side, O protector, now that my weary limbs lie down to rest. Guard me and embrace me in Your sheltering arms. Let me always be a light in the Lord, and let me never have fellowship with the unfruitful works of darkness. Grant that Your Word I have heard and learned may in the future spring up within me as a holy seed. Grant that its fruits may be perceived in my life by godliness, by fear of You, by being dead to the world and dedicated to You alone. Be my protection and my shade against the heat of affliction and the fiery darts of Satan. The Lord is my light and my salvation; whom shall I fear? The Lord is the stronghold of my life; of whom shall I be afraid? Turn from me and from my family fires, floods, and every misfortune, and let all who are in sorrow, sickness, or on the point of death enjoy Your rich grace. Then our mouth will be filled with Your praise at the break of day, and we will tell of Your goodness, which You have shown us in body and soul.

If I have not heard Your Word with the zeal I ought to, forgive me; do not on that account withdraw Your grace from me. During the coming week, cause me to be entirely renewed. Give me new love and desire for You, and new eagerness to serve and obey You. Grant that I may avoid and flee the sins that I have committed during the past week, in order that everyone will see that I have not heard Your Word in vain. Help me to ponder diligently that I have an immortal soul, in order that I may be more concerned about my soul than my body. O my God, I am turning my eyes to Your resting place; in doing so I remember my grave, where I shall rest until You raise me up on the Last Day with joy to the life that never ends. Go, then, my body, into your chamber and rest; but you, O my soul, enter into the wounds of Jesus. Amen.

HYMN

O Christ, who art the light and day,
Thou drivest night and gloom away;
  O Light of Light, whose Word doth show
  The light of heav'n to us below.

All-holy Lord, in humble prayer
We ask tonight Thy watchful care.
  O grant us calm repose in Thee,
  A quiet night, from perils free.

Our sleep be pure from sinful stain;
Let not the tempter vantage gain
  Or our unguarded flesh surprise
  And make us guilty in Thine eyes.

Asleep though wearied eyes may be,
Still keep the heart awake to Thee;
Let Thy right hand outstretched above
Guard those who serve the Lord they love. LSB 882:1–4

BELIEVING CHRISTIANS GIVE THANKS TO GOD AFTER HEARING THE DIVINE WORD

EXHORTATION

But be doers of the word, and not hearers only, deceiving yourselves. James 1:22

All divine blessings are misused by the children of the world. This applies also to the hearing of the divine Word. There is a big difference in this respect between the children of the world and the true children of God: The children of the world imagine that they may devote Sunday to their customary immorality and pleasures. They hold the view—utterly false—that, being at leisure, they may indulge their flesh. The children of the world, at best, go to church in the morning to observe a religious ritual, but in the afternoon they head out for sinful pleasures and come home late, filled with vain thoughts, sinful passions, and worldly follies, yes, maybe even drunk.

The children of the world do not heed the Word that was preached to them. When you ask them on Monday what they learned in church the day before—what they heard, what they remember—they can tell you nothing. Right away the devil has taken the Word out of their hearts, so that they should not believe it and be saved (Luke 8:12). And even when they still do remember a few things, they do not put them into practice. In the Old Testament, the Lord chose for the sacrifice animals that chewed the cud; He loves those most who chew on and ponder the Word they have heard or read, meditating on it and drawing from it new nourishment, strength, and vitality. That is how people are built up in their faith to eternal life.

PRAYER

O God, rich in grace, You have granted me time to celebrate Your praises this Sunday. But how can I ever thank You enough? How can I ever praise and glorify You adequately? You have permitted me to hear Your Holy Word today so that I should believe rightly, live piously, and finally die saved. You have revealed to me Your gracious will. You have taught me what things to shun and what to do. You have not left Yourself without witness, so that no one has an excuse. You give us Your Holy Word and Sacraments, that we should use them as Means of Grace for our salvation. Your Holy Spirit wants to employ these means to teach, enlighten, sanctify, strengthen, and confirm us in the faith.

O merciful God, keep me from being a forgetful hearer and make me a doer of Your Word. What good is all hearing to me, if I do not act accordingly? And so, O God, seal to my heart what I have heard and read. Make Your Word in me living, powerful, and energetic. O Keeper of the door, close my heart as soon as the Word of life has entered in for my edification, lest Satan rob me of it and I go home empty. Grant that I may take warning, O God, at the example of the thousands who hear Your Word but are not converted, do not become more godly or put away their wickedness, their evil doings, and their sinful habits, but instead grow more wicked and bold and never change. What good does their church attendance, their singing, their hearing, and their praying do for such people? Will not the Word condemn them the more because they have heard the Word of the Lord, have known it, and yet have not lived according to it?

O God, grant that I may become more pious and godly this week. Grant that I may daily ponder the Word that I have heard, and that I may talk about it with my family, that I may rejoice in it and always live according to it. I have heard from Your Holy Word that I am to be meek, humble, and merciful—grant me grace always to remember this! Keep me from lapsing into anger or from seeking revenge or from being proud and unmerciful. Grant me to love my enemies, deny myself, do good to the poor, and show kindness to the afflicted. I have been told that I must fight against my evil desires and thoughts, put off the old self and put on the new self, and live soberly, righteously, and godly in this present world. Grant me the strength and ability to daily practice these virtues and become proficient in them. Although I may at the start discover in myself a great deal of weakness, grant me to follow after holiness, so that I may more and more purify myself from all contaminations of flesh and spirit.

Lord, let me do with Your Word what the children of this world do with their earthly treasures: let me lock it away safe and secure in my heart. Grant me strength to keep in my heart, as precious and cherished treasures, Your holy truths, Your precious doctrines of faith, Your powerful exhortations to holiness of life. Yes, Lord, grant that I may daily increase my hoard of them, in order that in all difficult situations, in crosses, afflictions, sickness, and, above all, when the hour of my death arrives, that I may again and again take from them suitable texts for my comfort. Yes, grant me, O my God, that I may daily increase in stature, wisdom, and piety, in the fear of God, in the knowledge of Your will, and in favor with You and with all people.

Almighty God, Your Word is cast Like seed into the ground; Now let the dew of heaven descend And righteous fruits abound. Let not the sly satanic foe This holy seed remove, But give it root in every heart To bring forth fruits of love. Let not the world's deceitful cares The rising plant destroy, But let it yield a hundredfold The fruits of peace and joy. So when the precious seed is sown, Life-giving grace bestow That all whose souls the truth receive Its saving pow'r may know. Amen. *LSB 577:1–4*

HYMN

God's Word is our great heritage
And shall be ours forever;
To spread its light from age to age
Shall be our chief endeavor.
Through life it guides our way,
In death it is our stay.
Lord, grant, while worlds endure,
We keep its teachings pure
Throughout all generations. LSB 582

MORNING PRAYER
FOR MONDAY

Let me hear Your loving-kindness in the morning, for in You, O God, do I trust. Make me to know where I should walk, for to You I lift up my soul. O holy and good God, You alone are wise. You have created the heavens and laid the foundations of the earth. You have ordained the alternations of night to day and day to night, of labor to rest and rest to labor, so that people and animals may be refreshed. I praise and glorify You in this morning hour for Your wisdom and Your fatherly faithfulness. You have graciously heard my prayer. You have preserved me through the night from sickness and other ills. You have surrounded me and all that is mine with Your protection. Lord, great are Your works, which You reveal to us. Your mercy is in the heavens, and Your faithfulness reaches to the clouds. I slept while You kept vigil. Sleeping, I was like a person who is dead, but You have raised me up again to see the light of the sun.

O my God, be also today my helper and Savior, my friend and comforter, my refuge and the God who has mercy on me. Let Your eyes keep watch over me, that with Your safe conduct I may go about my calling unharmed and may, if it be Your will, reach the evening in safety. O my God, grant that Your blessing may attend me everywhere. In all that I begin in Your name grant me counsel and success, and let my will be wholly conformed to Your own. With the risen sun let the light of Your Holy Spirit arise in me, that I may spend the day in Your fear and love, and in obedience to You. Create in me a clean heart, O God, and renew a right spirit within me. Cast me not away from Your presence and take not Your Holy Spirit from me. Let the Spirit lead, teach, and guide me so that I may not knowingly sin against You this day. When I am tempted to sin, let Him remind me, and thus by His inward warning keep me from committing sin.

I put on my clothes; Lord Jesus, clothe me with the robe of Your righteousness. I wash my hands; Lord Jesus, wash me with Your holy blood from all my sins. Guard me, that I may never walk in the counsel of the ungodly, nor sin in the seat of the scornful. For to be their friend means to be Your enemy. If I would have the friendship of the world and would engage with the children of this age in their sinful and unholy ways, You would become my enemy. O my God, impress on my heart the words: "Walk before Me, and be blameless" (Genesis 17:1). Oh, how many begin a new week, but do not live to see the end of it! When the week is ended, they are sick or even in their graves! Therefore, grant that I may always pursue holiness, without which no one will see You. Make me zealous to be godly in my speech, blameless in my walk, and holy in my thoughts. May I always be found in a state of grace and shelter in Your wounds, O Jesus. May the grace of the Father keep me! May the love of the Son sanctify me! May the communion of the Holy Spirit make me fruitful in all good works!

My Maker, hold me in Your hand; O Christ, forgiven let me stand; Blest Comforter, do not depart; With faith and love enrich my heart. Amen. *LSB 876:4*

THE BELIEVING CHRISTIAN PRAYS FOR GOD'S BLESSING AT THE BEGINNING OF THE WEEK

EXHORTATION

And whatever you do, in word or deed, do everything in the name of the Lord Jesus, giving thanks to God the Father through Him. Colossians 3:17

We have reason to pray and to make requests of God at the beginning of each day; how much more should believing Christians lift up their heads and eyes to God when we are about to begin a new week! How many people were healthy and strong on Sunday, the first of the week, but buried the Saturday following! How many have begun the week happy and prosperous, but before the week was ended, misfortune overwhelmed them like a storm at sea and they closed the week in anguish and woe, with much weeping and hand-wringing. Now, my dear Christians, the same may happen to us. So we should turn to God in prayer at the very beginning of the week.

Believing Christians, however, should call upon God for His Holy Spirit to sanctify their hearts and to govern them, lest they fall into sins, offend God, do violence to their conscience, grieve their neighbor, and burden their souls. During the week they should not forget to pray and to worship God, but should be diligent in attending Divine Service and the prayer offices not only on Sunday but also during the week. In addition, they should daily read and ponder God's Word at home with the family. Because success does not depend on our rushing and hurrying to work, we should especially call on God for His blessing; and also have our thoughts on God while at work. We should begin, pursue, and end our work with prayer. We should be careful of what we say, should lead a Christian life, should have God always before our eyes, and remember that one week after another passes away until finally our last week arrives, when we must die and give an account of ourselves to the Lord. When believing Christians do this, they can begin the week with God's blessing and end it under His protection. Even if God permits that week to become filled with many crosses, believing Christians rejoice that God will be and remain their helper, Savior, and defender.

PRAYER

O loving and merciful God, with Your help I begin this new week. I do not know what will happen to me in the course of it. Much evil and misfortune can happen in a single day—how much more in a whole week! And so I come to You at the very beginning of the week and commend myself wholly to You. O my God, grant me Your Holy Spirit so that He may sanctify, lead, and govern me, bearing witness with my spirit that I am Your child. Bless me this week. Bless my going out and my coming in. Bless the labor of my calling and occupation. Bless every step I take. I lift my eyes to the hills. Where does my help come from? My help comes from the Lord, the maker of heaven and earth. O Lord, if You lead me, I shall not stray. If You keep me, I shall not fall. Let Your faithfulness and mercy guard me in all my ways. Bless all that I have, and let Your blessing prosper me.

O my God and faithful Father, protect and keep me from all harm, danger, and misfortune. Let me remain under Your gracious protection day and night. Guard my house on every side like the house of Job. Let the holy angels camp around me and my possessions, and I will dwell securely. Hear my prayer when I cry to You, and let me not leave the throne of grace without being heard. Keep me from grievous sins. Show me Your ways, O Lord; lead me in Your truth. Unite my heart to fear Your name. Grant that this week I may become more pious and godly, that I may increase in my knowledge and love of You. As I am leaving behind one week and entering another, grant that I may grow inwardly. Let me add to my faith, virtue; and to virtue, knowledge; and to knowledge, self-control; and to self-control, patience; and to patience, godliness. If the last week of my life has now arrived, grant me assurance of Your grace. If this week should become a week of crosses to me, strengthen me by Your Holy Spirit, that with Your mighty aid I may be able to endure and overcome them all. Be my helper in every need, and deliver me from every trouble. I commend myself, my body and soul, and all that I have, together with all pious Christians, to Your gracious and fatherly protection.

Direct, control, suggest this day All I design or do or say That all my pow'rs with all their might In Thy sole glory may unite. Amen. *LSB 868:5*

HYMN

Forth in Thy name, O Lord, I go,
My daily labor to pursue,
Thee, only Thee, resolved to know
In all I think or speak or do.

The task Thy wisdom has assigned,
O let me cheerfully fulfill;
In all my works Thy presence find,
And prove Thy good and perfect will.

Thee may I set at my right hand,
Whose eyes my inmost substance see,
And labor on at Thy command,
And offer all my works to Thee.

Give me to bear Thine easy yoke,
And ev'ry moment watch and pray,
And still to things eternal look,
And hasten to Thy glorious day.

For Thee delightfully employ
Whate'er Thy bounteous grace has giv'n,
And run my course with even joy,
And closely walk with Thee to heav'n. LSB 854:1–5

EXHORTATION TO EVENING PRAYER ON MONDAY

In peace I will both lie down and sleep; for You alone, O
LORD, *make me dwell in safety.* Psalm 4:8

Gratitude is a beautiful grace, delightful to both God and people. Accordingly, believing Christians should always consider when the evening arrives that it is God who permitted them to live through the day. It is deplorable that many persons spend days, weeks, months, yes, even years, without considering what God has done for them. These people enjoy His protection, aid, and help, yet never bother to thank Him. They regard it as a matter of course that they are well and happy and spend their time in prosperity. They think that God owes it to them to protect them and cause all to be well with them. And so, O Christians, withdraw from such ungrateful persons. When you have passed the day, aided and protected by God—when the sun is about to set, and it is toward evening—lift up your eyes toward heaven in thanksgiving and prayer.

Give thanks to God because He has kept you from misfortune during the day. Consider that while no harm has touched you, no doubt many people have suffered great misfortunes, perhaps have lost their health and find themselves sick in bed and in great pain this evening, though they were well this morning. Or think of those who have been reduced to poverty during the day by some disaster that they had no inkling of in the morning. Pray to God for the forgiveness of your sins. Think back over the day and consider your words and actions. Have you spoken anything against God or your neighbor during the day? Have you done anything against your conscience and the Christian faith? Do not prepare for or go to bed before you have asked God to forgive you. Consider that God may require your life this very night. Make your peace with Him before you close your eyes. Pray to God for His protection and the guardian care of His holy angels, that they may ward off all evil from you. Think of God even during the night, if you happen to lie awake. Give thanks to Him, and you will sleep calmly and peacefully in His arms and under the protection of His holy angels.

EVENING PRAYER FOR MONDAY

In peace I will both lie down and sleep, for You alone, O Lord, make me dwell in safety. O eternal and almighty God, these are my evening thoughts now that I am about to seek my rest. How shall I ever thank You enough for guiding my going out and my coming in so that I have not struck my foot against a stone? You have given me food and drink. You have comforted and refreshed me. Your visitation has strengthened my spirit, and through You and Your grace I still live this day. All these and all other mercies are voices that call me to praise You. And so, bless the Lord, O my soul, and all that is within me, bless His holy name! Bless the Lord, O my soul, and forget not all His benefits!

Forgive me, O Lord. In mercy, forgive me if I have not kept the example of my Lord Jesus before my eyes, but have put Your commandments out of my mind and lived with the world and according to its ways. Alas, O Lord, I accuse myself and repent in dust and ashes. The day is now spent. Cause my sins to vanish like mist, and remember them no more—now or ever. In true sincerity of heart I promise that I will strive to serve You from now on and to guide my steps by Your Word.

Protect me this night against all the wiles of the enemy, against misfortune and all evil. When I fall asleep, dear Lord Jesus, close my eyes and impress on my heart Your bleeding image, that I may never forget You. Grant that my yearning soul may dream about You. Grant that I remain firmly united to You, so that also in my sleep I may be Yours. Be my light in darkness, my help in trouble. When You said, "Seek My face," my heart said to You, "Your face, O Lord, I will seek." I do not know of any other helper but You, O almighty God. My Father is with me; why, then, should I fear, though I lie alone and sleep? My Jesus, the light of my soul, is with me, though my bodily eyes are closed. The Holy Spirit is with me and maintains His witness in my heart, assuring me that I am a child of God, though I lie heedlessly asleep. Since I am enfolded in the protection of the triune God, I sleep in safety like Jacob; I sleep unconcerned as a child on its mother's breast; I sleep protected like Peter.

Jesus, Savior, wash away All that has been wrong today; Help me ev'ry day to be Good and gentle, more like Thee. Let my near and dear ones be Always near and dear to Thee; O bring me and all I love To Thy happy home above. Amen. *LSB 887:2–3*

MORNING PRAYER FOR TUESDAY

Awake, O sleeper, arise from the dead and Christ will give you light! O merciful God, Your goodness and faithfulness are renewed every morning. I thank and praise You with all my heart that You have again permitted me to rise from bed in health, and have protected my body from harm and my soul from sin. How wonderful is Your loving-kindness, O God! The children of men put their trust under the shadow of Your wings and are sheltered there by Your might. The darkness is past, and I see again the light of the sun. Grant me grace to walk in Your light this entire day, and to flee from all the works of darkness. I count that day lost on which I have served the world, on which I allowed the world's speech, actions, and thoughts to dominate me. I know I will have to render a strict account for all these things one day before Your judgment seat.

Instead, let me consecrate myself wholly to Your service with body and soul. Grant that I may wish nothing, propose and think of nothing but what pleases You. Indeed, grant that I may always live, speak, and act as though I must die this day. Now that this dark night is past and I have reposed in Your arms as Your child and am granted a new lease on life, there is no place for me to turn but to You. I knock at the door of Your grace. I turn again to the fountain that flows with blessing after blessing and help after help. What You, O Lord, bless is blessed forever. When You open Your hand, You satisfy the desire of every living thing.

Give me good counsel when I need counsel. Direct my plans and purposes according to Your will. Kindle in me the flame of divine love, that this day I may show my faith by my works, abide in sincere love toward You and toward my neighbor, and reach the evening unharmed in conscience. To You, O Lord, do I cry! Do not be silent to me, lest I become like those who go down to the pit. Hear the voice of my prayer as I lift my hands toward Your holy sanctuary. Let the prayer of the afflicted, the downcast, the sick, and also the prayer of my family and of all God-fearing people find a hearing at Your throne of grace.

May we Thy precepts, Lord, fulfill And do on earth our Father's will As angels do above; Still walk in Christ, the living way, With all Thy children and obey The law of Christian love. Amen. *LSB 698:1*

BELIEVING CHRISTIANS REJOICE IN THEIR REBIRTH

EXHORTATION

Blessed be the God and Father of our Lord Jesus Christ! According to His great mercy, He has caused us to be born again to a living hope through the resurrection of Jesus Christ from the dead, to an inheritance that is imperishable, undefiled, and unfading, kept in heaven for you. 1 Peter 1:3–4

If any boast, let them boast in the Lord. If any rejoice, let them rejoice in those things that can make them eternally happy. Now, if there is anything in which believers may boast and at which they may rejoice, it is certainly at their rebirth, the blessed fact that they have been baptized and thereby made children of God.

In Holy Baptism we have obtained the status of being children of God. He is our Father and we are His children! He will sustain, preserve, and provide for us. He will never forsake us. We have also received the righteousness of Jesus Christ. All that Christ has obtained for us by His suffering and death has been given to us and made our own in Holy Baptism. We have truly been united to Him. He is the vine and we are the branches. Through Him we obtain new strength for every good work, light, wisdom, and grace. There has been imparted to us the indwelling of the Holy Spirit! He makes His home in us, sanctifies our hearts, governs our tongues and our lips, and enables us to order our lives according to the Word and will of God. By this indwelling power of the Holy Spirit we are more and more drawn away from evil, and we begin to grow in faith, in godliness, and in the fear of God—just like a newborn baby grows in years and strength. We also obtain everlasting salvation! When this life is over, we shall share eternal joy and glory.

When we ponder things like this, how can we not rejoice in God with all our heart? But we need to be on guard that we do not lose the grace so freely given us. We are to walk worthy of the great calling we have received, and not slip again into the ways of the unregenerate and worldly. Instead, as loving children, we are to obey our heavenly Father, follow our Lord Jesus, and not resist the promptings of the Holy Spirit. As we do these things, we will surely enjoy the love, grace, and assistance of the triune God in this age, and we will obtain everlasting life in the age to come.

PRAYER

O mighty God and dearest Father, how can I ever know, praise, and magnify Your love enough? You have been so deeply concerned for my soul, lest it should perish. What glory You have imparted to me in Holy Baptism by adopting me as Your own child! People boast about the happiness they derive from their noble birth, from the fact that they have risen to positions of honor, from their great wealth and pretentious possessions. But I know that greater than all of these is the happiness I enjoy in being Your child. For, if we are Your children, we are also heirs, heirs of God and joint-heirs with Christ, provided we suffer with Him that we may also be glorified together. Since I am a child of God, my heavenly Father will keep, govern, protect, and provide for me. Yes, He will never forsake me in any trouble. Since I am a child of God, I have in Him not only a powerful support in life but also great comfort in death. Since I am His child, He will refresh, restore, and comfort me, and when I leave this world, He will bring me safely to the life of joy that never ends.

O dearest Father, grant me Your Holy Spirit that He may continually remind me of this glory. I am still in this world and dwell among the children of Adam. Keep me from sinning and doing evil with the children whose hearts belong to this world, and from conforming myself to their ways. If I see anyone engaged in or speaking evil, remind me that I am a child of God and that such sins and evil habits are not fitting for me. Grant me the strength to say cheerfully: You whose portion is in this life, know that my birthright and heavenly heritage with God will not be bartered for your passing pleasures, vanities, and customs! O my Jesus, You know that I love You and that I am sincerely grieved that I do not at all times and in all ways love you as I should and as I desire to do. Be pleased to accept at least my good intention. Grant that I may lead a life of faith and godliness, of holiness and purity, of childlike humility. Let me love, honor, fear, and follow You, that I may live and die as Your child, and as Your child attain to heavenly joys.

In Baptism we now put on Christ—Our shame is fully covered With all that He once sacrificed And freely for us suffered. For here the flood of His own blood Now makes us holy, right, and good Before our heav'nly Father. O Christian, firmly hold this gift And give God thanks forever! It gives the power to uplift in all that you endeavor. When nothing else revives your soul, Your Baptism stands and makes you whole And then in death completes you.   *LSB 596:4–5*

HYMN

Baptized into Your name most holy,
O Father, Son, and Holy Ghost,
I claim a place, though weak and lowly,
Among Your saints, Your chosen host.
Buried with Christ and dead to sin,
Your Spirit now shall live within.

My loving Father, here You take me
To be henceforth Your child and heir.
My faithful Savior, here You make me
The fruit of all Your sorrows share.
O Holy Spirit, comfort me
When threat'ning clouds around I see.

My faithful God, You fail me never;
Your promise surely will endure.
O cast me not away forever

If words and deeds become impure.
Have mercy when I come defiled;
Forgive, lift up, restore Your child.

All that I am and love most dearly—
Receive it all, O Lord, from me.
Let me confess my faith sincerely;
Help me Your faithful child to be!
Let nothing that I am or own
Serve any will but Yours alone. LSB 590:1–4

EVENING PRAYER ON TUESDAY

The Lord is on my side; I will not fear, for what can anyone do to me? Thus, O gracious and loving God, I may speak to You in this evening hour. I give You humble thanks that You have allowed me to complete this day under Your fatherly protection, Your loving care, Your gracious guidance, and Your abundant blessings. Lord, Your goodness is great and Your mercy is without limit. The Lord is near to all who call upon Him, to all who call upon Him in truth. He will fulfill the desires of all who fear Him. He will hear their cry and save them.

But, my God, how swiftly the day has passed! Like an arrow shot from the bow, so swiftly do our years fly. And so, make me to know my end and the measure of my days so that I may remember always how frail I am. Behold, You have made my days a few handbreadths, and my lifetime is as nothing before You. We must all appear before the judgment seat of Christ, so that each one may receive what is due for what he has done in the body, whether good or evil. And so I enter into judgment with myself and inquire: My soul, how have you spent this day? Have you thought about anything good? Has God remained united with you, or have you driven Him from you by deliberate and intentional sins? My mouth, what have you spoken today? Have you spoken what is honest, chaste, and good? Have you spread abroad God's praises? Or have you overflowed with lewdness and foolish talk? Where have you gone, my feet? What acts have you performed and committed, my hands? What have you listened to, my ears? What have you looked at, my eyes? What has been your desire, study, and aim today, my heart?

O my God, if I am to answer all these questions, how shall I stand? O Lord, with the passing of this day remove my transgressions. O Jesus, blot out my sins with Your holy blood. O Holy Spirit, assure me of the forgiveness of all my sins before I fall asleep. When I am thus acquitted of my guilt, O Blessed Trinity, I shall calmly go to sleep, and tomorrow I shall be more careful to avoid all that may grieve You. My Father, let Your love cover me and all that is mine. My Jesus, in Your wounds I rest in peace and safety. O Holy Spirit, before I fall asleep, breathe in my heart the last sigh with which I commend my spirit into the hands of God.

I, a sinner, come to Thee With a penitent confession. Savior, mercy show to me; Grant for all my sins remission. Let these words my soul relieve: Jesus sinners doth receive. Amen.   *LSB 609:4*

MORNING PRAYER ON WEDNESDAY

When I awake, I am still with You, O gracious and loving God, my rock, my fortress, my deliverer, my shield, the horn of my salvation, and my strong tower! I lift up my voice at this early hour to the throne of grace and give You thanks because during the past night You have spread Your wings above me and preserved my body and soul from all harm. Blessed be the Lord every day, and blessed be His holy name forever and ever. My God, You continue my life from day to day, in order that I may prepare myself for eternity and yield my soul to You as Your possession and dwelling. You have created me for a life without end. You are not willing that I should perish, but that I should repent and live. Grant that I may employ this day in working out my own salvation in fear and trembling. It is now midweek. Three days have passed without ill fortune to me. If it pleases You, let me spend the remaining three under Your protection and grace. When I walk in the midst of trouble, refresh me. When my enemies gather around me, come to my rescue and help me. O Jesus, my mediator, make my heart Your dwelling place, that I may hurry to You in every event, trouble, distress, and in the hour of death, and obtain help from You. If God is for me, who can be against me? O dearest Savior, let me walk in Your holy footsteps today; let me live as You lived. Then I will readily escape the temptations of the world, and the wiles of my own heart.

Be at my side while I go about my calling. I say with full assurance: "Lord, I will not let You go unless You bless me." Bless me whether I sleep or wake. Bless every step. Bless me in all things. Let Your blessing rest on me. Let me be blessed by You, and never take Your blessing from me. As I go about my calling, let my heart diligently turn to You. When my heart inclines to become entangled in sin and to seek enjoyment in the desires of this age and its sins, give me strength to wrest it from these things and to sink it into Your love, O my Father, and into Your wounds, O Jesus, that it may not stray from Your fellowship, but may come to the evening in Your company. If a conflict awaits me today, help me to overcome. If a sinful thought suggests itself in my heart, or a naughty word rises to my lips, strengthen me that I may suppress it by Your Spirit. I commend all my household to You, and all who are afflicted or sick. Cause the light of Your grace to arise and shine in the midst of their suffering.

Let each day begin with prayer, Praise, and adoration. On the Lord cast ev'ry care; He is your salvation. Morning, evening, and at night Jesus will be near you, Save you from the tempter's might, With His presence cheer you. Amen.

LSB 869:2

Believing Christians Pray God to Wean Them from the World

EXHORTATION

Do not be conformed to this world, but be transformed by the renewal of your mind, that by testing you may discern what is the will of God, what is good and acceptable and perfect. Romans 12:2

When believing Christians reflect that the love of the world, like a weed, grows spontaneously in the soul, while the fear and love of God, like a beautiful and fragrant plant, must be planted in the heart and diligently and constantly tended, they will understand with what concern and anxiety they are expected to guard their hearts. According, they should be aware that the world is both inside and outside of them. Inside them there is the world in the form of evil lusts, wiles, desires, and thoughts of their heart. Outside them there is the world in the form of the examples, enticements, and temptations of evil people. All these evils true Christians must resist: the lusts and the thoughts arising in them, by prayer and supplication; the allurements of the world, by avoiding its society, habits, customs, and mode of living. Now, since it is not in their own power to do this, they must fervently pray God for help and assistance.

This separation of the world must not be effected by locking themselves away, shutting themselves in, and refusing to speak to or associate with anyone. It must consist in refusing to join the children of this age in their sins, declining to imitate their works and deeds. For if we were to have absolutely nothing to do with the children of this age, we would have to, as Paul indicates, go out of this world entirely. We are to be in the world, as Joseph was in Egypt, as Lot was in Sodom, as Daniel and his companions were in Babylon. All these did not practice the wicked ways of the people and cities where they lived. This separation from the world is not to be effected merely for show and for a few days, when we are about to go to confession and to the Lord's Supper, but we are to be constantly engaged in this work. The world must be turned out of our hearts every day, and every day Jesus must enter our hearts.

PRAYER

Merciful God, lover of mankind, how great is Your loving-kindness toward us! You patiently bear with our many faults and weaknesses. You do not punish us as our sins deserve. You have opened my eyes by Your Word, so that I now know myself and sadly have seen how depraved my heart really is. I feel the world both inside and outside me. I find the world inside me: the evil desires of my heart, my sinful inclinations and promptings to evil. I find the world outside me: evil people who would entice and mislead me by their sinful examples and temptations. O Lord, my heart, which is evil by nature, takes greater delight and pleasure in these things than in Your Holy Word. Woe is me, that I have such a long time, so often, and to such a degree allowed myself to be enticed and drawn away by this age! I am ashamed to lift up my eyes to Your presence when I think of the follies of my youthful years. Alas! I have served the world better than You, O my God! I have tried more to please the world than You. I have clung to the world more than to You. With these things I have offended You, have wounded my conscience, and aroused Your anger.

Behold, my God, I return and repent in dust and ashes. O my God, remove the love of the world from me so that You and You alone may possess and rule my heart. Let Your Holy Spirit sanctify me completely and drive all worldliness from me. Make me consider the sad end of the children of this age so that I cling to You and not to the world, that I obey You and not the world. Draw me back when I am about to run and sin with the world again. Keep me always in Your fear, and remind me constantly that You have created me for Your service, and that I should daily put on the new self created in God's likeness in true righteousness and holiness. Cause the world to become more and more distasteful to me. Let me with ever-growing relish strive after holiness, the fear of God, and the joys of heaven. Grant that I may constantly despise the lust of the world, which passes away. Grant me to run from the lusts and joys of this world, because after one has drained them, there follows nothing but anxiety, unrest, an evil conscience, and the destruction of the soul. Pluck from my heart whatever is still remaining in it of the world, and plant Your holy fear within me, so that I may carefully avoid all that is evil out of love for You.

Come, Holy Ghost, Creator blest, And make our hearts Your place of rest; Come with Your grace and heav'nly aid, And fill the hearts which You have made. To You, the Counselor, we cry, To You, the gift of God Most High; The fount of life, the fire of love, The soul's anointing from above. Amen.

LSB 498:1–2

HYMN

What is the world to me
With all its vaunted pleasure
When You, and You alone,
Lord Jesus, are my treasure!
You only, dearest Lord,
My soul's delight shall be;
You are my peace, my rest.
What is the world to me!

The world seeks to be praised
    And honored by the mighty
Yet never once reflects
    That they are frail and flighty.
But what I truly prize
    Above all things is He,
My Jesus, He alone.
    What is the world to me!

The world seeks after wealth
    And all that mammon offers
Yet never is content
    Though gold should fill its coffers.
I have a higher good,
    Content with it I'll be:
My Jesus is my wealth.
    What is the world to me?

What is the world to me!
    My Jesus is my treasure,
My life, my health, my wealth,
    My friend, my love, my pleasure,
My joy, my crown, my all,
    My bliss eternally.
Once more, then, I declare:
    What is the world to me! LSB 730:1–4

EVENING PRAYER FOR WEDNESDAY

I lay down and slept; I awoke, for the Lord sustained me. O holy, gracious, and only-wise God, this day is growing short and You have again shown me that You are the true Father, from whom the whole family in heaven and on earth is named. According to Your infinite goodness You have cared for me, so that I have not lacked any good thing. O Lord, I am not worthy of the least of all Your mercies, and of all Your faithfulness to me. What shall I render to You for all the benefits You daily bestow upon me, though I am but dust and ashes? Do not despise the humble offering of praise that I bring You in this evening hour, and continue to look upon me with Your favor.

Forgive me, O gracious God, whatever sins I have committed against You this day in thought, word, or deed. Help me to lay aside, with my clothes, every evil habit, impropriety, and sin. Grant that tomorrow and for the rest of my life I may hate and turn from them. Help me to put off the old self that belongs to my former manner of life and never let me put it on again. During the coming night let me, together with my relatives and the members of my household, sleep in peace and safety under Your protecting grace.

The sun has gone down; O Lord Jesus, the true sun of righteousness, shine with Your splendor in my heart. Fill me while I sleep with good impulses, so that when I wake up, Your name and the thought of You may fill my heart. Grant that in sleepless nights I may meditate on my bed and think of Your goodness, faithfulness, and gracious guidance, and thus drive away all useless cares and sinful thoughts. Renew my strength by sleep, so that I may wake up in the morning refreshed and cheerful. As the shepherd watches over his flock, even so let me be commended in body and soul to Your care, O my Good Shepherd.

But if for the trial of my faith, my patience and my hope, You would send affliction on me by day or night, remember, O my God, that I am Your child; that without You I can do nothing; and that it is for You, my Father, to send me deliverance and help from Your holy place. Cause me to rejoice in sorrow. Comfort me in affliction. When I am forsaken, kindly take me in. Let Your ever-present and all-seeing eye keep me by day and by night from sin. I lift up my eyes unto the hills. Where does my help come from? My help comes from the Lord, the maker of heaven and earth.

Now my evening praise I give; Thou didst die that I might live. All my blessings come from Thee; Oh, how good Thou art to me! Thou, my best and kindest Friend, Thou wilt love me to the end. Let me love Thee more and more, Always better than before. Amen.   *LSB 887:4–5*

MORNING PRAYER FOR THURSDAY

Give ear to my words, O Lord; consider my groaning. Give attention to the sound of my cry, my King and my God, for to You do I pray. O gracious and merciful God, I praise and magnify You in this morning hour, not only because like a father You have kept and protected me from my youth but also because You have been my protection and aid during the past night. You have permitted me once again to rise in health for Your praise and to behold the welcome light of day.

O Lover of life: what is man that You are mindful of him, and the son of man that You care for him? I lay in sleep, completely forgetful, but You have been with me and guarded my spirit. You have surrounded me and my house with Your angel hosts, so that no harm could touch me and no misfortune hurt me. You have refreshed me with sweetest rest, which many who are sick, sorrowing, or troubled have perhaps had to do without. And this You have done for me, even though I have deserved the same chastisement as any of them. Indeed, I have deserved far worse because I have not been grateful to You, my Creator, preserver, and redeemer—though I owe You unending thanks for the innumerable blessings I have received during all my life. I have not offered to You unceasing praise and humble thanks as I ought to have done.

By Your grace I will begin today to make amends for what I have neglected through my own fault. I promise in this morning hour that I will serve You with body and soul, and yield myself wholly to You. I am determined that my mouth will not offend today and load me down with heavy responsibility because of foolish or sinful talking. I will keep my feet from straying down sinful paths. My eyes shall not gaze longingly on forbidden things or people. I will not use my hands for any unrighteous deed. I will close my ears to all false teaching and bad language that can corrupt good manners. On the contrary, I will devote myself, O Blessed Trinity, to Your service. O Lord, dwell in me. Sanctify me. Guide and cleanse me more and more by Your grace.

Let me seek today the company of godly persons, and if, through my calling, I should unexpectedly be brought into the company of the wicked, protect my heart and conscience against their sinful words and polluting deeds. Bless my labors, so that I may perform them with joy and cheerfulness, in childlike reliance on Your providing care. Let me experience Your blessing at every point. And now, I lift up my eyes to the hills. Where does my help come from? It comes from the Lord, the maker of heaven and earth. It is He who shall bless, prosper, and preserve me, here in time and throughout an eternity of joy.

Abide with Your protection Among us, Lord, our strength, Lest world and Satan fell us And overcome at length. Abide, O faithful Savior, Among us with Your love; Grant steadfastness and help us To reach our home above. Amen. *LSB 919:5–6*

BELIEVING CHRISTIANS DESIRE TO FOLLOW JESUS

EXHORTATION

If anyone would come after Me, let him deny himself and take up his cross and follow Me. Matthew 16:24

Believing Christians should pray daily according to Psalm 139:24: "Lord, see if there be any grievous way in me." If careful travelers diligently inquire about their way, believers should just as diligently ascertain the way to heaven. Many deceivers have gone out into the world, says St. John, so true Christians take great care not to be deceived.

Accordingly, true Christians do not follow the children of the world who seek to entice them in their merry, but sinful, gatherings; for by so doing they would place their souls in very great danger. Still less do they follow the impulse of their evil thoughts, but every time a thought is suggested to them, they inquire, "Is it right?" Nor do believing Christians follow Satan and his allurements, but they follow the Holy Scriptures, which tell them what they are to believe, what they are to do, and what they are to leave undone. Scripture is their rule of life. What the Scriptures disallow, that they detest with all their heart.

In particular, they follow the Lord Jesus, who has given us an example that we should follow in His footsteps. The footsteps of Jesus are humility, chastity, kindness, and godliness. These virtues our Lord practiced in His life on earth for our imitation. To follow Him truly in a holy life means to practice these virtues. They also follow the examples of other good Christians. Whenever they observe that their fellow Christians are fervent in prayer, reverent toward God, charitable to the poor, or eager in other virtues, they strive to imitate them. They are to continue thus to follow after holiness until death. Then these words of St. John in Revelation 14:4 will be fulfilled: they "follow the Lamb" into the life that never ends!

PRAYER

O my God and Lord, my only desire is to live in such a way that after death I may enter into the joy of heaven! I always rejoice when I read in Your Word that the elect in heaven follow the Lamb wherever He goes. But I also know full well that whoever wants to follow the Lamb into glory must also follow Him here, while living on earth. When I ponder this, I am greatly concerned for my salvation. I see before me many who would become my guides, and I do not know who to follow. Satan invites me by his allurements to follow him; the world places before my eyes its examples, its ways, its society. But I fear that I would also have to follow them after death to where they end up: hell and damnation.

Therefore, O Jesus, I will follow You. Then I shall pursue the safest, best, and most blessed way. I will follow You in faith, love, humility, obedience, godliness, and chastity. Christ has left us an example that we should follow His footsteps. His example shall be constantly before my eyes. Following the example of Jesus, I will love and honor my heavenly Father and will do His holy will. Following His example, I will love my fellow human beings and will do good to them. Following His example, I will readily forgive my enemies. Following His example, I will be humble, for He says, "Learn from Me, for I am gentle and lowly in heart" (Matthew 11:29). This is my sacred purpose, but You must give me the strength to accomplish it.

Remind me of these things at all times, so that, when I see before me the behavior, speech, and vanities of the wicked children of this age, I may ask, "Where are you going, world? Your way is not directed toward Jesus and His salvation!" Help me always to inquire of myself, "Is this the true way to heaven?" Help me always to remember who I am and who I ought to be. I am called to be a child of God, a follower of Jesus. I am called to keep myself unspotted from the world. Help me constantly to persevere in this mind-set and to follow You until death.

Make me to walk in Thy commands—'Tis a delightful road—Nor let my head or heart or hands Offend against my God. Amen. *LSB 707:4*

HYMN

One thing's needful; Lord this treasure
*   Teach me highly to regard.*
All else, though it first give pleasure,
*   Is a yoke that presses hard!*
Beneath it the heart is still fretting and striving,
No true, lasting happiness ever deriving.
*   This one thing is needful; all others are vain—*
*   I count all but loss that I Christ may obtain!*

Wisdom's highest, noblest treasure,
*   Jesus, is revealed in You.*
Let me find in You my pleasure,
*   And my wayward will subdue,*
Humility there and simplicity reigning
In paths of true wisdom my steps ever training.
*   If I learn from Jesus this knowledge divine,*
*   The blessing of heavenly wisdom is mine.*

Nothing have I, Christ, to offer,
*   You alone, my highest good.*
Nothing have I, Lord, to proffer
*   But Your crimson-colored blood.*
Your death on the cross has death wholly defeated
And thereby my righteousness fully completed;
*   Salvation's white raiments I there do obtain,*
*   And in them in glory with You I shall reign.*

Therefore You alone, my Savior,
*   Shall be all in all to me;*
Search my heart and my behavior,
*   Root out all hypocrisy.*
Though all my life's pilgrimage, guard and uphold me,
In loving forgiveness, O Jesus, enfold me.
*   This one thing is needful; all others are vain—*
*   I count all but loss that I Christ may obtain!* LSB 536:1, 3–5

EVENING PRAYER FOR THURSDAY

When I lie down in bed, I remember You. When I awake, I speak of You. O bounteous and merciful God and Father, again I come before Your presence in this evening hour with a thankful heart because Your grace has showered numerous blessings on me. You have kindly regarded me and had pity on me as a father has pity on his child! Thus I have reached this evening unharmed. Your patience has spared me; You have not punished me as I have deserved. Pardon all my transgressions against you—whether done in secret or openly. I ought to become stronger in fighting against sin, more zealous in doing good works, more devout in prayer, more careful in speech, more godly in conduct. But who can discern his errors? Cleanse me also from hidden faults. Let me henceforth avoid diligently all those things with which I have offended You today. Though my sins are great, Your mercy is far greater. If You were not a merciful God, O Lord, who could ever live?

I now lay me down to rest. O God, shut the door after me, as You did to Noah's ark, that no flood of tribulation may sweep me away. Let Your holy angels take me into their protection, that neither visible nor invisible enemies may disturb my rest. Help me to remember, when lying down in bed, that I shall one day be covered with earth, but shall rise again on the Last Day. Let me spend and conclude all my days in such a way that I may be able to take comfort in the fact that I have a gracious God. Give me a good conscience that I may be ready at whatever hour You come to take me home.

As I lie sleeping and yet continue to breathe, so do You, O Jesus, remain united with me even in sleep. O Blessed Trinity, under Your shield and protection neither adversity nor death can harm me. Your love and protection, O Father; Your wounds, O Jesus; Your comfort, O precious Spirit, are a wall of defense around me within which I sleep in peace and repose in safety. Before this defense Satan must flee and run away. Let also my dear ones, and all who are poor and in distress, enjoy Your protection. Let me gather strength in sleep and, if it is Your will, let me behold the light of day again in the morning.

God, who made the earth and heaven, Darkness and light: You the day for work have given, For rest the night. May Your angel guards defend us, Slumber sweet Your mercy send us, Holy dreams and hopes attend us All through the night. Amen.   *LSB 877:1*

FOR USE IN HEALTH

MORNING PRAYER FOR FRIDAY

My heart is steadfast, O God, my heart is steadfast! I will sing and make melody. O gracious and loving God, my Father, redeemer, and sanctifier, I lift up my heart and my hands in this morning hour to the throne of Your divine majesty for all the blessings showered on all my life and also this past night. You have, during this night, been my strength, my protection, my deliverer, my strong tower, my helper in need, my comfort, my shield, indeed, my all. My God and Lord, I acknowledge that I am unworthy of all these blessings. You thought about me in the midst of darkness; and while the dark shadows were wrapped around me, Your fatherly care protected my body and soul against harm and danger. And so I praise You and magnify Your name. The Lord has done great things for me, and I am glad.

O loving God, be at my side this day; guide me and lead me with Your counsel and afterward receive me into glory. Whom do I have in heaven but You? And there is none upon earth that I desire besides You. Suggest to me all that I shall have to speak—both today and always—that I may not offend You with my lips. Teach me what I must do, so that I do not fall into evil. Let Your Spirit always knock with warning at my heart, whenever my thoughts are about to stray from You. O Jesus, when my flesh and blood excite sinful desires in me, let Your bleeding image stand before my eyes. Remind me that at the time of Your bitter sufferings it was on a Friday that You sweat drops of blood for me on the Mount of Olives; that You were cruelly scourged in the judgment hall, and were then nailed bleeding to the cross. If an occasion to sin should present itself today and my heart would incline toward it, then place Your bleeding image before me, that through it every desire to sin may be quenched, killed, and driven from my heart. Thus let this Friday suggest freedom to me: let it be to me a day of deliverance from sin and remain such all my life. Grant me to die to sin and to walk in newness of the spirit.

Remember also my bodily needs and bless me. Let me regard all earthly things as perishable possessions, lest I set my heart on them. Let me seek the things eternal. When I am at work, strengthen me. When I pray, hear me. When I go out, accompany me. When I return home, do not leave me. Surround me and those I love with Your protection like the house of Job. Watch over me as over Elijah, in order that with Your protection, I may reach the evening in safety. Let no sad message come to me, but let me hear joy and gladness.

Should some lust or sharp temptation Fascinate my sinful mind, Draw me to Your cross and passion, And new courage I shall find. Or should Satan press me hard, Let me then be on my guard, Saying, "Christ for me was wounded," That the tempter flee confounded. Amen.   *LSB 421:2*

BELIEVING CHRISTIANS PRAY FOR THE HOLY SPIRIT

EXHORTATION

Create in me a clean heart, O God, and renew a right spirit within me. Cast me not away from Your presence, and take not your Holy Spirit from me. Psalm 51:10–11

There is no more necessary and blessed petition than to ask for the Holy Spirit. In this present life we need a guide, a teacher, a comforter. All this, the Holy Spirit is! He guides us into all truth. He teaches us to know Jesus Christ, explaining His teaching to us. He comforts us in every affliction and trouble, and most especially in the hour of death. Everyone should pray for the gift of the Holy Spirit, whether old or young, great or small. Parents should ask for this gift for themselves and their children, since the Holy Spirit is the guarantee of our inheritance. Whoever does not have the Holy Spirit in the heart in this life cannot hope to be saved in the life to come. And so the most unfortunate people of all are those who do not have the Holy Spirit. They cannot become godly or lead God-pleasing lives. They fall and sin because they do not have the Holy Spirit to guide and govern them. And who can comfort them on their dying bed or cheer them in their last anguish? However, when God has given us His Holy Spirit, we must not drive Him away from us by willful sins or an ungodly life. We must pray daily: "Take not Your Holy Spirit from me!" Those who pray thus are truly in union with God and in a state of grace, as St. Paul testifies: "For all who are led by the Spirit of God are sons of God" (Romans 8:14).

PRAYER

O mighty God and holy Father, behold, I, Your poor child, come to You and pray for a necessary gift, for the Holy Spirit, whom You have graciously promised to give to all who ask You. Send Your Holy Spirit down from above, from Your holy habitation, into my heart, that He may be my guide, teach me to walk in Your counsel, and enable me at all times to do what pleases You.

I see before my eyes so many ways of error and of sin. I see so many people who walk in those ways, urging me to follow them—sometimes with kind words and sometimes with threats—trying to get me to join them in their sin and evil. O God, lead me in Your truth. Keep my heart steady so that I may fear Your name. Whenever the world with its sins becomes attractive to me, remind me where that broad way ends: in destruction and damnation. Grant me Your Holy Spirit, the Spirit of truth, to teach me! The Spirit of comfort, to revive me! The Spirit of joy, to gladden me in sorrow! The Spirit of rebirth, to make me a new creation, a new person! The Spirit of adoption, to assure me that I am Your child! The Spirit who is the down payment of my heavenly inheritance!

O precious Holy Spirit, sanctify me. You see that my heart is still filled with impurity, evil habits, and sins, and so nothing but unholy thoughts, words, and deeds come out of it. But You see also that by Your grace I heartily hate these things. I am sorry that I have ever grieved You and made light of Your warnings. I now yield myself wholly to Your holy guidance and rule. Be the life of my soul, the strength of my life, the comfort of my heart, the light of my understanding, the repose and firmness of my will, the treasury of my memory, the origin, beginning, and end of my spiritual life. Sanctify me wholly, that my spirit, together with my soul and body, may be kept blameless to the day of Jesus Christ. Make my heart Your temple and dwell there. Make my members Your instruments of righteousness, so that I may not sin purposefully and willfully. Make my heart a living sacrifice acceptable to God.

O sacred Fire, consume and drive from me all sinful desires, that I may use the powers of my body for Your glory. Govern me, and guide me always in Your paths, till You bring me to heaven. When my flesh and blood and the world would rob me of the comfort that I am a child of God, assure me by Your powerful consolation that neither life nor death shall separate me from the love of God. Remind me that the children of God have their crosses to bear, but they remain God's children nevertheless. Be and remain the constant tenant and Lord in my heart. Bear witness with my spirit that I am a child of God. In the hour of death, when all human help and support fail, then comfort me with the promise that I shall share the glory that my dear Jesus has acquired for me by His suffering and death.

Come down, O Love divine; Seek Thou this soul of mine, And visit it with Thine own ardor glowing; O Comforter, draw near; Within my heart appear, And kindle it, Thy holy flame bestowing. O let it freely burn, Till worldly passions turn To dust and ashes in its heat consuming; And let Thy glorious light Shine ever on my sight And clothe me round, the while my path illuming. Let holy charity Mine outward vesture be And lowliness become mine inner clothing—True lowliness of heart, Which takes the humbler part, And o'er its own shortcomings weeps with loathing. And so the yearning strong, With which the soul will long, Shall far outpass the pow'r of human telling; No soul can guess His grace Till it become the place Wherein the Holy Spirit makes His dwelling. Amen.

LSB 501:1–4

HYMN

Come, Holy Ghost, God and Lord,
With all Your graces now outpoured
*   On each believer's mind and heart;*
*   Your fervent love to them impart.*
Lord, by the brightness of Your light
In holy faith Your Church unite;
*   From ev'ry land and ev'ry tongue*
*   This to Your praise, O Lord, our God, be sung:*
*   Alleluia, alleluia!*

Come, holy Light, guide divine,
Now cause the Word of life to shine.
*   Teach us to know our God aright*
*   And call Him Father with delight.*

From ev'ry error keep us free;
Let none but Christ our master be
That we in living faith abide,
In Him, our Lord, with all our might confide.
Alleluia, alleluia!

Come, holy Fire, comfort true,
Grant us the will Your work to do
And in Your service to abide;
Let trials turn us not aside.
Lord, by Your pow'r prepare each heart,
And to our weakness strength impart
That bravely here we may contend,
Through life and death to You, our Lord, ascend.
Alleluia, alleluia! LSB 497:1–3

EVENING PRAYER FOR FRIDAY

The angel of the Lord camps around those who fear him, and he delivers them. O great and mighty God, let Your holy angels camp around me also in this coming night and surround me with their mighty protection. As You commanded them to guard me during the day and to keep me in all my ways, so let them stand around my bed at night like Solomon's mighty men.

I now lie down to rest, my Jesus. Cover the doorposts of my heart with Your holy blood so no harm may come near me. If You are with me, I have no fear. You have been at my side this day, wherever I have gone. You have put Your blessing on all my activities. You have prospered all that I have undertaken in Your name. Oh, that the words of Joseph had been my constant motto today: "How then can I do this great wickedness and sin against God?" (Genesis 39:9). Forgive me in mercy all the evil that I have done, spoken, or thought this day. With the waning day let also my sins and the punishment of my sins vanish, that they may be remembered no more at all.

If You, Lord, should keep a record of sins, O Lord, who could stand? I know full well that no one can be just in the sight of God. If one wished to contend with Him, no one could answer Him once in a thousand times. But I will pay with the blood of Jesus what I cannot pay out of my resources. My Jesus is mine. His righteousness is mine. His heaven is mine. Therefore, receive me, O my Keeper! My Shepherd, make me Yours! You

41

are the Fountain from which flows all my good. Let Your goodness lead me to repentance, for You have loved me with an everlasting love, and with tender mercies You have drawn me. Let the warmth of Your blood and Your faithful love warm my cold heart, that I may never again intentionally offend You, who have shown me so many acts of kindness.

I lay me down to rest. This night may be my last. I know how to lie down to sleep, but I do not know how I will arise. That rests with You alone, for You are Lord over the days of my life. But this I know for certain: that when I fall asleep in Your name, my Father; in Your wounds, O Jesus; in Your fellowship, Holy Spirit, I die a blessed death, even though I should not rise again for this earthly life.

All-holy Lord, in humble prayer We ask tonight Thy watchful care. O grant us calm repose in Thee, A quiet night, from perils free. Amen.

LSB 882:2

MORNING PRAYER FOR SATURDAY

Lord, make me to know my end and the measure of my days so that I may realize how frail I am. Such are my thoughts, O strong and almighty God, now that I have reached the end of the week. You have permitted me to wake up healthy this last day of the week. I praise You this morning because You have so gloriously protected and so mightily defended my body and soul, that no danger or affliction has been able to disturb me. O my God, as little as the stars in the heavens, the sand on the shore, the drops in the ocean can be counted, as little can I number the blessings that I have received from You during all my life and also during this past week. You have not left me during the night. You have warded off every calamity. You said: "Lie still, My child, confiding, The tempter's wiles deriding; No nightly terror frighten Your sleep till morning brighten. 'Tis done; the light is shining Upon me, and from pining And fear I am recovered; Your love about me hovered."

Let me constantly deny this day all ungodliness and worldly lusts, and pass the day in a sober, righteous, and godly manner. With my clothes let me also put on cordial pity, kindness, meekness, humility, and patience. Help me to put off the old man with his works: unrighteousness, insincerity, lying, anger, strife, discord, impurity, and malice. Consecrate my heart to be Your temple. Grant that nothing that I say or do today may be displeasing to You.

My Jesus, You are the Alpha and the Omega, the beginning and the end. It is by Your grace that I have reached again the end of a week. Let me bear in mind that the last week and the last day of my life will come one of these days. Let me begin, continue, and end each week and day in such a way that I may not have to be ashamed or regret that I ever lived. Let me also spend this day in Your holy fear. Preserve my going out and my coming in. Bless my labor. Assist me in every difficulty and direct all my undertakings and plans according to Your will. Destroy the record of the sins that I have accumulated during this week and cancel them with Your blood. Let me become more godly, sincere, and God-pleasing during this week. I rejoice even now at the thought of the approaching Sunday, when I shall rest from the works of my earthly calling, in order that You may do Your work in me for my edification and sanctification.

O Holy Spirit, enter in, And in our hearts Your work begin, Your dwelling place now make us. Sun of the soul, O Light divine, Around and in us brightly shine, To joy and gladness wake us That we may be Truly living, To You giving Prayer unceasing And in love be still increasing. Amen.

LSB 913:1

BELIEVING CHRISTIANS RETURN THANKS TO GOD AT THE END OF THE WEEK

EXHORTATION

What shall I render to the LORD for all His benefits to me?
Psalm 116:12

Day after day and week after week we come nearer to our dying hour. Meanwhile, our good God is so merciful that He has shown us many benefits in body and soul, and has filled our hearts with food and gladness. With thoughts such as these, believing Christians are occupied at the end of the week.

They thank God for the blessings they have received, for the protection that has enabled them to spend the week in safety, for the help they have obtained and for which they asked God in prayer. If they are informed during the week that others have suffered misfortune, have met with sorrow, have fallen from grace, have incurred loss, and have not been relieved from their misery and grief, they feel pity for them and yet praise the goodness of God who has spared them such afflictions. Believing Christians resolve in their mind that by such constant manifestations of His goodness God wants to lead them to repentance. Therefore, on the last day of the week they repent of the evil each day, and thus make the last day of the week their day of reconciliation, of prayer, of repentance, and of thanksgiving.

For the coming week they pray for continued protection, goodness, and mercy. They commend themselves to God and His grace. They reflect that all weeks, one after the other, thus pass until at length the week arrives in which they will die. For that week they prepare themselves by true faith in Jesus Christ and a holy and repentant way of living. Such sacred meditations should make people devout, careful, grateful, and godly, causing them to look to God as the source on high from which every good gift comes. They commit themselves to divine grace and to remain in the love of Jesus. Thus they are in a condition to live as saved sinners, according to God's will, and to die when their dying hour comes.

PRAYER

The Lord has done great things for me, and for this I am glad. Up to the present moment the Lord has helped me. It is fitting for me to talk this way, my God and Lord, now that I have reached the end of the week in safety. How excellent is Your loving-kindness, O God! Therefore, the children of men take refuge in the shadow of Your wings. You shield them, You keep them, You preserve them, and Your mercies are new every morning. O my God, You have spread Your wings over me. You have kept me in health and blessed me. You have been my companion and preserved me. You have shown me many benefits in body and soul and also allowed those dear to me to enjoy Your protection and grace. Surely, it is God who has done this. It is the Lord's doing that I have safely passed through this week. And so, bless the Lord, O my soul, and all that is within me, bless His holy name. Bless the Lord, O my soul, and forget none of His benefits.

Sadly, how many have fallen during this week, while I stand only by Your grace! To many, this past week been a sad week of sorrow and crosses, while You have allowed me to conclude it in peace and quietness. How many have suffered misery and anguish, while I have remained unharmed under Your protection! For all this let me offer You my love, praise, and fervent exaltation from my inmost soul. Receive my thanks for Your protection and Your grace. Receive my thanks for Your love and mighty aid. Receive my thanks for all the benefits You have bestowed on me in body and soul.

O my God, forgive me in mercy all the evil I have done this week. I am sorry. I repent. I am in distress on account of my sins; and I ask for mercy and forgiveness for all the ways I have been unfaithful to You. For the sake of the blood and wounds of Christ, spare me, and reward me not according to my works. In the strength of Your Spirit during the coming week I will strive to avoid the sins that I have committed and to serve You in holiness and righteousness all the days of my life.

The will of God is always best And shall be done forever; And they who trust in Him are blest; He will forsake them never. He helps indeed In time of need; He chastens with forbearing. They who depend On God, their friend, Shall not be left despairing. God is my comfort and my trust, My hope and life abiding; And to His counsel, wise and just, I yield, in Him confiding. The very hairs, His Word declares, Upon my head He numbers. By night and day God is my stay; He never sleeps nor slumbers. Amen.

LSB 758:1–2

HYMN

O God of love, O King of peace,
Make wars throughout the world to cease;
The rage of nations now restrain:
Give peace, O God, give peace again!

Remember, Lord, Thy works of old,
The wonders that Thy people told;

Remember not our sins' dark stain:
Give peace, O God, give peace again!

Whom shall we trust but Thee, O Lord?
Where rest but on Thy faithful Word?
None ever called on Thee in vain:
Give peace, O God, give peace again!

Where saints and angels dwell above,
All hearts are knit in holy love;
O bind us in that heav'nly chain:
Give peace, O God, give peace again! LSB 751:1–4

EVENING PRAYER FOR SATURDAY

When I walk in darkness, the Lord is my light. O loving and gracious God, the day and the week now are ending, but Your mercy goes on forever. The mountains may depart and the hills be removed, but Your kindness will not depart from Your children. It is by Your everlasting grace that I have been permitted to live through this week. What I did not know at the beginning of the week I know now: it was Your will that I should reach the end of this week in safety. Your blessings on me have been numerous this week. You have heard my prayer, preserved me, imparted good counsel to me, and stayed at my side. Not a day passed without receiving from You gifts of grace, love, and bounty. Not an hour passed without the rich streams of Your blessings being poured out on me. I have now received what I wished for at the beginning of the week. How great and inexpressible Your grace, Your love, Your mercy!

But now that the week draws to a close, I remember my sins. Numerous were my transgressions in thought, wish, desire, by commission and omission. I have not cared for my soul as faithfully as it was my duty to. O Lord, forgive me! Jesus, blot out with Your holy blood the entire record of my sins during this week forever! O Lord, rebuke me not in Your anger, nor discipline me in Your wrath! Be a wall of fire around me this night. Let no misfortune, harm, or danger touch me and mine. Help me to cast all my worry on You, and under Your loving care, O my Father, let me sleep in peace.

I am now a week older and a step nearer to eternity. The end of this week reminds me of the end of my days, and that the last week, the last day, and the last hour of my life will surely come, and after that endless eternity. Help me, then, to use the coming week, day, and hour that I may not be terrified when I behold You. Help me every day to make my heart ascend there, where I long to be eternally. I am a pilgrim here, and can claim only a night's rest on earth. My home and my eternal mansions are in heaven, where You will wipe away all tears from the eyes of Your children, give them the glorious bounties of Your house, and refresh them with a joy that never ends.

I now lay aside my occupation and the works of my calling. I prepare myself for the coming Sunday, when I shall hear the preaching of Your Holy Word. So that I may hear it to my benefit, grant me the strength of Your Holy Spirit that I may not be hindered in my devotion either by others or my own wayward heart.

Oh, may my soul in Thee repose, And may sweet sleep mine eyelids close, Sleep that shall me more vig'rous make To serve my God when I awake! Amen.

LSB 883:4

A CHILD'S EVENING PRAYER

Blessed Savior, hear me now,
Lowly at Your feet I bow;
Let Your watchful care this night
Keep me safe till morning light.

Bless, O Lord, my parents dear;
Keep them in Your holy care;
Bless my brothers, sisters, too,
And our evil hearts renew.

Bless the sick on beds of pain;
Savior, give them health again;
Or prepare them, should they die,
For Your mansions in the sky.

Bless the poor with needful good,
Clothe and give them daily food;
You who make even birds Your care
Bless Your creatures everywhere.

Lord, give to me a grateful heart
For the gifts You now impart;
All my trust I rest in You,
Make my heart be ever new.

All my sins, O Lord, forgive;
Fit me with Yourself to live
In that glorious home above
Purchased by Your dying love.
Amen.

Part Two : For the Festival Seasons

DEVOTIONS DURING HOLY ADVENT

MORNING PRAYER

Gladdened because of the multitude of blessings Your coming in the flesh has brought us, only-begotten Son of God, I rise from my bed and lift up my hands to You, from whom comes all my help. You come to be a guest in this world to rescue and save it. Since I am part of the world, You came also for my benefit—to bless me, that I may have life in You, and have it abundantly. How, then, could I not rejoice? How could I not be glad?

O Jesus, You have appeared in the form of sinful flesh for my benefit. You have come into the world for my sake. Come to me and dwell in my heart! Sanctify my heart wholly and prepare it for Yourself so that it may become Your dwelling place. Strengthen my faith, and fill me with Your love, that I may choose You above the world and its pleasures.

When the world with its sins, such as haughtiness, pride, anger, boastfulness, and other works of the flesh, approaches me and says, "In this heart we will dwell! Here we will reign! Here we will take up our abode!", let me resist them in Your strength and stoutly reply, "Depart from me, sins! Be gone, world! Here is the temple of the Lord! Away with you! There is no place for you! I have no room for you! You cannot make your home with me. My Jesus is with me. To Him alone I have yielded myself entirely. He shall reign over me, and I shall remain His own in time and eternity." How happy I shall be if You abide with me and I am enabled by You to overcome the world and all the enemies of my soul.

O my Savior, You came into the world to save sinners; receive me and enter my heart. You have long ago, even before my birth, chosen my soul for Your dwelling. You prepared it for this purpose in Holy Baptism, when I was washed with Your precious blood and purified from all pollutions of the flesh. But I have departed from You, again defiling my soul with many grievous sins. By my ungodly conduct I have often broken my baptismal covenant. I now return to You. I open the door of my heart again to You. I long for You with great earnestness. As the deer pants for streams of water, so my soul longs and pants for You, my God and Savior. May it please You to come and enter my heart. I vow eternal faithfulness to You. Unite Yourself with me, that nothing may separate us. Let Your Spirit from now on be joined to my spirit, and lead me always in a straight path, that I may always follow You, cling to You, and through You obtain eternal salvation.

Love caused Your incarnation; Love brought You down to me. Your thirst for my salvation Procured my liberty. Oh, love beyond all telling, That led You to embrace In love, all love excelling, Our lost and fallen race. Amen.

LSB 334:4

EXHORTATION

Rejoice greatly, O daughter of Zion! Shout aloud, O daughter of Jerusalem! Behold, your king is coming to you; righteous and having salvation is He; humble and mounted on a donkey, on a colt, the foal of a donkey. Zechariah 9:9

If there is a time that people consecrated to God love to spend in devotion, it is certainly the time of the holy festivals on which the Christian Church contemplates the mercies of God. True, many who are Christian only in name spend the holy festival seasons partly in high living and luxury, partly in pride and in parading new clothes, partly in idleness and unbecoming talk. Because of this, they do not take the love and grace of the Most High to heart. But believing children of God have an altogether different mind. For they hail with joy each coming festival season because in their devotions they are going to place before their mind the gift that the goodness of God has given them.

During the holy season of Advent, they meditate on the love of their heavenly Father, who spared not His only Son but sent Him into the world to suffer and die, and thus acquire salvation for all people. They consider the ardent love of Jesus, who was clothed with our flesh and blood in order that He might bring us to heaven and give us unending happiness. They give praise for the grace of the Holy Spirit, who has placed the gifts lavished on our human race before the souls of believers, who has made them their own, and who causes them to recognize these gifts in such a vivid and effectual manner that they seem to have been given this very day. Accordingly, they make this holy season a time of devotion and prayer, and begin and end it with hearing and meditating on the Word of God, with singing festival hymns, and with a quiet and godly way of living.

PRAYER

O merciful Jesus, You have come to seek and to save what was lost. I thank You that through Your protection and by Your grace I have been permitted once more to reach this holy season. Grant me the strength of Your Holy Spirit that I may spend this time in Your fear, in holy meditations, and to the edifying of my soul. Everlasting Son of God, who was before the foundations of the world were laid, You came in the flesh and were made a true man, in order to make us happy and to save us. On account of our grievous fall into sin we could not come to You in heaven, so You came to us on earth to lead us all to life everlasting. Through sin we had become aliens, yes, prisoners of Satan and enemies of God. But by Your most holy Advent all our losses are made good. O grace abounding! Love unspeakable! For Your sake, O Jesus, the strangers are made friends, the prisoners set free, the enemies of God are made His beloved, sinners become God's children, and the fallen are raised. O holy Advent, by which we who were condemned to death obtain life, by which we who were fallen from grace are clothed with glory and honor on Your account. For this is a faithful saying and worthy of all acceptance: that Christ Jesus came into the world to save sinners.

Dearest Jesus, save me and lead me into the joys of Your kingdom. Give me an attentive and obedient heart in this holy season, that I may diligently and reverently hear Your Holy Word, and receive and keep it in my heart. Let me grow in faith and in Your knowledge and love during these holy days. Let me show forth the fruits of faith, such as chastity, humility, meekness, obedience, and godliness, that Your Advent may be also for me a blessed and salutary Advent. Preserve me, that it may not be said of me: He came to His own, and His own did not receive Him.

O Lord Jesus, I receive You in faith; I love You! Enter in, You blessed of the Lord. Why are You standing outside? By Your grace I have prepared my heart for You. Enter into my heart. I will embrace You as my only Redeemer and Savior. I will make Your merit and righteousness my own. Enter into my heart. For love of You I will gladly shun all worldly vanities, amusements, sins, and wickedness, so that You alone may be the occupant of my soul and the ruler of my heart. Dwell in me, sanctify me for Your possession, and keep me in Your grace. I repent of the sins I have committed and seek grace in You. Therefore, my sins shall no more condemn me. For if the Son shall make me free, I shall be free indeed. If God is for me, who can be against me?

O Jesus, You came as a king. Reign from now on in my heart, that sin may have no more dominion over me. You came as the Righteous One. I am unrighteous and a sinner worthy of condemnation. Make me righteous and bestow on me the robe of Your perfect righteousness. I will greatly rejoice in the Lord, my soul will be joyful in my God, for He has clothed me with the garments of salvation. He has covered me with the robe of righteousness. You came in poverty to make me spiritually rich in faith and to give me imperishable heavenly treasures. You came in humility; make me humble, that I may learn from You meekness and humility. Grant me to practice these virtues on all occasions in my life. O King of glory, enter by the gate of my heart. Behold, enabled by Your strength, I open it wide for You. Govern me from now on with Your Spirit, so that I may remain Your dwelling and temple until my blessed end.

Come, Thou precious Ransom, come, Only hope for sinful mortals! Come, O Savior of the world! Open are to Thee all portals. Come, Thy beauty let us see; Anxiously we wait for Thee. Enter now my waiting heart, Glorious King and Lord most holy. Dwell in me and ne'er depart, Though I am but poor and lowly. Ah, what riches will be mine When Thou art my guest divine! My hosannas and my palms Graciously receive, I pray Thee; Evermore, as best I can, Savior, I will homage pay Thee, And in faith I will embrace, Lord, Thy merit through Thy grace. Hail! Hosanna, David's Son! Jesus, hear our supplication! Let Thy kingdom, scepter, crown, Bring us blessing and salvation, That forever we may sing: Hail! Hosanna to our King. Amen. *LSB 350:1–4*

HYMN

Hark the glad sound! The Savior comes,
The Savior promised long;
Let ev'ry heart prepare a throne
And ev'ry voice a song.

He comes the pris'ners to release,
In Satan's bondage held.
The gates of brass before Him burst,
The iron fetters yield.

He comes the broken heart to bind,
The bleeding soul to cure,
And with the treasures of His grace
To enrich the humble poor.

Our glad hosannas, Prince of Peace,
Thy welcome shall proclaim,
And heav'n's eternal arches ring
With Thy beloved name. LSB 349:1–4

PRAYER

"Yes, He loves the people!" Thus, O loving and lovable Lord, I am forced to exclaim, filled with wonder, at the close of this day. I have become convinced of the boundless love that You have for us poor mortals, not only in the innumerable blessings that You have shown to me and to others in body and soul, but above all in this: that You did not spare Your only-begotten Son, but delivered Him up in the place of all the lost children of Adam, and hence in my place.

What an exceptional proof of Your love You have given me by such a gift! For my sake, You caused Your only-begotten Son, the Son of Your love, Your only Child, to become a human man, that as man He might be able to suffer torture, scourging, stripes, and even death, and thereby render satisfaction to Your offended majesty, and redeem, justify, and save me. If some great man of this world were to sacrifice his most beautiful ring, his most valuable jewels, his choicest treasure, to save some wretched human being from his misery and make him happy, such an act would be admired and praised everywhere as an instance of the highest degree of man's love for man. If a king were to deliver one of his sons into captivity to obtain release of some prisoner of lesser rank from his chains and dungeon, people would imagine that they could not sufficiently extol and praise the love of such a monarch for his subjects. And yet, all this is as nothing in comparison with the love that You have shown to the children of men by clothing Your beloved Son in their flesh and blood, by sending Him in the fullness of time as man into this world.

A person who has once been delivered out of misery by a great benefactor may come into better circumstances again, and then render his benefactor many a useful service. This would in some measure repay the benefits shown him. A person who has been freed from hard bondage by the goodness of his king can render himself useful after he has obtained liberty. But we human beings can never repay You for what You have done for us. We have nothing to give You; we are not able in the least to repay You for rescuing us from the lost condition in which we found ourselves by nature and for setting us free from the bonds of death that held us fast. All these blessings came to us because Your Son became man. Your love has no equal—it passes all understanding! We can do nothing but humbly thank You, praise You, and magnify You. This is the only tribute by which our hearts can express their affection for You.

And so, blessed be Your holy name for the manifestation to me of Your infinite love in sending Your Son into the world. Let this love urge me to love You in return with all my heart, with all my soul, and with all my strength. Give me the ability to live according to Your will and to cling to You. Wean my heart from the love of the world, its vanities and sins, and kindle within me the flame of Your divine love, that I may always please You. Grant that I may increase in love and in knowledge of You, that I may abide in faith, and so worship You in spirit that I may taste even here and now in my heart Your sweetness, and may ever thirst for You. Amen.

HYMN

Lift up your heads, ye mighty gates!
Behold, the King of glory waits.
The King of kings is drawing near;
The Savior of the world is here.
Life and salvation He doth bring;
Therefore rejoice and gladly sing.
To God the Father raise
Your joyful songs of praise.

A righteous Helper comes to thee;
His chariot is humility,
His kingly crown is holiness,
His scepter, pity in distress.
The end of all our woe He brings;
Therefore the earth is glad and
sings.
To Christ the Savior raise
Your grateful hymns of praise.

How blest the land, the city blest,
Where Christ the ruler is
confessed!
O peaceful hearts and happy
homes
To whom this King in triumph
comes!

The cloudless sun of joy is He
Who comes to set His people free.
To God the Spirit raise
Your happy shouts of praise.

Fling wide the portals of your
heart;
Make it a temple set apart
From earthly use for heav'n's
employ,
Adorned with prayer and love and
joy.
So shall your Sov'reign enter in
And new and nobler life begin.
To God alone be praise
For word and deed and grace!

Redeemer, come and open wide
My heart to Thee; here, Lord,
abide!
O enter with Thy grace divine;
Thy face of mercy on me shine.
Thy Holy Spirit guide us on
Until our glorious goal is won.
Eternal praise and fame
We offer to Thy name. LSB 341:1–5

BELIEVING CHRISTIANS MEDITATE AT CHRISTMAS ON THE BIRTH OF JESUS CHRIST

MORNING PRAYER

In You, my God and Savior, my spirit rejoices at the moment that I rise from sleep and think of Your holy conception and birth. My limited and feeble understanding cannot truly comprehend and grasp the mystery great without controversy: God was manifest in the flesh. Yet my soul is delighted with the contemplation of the mystery because Your

Word, which is the truth and cannot deceive me, assures me that this event has certainly taken place, and also reveals to me with clarity the mode and manner in which it occurred. But even here my reason must be silent, for it beholds a veil spread over these matters which it cannot penetrate, and which shall be drawn aside only in eternity.

Your revealed Word describes beautifully Your conception and birth in the words of the angel announcing these events to Mary: "The Holy Spirit will come upon you, and the power of the Most High will overshadow you" (Luke 1:35). In this description I find reasons enough for joy. When I reverently contemplate it, joy flows through me like a river of life. I picture to myself how the Holy Spirit, as an all-wise and almighty architect, approached Mary and how He cleansed from all sins the tabernacle which Your divinity was to occupy, filling it with His most holy gifts. I picture to myself next how this sanctified tabernacle was occupied by You, the Power of the Highest, and whose name is Wonderful Counselor, Mighty God, Everlasting Father, Prince of Peace; how this tabernacle became united with Your divinity, and all Your divine properties and prerogatives were communicated to the human nature that You assumed. I picture to myself how by this very act, namely, by taking upon Yourself flesh and blood in the same manner as the children do, You have sanctified our human nature and made us accepted with Your Father in heaven.

What streams of delight must descend upon me when, on waking, I ponder these matters in sacred solitude! O my Jesus, by Your incarnation You have become my Brother. How rich, how happy You make me! In You I now have all things. By You I can obtain all things. With You I can understand and accomplish all things. From now on I will not despair in any tribulation, but will turn to You and confidently say, "Jesus, my Brother, help me!" No distress and no affliction will ever discourage me. I will firmly rely on You because You are my Brother, and as such, You love me and will surely have mercy on me.

In Your incarnation, O my Jesus, You have assumed my nature, and in doing so, become united with me. Make me also to share Your divine nature, that I may lead a godly life and submit myself wholly to the power and the ruling of Your Spirit. Let the noble relationship in which I now stand to You keep me at all times from sin and from the fellowship of the world, that I may do nothing that would offend You. Let me prize Your friendship higher than everything in the world. Let me serve You in holiness and righteousness all the days of my life. Let me love You constantly—for to love You is better than all else—in order that in life and in death, in time and in eternity, I may be found in Your fellowship. O my Brother, my chosen Friend, what joy shall be mine when in the joy everlasting I will see You crowned with majesty, whom even here I have fervently loved, and when I shall be united with You forever! As I anticipate these joys, my spirit rejoices and my heart is filled with gladness. And why should I not rejoice, since by hope I am even now blessed and in heaven with Jesus, my Brother?

Behold, the world's creator wears The form and fashion of a slave; Our very flesh our maker shares, His fallen creatures all to save.

LSB 385:2

EXHORTATION

But when the fullness of time had come, God sent forth His Son, born of a woman, born under the law, to redeem those who were under the law, that we might receive adoption as sons.
Galatians 4:4–5

If the birth of a royal prince causes comforting reflections and joy in the entire kingdom, the birth of Jesus Christ cannot fail to be a cause of joy to all people. The angels rejoice in the heavens above and proclaim to all tidings of great joy; how then could the children of God not rejoice? They rejoice over the love and mercy of God, who spared not His Son but delivered Him up for us all. They rejoice over the loving-kindness of Jesus, who though He is God and the Son of God, does not refuse to take on Himself the nature of man in a lowly virgin and to become a little child.

In quiet moments of devotion, believers marvel at the wonderful counsel of God for our salvation, which no human and no angel could ever have conceived—that the Son of God was to suffer in the place of humanity and thus reconcile all to God. They marvel at the unmerited grace that God offers to human beings who were His enemies (Romans 5:10), and for which they did not pray, no matter how much they needed it. Therefore, they return all the more fervent thanks to Him once the counsel of God for our salvation has been revealed to them. They enter gladly into the order of salvation by clinging to Jesus in faith and by following Him in a godly and pious life. And thus the holy Christmas days become to them days of prayer, rejoicing, and thanksgiving.

PRAYER

This it the day the Lord has made, we will rejoice and be glad in it! Save us, we pray, O Lord! O Lord, we pray, give us success! Blessed is he who comes in the name of the Lord. Arise my soul. Use this festival for the glory of God and for your edification and say: O Holy Trinity, Father, Son, and Holy Spirit, would that every drop of my blood were a tongue, that I might praise Your love, grace, and mercy!

God is love! This truth my heart and mind perceive on this holy festival. Your love has found a means for bringing grace to humanity, of which neither angels nor human beings would have dared to think! Namely, that the Second Person of the Godhead was to become man, to sanctify and cleanse our human nature. O gracious Jesus, everlasting praise and thanks to You for Your incarnation and birth. You became a child of man that we might become children of God. Now our human nature is truly exalted: You have united it with Your divinity and brought it into the council of the Holy Trinity. O love! O grace! As surely as the human nature is united with the divine, so surely everlasting friendship, everlasting reconciliation, everlasting peace, and everlasting love has been established between God and all people. When God beholds us in His Son, He cannot but be gracious to us. For He who spared not His beloved Son but delivered Him up for us all, how shall He not with Him freely give us all things—the forgiveness of sins, righteousness, peace, life, and salvation?

Oh, the greatness of the love of Jesus, who chose to be born a tender infant, that He might sanctify our sinful birth! He increased in wisdom and stature that He might sanctify our youth. "Welcome to earth, O noble Guest, Through whom the sinful world is blest! You came to share my misery That You might share Your joy with me" *(LSB 358:8)*. What thanks shall I return to You? O dearest Friend of souls! My Brother! I now have in You a helper in affliction, a deliverer in tribulation, a Savior when my sins terrify me, an aid in need, a support in death. You are my light; enlighten me! You are the Way that leads me to the Father. You are the Truth that teaches me to know that life which gives life. You are my righteousness; You justify and save me. You are my High Priest, who intercedes for me and blesses me. You are the lamb sacrificed for my trespasses, the full ransom for all my transgressions.

O precious Holy Spirit, how great is Your love in having this comfort, this joy, this salvation proclaimed to me again! From my heart I rejoice on this holy festival and say: My Jesus is mine; His heaven is mine. This Child is born for me, yes, truly for me. This Son is given for me, yes, truly for me. He has obtained and given also to me, yes to me, the grace of God, sonship with Him, and the eternal inheritance that is reserved for us in heaven.

O Jesus, whom in spirit I behold and gaze upon in the manger, how lovely, how kind You are! Grant me grace never to forget You, but to keep You ever in my heart, on my lips, and before my eyes. O my Salvation, sanctify me! I yield myself to You with all that I am and have. O my Bridegroom, embrace me. For You I will live, You I will serve, from love of You I renounce the world and all the pleasures of this life. Let my heart be Your manger and Your dwelling in time and in eternity. Enfold and keep me in Your love, that I may have rest, peace, comfort, safety, and the salvation of my soul. Now that my Jesus has become man, I am not lost. Since I believe in Him, I will not perish, but have everlasting life. God is my friend because by faith I am in Jesus, and because Jesus is in me. I do not fear death, for in Him I have life. I do not fear the accusation of my conscience on account of my sins, for Jesus, my Advocate, is with me.

Thou Christian heart, Whoe'er thou art, Be of good cheer and let no sorrow move thee! For God's own Child, In mercy mild, Joins thee to Him; how greatly God must love thee! Remember thou What glory now The Lord prepared thee for all earthly sadness. The angel host Can never boast Of greater glory, greater bliss or gladness. Amen.   *LSB 372:4–5*

HYMN

We praise You, Jesus, at Your birth;
Clothed in flesh You came to earth.
The virgin bears a sinless boy
And all the angels leap for joy.
Alleluia!

Now in a manger we may see
God's Son from eternity,
The gift of God's eternal throne
Here clothed in our poor
flesh and bone.
Alleluia!

The virgin Mary's lullaby
Calms the infant Lord Most High.
Upon her lap content is He
Who keeps the earth and
sky and sea.
Alleluia!

The Light Eternal, breaking
through,
Made the world to gleam anew;

His beams have pierced the core of
night,
He makes us children of the light.
Alleluia!

The very Son of God sublime
Entered into earthly time
To lead us from this world of cares
To heaven's court as blessed heirs.
Alleluia!

In poverty He came to earth
Showing mercy by His birth;
He makes us rich in heav'nly ways
As we, like angels, sing His praise.
Alleluia!

All this for us our God has done
Granting love through His own Son.
Therefore, all Christendom, rejoice
And sing His praise with
endless voice.
Alleluia!   *LSB 382:1–7*

EVENING PRAYER

My Jesus—my Immanuel, my King, and my Kinsman—I am still kneeling in spirit at Your manger and pondering Your holy incarnation. How could I better close this day the Lord has made, and prepare for a sweet and refreshing sleep, than by such meditations? I acknowledge You, O incarnate Savior, as the true Messiah, as the Redeemer of the world, sprung from the house and lineage of David. You are the Messiah in whom all things that the prophets spoke have been fulfilled. You were born at the exact time, at the exact place, in the particular family and of the chosen mother, appointed, indicated, and made known by the heavenly Father through His messengers even in the days of the old covenant. Why, then, should I not acknowledge You as the true Savior of the world, and rejoice with all my heart at Your manifestation in the flesh? "What the fathers most desired, What the prophets' heart inspired, What they longed for many a year, Stands fulfilled in glory here" *(LSB 352:4)*.

When I think of this event and ponder the infinite blessings that have come to me on account of it, my heart leaps for joy. You are the supreme and exalted God. You were before the mountains were brought forth, or even before the earth and the world were formed. You shall remain when all these have fallen into ruin. You are the eternal Yahweh, Alpha and Omega, the beginning and the end, who is, who was, and who is to come. And yet You do not despise the human race. To save humanity You become the humblest, the most despised and rejected of men. O the depth of Your grace and love! How happy I am to behold such a Redeemer as You, lying in the manger!

Do not let me part from Your manger without having my soul stirred. Let all that I observe in Your human birth contribute to my sanctification and the strengthening of my faith. You are born at night; help me to flee the darkness of sin and walk as in the day, in Your light. You came on earth when stillness and rest prevailed everywhere; let me in You attain true rest of my soul and escape the turmoil of the world, so that when my heart is quieted, You may be my guest. Seeking You diligently in spirit, O my Immanuel, I find You at an inn; grant me the grace to regard this world as an inn, in which I am to tarry only for a few years and hours, that I may in time direct my heart to that place where I wish to be forever, and that I may not neglect to enter into Your rest, nor give up the race. You chose to enter this world in a dark stable, an unbecoming place; grant that I may renounce all ease, and that in this life I may be content with whatever Your goodness sends me, or in whatever condition it may place me. You are lying in a manger wrapped in swaddling clothes; wrap Yourself in my heart and let it be Your dwelling place.

How happy shall I be if You will graciously fulfill all these desires of my heart! I doubt not that You hear me. I firmly believe that You will still my longing. Perfectly quiet and content, therefore, I now lay me down to sleep and rest in Your arms, and pray:

Ah, dearest Jesus, holy Child, Prepare a bed, soft, undefiled, A quiet chamber set apart For You to dwell within my heart. Amen.   *LSB 358:13*

THE POVERTY OF CHRIST

Foxes have holes, and birds of the air have nests, but the Son of Man has nowhere to lay His head. Matthew 8:20

O my King, and was it so,
Did You suffer all this woe?
Did You wander thus forlorn,
Bearing poverty and scorn;
Lord of all the realms above,
'Reft of home and human love,
In the world that You had made
Nowhere could You lay Your head?

If we could at all conceive
All the glory You did leave;
All the splendor of the throne
That for us You did disown;
Catch but one imperfect ray
Of Your everlasting day,
And in that supernal light
See Your majesty aright, —

How could we believe that You
All our grief and sorrows knew;
How, amidst these lower things,
Recognize the King of kings:
Washing the disciples' feet,
Sitting with the poor at meat,
Bearing daily pain and loss,
Dying on the shameful cross?

Only as Yourself have shown
What the glory of Your throne;
What, in all the realms of light,
Is the source of chief delight;
What in all You made below,
Made You bear Your load of woe;
By the truth all truth above,
We know You, for "God is love."

EPIPHANY

As with gladness men of old
Did the guiding star behold;
As with joy they hailed its light,
Leading onward, beaming bright;
So, most gracious Lord, may we
Evermore be led by Thee.

As with joyful steps they sped,
Savior, to Thy lowly bed,
There to bend the knee before
Thee, whom heav'n and earth adore;
So may we with willing feet
Ever seek Thy mercy seat.

As they offered gifts most rare
At Thy cradle, rude and bare,
So may we with holy joy,

Pure and free from sin's alloy,
All our costliest treasures bring,
Christ, to Thee, our heav'nly King.

Holy Jesus, ev'ry day
Keep us in the narrow way;
And when earthly things are past,
Bring our ransomed souls at last
Where they need so star to guide,
Where no clouds Thy glory hide.

In the heav'nly country bright
Need they no created light;
Thou its light, its joy, its crown,
Thou its sun which goes not down;
There forever may be sing
Alleluias to our King. LSB 397:1–5

BELIEVING CHRISTIANS PRAY AND GIVE THANKS TO GOD AT THE CLOSE OF THE YEAR

MORNING PRAYER

O Lord, my God, the Father of all mercies, as I open my eyes, I now behold the light of day for the last time this year, in which I have realized that You are gracious, full of compassion, patient, and abundant in goodness and truth. Not a day, not an hour of the year that is now departing, has passed away without You showing all these glorious attributes to me.

You have been gracious toward me. You have shown me many favors without any merit or worthiness on my part. You have given me food, drink, nourishment, and have not allowed me to lack any good thing. You have been gracious to me. When I called upon You, You have forgiven my sins and iniquities for the sake of my Redeemer. You have been gracious to me. You have taken away all punishments I had accumulated by my malice, transgressions, and sins. Instead of inflicting punishment on me as I deserved, You have showered on me the blessings of Your salvation.

Your compassion toward me has been equal to Your grace. No need, no misery, no tribulation was allowed to befall or come near me, but Your tender, fatherly heart melted with compassion, and You had pity on me. Scarcely had my need reached its extremity, when it was to be Your opportunity. Scarcely had sorrow visited me, when You began to turn my sorrow into joy. Scarcely did I cry to You, when You heard me. Indeed, You answered me before I cried a second time.

Oh, the mercy of my God, who has also in this year borne with me in patience and long-suffering! When I was overtaken by weakness, You did not abandon me. When I sinned against You in my haste, You cancelled the debt I had incurred. When after leaving You, I came back a humble penitent, You received me again. Oh, the riches of the patience and long-suffering that You have thus shown me!

And in the same way You have shown by how You have treated me that You are abundant in goodness. By Your goodness You have preserved my life, sustained and kept me in health, so that I can now glorify Your love and can say to Your praise that You have done all things well and that all, yes, all things have been arranged by You.

It is from Your great truth and faithfulness that all Your dealings with me have their source. In accordance with Your faithfulness, You fulfill all promises that You have made. You keep faith with humanity. In accordance with Your faithfulness, therefore, so many blessings have been showered on me that I am not able to recite them all. What now shall I render to you, O my God, for all Your benefits to me? I am altogether unable to pay You. For the time being, then, mercifully accept my feeble stammering as an offering of praise and gratitude: Thanks to You for all Your mercies! Thanks to You for all Your grace!

Deal with me in the future as You have dealt with me in the past. Let me spend this day in Your fear, that today as well as through all eternity I may praise and glorify Your name.

Oh, that I had a thousand voices To praise my God with thousand tongues! My heart, which in the Lord rejoices, Would then proclaim in grateful songs To all, wherever I might be, What great things God has done for me. O all you pow'rs that He implanted, Arise, keep silence now no more; Put forth the strength that God has granted! Your noblest work is to adore. O soul and body, join to raise With heartfelt joy our Maker's praise. Amen.   *LSB 811:1–2*

EXHORTATION

Bless the Lord, O my soul, and all that is within me, bless His holy name! Bless the Lord, O my soul, and forget not all His benefits. Psalm 103:1–2

If devout souls and grateful hearts rejoice greatly in God when He has permitted them to pass a week or a month in safety, why should their joy not increase much more when, with God's help, they have lived through an entire year? Just think of how much suffering may come our way on a single day! How much more in a whole year! When pious Christians behold the end of a year, they lift up their hearts, voices, and hands to heaven, and conclude the year with prayer, praise, and thanksgiving.

Nor are they satisfied merely to repeat such things as: "God be praised and thanked; this year, too, is past!" No. Rather, they thank God because through the year His Holy Word has been proclaimed for the sanctification of their soul, and they have been shown the way to heaven. Likewise, they thank God because through the Lord's Supper He has repeatedly furnished them new strength and ability to practice godliness and bring forth fruits of faith. They ask themselves whether they have grown in piety during the year; and what age they have attained in the inner self according to the new birth, now that they have rounded out another year according their old sinful birth. They pray God heartily and fervently to forgive them all the sins they have committed, whether knowingly or unknowingly. Further, they praise God for the many temporal blessings He has granted them by sustaining them, providing for them, protecting, delivering, preserving, blessing, guarding, and attending them.

If God did send sickness, sorrow, or tribulation, and again delivered them from these evils, they should offer special thanks, and at the end of the year recall, as far as possible, the blessings they or their family received each week and each month, so that the last days of the year may become days of praise, prayer, thanksgiving, and repentance. And while doing these things, they also invoke the grace of God for the upcoming year.

PRAYER

What shall I render to the Lord for all the goodness and faithfulness He has shown me? The Lord has done great things for me, and I am glad. Thus, O triune God, Father, Son, and Holy Spirit, my soul speaks, rejoicing in Your grace now that I have completed another year in safety. How excellent is Your loving-kindness, O God; that is why the children of men put their trust under the shadow of Your wings. They shall be abundantly satisfied with the goodness of Your house, and You will make them drink of the river of Your pleasures. With You is the fountain of life; in Your light we see light.

My God, the days in a year are many, but Your benefactions are more. The hours and minutes in a year can be counted, but the benefits You have shown me cannot be numbered. I thank You that during this year

You have caused Your Word to be preached to me in truth and purity, and through it have shown me the way to heaven and my everlasting salvation. Seal all that I have heard in my heart, and grant me Your Holy Spirit that I may order my life accordingly. I thank You that You have many times given me Your holy body and blood to eat and drink in the Holy Supper; grant that it may strengthen my faith and the sanctification of my life. I thank You that You have oftentimes forgiven my sins and turned aside the punishment that I had deserved. Give me strength to avoid sins in the coming year and not to commit them willfully again. I thank You that You have blessed my calling, provided me food and clothing, granted me health, turned away misfortune, lightened my cross, and graciously guarded me in distress. You have guarded me as the apple of Your eye. You have shielded me from my foes all around who sought to destroy my soul. You have heard me in the day of trouble and permitted my prayer to ascend beyond the clouds and to come to Your throne. In my sorrow You have sent help from the sanctuary and strengthened me out of Zion. You have poured blessings upon me. When I cried to You, You did not hide Your face from me.

O loving Father, You have led me by Your hand as Your child. Mighty King, You have protected me, Your subject, against all my foes. Faithful Shepherd, You have led me, Your sheep, to lie down in green pastures. You have preserved my life, while others went to destruction. Your goodness and faithfulness have followed me everywhere, from the beginning to the end of the year. Your wisdom has led me. Your love has covered me. Your help has made me glad. Your grace has kept me. Your almighty power has rescued me on all occasions. Your tender, fatherly hand has given me everything. Your all-seeing eye has kept watch over me and preserved my going out and coming in. No evil has befallen me. Indeed, I have tasted and seen that the Lord is good! Behold, what great things He has done for my soul!

If at times You made me experience great and many moments of anguish, You also granted me life again. If at times my heart was sorely troubled, Your comfort delighted my soul. If sometimes danger or distress were near, Your help was nearer, and Your angel kept me in all my ways and delivered me from the lion's mouth.

O my God, mercifully forgive all my sins that I have committed this year. Do not punish me in the new year on account of them, but pardon me for Jesus' sake. Lord, remember not the sins of my youth or my transgressions; according to Your mercy remember me for Your goodness' sake.

O Lord God, I will now close this year with prayer, praise, and thanksgiving. I humbly asked You to remain my shield, my gracious God, also in this new year. Keep Your protecting hand over me, and in the days to come let me be commended to Your care, Your love, and Your grace.

Sing praise to God, the highest good, The author of creation, The God of love who understood Our need for His salvation. With healing balm our souls He fills And ev'ry faithless murmur stills: To God all praise and glory! Amen.   *LSB 819:1*

HYMN

Across the sky the shades of night
The New Year's Eve are fleeting.
We deck Your altar, Lord, with
light,
In solemn worship meeting;
And as the year's last hours go by,
We raise to You our earnest cry,
Once more Your love entreating.

Before the cross subdued we bow,
To You our prayer addressing,
Recounting all Your mercies now,
And all our sins confessing;
Beseeching You this coming year
To keep us in Your faith and fear
And crown us with Your blessing.

We gather up in this brief hour
The mem'ry of Your mercies:
Your wondrous goodness, love,
and pow'r
Our grateful song rehearses;
For You have been our strength
and stay

In many a dark and dreary day
Of sorrow and reverses.

We now remember, as we pray,
Our dear ones in Your caring
Who brightly shine in endless day,
Past death and all despairing.
At our life's end, Lord, as Your
own,
Bring us with them around Your
throne,
The joys of heaven sharing.

Then, gracious God, in years to
come,
We pray Your hand may guide us,
And, onward through our journey
home,
Your mercy walk beside us
Until at last our ransomed life
Is safe from peril, toil, and strife
When heav'n itself shall hide us.
LSB 899:1–5

EVENING PRAYER

For the last time in this year I now bend my knees before You, O my God. You have had mercy on me, and now I seek nothing but Your grace and peace. I know that I have many times angered and grieved You in the past twelve months. I know that I have often transgressed Your commandments, and have not always walked before You as I should. I know that by my disobedience I have justly deserved Your wrath, displeasure, and punishment. But I also know that You graciously receive penitent sinners for Jesus' sake and forgive them their iniquities, rebellions, and sins.

And so I now cast myself before Your throne and plead for mercy. O Lord, remember not the sins of my youth; according to Your mercy remember me for Your goodness' sake. Enter not into judgment with me, for I can no more be justified before You than any sinful being. Cleanse me from all sins, also my secret faults. If during this year I have failed to listen as devoutly and attentively as I ought to Your revealed Word, which makes me wise unto salvation, forgive my inattention, and let me from now on be changed from being a mere hearer into a doer of Your Word. If I have not loved You and my neighbor as I should have, remove from my heart all coldness and kindle the fire of divine love in my soul so that I can love You with my all and my neighbor as myself. If in my vocation and in the works of my calling I have not shown proper faithfulness, forgive me in Your great mercy, and grant that in the future I may better apply the talent You have entrusted to me. At all times may I be found a good steward, ready to face You when You shall call me to render an account of my trust. There is forgiveness with You, O God; and so I seek forgiveness with You. Now that the year is closing, blot out the record of my guilt, which is great indeed. Cancel it with the precious blood of my Savior, which I make my own by faith. Let my sins vanish like mist from before Your eyes. Remove them far from me and remember them no more ever again, lest in the new year I should have to appear in Your sight as a debtor.

Further, take me under Your gracious protection this night and be a wall of fire around me, that no harm befall me. Should this night prove the last for me in this dark vale of tears, then lead me, Lord, to heaven to

You and to Your saints in glory. May I thus live to You and die to You, O Lord of hosts! In life and death You help me in every fear and need. But if according to Your counsel I am appointed to live on for more years; if on waking, I am to enter a new year, let Your goodness accompany me. Lead me in Your paths. Make me godly in word and deed. Guide me in an even way, and do not take Your Holy Spirit from me, that I may live for You, serve You, and obey You. Yes, my God, this is the only thing I ask of You before I fall asleep: give me a new mind and spirit in the new year, a spirit which shall unhesitatingly perform what Your commandment bids me do, that my spirit, together with my soul and body, may remain the abode of Your Holy Spirit.

Jesus, guard and guide Thy members, Fill them with Thy boundless grace, Hear their prayers in ev'ry place. Fan to flame faith's glowing embers; Grant all Christians, far and near, Holy peace, a glad new year! Joy, O joy, beyond all gladness, Christ has done away with sadness! Hence all sorrow and repining, For the Sun of Grace is shining! Amen.   *LSB 897:4*

BELIEVING CHRISTIANS PRAY AT THE BEGINNING OF A NEW YEAR

MORNING PRAYER

O my God and Father, what am I to ask of You as I appear in prayer before Your throne during the first hours of this year that Your goodness has granted me to enter? Three things I ask of You in childlike confidence, and I trust that You will not deny me any of them.

My first request is that You would protect, cover, and sustain me in this new year with Your strong and mighty arm. During our earthly pilgrimage, we human beings are subject to many changes and exposed to countless danger that can easily ruin and destroy us, if we are not guarded and delivered by Your divine power. Graciously avert from me the manifold calamities that could overtake me. When I am threatened with danger, take me under Your wings that it may not reach me. When sorrow, tribulation, and trouble would approach me, be my protector and guard me from them. But if it is Your will that I suffer some of the afflictions of the present time, let me patiently bear them, accept them as fatherly corrections from Your hand, and submit my will to Yours. Be present with me in the hour of anguish, and let me not lose heart. Finally, let me speedily behold Your help, and let me find delight in Your favor.

My second request that I offer most humbly is that You would let Jesus dwell in my heart at all times. My Savior has prepared my heart for His temple at my Baptism. He has occupied it as His dwelling and united Himself with me before I had knowledge of myself. Yes, though I have often driven Him from me by my sins and forfeited His communion, He has returned and entered me again when His grace led me to repentance. O, Lord, let not this precious treasure be taken from me! Strengthen my faith in His name. Let me love and esteem my Jesus above everything. Let me by Your power follow in His holy footsteps, and ever let that mind be in me that was in Him also, so that at all times I may be most intimately united with Him and please You for His sake.

Finally, I ask You, in deepest humility of heart, to let Your holy angels be with me during this year and accompany me in all my ways. You send forth these ministering spirits to serve the heirs of salvation. Further, You are not willing that any should perish, but that all should inherit eternal life. Accordingly, I am one of those who are to derive comfort from the blessed service of these perfect spirits who are ever before Your throne. For this very reason I pray earnestly for the companionship of Your angels. Give them charge over me that they may keep me in all my ways. Let them encamp and be a fortress surrounding me that no evil can come near me. That way even Satan, though he were transformed into an angel of light, can have no power to harm or overwhelm me. Let me ever bear in my mind that Your angels are with me, that I may be careful not to sin, and that I may allow myself to be guided in an even path.

O my God and Father, if You will grant me this threefold request, I shall remain unharmed during this year, and this year will be one of which I shall have to say at its close: "It has pleased me." Then my soul will remain full of light, power, and strength. I shall grow in faith and holiness, and pursue my calling in good health. Therefore, if You will grant me what I have now asked of You, I shall have everything in bodily and spiritual blessings that can make me happy. And since You desire the true happiness of all people, graciously grant me for this new year what I have requested. Hear my first prayer to You in this year. Give me what I have desired in meekness and be merciful to me. I shall ever praise You with joyful lips, and tell what You have done for me.

God, Father, Son, and Spirit, hear! To all our pleas incline Your ear; Upon our lives rich blessings trace In this new year of grace. Amen.

LSB 896:7

EXHORTATION

Let the favor of the Lord our God be upon us, and establish the work of our hands upon us; yes, establish the work of our hands! Psalm 90:17

Presumptuous, and at times even timid, folk would like to know at the beginning of a new year whether it will be a prosperous one. However, it is in no one's power to make this known to another. The Lord alone knows what is going to be. Accordingly, this advice may be given to each and every person—and it is also a precious custom of godly persons—that on entering a new year we should begin it with thanksgiving, praising the goodness of the Most High, who has permitted us to begin a new year despite the many tempests of suffering and floods of troubles through which we have had to pass. To be sure, if a ship has been blessed with a great good fortune when it has passed through storms and billows, we, too, have to fall to our knees and thank God when He has permitted us to begin a new year in health and happiness.

Devout hearts will turn from thanksgiving to prayer, asking the goodness of the Most High to protect, govern, and keep them in the future. They pray: leave me not, neither forsake me in this new year, O God of my salvation! They commit to the gracious protection of God their body, their soul, and all that is dear to them.

Further, they are zealous in the new year to become more devout and godly. They resolve that, with the help of God, this year will belong to the new life into which they were born in Baptism. Surely, when aged people boast the great number of years they have lived, and yet are earthly-minded and devoted to the world, they have no greater honor than any aged non-Christian, who may even surpass them in years. For godliness, being a fruit of faith and indwelling grace, is an ornament to both young and old.

PRAYER

Lord, Lord, merciful and gracious, ever patient and of great faithfulness, You are from everlasting to everlasting, and with You there is no variation or shadow due to change. Under Your protection I have again entered upon a new year. How excellent is Your loving-kindness, O God; therefore, the children of men take refuge under the shadow of Your wings. They shall be abundantly satisfied with the goodness of Your house; the river of God is full of water.

My God and Father, during the past year I have fully experienced all this. And so I begin the new year in Your name with prayer, sighing, and supplication. Lord, be pleased to hear my voice early, on the very threshold of the new year. Give ear to me in its first hours. O Lord, I know not what may befall me during this year. A year is long; its days are many. Human misery is manifold, and the calamities that may befall us are countless. And so I come to You, O mighty and loving God, and wish to commend myself at its very beginning to Your mercy and faithfulness.

Now that all things are about to be made new; the earth again to be covered with green vegetation; the sun ascending higher and higher, and everything is to be filled with new vigor, let Your goodness and mercy be renewed upon me. I commit my soul into Your fatherly mercy and protection. Guard it against sin, that I may not contaminate it by willful and intentional rebellion. Lord Jesus, sanctify, wash, and cleanse me with Your holy blood. God the Holy Spirit, dwell in my soul, and let it be Your temple. What a blessed year it will be for me, if I, heavenly Father, abide in Your grace and live as Your child! How happy I will be if I continue in Your fellowship, O Jesus! How beautifully shall I be arrayed, O precious Holy Spirit, if You dwell in me and rule me! If the King's daughter is all glorious within, I too, thus adorned, will be pleasing to You.

And since You have up till now bestowed on me the precious gift of life and health, be pleased, if it is Your fatherly will, and if it is for my salvation of soul, graciously to preserve this gift to me during this year, that I may become more fit to serve You and fulfill the duties of my calling. But if it should please You in Your holy counsel to visit me with sickness or pain, do not depart from me. When I suffer, alleviate my pain, and let me also welcome with joy the hour You will refresh me and relieve me of my burden. O Lord, my God, hold Your protecting hand over my loved ones and my possessions. Be a wall of fire around us, as You were around Elisha. Hedge us all around as You did the house of Job.

Grant me the power of Your Holy Spirit that I may become truly godly during this year and live as a true child of God, that I may be devout in my prayers and be a careful hearer and doer of Your Word. Grant that in the new year the condition of my heart may be described like this: "The old has passed away; behold, the new has come" (2 Corinthians 5:17). Let there be in me new longings for You, new love toward my fellow human beings, a new zeal to enter into communion with You and to abide in it. Sanctify me wholly, that my entire spirit, soul, and body may be kept blameless until the day of Jesus Christ. Give me new zeal in my Christian faith that I may grow and increase in whatever is good. Bless my calling and labor, my going out and my coming in. Give me whatever blessings You have in store for me.

However, let me also remember that some time the last year of my life will begin. Grant that I may always keep myself in readiness, live in a state of repentance and faith, have my lamp burning and dressed to welcome You, my Bridegroom and my gracious God, and to enter into the Kingdom You have prepared for me from the foundation of the world. Give me a new mind and a new spirit in conformity with Your will, teach me unwaveringly to fulfill what You command, and keep me, body and soul, a habitation of Your Spirit.

Now greet the swiftly changing year With joy and penitence sincere. Rejoice! Rejoice! With thanks embrace Another year of grace. Amen.

LSB 896:1

HYMN

Jesus! Name of wondrous love,
Name all other names above,
Unto which must ev'ry knee
Bow in deep humility.

Jesus! Name decreed of old,
To the maiden mother told,
Kneeling in her lowly cell,
By the angel Gabriel.

Jesus! Name of priceless worth
To the fallen of the earth
For the promise that it gave,
"Jesus shall His people save."

Jesus! Name of mercy mild,
Given to the holy Child
When the cup of earthly woe
First He tasted here below.

Jesus! Only name that's giv'n
Under all the mighty heav'n
Whereby those to sin enslaved
Burst their fetters and are saved.

Jesus! Name of wondrous love,
Human name of God above;
Pleading only this, we flee
Helpless, O our God, to Thee.

LSB 900:1–6

EVENING PRAYER

Great and exalted God, the trust I placed in You has not been put to shame on this first day of the year. I have tasted Your goodness and love today. You have given me a cheerful heart. You have caused Your Word to be proclaimed to me. You have satisfied and overwhelmed me with many blessings. Praise, glory, and thanksgiving to You with all my heart.

You have graciously heard my prayer up till now; listen again as I pray to you before going to rest. At the dawn of the day and year I prayed for Your favor, grace, and blessing. I now add a humble request on behalf of others because according to Your commandment I am to make supplications, thanksgiving, and prayers for all kinds of people. Let those whom You have appointed to serve in government on earth discharge their duties with uninterrupted prosperity. Crown all who bear Your image and are Your servants with health. Make them careful and give them wise counsel to carry out the duties of their office properly. Let them always remember that they have been placed above others by You, in order that they may administer justice, reward good, and punish evil, that all who are subject to their rule may lead a quiet and peaceful life in all godliness and honesty.

Furnish those whom You have sent out to proclaim the Gospel of peace with the manifold gifts of Your Spirit. Give them the ability and strength to conduct their important office. Let them always open their mouths joyfully to Your praise. Grant that they may freely and without fear proclaim the divine truth, so that through their ministry Your kingdom on earth may spread ever further, and a communion of people be gathered who will take comfort in Your grace. Let the entire Christian Church be commended to You also in this year. Deal with each and every one as a loving Father who has been reconciled through Christ. Do good to them as to Your children. Bless their occupation, profession, and calling. Avert from them every misfortune and always be their Sun and Shield.

Having thus provided for them in all bodily things, show them Your grace and goodness also in spiritual matters. Let sinners be led to repentance by Your goodness so that the angels in heaven may rejoice over them. Strengthen, establish, and confirm in their good estate those who are in grace, that nothing may rob them of their crown and of that which they have committed to You. Gladden the hearts of all who are afflicted and sorrowful. Strengthen and heal the sick and the feeble. Comfort and refresh the forsaken. Have mercy on all men.

These, O Father of mercies, are the supplications I bring before You. Graciously hear them and add to them Your "Yes and Amen." In this manner bless us, O God, our God in whom we trust. Yes, bless us in spiritual and temporal things, until in eternity we shall reap blessings without end from Your hand and enter into the possession of the glories of Your house. In confident trust that You will certainly hear my request, I close my eyes and say:

Abide, O faithful Savior, Among us with Your love; Grant steadfastness and help us To reach our home above. Amen. *LSB 919:6*

Believing Christians, on Entering the Holy Season of Lent, Meditate on the Suffering of Jesus Christ

MORNING PRAYER

Jesus, I will ponder now On Your holy passion; With Your Spirit me endow For such meditation. Grant that I in love and faith May the image cherish Of Your suff'ring, pain, and death That I may not perish *(LSB 440:1)*. Thus, O faithful Savior, I beg Your gracious assistance, when in spirit I behold You journeying to that city in which the sentence of death already awaits You, where Your enemies who hate You rejoice without cause at Your coming.

This present season, which Your infinite goodness has again permitted me to reach, reminds me of the bitter suffering that You willingly submitted to in accordance with the counsel of Your heavenly Father. You did it as the Lamb of God that You might take away the sins of the entire world and render satisfaction for them. No man can by any means redeem his brother, nor give to God a ransom for him; for the redemption of their souls is costly, and it never ends. And so You took pity on those whose flesh and blood You assumed in the fullness of time. By Your bloody atonement You have regained for them the peace that they had broken and lost by their sins.

Make me able to ponder these important matters in a fruitful manner by Your power, for without You I can do nothing. Enlighten my understanding that in Your light I may behold the greatness of Your love and compassion, and may be prompted to render to You due thanks. Sanctify also my will that I may accept and apply to my benefit the blessings that You acquired by Your death. You loved me before I knew You. You gave Yourself for me at a time when I knew nothing of You. You suffered shame, scorn, disgrace, and manifold afflictions to gain happiness for me. All this You have done for me, for my benefit. Ought I not then to sing Your praises? Ought I not laud and magnify You on account of Your passion? Yes, thousand, thousand thanks shall be, dearest Jesus unto Thee *(LSB 420)*. A thousand times, dearest Jesus, shall praise and glory be given to You, O conqueror of hell and death!

I am now Your own, and You are my joy and my delight. May I soon behold You, most beautiful Sun, in Your glory, now that Your suffering is ended! Come to me, faithful friend of my soul, and unite Yourself with me. You died for all, hence also for me, in order that those who live might no longer live for themselves but for Him who died and rose again. And so enter my soul and give it life. Let me ever contemplate how much my redemption has cost You. Let me ever bear in mind that You chose to endure the most shameful death, in order to deliver me from eternal death. Let that fact ever be before my eyes as a solemn reminder that You chose to lose Your life because I chose to live for myself and for the world; and let me also be moved by it, to live for You and to follow You. Pluck me as a brand from the fire, that Your suffering for me may not have been in vain.

Let me become Your disciple, whom nothing shall be able to separate from You. And grant me Your Spirit, that during this holy Lententide, He may bring home to me all that I hear and perceive of Your bitter suffering and death. Give me grace to be constantly occupied with You in these days, and to find my delight in You, and thus to secure for myself a blessing that abides forever. If the world tries to tempt me to depravity and ease, if Satan tries to disquiet and distract me by all kinds of disturbances, if my corrupt flesh and blood draws me away and entices me to evil, let me think of Your suffering, and with firm faith resist all these temptations, that they may not overcome and vanquish me. Help me to keep You in remembrance at all times, that I may be kept from sin, and finally enter into that glory to which You have provided me access by Your suffering and death.

Should some lust or sharp temptation Fascinate my sinful mind, Draw me to Your cross and passion, And new courage I shall find. Or should Satan press me hard, Let me then be on my guard, Saying, "Christ for me was wounded," That the tempter flee confounded. Amen.   *LSB 421:2*

FOR USE IN HEALTH

EXHORTATION

For our sake He made Him to be sin who knew no sin, so that in Him we might become the righteousness of God. 2 Corinthians 5:21

Among the early Christians the holy season of Lent was a season of devotion and prayer, and it was spent in special meditations on the sufferings of Jesus. This custom is observed among Christians to this day. While Satan has induced the children of the world to enter the season of Lent not with prayer and devotion but with all the drunkenness and follies of Mardi Gras, showing that they care nothing for crucified Lord Jesus and trample His blood underfoot, the children of God have a very different spirit. They regard this worldly revelry with horror.

The children of God begin this season with prayer and singing, preparing their hearts to contemplate the suffering of their Lord. They place before their eyes the entire account of the Passion: from Gethsemane to the council, to Pilate, to Golgotha and the cross. And as they contemplate each detail, they say: "All this He did for me."

While they participate in these sacred meditations at home or at church, they are not satisfied merely to recall the history of these events, nor does their devotion vanish with the passing of Lent. Since they intend to draw comfort from the wounds of Jesus throughout the days of their life, and most especially at the hour of their death, they remember the crucified Lord Jesus as long as they live. Such remembrance prompts them to crucify their sinful desires, so that they live no longer in the manner of the lost world with its purposeful sinning, but they die to sin and rise to new life in spirit. God blesses such diligence, zeal, and desire for the sanctification of their lives.

PRAYER

O Jesus, my Jesus, how great is Your love, which was revealed in Your bitter suffering! You are the only-begotten Son of God. You are the Lamb without spot, the Lord of glory, the Most Holy, in whom there is no sin. And yet You surrendered Yourself into the most shameful death and the most cruel suffering for me, an unrighteous person, a sinner, a child of death. Oh, how great is Your unspeakable mercy! The Holy One bears my unholiness; the Perfect One, my wickedness; the Innocent One, my guilt.

My sins were laid on You so that Your righteousness could be laid on me. My Jesus, in Your suffering I behold the wrath of God against sin, the abomination of sin, the punishment of sin. For, if God on account of the iniquities of others and for imputed sins has so miserably afflicted You on the Mount of Olives—You, the innocent Lamb—and has permitted You to become so awfully disfigured by the treatment of Your enemies, how grievously will those be punished in the end who are not moved to repentance and faith by this suffering? How wretched shall they be when they have to pay for their sins themselves!

My Jesus, I approach You now. With a believing heart, I contemplate Your suffering. You entered the Garden of Gethsemane, and Your sweat is great drops of blood. Lord, have mercy! This was done for me that I might be delivered from the power of Satan. You are brought before the judgment seat, accused and condemned to death. This was done for me that I may be acquitted, when after death I will be placed before the judgment seat on the Last Day. At Your trial there were only accusers, but no advocate. This is done for me that You may be my Advocate, when my sins and my conscience accuse me. You are scourged and Your body is dyed with blood. The plowers plowed deeply on Your back. This is done for me that I may not be punished for my sins. You are led forth to death. This is done for me that my departure may be in peace, and may be my entrance into heaven, my return to the Father. You are crucified. This is done for me that through Your death I might have life. You are buried. This is done for me that You may sanctify my grave. Truly, this is love, this is mercy, that by Your bitter suffering I obtain life, grace, and forgiveness of all my sins. The chastisement of all my sins is on You that I may have peace and be delivered from punishment.

I will now place this suffering before my eyes, and wherever I may be, it shall be my constant delight. Until body and soul are sundered, Your suffering and death shall ever be enshrined in my heart. The Israelites were free from all guilt and punishment when in faith they brought a lamb for sacrifice before God and beheld the shedding of its warm blood. So I, too, know that I have been pardoned and reconciled to God, when I believe that You, O Jesus, the Lamb of God without spot or blemish, have been slain for me and have poured out Your heart's blood for me in abundance. Your blood is the true sacrificial blood, the blood of reconciliation, the blood of purification, the blood of atonement.

O my Jesus, when my heart tries to mislead me into sin, I will remember the sufferings You endured and the blood You shed. When the world by its evil example would entice me to follow its ways, I will place before my eyes Your bleeding image on the Mount of Olives, at the scourging, and on the cross. In the terror of my sins, I will flee to Your wounds. When my conscience fills me with fear, I will receive Your blood as my ransom. Yes, in my dying hour I desire to know nothing but You, O Jesus. Your holy name, O Jesus, shall be my last word. Your bleeding image, my last thought. Your last word from the cross, my last sigh in death. With You I will say: "Father, into Your hands I commit my spirit!" (Luke 23:46). In that last hour, Jesus, be my comfort, my joy, my consolation, my defense. Amen.

HYMN

O sacred Head, now wounded,
  With grief and shame weighed down,
Now scornfully surrounded
  With thorns, Thine only crown.
O sacred head, what glory,
  What bliss till now was Thine!
Yet, though despised and gory,
  I joy to call Thee mine.

What Thou, my Lord, hast suffered
  Was all for sinners' gain;
Mine, mine was the transgression,
  But Thine the deadly pain.
Lo, here I fall, my Savior!
  'Tis I deserve Thy place;
Look on me with Thy favor,
  And grant to me Thy grace.

What language shall I borrow
  To thank Thee, dearest Friend,
For this Thy dying sorrow,
  Thy pity without end?
O make me Thine forever!
  And should I fainting be,
Lord, let me never, never,
  Outlive my love for Thee.

Be Thou my consolation,
  My Shield, when I must die;
Remind me of Thy passion
  When my last hour draws nigh.
Mine eyes shall then behold Thee,
  Upon Thy cross shall dwell,
My heart by faith enfold Thee.
  Who dieth thus, dies well.

LSB 449:1–4

EVENING PRAYER

O my Jesus, my King and my Head, before I lay my weary limbs to rest and fall asleep, I must yet commune with You and commend myself to Your keeping. The meditation I began today on Your sufferings has awakened in me the sweetest of emotions. With these in my heart, let me quietly fall asleep, and let the remembrance of You go on bearing fruit in me.

By Your suffering, dearest Jesus, You have hallowed all the afflictions which may, and must, come to Your members, and hence also to me. You were sorrowful unto death. Yes, You experienced how a person feels who is utterly forsaken. You went through these sufferings, that whenever I am in similar distress, I may be delivered from it by You. And so, my Helper in need, do not be unkind to me in such hours. When I cry, do not be silent to me. I am frightened when You seem not to hear me. Trembling and anguish overtake me when You hide Yourself from me and seem not to know more or to care about me. Terror and dismay seize me when You seem to turn away from me in my temporal afflictions or my spiritual distress, as though I had no right to speak to You. And so, O Son of Grace, do not hide Yourself from me. In such dark hours, rouse my faith that I may firmly cling to Your promises and to Your love, and may confidently hope that You will turn my mourning into dancing, putting off my sackcloth and transforming my sadness into joy.

Indeed, my Jesus, speak words to cheer my soul in affliction. Don't leave me or withdraw Your hand from me. Let me behold Your fair likeness; let me consider that Your suffering ended gloriously. Let me firmly trust in Your goodness and mercy. Let me also become like You in my suffering, and let me follow Your example. Let me willingly submit to all that Your wise and eternal providence chooses to lay on me. Let me be patient when tribulations rush on me like a flood. Let the same mind be in me always that was in You, O Jesus. In my requests, keep me from presuming to instruct You on the time and the hour when You are to help me. Teach me to say with You: "Father . . . not My will, but Yours be done" (Luke 22:42). In the hours of sorrow, let me so conduct myself, following Your example, that at last I may enter with You into the joy that never ends. Let me remember You, and my sadness will soon flee away. The remembrance of You, O Jesus, makes my sad heart sing for joy. Hold Your bleeding image ever before my eyes, and I will never be without comfort, but will be powerfully refreshed and comforted in You.

Be with me also during this night. When I wake tomorrow and every time I greet the new day, let me be satisfied with beholding You. Strengthen me continually with Your hand until my end arrives. And when it arrives, when death knocks at my door, let me look forward in faith to my transformation and fall asleep in blessed peace. Receive my spirit in that hour. Let Your suffering be before my eyes. From it, let me draw comfort, strength, and peace in abundant measure. Amen.

BELIEVING CHRISTIANS PONDER ON THE DAY OF JESUS' DEATH, GOOD FRIDAY

EXHORTATION

Surely He has borne our griefs and carried our sorrows; yet we esteemed Him stricken, smitten by God, and afflicted. But He was wounded for our transgressions; He was crushed for our iniquities; upon Him was the chastisement that brought us peace, and with His stripes we are healed. Isaiah 53:4–5

Good Friday is the real day of the Passion of our blessed Lord Jesus; on this day He died. It is true that even worldly people, from a sense of decency or because they fear the opinion of their fellow human beings, pass this day quietly. But Christians have chosen this day as a day of special devotion.

They ponder on this day the suffering of Jesus that He took upon Himself out of love. Oh, what a great love! O love, how deep, how broad, how high, which prompted You, O Jesus, to enter upon this way of sorrows! Love impelled Jesus to become man; love moved Him to give Himself for us and to die upon the cross. Christians ponder the sufferings of

Christ as innocent sufferings. We are not to think that the Savior had done the least thing deserving of punishment. He was holy, undefiled, set apart from sinners. He did no sin, and there was no deceit in His mouth. Hence, on the part of Jesus it was wholly undeserved suffering; but He freely chose to take it upon Himself for our sake. His suffering was appointed for Him and sent to Him by His heavenly Father. Since Jesus suffered according to the determined plan of God (Acts 2:23), He knew beforehand what awaited Him. This, however, does not free the Jews from guilt. No. God would have been able without the aid of the Jews completely to exhaust and slay His Son. He had begun to do so already in Gethsemane, when Christ lay prostrate on the ground and His sweat was, as it were, great drops of blood. For His own purpose, God made use of the stubbornness and the malice of the Jews; their purpose was not to do the will of God, but to vent their ill will and spite against Christ. In a similar manner, Joseph's brothers did not sell him into slavery to make him a great lord, but they meant to do evil to him. God, however, turned the tables and brought good out of it (Genesis 50:20). The suffering of Christ was real suffering. He keenly felt every wound and smarted under every pain.

Believers consider all these things and use them as a mirror that reflects the anger of God over man's sin and, even more, the love of God working for man's salvation.

PRAYER

O loving and blessed Jesus, I come before You to meditate with true devotion of heart on Your bitter suffering. Lord, let Your woes, Your patience, inspire my heart with strength to vanquish every temptation and spurn every unworthy desire. This is what my heart would cherish most of all. What pain my soul's redemption has cost You, O Savior! O Lamb of God slain in innocence! You suffered because of all my sins. Yes, the sins, debt, iniquities, unrighteousness, and wickedness of all people were laid squarely on You and You claimed them as Your very own, so that in the judgment of God You became the greatest sinner of all, yes, sin itself. And as our sins were all on You, so on You also came our punishment, overwhelming You like a flood. During Your public ministry as a teacher, Your lot was contempt, vilification, and blasphemy. But during Your Passion all these things were poured on You with multiplied force. Not satisfied with raising accusations against You and forcing You to stand trial in two courts, the spiritual and the secular, and suffering Yourself to be sentenced to death by both, You were also made to suffer the cruelest physical pains. Your holy body was wounded, scourged, torn, and suffused with blood.

Behold, children of Adam, was there ever grief like the grief of our Jesus? His head was crowned with thorns. His body was covered with blood and bruised from His bonds. On the cross, nails were driven through His feet and hands. His side was pierced by a spear. He could truthfully say, "I am a worm and no man." But not only was His holy body so miserably maltreated, He had to suffer also the most extreme agony in His soul. His soul was sorrowful even to death. The waves of God's wrath rushed upon Him, and the pains of hell took hold of Him with such violence that He cried out from His cross: "My God, My God, why have You forsaken Me?" (Matthew 27:46). And then, at last, death followed.

O Lamb, slain by God, all this You have suffered and endured for my good, for my benefit, for my comfort, for my peace, for my redemption, for my welfare, and for my salvation. If Christ had not come into this world and assumed our miserable form, if He had not willingly died for our sins, we would have had to suffer eternal damnation. But now, when we believe in You and in the confidence of faith make Your holy blood our own, we shall not be condemned but shall have eternal life through You.

O my Jesus, let Your bitter pains ever be before my eyes and in my heart. Let me draw from them comfort and obtain righteousness from it, and by it be made a godly person. Let me not spend a day on which Your bleeding image is not before my eyes. Let Your suffering, Your blood, Your wounds be written on my hands and in my heart so that with each breath nothing but Your Passion, Your death, You blood, may be in my thoughts. Thus You will wean me from the world, sanctify, wash, and purify me.

My Jesus, as Your suffering raises me up, gladdens, comforts, awakes, and edifies me, so do the seven words You uttered upon the tree. It also for me that You prayed: "Forgive them!" It was for me that You cried: "My God, My God, why have You forsaken Me?" that I might never be forsaken—not in the hour of death, not in my crosses, not in my affliction, not at the judgment on the Last Day, not in time or in all eternity. For me You said: "I thirst." Grant me in turn to embrace You by faith and pant after You as the deer pants after the streams of water, so that I may be delighted and refreshed in Your love. For me You said: "Behold, your mother!" (John 19:27). Although I may stand like Mary beneath the cross, forsaken by all people in my tribulation, You will cordially receive me, have mercy on me, take care of me, help me, and be gracious to me. Let me hear, in my dying hour, Your voice saying: "Today you will be with Me in Paradise" (Luke 23:43). Give me the assurance in the days of my health, repeat it to my on my deathbed, and after I have departed let it be fulfilled in me. For me You said: "It is finished!" Everything has now been done that I ought to have done. All has been suffered that I ought to have suffered. Salvation, life, peace, joy, comfort, bliss, the crown of life, and the white garments have been procured for me. Yes, Your last word upon the cross shall become a word of comfort and cheer also when I die: "Father, into Your hands I commit My spirit!" (Luke 23:46). Thus will I pray, repeating the words after You. Amen.

HYMN

O dearest Jesus, what law hast Thou broken
That such sharp sentence should on Thee be spoken?
Of what great crime hast Thou to make confession,
What dark transgression?

They crown Thy head with thorns, they smite, they scourge Thee;
With cruel mockings to the cross they urge Thee;
They give Thee gall to drink, they still decry Thee;
They crucify Thee.

Whence come these sorrows, whence this mortal anguish?
It is my sins for which Thou, Lord, must languish;
Yea, all the wrath, the woe, Thou dost inherit,
This I do merit.

What punishment so strange is suffered yonder!
The Shepherd dies for sheep that loved to wander;
The Master pays the debt His servants owe Him,
Who would not know Him.

The sinless Son of God must die in sadness;
The sinful child of man may live in gladness;
Man forfeited his life and is acquitted;
God is committed.

There is no spot in me by sin untainted;
Sick with sin's poison, all my heart had fainted;
My heavy guilt to hell had well-nigh brought me,
Such woe it wrought me.

O wondrous love, whose depth no heart hath sounded,
That brought Thee here, by foes and thieves surrounded!
All worldly pleasures, heedless, I was trying
While Thou wert dying.

O mighty King, no time can dim Thy glory!
How shall I spread abroad Thy wondrous story?
How shall I find some worthy gifts to proffer?
What dare I offer?

For vainly doth our human wisdom ponder—
Thy woes, Thy mercy, still transcend our wonder.
Oh, how should I do aught that could delight Thee!
Can I requite Thee?

Yet unrequited, Lord, I would not leave Thee;
I will renounce whate'er doth vex or grieve Thee
And quench with thoughts of Thee and prayers most lowly
All fires unholy.

But since my strength will nevermore suffice me
To crucify desires that still entice me,
To all good deeds O let Thy Spirit win me
And reign within me!

I'll think upon Thy mercy without ceasing,
That earth's vain joys to me no more be pleasing;
To do Thy will shall be my sole endeavor
Henceforth forever.

Whate'er of earthly good this life may grant me,
I'll risk for Thee; no shame, no cross, shall daunt me.
I shall not fear what foes can do to harm me
Nor death alarm me.

But worthless is my sacrifice, I own it;
Yet, Lord, for love's sake Thou wilt not disown it;
Thou wilt accept my gift in Thy great meekness
Nor shame my weakness.

And when, dear Lord, before Thy throne in heaven
To me the crown of joy at last is given,
Where sweetest hymns Thy saints forever raise Thee,
I, too, shall praise Thee. LSB 439:1–15

BELIEVING CHRISTIANS REJOICE OVER THE RESURRECTION OF JESUS CHRIST

MORNING PRAYER

O my Jesus, as I now open my eyes and look into the bright day, I seem to begin life anew after having lain in death, as it were, during the peaceful slumber of the night. Yes, now I begin really to live, since You live and have risen from the dead. By Your resurrection You have won for me this happiness, that in You I may have life and have it abundantly. Let me truly realize the happiness that comes from Your return to life! Let the noble life that is in You be gloriously manifested and break forth in me, so that not only I experience it, but others may also see this new life in me. If in the realm of nature it can plainly be seen when the sap and the new life is rising in the trees, how much more must it be manifested in the realms of grace when Your holy life has entered the soul. Since, then, by Your resurrection I have also become a partaker of Your life, let me reveal it in Your strength and shine with it before all the world.

Let me manifest this life toward God by diligently keeping Him in my thoughts, by making Him attend my going out and my coming in, by beginning and accomplishing all things with Him. Accordingly, let me not be ashamed to speak of Him, to praise Him everywhere as my best and truest Friend, and to praise His goodness in every place. Guard me, though, from doing these things with a false motive, from showing off. Instead, let me praise Him with sincere love and so glorify His holy name.

Let Your life, furthermore, be manifest in me toward my neighbors, that I may be concerned for them, talk to them about the condition of their soul, with them take delight in You. Consecrate my time for Your purposes that I may never spend it in vain conversation and sinful amusements. When I speak of You to others, let it always be done with the profoundest reverence, that when speaking of You I do not seek to show off my wisdom but rather to increase Your honor.

Finally, let Your life be manifest in those duties that I observe toward myself. Let me gladly be in Your company and commune with You. Let me always find my joy in You and never tire of striving to form a closer acquaintance with You and to enter an ever more intimate relationship with You. In this way make me happy here in time and hereafter in eternity. I am under the strongest obligation to make this my top priority in life. Help me, O risen Savior, that I may keep what I have and that no one may take from me my crown that I even now possess in believing hope. Let me never in any way forsake You. Let neither height nor depth, neither death nor life, neither angels nor principalities nor powers, nor things present nor things to come, nor any other creature ever separate me from Your love, from Your fellowship, from my union with You.

Let me not only esteem very highly and prize above all else the gifts of grace that You impart to me and bestow upon me while I live in You, but let me also use them properly, that I may reap the sweetest fruits from them. Then, when my heart is aglow with Your love, when my knowledge is growing and increasing, let me constantly continue in such growth, and let me labor without tiring to convert others from the error of their ways and to save their souls from death.

If You, O my Savior, who I constantly trust because of Your goodness, will grant me this grace for which I ask—namely, that I may live in You and by my conversation everywhere manifest and reveal the new life You have given—then let me not fall again into sleep and death, but daily rise again, continue to walk a new life, and bring forth good fruits until at the appointed time You lead me into life everlasting.

Jesus lives! For me He died, Hence will I, to Jesus living, Pure in heart and act abide, Praise to Him and glory giving. All I need God will dispense; This shall be my confidence. Amen. *LSB 490:3*

EXHORTATION

*I am the first and the last, and the living one. I died, and
behold I am alive forevermore, and I have the keys of Death and
Hades.* Revelation 1:17–18

Holy Eastertide is a time of joy for all the children of God, for they
rejoice from their heart in their risen Jesus. They rejoice because their redemption is completed. For, after Jesus, who had offered Himself to make
satisfaction for us, has been raised from the dead, a complete ransom has
been paid for us! God is reconciled and has accepted the death of His Son
in place of our death and has granted us life for His sake. Believing souls
rejoice over the glorious witness and testimonies of the resurrection of
their Jesus. Is it not a glorious testimony to be told that He was seen ten
times after His resurrection; that on one occasion He appeared to five
hundred brothers (1 Corinthians 15:6); that He spoke with individual
disciples, ate with them (Acts 10:41), and permitted them to touch and
handle Him (John 20:25; 1 John 1:1)? All these testimonies at once dispense with all cause for unbelief. Yes, unbelief is still conquered by every
believer because, according to Galatians 2:20, Jesus lives in us! Hence He
must have risen and still be alive. They rejoice because they have received
the seal and assurance of the gracious forgiveness of their sins, of their
peace with God, and know that as believers in Christ they can fearlessly
approach God and that He, in turn, will come to them. They are assured
that the resurrection of Jesus will comfort them also in their dying hour.
By His death Jesus sweetened death for them and hallowed their graves,
assuring them that they will rise to life everlasting.

Accordingly, they spend holy Eastertide, like other festivals, in heartfelt devotion, prayer, praise, and contemplation of the blessings of God.
They endeavor to rise spiritually every day and to quit the grave of their
sins, that is, their evil habits, naughtiness, and iniquities. They strive to
spend the remainder of their lives in faith and holiness to the glory of
the Lord.

PRAYER

The voice of rejoicing and salvation is in the tents of the righteous.
The right hand of the Lord is exalted! The right hand of the Lord has done

valiantly. O risen Jesus, mighty victor, Jesus Christ, conqueror of death, powerful Samson, Your resurrection fills my heart with pure joy, now that by Your grace I may celebrate this holy festival. On bended knees, with folded hands, I say: "Thanks be to God who gives us the victory through our Lord Jesus Christ!" "Christ is risen from the dead! He is risen indeed! Alleluia!" This is a joyful message. Our Surety has been released from the prison of the grave; so our sin must be canceled, God reconciled, our debt paid in full. Who will condemn us now? It is Christ who died, yes, who has been raised again and is even now at the right hand of God, making intercession for us. Jesus has abolished death and brought life and immortality to light.

O Jesus, dearest friend, Your resurrection brings me a threefold comfort. I say on this festival: The resurrection of Jesus is my victory. Now my sins can no more condemn me. By the blood and wounds of Christ, by His resurrection, I have obtained forgiveness of all my sins, no matter how many or how great and grievous they may be. Here is an all-sufficient ransom, a perfect redemption. In Christ, we have the redemption through His blood, namely, the forgiveness of sins. Death cannot harm me, for Christ has overcome death. Yes, He has changed death into a sweet sleep and made it my departure to my Father in heaven. Satan is a vanquished foe. He may roar, but he cannot devour me. He may accuse me, but Jesus intercedes for me and bestows on me His righteousness, in which I am justified in the sight of God and saved. Hell does not terrify me, for Christ has rescued me from hell. "Whoever believes in Him should not perish but have eternal life" (John 3:16). O glad day, on which my salvation is sealed and happiness is confirmed to me! Jesus lives and I will live also! I am united with Him now in faith and will be after this life in glory.

Rejoicing in the risen Redeemer, my soul says: the resurrection of Jesus is my own resurrection. Since the Head has risen, the members cannot remain in death. However, on the Last Day I will not simply rise like all others, but I will rise as a child of God, a joint-heir with Christ, by virtue of His merit and atonement. And so I do not fear the grave. I regard it as a chamber of rest where my Savior will let me sleep until He speaks and says: Arise, O dead, and appear before the judgment seat. Oh, the greatness of the glory that my Savior has gained for me! Risen Jesus, how can I ever announce, glorify, and praise Your goodness enough? Oh, the love that bestows on me life and salvation! Now all injury caused by the fall of Adam has been superabundantly repaired.

And my Savior, Your resurrection yields me a very strong comfort also in my sufferings. You lay locked in the tomb, but came forth the victor. Thus the night of my affliction will also pass, and the sun of Your joy, grace, help, and refreshing will rise for me again. O Jesus, only three days did You remain in the grave. And so, after my tribulation, the day of deliverance is appointed also for me. After the weary years of suffering will follow the glad year of jubilee. You arose in a glorified body. Your wounds and nail-prints were no longer bloody, nor did they cause You pain, but were radiant like the sun. Thus my body also will be transformed and glorified when You awaken me from the dust. My former body will be restored to me; I will be clothed in my former flesh. This body with all its members, which I have consecrated to Your service, will share in the splendor of heaven and be glorified. Yes, since You, O Jesus, live, I have in You a faithful and constant friend. You will provide for me while I live, sustain me while I suffer, protect me from my enemies, gladden me in affliction, refresh me in my dying hour, keep me while in the grave, and finally receive me to glory and adorn me with the crown of life, which You have promised also to me. Amen.

HYMN

Awake, my heart, with gladness,
  See what today is done;
Now, after gloom and sadness,
  Comes forth the glorious sun.
My Savior there was laid
Where our bed must be made
  When to the realms of light
  Our spirit wings its flight.

The foe in triumph shouted
  When Christ lay in the tomb;
But lo, he now is routed,
  His boast is turned to gloom.
For Christ again is free;
In glorious victory

He who is strong to save
Has triumphed o'er the grave.

This is a sight that gladdens—
  What peace it doth impart!
Now nothing ever saddens
  The joy within my heart.
No gloom shall ever shake,
No foe shall ever take,
  The hope which God's own Son
  In love for me has won.

Now hell, its prince, the devil,
  Of all their pow'r are shorn;
Now I am safe from evil,

And sin I laugh to scorn.
Grim death with all its might
Cannot my soul affright;
It is a pow'rless form,
Howe'er it rave and storm.

The world against me rages,
Its fury I disdain;
Though bitter war it wages,
Its work is all in vain.
My heart from care is free,
No trouble troubles me.
Misfortune now is play,
And night is bright as day.

Now I will cling forever
To Christ, my Savior true;

My Lord will leave me never,
Whate'er He passes through.
He rends death's iron chain;
He breaks through sin and pain;
He shatters hell's grim thrall;
I follow Him through all.

He brings me to the portal
That leads to bliss untold,
Whereon this rhyme immortal
Is found in script of gold:
"Who there My cross has shared
Finds here a crown prepared;
Who there with Me has died
Shall here be glorified."

LSB 467:1–7

EVENING PRAYER

O living Savior, Lord Jesus Christ! Abide with me, for it is toward evening and the day is far spent. You have shown me Your bountiful grace. You have not only granted me health so that I have once more been able to celebrate the triumph of Your resurrection from the dead—for which mercy I owe You thanks without end—but from the fact that You have assumed life again You have enriched me with abundant comfort and caused this joy to be proclaimed to me. Do not let the manifestations of Your love depart from me. Abide with me in Your grace, and hear my prayer I bring to You before I fall asleep.

At the first glimpse of this day, when I remembered Your blessed resurrection, I called upon You fervently that You would manifest Your life in me in every way. Call to me with Your strong voice: "Awake, O sleeper, and arise from the dead, and Christ will shine on you" (Ephesians 5:14). Let me hear this voice and heed it; give me Your light! Cause me to rise spiritually, that I may not remain dead in my sins. I cannot accomplish this by my own strength. Although I read such books as might edify me, though I listen zealously to others who show and point the way, yet I cannot achieve this result, that I become a new person and live in You. This is Your work alone. You must accomplish it. You must work in me both to will and to do. And so let Your grace in me be powerful and awaken me from the sleep of sin.

Give more light to my intellect that I may know You and the ways in which I must go. Grant my will a greater conformity to Yours. Implant in my heart a better and more sincere intention to do everything for Your glory. Give to the faculties of my mind a willing obedience that You may govern me and have Your mind live in me. O my Savior, if You will do this, I will rise from sleep and show that I have become a new creation in You.

After Your blessed resurrection not only was Your holy body glorified, but from the moment you left the grave You had a new sort of life entirely. And so let me, when rising spiritually with You, truly experience and perceive this spiritual resurrection and new life that You have given me. Let others also notice and perceive it in me, so that everyone may see by my godly way of life that I no longer live in the darkness, but in Your light. Truly You have transferred me from the kingdom of darkness into Your marvelous light. From now on let me renounce all ungodliness and worldly lusts. Instead, let me live righteously, soberly, and godly in this present age. Let me turn from the world and live only for You so that You may live in me and walk in me. Keep my eyes constantly open so that I may always be wakeful, and may not lose my new spiritual life. Let me pass from glory to glory, from knowledge to knowledge, until at last I will be united with You and live with You forever. Amen.

BELIEVING CHRISTIANS MEDITATE ON THE ASCENSION OF CHRIST

AN EVENING PRAYER FOR ASCENSION

Suggested by the promise of the ascending Lord: "Behold, I am with you always!"

As low the light of day descends,
And fall the shadows wide;
As now, O Lord, the journey ends,
With me, I pray, abide!

The path together we have walked
Throughout the sunny day,
And You of heavenly things have
* talked;*
Abide now here, I pray!

My heart has burned, as yonder
* burn*
The stars within the sky;
And still, O Lord, my soul does
* yearn*
To have Your presence nigh.
A plenteous board I cannot spread
Before You as my Guest;
But in the breaking of the bread
I shall myself be blest!

This very eve come dine with me,
Whatever may be my fare;

And in the lifting of the cup,
I shall a blessing share!

Abide with me through all the
* night*
And converse with me hold,
Until the sun the eastern height
Shall climb in robes of gold.

Yes, gracious Master, e'er abide
With me and be my Friend!
I wish no other friend beside
With whom my life to blend.

You have a charm of voice and
* speech*
That thrills me to the core.
O hear my prayer, I now beseech,
Abide till life be o'er!

MORNING PRAYER

Eternal High Priest, glorified Jesus, You are holy, undefiled, and separate from all sinners. After You had made atonement, You ascended on high, yes, above the heavens, and prepared for Your redeemed the place to which they shall come when they have finished their course and kept the faith. You intercede for them and will finally gather them around You that they may be forever where You are. I am also one of those whom You have purchased and redeemed with Your precious blood. The blood that flowed from Your pierced side was shed for all people. Oh, how I rejoice over Your triumphant ascension! By it You are making a way for me and directing me to the place where I shall go when I depart this life as Your servant. How delighted I am at this moment when I awake and in spirit hear the angelic choirs of heaven singing their joyful chorus: Alleluia! For the Lord God almighty reigns! And so I learn that I shall join those perfect spirits in singing hymns of praise and gratitude to Your honor throughout eternity, when by a blessed death I shall at last enter that realm of joy to which You have made a way for me by Your ascension to Your Father and my Father, to Your God and my God.

However, O Prince of Life, since Your ascension cannot be of any benefit to me if I remain lying in the dungeon of my sins; since the victory You have gained over sin, death, and hell will profit me nothing if I do not myself fight against these enemies of my soul; since I cannot attain to that heavenly glory You entered by Your ascension on high if I do not become heavenly minded here on earth; O dearest Redeemer, grant me Your grace! Give me strength to enter upon a new spiritual life and become heavenly minded. Kindle in me a heartfelt desire to know the treasures of Your grace which You have obtained for me by Your suffering and death, by Your ascension, by Your sitting at the right hand of the Father. I find these treasures described in the revealed Word of God; grant that this Word may urge me to love You fervently and to prefer You above all else. And when I have learned to know the glory, the righteousness, the peace, and the grace You have obtained for me, let me zealously strive to enter into true and intimate friendship with You. Let this be accomplished through living faith, which places me within Your wounds and You within my heart, and which unites with You so closely that I live in You and You in me. Let this be accomplished also by my continuous communion with You, by my persevering, by my continuous prayer, and by my untiring remembrance of You. Thus will my heart always be where my treasure is.

Preserve me, lest I allow myself to be drawn away from this heavenly disposition by the lust of the world. Keep me from coveting earthly things that burden my mind and draw me to the earth with their powerful weight, thus rendering me unfit for ascending to heaven. Let me always direct my heart to that place where I long to be forever. Let me wish to die only from a desire to be with You. Lead me thus by Your side, as long as I must, according to Your counsel, continue in this valley of sorrow. And when at last my eyes shall close, and I shall yield my spirit into Your hands, take me to Yourself in heaven.

How beautiful, how lovely, how glorious, how peaceful I shall be when I am with You! Even now I rejoice when I think of what I shall be. I confidently hope to be with You forever. Let not my hope be put to shame, but grant my desire, and let me persevere and remain constant in the blessed state of grace, so that when I die, I may behold Your face, and when I awake again, I may be satisfied with Your likeness, and then may never again be moved from Your side. Amen.

EXHORTATION

I am ascending to My Father and your Father, to My God and your God. John 20:17

The contemplation of the ascension of Jesus, our Savior, cannot fail to comfort and edify believers. It reminds us of the certainty of our redemption. Since the Victor returns to the place from which He came—to heaven—He has finished the work He was sent to do. When He was conceived and born, He came forth from the Father, and in His ascension He returns to the Father, having obtained for the children of Adam and Eve peace, joy, forgiveness of sins, righteousness, and salvation.

The ascension of Christ reminds a believing soul of the fact that we have here no lasting city, but we seek one to come. Neither the godly nor the ungodly have a permanent dwelling place on earth. The godly do not desire such a habitation because they know of a better one. The ungodly, though they desire it, do not obtain it. It is appointed to men once to die, and after that comes the Judgment. Now, then, since there is no permanent dwelling place for people here on earth, the godly direct their hearts to that place where they wish to be forever. Yes, they are reminded everyday, when looking at their homes, their clothes, their possessions, and their relatives, that they must leave all these things behind them.

In order that their place of glory may be found prepared for them when the hour of their deliverance from the misery of this life comes, they are diligent to ascend to heaven in a spiritual manner. Earth is cast out of their thoughts; they are mindful of heaven. The world is denied a share of their love; they cling to Jesus by faith. The world is not permitted to determine their life; they live according to the will of God, not the customs of this passing age. And so, whenever they lift their eyes toward heaven, they say to themselves: "Yonder is my fatherland, my heritage, my eternal home."

PRAYER

The Lord has gone up with the sound of the trumpet! Sing praises to God! Sing praises to our King! Thus, O my Jesus, mighty victor, I celebrate Your ascension. You have entered into glory, having finished the work of redeeming the human race. Now all our enemies—the devil, the world, sin, and death—lie prostrate beneath Your feet. You have delivered us from them. You have cleansed us from our sins and now have taken Your seat at the right hand of the Divine Majesty in heaven.

O my Jesus, all this is a very great comfort to me, and I rejoice over it from my inmost soul. As I rejoiced at Your coming to earth, so I take comfort in Your ascension. You sit at the right hand of God and intercede for us. And so when I pray, I am not praying alone. Your Spirit prays in me and Your Son prays for me. Thus my poor, feeble prayer will graciously be heard for Your sake.

I rejoice when I remember Your words: "And if I go and prepare a place for you, I will come again and will take you to Myself, that where I am there you may be also" (John 14:3). This promise refreshes my spirit because I know that You have prepared a place for me. When I die, I shall find a place where I shall abide and remain forever. You have been crowned with glory and honor, and laid up for me the beautiful crown of righteousness, which You, the righteous Judge, will give to all who have loved Your appearing. You have taken possession of Your kingdom, and rule over heaven and earth, in the realm of nature, of grace, and of glory. And the day will come when You will say to me and all believers: "Come, you who are blessed by My Father, inherit the kingdom prepared for you from the foundation of the world" (Matthew 25:34).

According to Your human nature, You have received gifts for humanity that You might distribute them to us, Your brothers and sisters, who believe in You. O my Jesus, grant me a twofold portion; for I need double strength and comfort. Grant me Your Holy Spirit! Give me Your righteousness, sonship with God, life, peace, and finally heaven's glory and everlasting salvation. Now that You, my Head, have been exalted, You will draw me, Your member, after You. Since Your Spirit gives me life, I will be with You in eternity. What comfort, what joy, what glory this my Savior promises to His believers, His disciples, saying: "Where I am, there will my servant be also!" (John 12:26). O my Jesus, let me be where You are. Draw me to Yourself, to the place where You are exalted at the right hand of God. Bring me to the company of the holy angels and all the saints. Let me behold Your glory, the glory You have prepared for Your believers.

Although, dearest Friend of my soul, by ascending on high You have withdrawn from me Your visible presence, still You are with me invisibly as You have promised: "Behold, I am with you always, to the end of the age" (Matthew 28:20). And so I am everywhere content. I know You are with me in the hour of need. You deliver me from danger. You comfort me in affliction. You refresh me in suffering. You protect me in all adversities. And so I am of good courage; the Lord Jesus is on my side. I will not fear; what can anyone do to me? Though I do not see You, yet I love You and rejoice in You with joy unspeakable. I will see You when my soul after its blessed departure from this body ascends to heaven. I will also see You with my own eyes on the last day, when You will raise the dead.

And so I want to ascend to heaven each day and contemplate with the eyes of faith my future home, my future crown, my dwelling place, my robe of white. As long as I am in the world, I will shut out the world from my heart, from my love, from my life. I will flee the world with all its vanities, habits, and sins, because these hinder me from ascending to heaven in this spiritual manner. Thus, while I live, I live to the Lord, and when I die, I die in the Lord. Amen.

HYMN

See, the Lord ascends in triumph;
  Conqu'ring King in royal state,
Riding on the clouds, His chariot,
  To His heav'nly palace gate.
Hark! The choirs of angel voices
  Joyful alleluias sing,
And the portals high are lifted
  To receive their heav'nly King.

Who is this that comes in glory
  With the trump of jubilee?
Lord of battles, God of armies,
  He has gained the victory.
He who on the cross did suffer,
  He who from the grave arose,
He has vanquished sin and Satan;
  He by death has crushed His
  foes.

While He lifts His hands in blessing,
  He is parted from His friends;
While their eager eyes behold Him,
  He upon the clouds ascends.
He who walked with God and
pleased Him,
  Preaching truth and doom to
  come,
He, our Enoch, is translated
  To His everlasting home.

Now our heav'nly Aaron enters
  With His blood within the veil;
Joshua now is come to Canaan,
  And the kings before Him
  quail.
Now He plants the tribes of Israel
  In their promised resting place;

Now our great Elijah offers
  Double portion of His grace.

He has raised our human nature
  On the clouds to God's right hand;
There we sit in heav'nly places,
  There with Him in glory stand.
Jesus reigns, adored by angels;
  Man with God is on the throne.
By our mighty Lord's ascension
  We by faith behold our own. LSB 494:1–5

EVENING PRAYER

O living and exalted Savior, You have ascended on high and have sat down, also according to Your human nature, at the right hand of the majesty of God. By this act, as also by Your blessed incarnation, You have ennobled my nature and acquired for me a title in heaven. Praise, glory, and thanks to You for this grace!

But I pray You to let the purpose of Your ascension be accomplished in me. Your purpose is that all believers are to be with You forever, and that they are to be one with You as You are one with the Father. Oh, how my spirit is filled with joy when I think of these things! Let me not experience this joy in vain. Let me arrive at its full fruition in eternity. O merciful Lord, let me even in my present life attain to the blessedness of being one with You. Let me as a member be attached to You, my Head. Never again let me be sundered from You. Let me obtain in You power, strength, and increase in all good works, in order that I may be able to remain with You in eternity.

To this end let me from now on be one with You and all Your believers as regards the glorious treasure you have acquired for us by Your suffering and death. Let me, together with all my fellow-Christians, become partakers of those treasures, and in that way obtain as my own Your peace, the forgiveness of sins, righteousness, access to the throne of grace, and the assurance of life everlasting.

Let me be one with You and all believers in spirit. Let Your Spirit—not the spirit of the world—guide, enlighten, sanctify, govern, glorify, and unite me with You. Let me by this Spirit be in You and with You. Yes, let me be Your own, even as You are united with the Father in one Spirit and life. Let me be one with all believers in love, that I may cherish them with a sincere and constant love, and may wish, do, and procure for them whatever I would wish for myself. Let my love toward them be fervent, zealous, and constant.

True love is the bond of perfection and it holds together all the virtues that are fitting for Christians and causes them to be put to use. As You are united with Your Father in unspeakable love, so let me be one with You and with Him. Let me heartily love You and Him who sent You. Let me consecrate to You and to Him my will, my intellect, my affections, and my entire life. O my exalted Savior, if I obtain this grace from You, I shall be truly happy, truly blessed during my pilgrimage on earth and after my pilgrimage here has drawn to a close. When I have attained to unity with You by Your Spirit, You are mine and I am Yours. I can at all times derive a sure comfort from Your assistance, Your graciousness, Your love, Your blessing. I can always put my trust in You. I need fear no trouble. I may hope for every good thing from You. Is this not a blessedness to be envied that I receive in and through You?

But this blessedness does not end when I cease to live here. In fact, it rises to a higher stage and reaches greater perfection. When resting in Your arms, in which You will constantly hold me as Your own, You will glorify and receive my spirit with You into glory when I have closed my eyes and yielded up my spirit. For, could the Head rise and leave His members dead? You will unite me with You forever and let me taste joy, rapture, and pleasures at Your right hand forevermore. You will grant me to occupy the place You have prepared for me by Your death and by ascending into the kingdom of Your Father. You will lead me into the everlasting habitations of peace. Oh, what blessedness, then, is in store for me, when I will have become one with You as You are with the Father! What happiness awaits me yonder when I will have entered fully into Your fellowship! I rejoice even now at the thought of this great glory. Let my rejoicing not be in vain. Let me while I am here have a foretaste of heaven. Yet yonder in the eternal home, let me, together with all believers, be fully united with You, with Your Father, and with the Holy Spirit forever and ever. Yes, before I fall asleep, assure me by Your Spirit that my prayer has certainly been heard. Let it not have come before You in vain, that I may from now on become, and forever remain, one with You.

He has raised our human nature On the clouds to God's right hand; There we sit in heav'nly places, There with Him in glory stand. Jesus reigns, adored by angels; Man with God is on the throne. By our mighty Lord's ascension We by faith behold our own. Amen. *LSB 494:5*

BELIEVING CHRISTIANS MEDITATE ON THE OUTPOURING OF THE HOLY SPIRIT AT THE HOLY FESTIVAL OF PENTECOST

MORNING PRAYER

O Spirit of Grace, who from eternity proceeds from the Father and the Son, You were visibly poured out on the apostles after the triumph and ascension of my Jesus. I gladly call to mind that fact today, for by that event they were fitted for the discharge of their office. I pray that You would enter also into my soul, that it may become a temple of the living God, prepared by You and fit to obtain that eternal life for which I was created and purchased by my Redeemer.

You are the down payment of our adoption and our inheritance. Come to me and assure me that I am a child of God, that I have a well-grounded claim to the inheritance of the saints in light. Lead me into a true quietness of heart and mind, that I may have no pleasure in the bustle of the world and its sinful unrest. Rather, let me flee from it and delight myself solely in You and with You. Sweep my heart clean of all impurity, wickedness, and sin, in order that with each year, each week, yes, with each day I may become more pure. Remove farther and farther from me all evil, that it may become manifest that I have become a new and better human being. Sanctify me, for how otherwise should I be able to see the Lord? Kindle in me also the true light that I still lack, in order that I may grow in Your knowledge, have a desire to understand the ways of heaven, and make every effort to enter them and walk in them without growing weary.

Let me keenly perceive my misery, my lost state, and the need I am in, in order that by such knowledge I may be brought to true humility of heart. Let me also recognize to what majesty and glory I have attained by Your gracious indwelling, in order that I may be induced to love You more fervently. Let me become obedient to You by love; let me follow You in love and yield my heart to You. Whenever You work in me, grant that I may not resist You, but may let myself be restrained by You from all evil and urged to all good. Let me always follow Your promptings. Let me hear and heed Your admonitions. Let me be guided by You through all my life in a straight path, and I shall continue to walk in the right way and travel toward heaven.

However, O precious Holy Spirit, when You have thus worked in me, when You have proved Your power in my weakness, let me also, like the messengers of Jesus after You rested on them, speak with new tongues, so that everyone may hear that the old, sinful, unseemly words (which are so unbecoming of Christians) have now been removed far from my lips. Let all who come to know me see that I have become a different human being, and let everyone perceive that it is all due to You, O Spirit, dwelling in me. And then sanctify me more and more, and let me thoroughly become Your temple in my body and soul and remain such forever. Thus, let me here in time attain to a firm assurance of my salvation and to the possession of the righteousness of Jesus, of the divine peace that He has acquired, and find my joy in You. After this life, let me attain the inheritance incorruptible, undefiled, and that does not fade away, reserved in heaven for me. Let me come to the possession of a glorious crown, a beautiful robe of white, and let me praise and magnify You with the Father and the Son unto the ages of ages!

Come, Holy Ghost, Creator blest, And make our hearts Your place of rest; Come with Your grace and heav'nly aid, And fill the hearts which You have made. Amen. *LSB 498:1*

EXHORTATION

If you then, who are evil, know how to give good gifts to your children, how much more will the heavenly Father give the Holy Spirit to those who ask Him! Luke 11:13

Not only has the merciful love of God planned from eternity to grant us many blessings, not only has Jesus purchased us with His holy blood, but the Holy Spirit, who is the most glorious, most necessary, most blessed gift, desires to lead, sanctify, and govern us even in this valley of sorrow.

The Holy Spirit is the most glorious gift. For what greater or nobler thing could God do for us than to give us His Spirit for our leader and guide? The everlasting love of God was not content with having appointed the holy angels as our guardian keepers to be at our side, to surround us, and to accompany us in all our ways; but the Holy Spirit was also to dwell in us, so that our body and soul might be truly kept and preserved from evil. The Holy Spirit is the most necessary gift. We can lack wealth, honors, and great possessions, and yet live happily in this world; but without the Holy Spirit we cannot be truly happy either here in time or hereafter in eternity. For this reason the Holy Spirit is the most blessed gift. He is the down payment of our inheritance, the seal of our being God's children. Through Him we are assured that we are God's own children and heirs of eternal life. We need Him most in sadness, in affliction, and temptation. Then He comforts us that we are nevertheless in a state of grace. When we are unable to offer prayers, He intercedes for us before God with groans that cannot be expressed in human words.

God desires to give this glorious, necessary, and blessed gift to all who ask Him. We have no such promise about temporal and earthly things because they are not always salutary for us. But the gift of the Holy Spirit God will refuse no one. The Holy Spirit purifies the hearts of Christians from love of the world and sin, so that He, who is good and pure, may take up residence in them.

PRAYER

"For I will pour water on the thirsty land, and streams on the dry ground; I will pour my Spirit upon your offspring, and my blessing on your descendants. They shall spring up among the grass like willows by flowing streams" (Isaiah 44:3–4). O dearest Jesus, You fulfilled this gracious promise on the holy festival of Pentecost, when You poured out Your Spirit abundantly on the apostles and thus equipped them for their work of proclaiming to all nations grace, salvation, and the forgiveness of sins in Your blood. Faithful Savior, impart this gift also to me. Give me also this glorious blessing.

Descend upon me in abundant measure, O blessed Holy Spirit, You who were revealed in flames of fire upon the apostles. Enlighten me to life everlasting. Enlighten my understanding, that I may know Jesus Christ. Sanctify my will, that I may desire and wish for nothing but what is pleasing to You. O Spirit of power, as God gave the apostles strength from on high, so strengthen my faith. Give me courage and strength to walk in Your ways, to overcome the world, to resist sin, and to live as a true child of God. O gracious Rain, make me fruitful in all good works. Refresh me in the heat of temptation. Grant that I may bring forth abundant fruits in a life of faith.

O Spirit of grace and prayer, seal to me the joyful comfort that I am in a state of grace. Pray in me and with me. Teach me to pray with true devotion. Stir me up to devotion and to the praise of God. Spirit of wisdom, rest on me, that I may know and do what pleases God. Spirit of knowledge, rest on me, that I may walk in Your truth. Unite my heart to fear Your name. Guard my understanding against error. Dispel from it all darkness of ignorance and self-love. Kindle in me the light of Your knowledge, that I may daily increase in Your love and knowledge. Spirit of the fear of God, rest on me. Implant in my heart Your holy fear, that I may nevermore sin knowingly and willfully. Spirit of love, rest on me. Remove from my heart all anger, stubbornness, envy, wickedness, and vengefulness.

Be my comforter in affliction and sorrow, when the floods are about to overwhelm me and the waves would engulf me. Be my strength when I am weak. Help me to quench the lust of the flesh. Let faith, love, humility, hope, and patience grow in me. Be my guide, and lead me always in a straight path that I may not stumble, fall, or act contrary to the commands of God. Be my teacher and lead me into all truth and glorify Jesus in me. O Pure Water, wash me! Grant that I may grow in all that is good and bring forth much fruit. Help me by Your power that I may truly call Jesus Lord, and acknowledge Him as my Jesus, my Redeemer, my Savior, the foundation of my salvation and my eternal happiness.

O Light of my soul, see how I am surrounded in this world with innumerable temptations, for many deceivers have gone forth. Therefore keep me, lest I stray from You. Show me the way in which I must walk, for to You I lift up my soul. If I would be my own guide, I would certainly go astray; but when You lead me, I shall walk in the way of Your teachings.

O blessed Holy Spirit, if I have up till now grieved You, I am heartily sorry for it. Behold, my heart is open to You; O enter in and fill it with the rich gift of Your grace, with all Christian virtues. Establish me, make me firm, and preserve in me the good work that You have begun in me. Create in me a new heart. Remove from it all naughtiness, all evil habits, all dominion of sin. Take away from me the heart of stone and give me a heart that is sanctified and changed by Your grace. Dwell in me, and let me be Your temple and dwelling. Thus I have the earnest promise of my inheritance and adoption; and thus I know for certain that I shall obtain everlasting salvation.

O Holy Spirit, abide with me in every time of need and in death. Cry "Abba, Father!" in me at that hour. Give me a glimpse of the eternal glory and a foretaste of the eternal joy into which I shall enter, when after the fight I shall obtain the crown, and after the sorrows of this age, the unending joys of heaven.

To You, the Counselor, we cry, To You, the gift of God Most High; The fount of life, the fire of love, The soul's anointing from above. Amen.

LSB 498:2

HYMN

O Holy Spirit, enter in,
And in our hearts Your work begin,
Your dwelling place now make
us.
Sun of the soul, O Light divine,
Around and in us brightly shine,

To joy and gladness wake us
That we may be
Truly living,
To You giving
Prayer unceasing
And in love be still increasing.

*Give to Your Word impressive
pow'r,
That in our hearts from this good
hour
As fire it may be glowing,
That in true Christian unity
We faithful witnesses may be,
Your glory ever showing.
Hear us, cheer us
By Your teaching;
Let our preaching
And our labor
Praise You, Lord, and serve our
neighbor.*

*O mighty Rock, O Source of life,
Let Your dear Word, in doubt and
strife,
In us be strongly burning
That we be faithful unto death
And live in love and holy faith,
From You true wisdom learn-
ing.
Your grace and peace
On us shower;
By Your power
Christ confessing,
Let us see our Savior's blessing.*

LSB 913:1–3

EVENING PRAYER

Holy Spirit, light divine, Shine upon this heart of mine; Chase the shades of night away, Turn the darkness into day. Let me see my Savior's face, Let me all His beauties trace; Show those glorious truths to me, Which are only known to Thee. Holy Spirit, pow'r divine, Cleanse this guilty heart of mine; In Thy mercy pity me, From sin's bondage set me free. Holy Spirit, joy divine, Cheer this saddened heart of mine; Yield a sacred, settled peace, Let it grow and still increase. Holy Spirit, all divine, Dwell within this heart of mine; Cast down ev'ry idol throne, Reign supreme, and reign alone *(LSB 496:1–5)*. Thus, O greatest comforter in every sorrow, O blessed Holy Spirit, I find that, before going to bed, I must pray for Your gracious indwelling and Your heavenly gifts because I have been convinced today that You would gladly set up and prepare a temple of God among human beings. Make also my heart Your temple because it longs with yearning for this blessing.

To this end, glorify Jesus in my soul, so that I may begin to love and receive Him and thus obtain power to become a child of God and His temple. Glorify Him in me, as regards His person, His blessing, and the grace He has obtained for me, that I may accept Him as my only Savior, and seek and find forgiveness of sins in His name. Glorify Him in me, as regards His virtues and His way of life among us, that I may follow Him. Let His glory, His humility, His meekness, His holiness, His purity, His love, His sincerity, and His truth be reflected in my heart and shine as a bright light, manifesting themselves in my entire life. Glorify Him in me as regards His majesty and glory, which for my sake He did not use fully during His state of humiliation, but resumed after the work of redemption was completed. Clothed in that glory now He is seated at the right hand of His heavenly Father. Grant that I may worship, adore, and serve Him as the only Mediator between God and myself. If You will thus glorify Jesus in me, I shall be united with Him by faith, conformed to His image by fellowship with Him, and by following Him be led to the Jerusalem above.

O Spirit of grace, help me to attain to this blessedness. Without You I cannot call Jesus my Lord. Work me in a true and living faith. Work and accomplish in me all that is necessary so that Jesus may be formed in me and I may become His own. Hear my sighing, give ear to my supplications, accept my prayer, and grant me this grace that I desire.

When You have done this, when Jesus has been glorified in me, let me bear witness of Him as His apostles did after You had been poured out on them in abundant measure. Let me bear witness of Him in my entire life, that I may order my life, conversation, and conduct in obedience to His Word and will. Let me bear witness of Him in my heart by acknowledging Him as the true Messiah and the true God, by serving Him and by believing in Him. Let me bear witness of Him with my lips, by praising and magnifying Him both in private and in public, and by confessing Him at all times, trusting His promise then to confess me before His Father in heaven. Let me also bear witness of my Jesus in afflictions, by cheerful trust in Him, by firmly hoping and relying on Him, and patiently awaiting His help. Finally, let me bear witness of Him also in death, by remaining faithful even in that hour and by hoping in faith to receive the crown of life from His hand.

If You will in this way make me constantly bear witness of my Savior, He will in due time bear witness of me also, and confess me before His Father who is in heaven. How happy and blessed I shall then be! O Spirit of Jesus, guide me to this blessedness. I trust in You; let me never be ashamed. I surrender myself to You. Bring me to heaven and never allow me to be led astray into wrong paths. Amen.

BELIEVING CHRISTIANS CONTEMPLATE THE MYSTERY OF THE HOLY TRINITY

MORNING PRAYER

Holy, holy, holy is the Lord of hosts; the whole earth is filled with His glory. With these words, it is fitting for me, now as I arise from sleep, to praise Your exalted name, O adorable God. You have manifested Yourself as one in essence, yet distinct in persons. This day that your goodness has permitted me to see moves me to consider this great and blessed mystery of the Godhead and to employ it for my profit. Oh, grant me grace to accomplish my purpose! Manifest Yourself to me as my God, that I may be encouraged and prompted to show myself Your obedient creation.

Father of mercies, Your hand has fashioned me. Your power created me when I was yet in my mother's womb and brought me out into the light of day. Your faithfulness has preserved and maintained my spirit. Do not cease to be faithful to me, but forever show Yourself to me as my loving Father. But let me also conduct myself toward You with the humbleness and reverence of a child, and by Your grace strive for the highest degree of perfection.

Lord Jesus Christ, only-begotten Son of the highest, my mediator, Redeemer, and Savior, do not cease to hold Your merit and Your blood before Your Father whenever my trespasses, iniquities, and sins would give Him just cause in anger to condemn, reject, and cast me from Him. O eternal High Priest, do not cease to intercede for me. Do not cease Your work in me. Do not grow weary of calling me to grace, but work in me that Your image may be formed in me. Let none of Your redeemed be lost; and so let me also have light in You ever more abundantly.

O Spirit of Grace, have mercy on me and be not far from me with Your gifts. Comfort and refresh my poor soul when I am grieved. Hold me when I stumble and set me on my feet again. When I stray, point me to the right way and lead me on a plain path. Pray with me whenever I pray, and give my feeble words and sighs power to move the heart of my Father in heaven, to touch His heart, to procure His help.

O triune God, manifest Yourself in this way to me, and I will praise Your name, spread abroad Your glory, live according to Your will, and finally, when You summon me, gladly leave this world of trouble and look for a gracious reward from Your mercy. When my depraved reason stirs up all manner of doubt in me, as if it were impossible that You, O hidden God, who dwells in light no one can approach, are one in essence and three in persons, let me take my reason captive in the obedience of faith. Let me not lend my ear to its suggestions. Strengthen my faith in You, and let me cling so firmly to Your Word and testimonies that even the gates of hell shall not be able to prevail against me or rob me of my faith. When my sluggish flesh and blood resist following You and living according to Your will, grant me strength and ability from Your inexhaustible divine fullness to submit myself to You and to become obedient to You in all my life. Let me show my faith by my works, adding to my faith, virtue; and to virtue, knowledge; and to knowledge, patience; and to patience, kindness; and to kindness, love. So let me walk before You here in holiness and righteousness, and let me finally pass from believing to seeing. Then, when I shall see You face-to-face, with all the saints I will praise You forever, even as I now make a beginning and say with a heart that has been touched by Your love:

The Lord, my God, be praised, My God, the ever-living, To whom the heav'nly host Their laud and praise are giving. The Lord, my God, be praised, In whose great name I boast, God Father, God the Son, And God the Holy Ghost. Amen. *LSB 794:4*

EXHORTATION

The grace of our Lord Jesus Christ and the love of God and the fellowship of the Holy Spirit be with you all. 2 Corinthians 13:14

When believers are about to begin a meditation on the mystery of the Holy Trinity, they must be like those who want to obtain light and benefit from the sun and make the sun serve them. If they look into the sun with unprotected eyes, they become blinded; they see nothing but darkness, indeed, nothing at all. But if they keep their eyes cast down and thus use the light and splendor of the sun, they see much. Indeed, they see all that they ought to see.

The mystery of the Holy Trinity is a mystery incomprehensible to reason. We cannot comprehend this statement: one essence and three persons. Accordingly, many have stumbled at this doctrine of the Creed. People stumble over this right up to the present day. Nevertheless, the mystery of the Trinity is clearly described in the Holy Scriptures. It is declared in some of the choicest passages of the Old and New Testaments. For example, at the Baptism of Jesus in the Jordan three persons were revealed (Matthew 3:16–17). The works and the properties of the triune God are also clearly described and manifest before our eyes. Devout Christians believe this Word of life, until in the life everlasting they will come to see what they have believed.

In the meantime, they worship the thrice-holy God with humbleness of heart. They praise their Creator because of all the benefits He has bestowed on them, on both body and soul. They thank their Redeemer because He has delivered them from death, from sin, from the devil, and from the power of hell. They surrender their hearts and their entire life to the Sanctifier, seek to obey the triune God, and rest assured that they will at last behold in glory what they have believed on earth. For blessed are they that have not seen and yet have believed.

PRAYER

Holy, holy, holy is the Lord of hosts; the whole earth is full of His glory. With these words, O triune God, Father, Son, and Holy Spirit, I now join all the seraphim and cherubim in their hymn of praise and sing of Your sovereign rule, Your majesty, and glory. You, O God, are self-existent, unfathomable, and incomprehensible! My faith firmly clings to Your Holy and revealed Word alone, through which You have gloriously revealed yourself to me. This is eternal life that people may know You, O Father, the only true God, and Jesus Christ, whom You have sent.

O Father of all grace and mercy, You have made Yourself known to me as my Father. I worship You. I honor and praise You. From eternity You have begotten Your only Son, Jesus Christ, and You are also the true Father from whom the whole family in heaven and on earth is named.

You have to this day, as a gracious and loving Father, nourished, sustained, kept, and preserved me. O merciful Father, look upon me still with cordial and fatherly compassion as Your own child.

Lord Jesus, Son of God, I have learned to know You from Your Holy Word as the Second Person of the Holy Trinity, eternally begotten of the Father in heaven, God of God, Light of Light, sprung into being in a manner incomprehensible to us. I have also learned to know You as my brother and kinsman, who took upon Himself our human nature and redeemed me and all people from sin, death, the devil, and hell. And so I rejoice in You and worship You. You are my righteousness, my Redeemer, my Advocate, my High Priest, my Mercy Seat, my mediator, my Immanuel, my Savior, and my Shepherd. In You I have life and have it abundantly. You are the Paschal Lamb who was given for my sins. Your precious blood is the cleansing of my iniquities. Through You I have access to grace and life. In You I am saved, here in time and hereafter in eternity.

O blessed Holy Spirit, You have revealed Yourself to me in Your Word as the third person of the Godhead, proceeding from the Father and the Son, of one essence, of equal majesty and glory with them. You have given me a new birth in Holy Baptism. Through You I have been brought to grace, to light, and to the life that is from God. You are my sanctifier. You enlighten, sanctify, and keep me in true faith. You comfort me in suffering, cheer me in sadness, and refresh me in tribulation. O Spirit of grace and of prayer, seal to me the comfort that I am in a state of grace. Bear witness with my spirit that I am a child of God. Stir me up to prayer. Give me the spirit of devotion while praying, and joyfulness when I have prayed.

Oh, come, let us worship and bow down and kneel before the Lord, the triune God who has made us, for we are His people and the sheep of His pasture. His judgments are unsearchable, and His ways past finding out. Of Him and through Him and to Him are all things. To Him be praise, honor, and glory forevermore. The Father is made of none, neither created nor begotten. The Son is of the Father, neither made nor created but begotten. The Holy Spirit is of the Father and of the Son, neither made, nor created, nor begotten, but proceeding. Among these three persons none is first and none is last; none the greatest and none the least, but all three are equal. The Father is God, the Son is God, and the Holy Spirit is God. And yet there are not three gods, but one God. The Father is Lord, the Son is Lord, and the Holy Spirit is Lord. And yet there are not three Lords, but one Lord.

O triune God and Lord, grant that I may ever grow and increase in this knowledge, that I may embrace You in faith and may firmly cling to Your Holy Word as the norm of my faith and life. Grant that what I cannot grasp with my mind I may nevertheless believe from my heart, until I shall pass from faith to sight. Meanwhile, my Father, cover me with the wings of Your grace and bless me. O Jesus, wash me with Your holy blood and bless me; make me righteous and save me forevermore. Lord God, the Holy Spirit, enlighten me and bless me, that I may walk in Your light and in Your light may behold the light of joy in heaven above. Amen.

HYMN

Father most holy, merciful, and tender;
Jesus, our Savior, with the Father reigning;
Spirit of comfort, advocate, defender,
Light never waning.

Trinity blessed, unity unshaken,
Goodness unbounded, very God of heaven,
Light of the angels, joy of those forsaken,
Hope of all living.

Maker of all things, all Thy creatures praise Thee;
All for Thy worship were and are created;
Now, as we also worship Thee devoutly,
Hear Thou our voices.

Lord God Almighty, unto Thee be glory,
One in three persons, over all exalted!
Glory we offer, praise Thee and adore Thee,
Now and forever. LSB 504:1–4

EVENING PRAYER

O holy triune God, filled with joy and gladness I once more appear before Your throne before hastening to my place of rest, because I have today heard the glad tidings and have been convinced that You come to dwell in the hearts of those who love You. I regard this as the greatest glory a rational creature is capable of, and my soul is glad and leaps for joy.

True, the world judges otherwise and regards those as unhappy who yield their heart to You for Your habitation. They think Christians are unfortunate because You call them to deny themselves all worldly pleasures and to wrestle and fight daily, lest sin gain dominion over them. But I know and am persuaded that it is well with the righteous, and that great glory and blessedness are prepared for them. Therefore, I long for Your indwelling and experience a fervent desire for it.

Come, O triune God, come into my soul and dwell in me. Make me entirely new. Let me no longer live for myself, but for Him who died for me and rose again. I know that Your indwelling is no mere fantasy, such as the perverted world imagines it to be. It is not the mere bestowal of Your gifts. And it certainly does not mean that man is changed into God. Rather, You come to us according to Your essence, not in the manner in which You are present with all the ungodly, but by Your special grace, so that we are united with You as intimately as the branch with the vine, the head with the members, the soul with the body. What unspeakable grace! How greatly You ennoble those who are Yours, O God, in making them partakers of Your Spirit and Your power! When You enter into my soul, it is no longer I that live, but You live in me, You speak through me, You walk and work all things in me.

Let me, then, continually grow in Your strength, that it may always be said: Behold, the tabernacle of God is with me! Do you not know that Jesus Christ dwells in you? This is the source of my true blessedness, in which I delight with all my heart and which I anxiously desire. A bright light now arises in me, causing me to see my sins and Your grace, and urging me to flee the former and to seek the latter. With You new life comes into me. Now I am no longer powerless, carried away by every sin, but I can do all things through You who strengthen me. Now I have comfort in every sorrow, in all changes and trials. How happy, then, I am even in this present life! And how blessed will I be in eternity, when I will remain in Your fellowship and see You as You are! O grant me this in mercy! Let me remain in a state of grace and grow in it. Let me never again drive You from me, but be united with You until in eternity I behold You forever and ever.

Glory be to God the Father, Glory be to God the Son, Glory be to God the Spirit: Great Jehovah, Three in One! Glory, glory While eternal ages run! Amen.

LSB 506:1

BELIEVING CHRISTIANS MEDITATE ON THE GUARDIANSHIP OF THE HOLY ANGELS ON ST. MICHAEL AND ALL ANGELS DAY

EXHORTATION

Are they not all ministering spirits sent out to serve for the sake of those who are to inherit salvation? Hebrews 1:14

The holy angels were created by God for His service and glory, and were appointed to stand around His throne continually and to carry out His commands. If a great king were to appoint his bodyguards and attendants for the service of another, that would be a token of love and grace. Accordingly, believing Christians thank God for this special grace that God has not only given Himself with all His blessings and gifts for their enjoyment, has not only sent Jesus Christ for the salvation of their souls, has not only appointed the Holy Spirit as their Comforter and Guide, but has also made the holy angels to keep guard over them.

Therefore, Christians do not drive the holy angels from them by willful sins, but they give the holy angels cause for joy by their repentance and godly conversation. Christians strive, while still on earth, to become like the angels, by daily praising and glorifying God, returning Him thanks, and by rendering to Him acceptable service. Whoever in this life remains a devil—that is, a stiff-necked, obstinate, unconverted person, and a brazen sinner until death—can never after death become like the angels. Believing Christians, in accordance with the Third Petition, diligently seek to do God's will on earth as it is done in heaven. Believers do not worship the angels, for such honor belongs only to the Lord of the angels, and not to fellow servants (see Revelation 19:10).

In this condition of faith, love, godliness, and the fear of God, believing Christians persevere to their end, knowing that the holy angels of God will not only keep them from harm in the works of their calling and in the paths appointed for them by God, but that the holy angels will attend their dying hour, and when the Christian dies, they will carry them to the bosom of Abraham.

PRAYER

The angel of the Lord encamps around those who fear Him and delivers them. O merciful and loving God! Now I rejoice that You have given Your holy angels for my protection and defense. Lord, Lord, what is man that you are mindful of him, or the son of man that you visit him and regard him so highly? It is a high honor when a king assigns his bodyguards and attendants to look after a humble person. How much greater glory is it when the holy angels are sent to act as protectors and companions to us poor human beings!

O God of love, in Your unspeakable goodness You have not only appointed all visible creatures, heaven, earth, sun, air, sea, all fruits and products of the earth, for our enjoyment, but You have also appointed the invisible creatures, the holy angels, for our service, that no evil may befall us. You know, O loving Father, how Your children on earth are surrounded by many dangers and much misery. And so You have appointed watchmen to guard Your children night and day and to turn from them all evil. You know how many and strong enemies Your believing children have around them: the prince of darkness, Satan, and his host. So You have provided them with mighty heroes who can resist those foes and guard Your loved ones.

O my God, when weeks, months, yes, years pass, one after another, and I remain uninjured in life and limb, suffer no harm in house, home, or property, when I am not persecuted in my pursuits, no misfortune coming near me, should I not ascribe all of this to Your fatherly faithfulness, love, and mercy? You have kept and preserved me through Your ministering spirits. How many dangers of which I was not even aware have You turned aside by the mighty protection of Your holy angels! Let me then, O my God, fervently love and praise You now and forever.

However, O loving Father, I pray You to command Your angel also in the days to come to attend and guard me as Your own. Let Your angel turn from me all danger and misfortune, as happened to Jacob when he was met and accompanied by the hosts of God when great danger at the hand of Esau threatened him. Fortify my house, surrounding it with Your angel host, as was done for the house of Job. Let them be with me in adversity, as they were with Daniel. Let them drive all misfortune from me, as they turned away the flames from the three children in the fiery furnace. Let them guard my business and my daily bread, as they brought food and drink to Elijah. Yes, let them encamp around me, accompany me, and assist me in my journeys, as they did Tobias.

O gracious God, grant Your Holy Spirit that I may not grieve these creatures of Yours by my sins, nor drive them from me by reckless living, forcing them to stand far off and to forsake me because of my wickedness. Grant that even in this life I may become like the angels by serving, praising, obeying, and glorifying You, so that at last I may be like the angels also in the joys and bliss of the life that never ends. Your will be done on earth as it is in heaven—let this prayer resound in my ears and in my heart from now on and forevermore. My God, let Your holy angels remain with me in death that they may carry my soul to Abraham's bosom and accompany me to glory. There let me forever be in their fellowship and company, rejoice with them over Your glory and majesty, and chant with them: Holy, holy, holy is the Lord God of hosts! And so I will praise You for this and for all Your blessings forever and ever.

Stars of the morning, so gloriously bright, Angels in heaven, resplendent in light, These, where no darkness the glory can dim, Praise the Thrice Holy One, serving but Him. These are Your ministers, these are Your own, Lord God of Sabaoth, nearest Your throne; These are Your messengers, these whom You send, Helping Your helpless ones, Helper and Friend. Then, when the earth was first poised in midspace, Then, when the planets first sped on their race, Then, when were ended the six days' employ, Then all the sons of God shouted for joy. Still let them aid us and still let them fight, Lord of angelic hosts, battling for right, Till,

where their anthems they ceaselessly pour, We with the angels may bow
and adore. Amen.   *LSB 520:1–4*

HYMN

Lord God, to Thee we give all praise,
With grateful hearts our voices raise,
That angel hosts Thou didst create
Around Thy glorious throne to wait.

They shine with light and heav'nly grace
And constantly behold Thy face;
They heed Thy voice, they know it well,
In godly wisdom they excel.

They never rest nor sleep as we;
Their whole delight is but to be
With Thee, Lord Jesus, and to keep
Thy little flock, Thy lambs and sheep.

The ancient dragon is their foe;
His envy and his wrath they know.
It always is his aim and pride
Thy Christian people to divide.

As he of old deceived the world
And into sin and death has hurled,
So now he subtly lies in wait
To undermine both Church and state.

A roaring lion, round he goes,
No halt nor rest he ever knows;
He seeks the Christians to devour
And slay them by his dreadful pow'r.

But watchful is the angel band
That follows Christ on ev'ry hand
To guard His people where they go
And break the counsel of the foe.

For this, now and in days to be,
Our praise shall rise, O Lord, to Thee,
Whom all the angel hosts adore
With grateful songs forevermore. *LSB 522:1–8*

Part Three: Prayers for Various Spiritual and Bodily Blessings

BELIEVING CHRISTIANS PRAY FOR TEMPORAL, SPIRITUAL, AND ETERNAL BLESSINGS

EXHORTATION

God, our God, shall bless us. God shall bless us; let all the ends of the earth fear Him! Psalm 67:6b–7

All Christians ask something of God in prayer. However, when doing so, they should carefully consider how and for what they pray. Christians pray for temporal things, such as health, prosperity, food, the warding off of danger, help and deliverance from trouble, and support in suffering. Such prayers God does not decline because He has promised us all these things in His Holy Word.

But Christians do not stop at these blessings, which are of lesser importance. They pray for spiritual blessings: for the Holy Spirit; for a godly heart; for the kingdom of God, which is "righteousness and peace and joy in the Holy Spirit" (Romans 14:17). Christians pray for enlightenment, growth in godliness, sanctification, and for the gifts of the Holy Spirit. These are the chief blessings they can ask and obtain from God, and when they are granted, Christians regard them as their greatest treasures.

Christians also pray for eternal things: for a blessed end; for a joyful departure from this world; and for entrance into the life of joy they have desired, that after this conflict is over they may behold the face of God, be robed in white garments, and forever rejoice in Him. So, believers pray chiefly for spiritual and heavenly blessings if they want to pray correctly and in a way that pleases God. At the same time they are to study to lead a blameless Christian life, lest their prayer be hindered by an evil conscience.

PRAYER

O bountiful and gracious God, how great and glorious, how rich and mighty You are! You possess all things and can give all things. Behold, I, Your child, come to You and ask You for Your gifts. You know that I have brought nothing into this world; I have nothing of my own, except my sin. And so any good thing that I possess has come from You, since every good and perfect gift is from above. Yes, what do I possess that I have not received at Your hand?

O my God and Father, make me, above all, rich in my soul. Give me Your Holy Spirit. Give me a godly heart. Convert and enlighten me that daily I may become a new creation. Help me to struggle and labor, that I may conquer evil desires, put away bad habits, separate myself from the world, and surrender my body and soul to You as a living sacrifice, holy and acceptable to You through Jesus Christ. Behold, my God, how many dangers and temptations I am exposed to in this world. Guide me by Your power, lest I be led astray or depart from You. Dwell in my soul, govern my heart, and grant me grace to be a living member of the body of my Jesus, and a new creation; then I shall be rich indeed, honored and blessed in this world.

O generous God and Father, provide for me also in earthly things. You know what I need; You see what I lack. However, do not give me anything according to my will, but all things according to Your will. If health is good for me, give me a sound body that I may successfully perform the duties of my calling. Give me food and clothing, for You know that without these I cannot live. Accompany me in all my ways. Preserve me from evil. Add Your blessing to my labor, for what You bless, O Lord, is blessed indeed. You have placed me in this world; You will also know how to sustain and provide for me. I cast all my burdens and all my cares on You. O God, care for Your child, preserve Your child, and let me always experience abundantly Your fatherly faithfulness and grace.

But since You, great God and Father, have not created me for this life only, I hope for still greater blessings. For if I had nothing to expect from You than what I have received for this life, I would be the most wretched of human beings. And so, my Father, give me also heavenly blessings. Keep me in faith until my blessed end. Let me depart this life trusting in the death of Christ. Receive my soul into Your heavenly mansions, into Your eternal joy. If it is Your will, grant me to die in the possession of my right mind. After my departure from this life, bring me to the company of the elect in heaven, that with them I may be crowned, glorified, clothed in robes of white, behold Your face, and rejoice in You forever.

O my God, hear the voice of my supplication and do not refuse the prayer of my lips. Give me of earthly things as much as it pleases You to give, and such as are salutary and useful for me. As regards spiritual and heavenly things, give me a rich measure of Your grace, and at the proper time bring me, Your child, to the assembly of saints in light, that I may be united with You here by faith and love, and in heaven forever and ever. Amen.

HYMN

All depends on our possessing
God's abundant grace and blessing,
Though all early wealth depart.
They who trust with faith
unshaken
By their God are not forsaken
And will keep a dauntless
heart.

He who to this day has fed me
And to many joys has led me
Is and ever shall be mine.
He who ever gently schools me,
He who daily guides and rules me
Will remain my help divine.

Many spend their lives in fretting
Over trifles and in getting
Things that have no solid ground.
I will strive to win a treasure
That will bring me lasting pleasure
And that now is seldom found.

When with sorrow I am stricken,
Hope anew my heart will quicken;
All my longing shall be stilled.
To His loving-kindness tender
Soul and body I surrender,
For on God alone I build.
Well He knows what best to grant
me;
All the longing hopes that haunt
me,
Joy and sorrow, have their day.
I shall doubt His wisdom never;
As God wills, so be it ever;
I commit to Him my way.

If my days on earth He lengthen,
God my weary soul will strengthen;
All my trust in Him I place.
Earthly wealth is not abiding.
Like a stream away is gliding;
Safe I anchor in His grace.

LSB 732:1–6

BELIEVING CHRISTIANS THANK GOD FOR THEIR HEALTH

EXHORTATION

Better is the poor, being sound and strong of constitution, than a rich man that is afflicted in his body. Health and good estate of body are above all gold, and a strong body above infinite wealth. There is no riches above a sound body, and no joy above the joy of the heart. Ecclesiasticus 30:14–16 (KJV)

God distributes diverse spiritual and bodily gifts to people. Of bodily gifts, health may be reckoned among the foremost. A healthy person, if that person is godly, is a happy person; on the other hand, if the person is ungodly, he is the most unhappy. A healthy person is happy because he can serve God and the neighbor without hindrance, attend to what God has called him to, and accomplish much good. But if a person sound in health is not godly, such a person makes the most appalling misuse of this gift by committing many sins and iniquities. How wholesome it would be for many a person to be lame, dumb, blind, or afflicted with pain, so that the sins of feet, tongue, eyes, and body would be hindered! On Judgment Day, then, people guilty of such an abuse of healthy limbs will face a great reckoning, and a well-merited eternal punishment will follow.

True Christians recognize the noble blessing of good health, and so they thank God whenever they think about their healthy limbs. They put these healthy limbs into the service of God by reverently attending the Divine Service at God's house and by growing in their Christian faith. They also offer service to their fellow human beings by attending to the duties of their calling in a faithful and honest manner.

They recognize that health is not an abiding and permanent blessing; that, when God wills it, pain and sickness, lameness and disease, may be visited on them. Accordingly, in the days of health, they do not abuse their health by wantonness, recklessness, and malice, lest, when days of sickness and suffering come upon them, their conscience would accuse them: "This is God's punishment for the abuse of your health." God must put bit and bridle to many a healthy person who is obstinate by visiting such a one with bodily infirmity so that person may cease sinning. Pious Christians are diligent in prayer in the days of health because they do not know whether they will have the strength in days of sickness; they employ their health to good purpose.

PRAYER

O gracious and merciful God, how great is Your love and goodness to me, not only in keeping me in Your gracious protection but also by permitting me to begin and complete one year after another in good health! O my God, I acknowledge that this is one of those good gifts that comes down from above, from You, the Father of lights.

Lord, who am I, that You should show such mercy to me? Daily I see before me people who are sickly, suffering, and infirm. I hear many complaining that they must spend their days bored on their bed, confined by some illness—many who most likely are much more God-fearing and pious, and who pray with greater devotion than I. Yet to me You have given good health, strength, and vigor. O Lord, I am not worthy of all the mercies You have bestowed on me up till now and continue to shower down on me.

Preserve me, O my God, that I may not abuse this noble gift of health by wasteful living, depravity, pride, and insolence. Instead, make me to understand that by this gift You would stir me up to gratitude and godliness. As long as I may still have to live, help me use my health for Your praise and honor, for the benefit of my neighbor, and for accomplishing the duties of my calling. If it is in accordance with Your holy counsel and will, preserve my health and my soundness of body, so that without hindrance I may frequently and diligently come to Your house and sing hymns of praise and thanksgiving in Your temple.

Give me Your Holy Spirit, that I may consecrate my limbs to Your service and my understanding to growing in Your knowledge. O my God, grant me strength and ability to increase in the inner self, that I may be sound in faith, fervent in spirit, patient in trouble, devout in prayer, sincere in my love to You and my fellow human beings, Christlike in my conversation, rejoicing in hope, and confident in death. Sanctify me. Bless me. Let Your good Spirit lead me into the land of uprightness! Amen.

HYMN

O God, my faithful God,
True fountain ever flowing,
Without whom nothing is,
All perfect gifts bestowing:
Give me a healthy frame,
And may I have within
A conscience free from blame,
A soul unstained by sin.

Grant me the strength to do
With ready heart and willing
Whatever You command,
My calling here fulfilling;
That I do what I should,
While trusting You to bless
The outcome for my good,
For You must give success.

Keep me from saying words
That later need recalling;
Guard me lest idle speech
May from my lips be falling;
But when within my place
I must and ought to speak,
Then to my words give grace
Lest I offend the weak.

Lord, let me win my foes
With kindly words and actions
And let me find good friends
For counsel and correction.
Help me, as You have taught,
To love both great and small
And by Your Spirit's might
To live in peace with all.

Let me depart this life
Confiding in my Savior;
By grace receive my soul
That it may live forever;
And let my body have
A quiet resting place
Within a Christian grave;
And let it sleep in peace.

And on that final day
When all the dead are waking,
Stretch out Your mighty hand,
My deathly slumber breaking.
Then let me hear Your voice,
Redeem this earthly frame,
And bid me to rejoice
With those who love Your
name. LSB 696:1–6

BELIEVING CHRISTIANS ASK GOD TO SANCTIFY THEIR HEARTS

EXHORTATION

Strive for peace with everyone, and for the holiness without which no one will see the Lord. Hebrews 12:14

When believing Christians view themselves in their natural depravity, they remember that they cannot make themselves holy, but that this is a work of God. And so, they use the means appointed by God for their sanctification. They remember their Holy Baptism, in which the Holy Spirit was poured out on them and took up His abode in their heart. They honestly ask themselves whether they have driven the Holy Spirit away since then with intentional sins. They know that the Lord's Supper is a food for sanctification. When they receive it, they ask that through it God would sanctify their soul, body, and all its members. They listen reverently to the Word of God and treasure up in their hearts what they have heard, that they can grow in holiness. For the sanctification of their body and soul to be accomplished they know that this can only happen by God's power and the working of the Holy Spirit. If the soul is sanctified, the entire life will be spent in true sanctification: all thoughts, words, and deeds are to be shaped by the rule of holiness.

This sanctification must take place in the present; it must not be deferred to old age or to the hour of death. It must begin while a person is still able to pray and to use the means of sanctification intelligently. This sanctification, in addition, is to be manifested at all times, on all occasions, even when a person happens to be among those whose hearts are set on this age. We are to show by our conduct, words, and deeds that we have a sanctified heart and that the Holy Spirit governs our lips and our entire life. Such a sanctified soul will one day be admitted to the place where the saints dwell in light.

PRAYER

O Holy Spirit, I am seized with fear whenever these divine words strike my ears: "You shall be holy, for I am holy" (1 Peter 1:16) and again, without holiness "no one will see the Lord" (Hebrews 12:14). When I ponder these sayings and measure against them my unholy heart, my unholy thoughts, my unholy words, my unholy actions, I am often thrown into great anguish, and I become ashamed of the unbecoming and unholy life that I have led. For, sadly, obeying the promptings of my heart and the habits of the world, I have sinned and have offended You in word and action. Oh, if no one shall see Your face without holiness, how few will be saved and how many damned! Help, Lord! For the godly disappear!

And so, O Holy God, make me understand all these things well, so that I may with sincere earnestness seek for true inward and outward holiness. O Jesus, sanctify me by Your righteousness, by Your merit and Your blood. Give to me, who by nature am unholy, Your holiness, that clothed in it as my most beautiful robe, I may be able to appear and stand before Your heavenly Father. Sanctify my life by Your Holy Word. Sanctify my heart, that it may always be occupied with good thoughts. Sanctify my lips, that they may speak nothing that is unfitting, unchristian, or wicked. Sanctify my will, that I may desire and do only what pleases You. O Holy God, draw me away from the world and unite me to You, that through Your Holy Spirit I may have the witness in me that I am born again, that I am a child of God and in a state of grace.

But let this sanctification be real, that I may not be holy only outwardly, seeking holiness while at church, while attending the Lord's Supper, or when I am engaged in other sacred actions; but let me be truly holy and follow after holiness in all places, at all times, on all occasions, even when I must live entirely in the company of godless people. Let me under such circumstances speak, live, and act as a child of God, and remain in such a blessed state until death, when You will bring me to the company of the saints and elect in the everlasting light of joy. Amen.

HYMN

O Holy Spirit, grant us grace
  That we our Lord and Savior
In faith and fervent love embrace
  And truly serve Him ever.
The hour of death cannot bring loss
When we are sheltered by the cross
  That cancelled our transgressions.

Help us that we Thy saving Word
  In faithful hearts may treasure;
Let e'er that Bread of Life afford
  New grace in richest measure.
O make us die to ev'ry sin,
Each day create new life within,
  That fruits of faith may flourish.

And when our earthly race is run,
  Death's bitter hour impending,
Then may Thy work in us begun
  Continue till life's ending,
Until we gladly may commend
Our souls into our Savior's hand,
  The crown of life obtaining. LSB 693:1–3

BELIEVING CHRISTIANS PRAY GOD TO GOVERN AND GUIDE THEM

EXHORTATION

Teach me Your way, O LORD, that I may walk in Your truth;
unite my heart to fear Your name. Psalm 86:11

This life is nothing else than a journey. We enter upon it at our birth; and when we die, the journey is ended together with our life, and we pass into eternity. The question is: which way are we headed during this life? If we are traveling a good way—the way of faith and the fear of God—our journey ends in the glory of heaven. If we are walking the broad way—

the way of unbelief, malice, or wickedness—our journey will end in hell, in eternal damnation.

When Christians think about these facts, they should picture to themselves the two ways that lie before them in this life: the narrow way leading to heaven and the broad way leading to hell. They should give every effort toward walking the way to heaven. In order that they may enter and remain on the narrow way, they should pray God to guide and govern them. If they pray God for His holy guidance and direction, they must not look around to see how the children of this world live and on what ways they are traveling; for if they end up following those errant ways, God's Spirit ceases to guide them. In fact, He departs from them.

Now, just as a traveler needs a guide to show the right way, so believing Christians need the Spirit of God to show them the right way in which they should walk. And so the indwelling of the Holy Spirit in the heart is a necessity, that it may be said of Christians: "Do you not know that you are God's temple and that God's Spirit dwells in you?" (1 Corinthians 3:16). If we have this trusty guide in us and with us, He will also regulate our thoughts, our lips, our senses, and our desires. Believing Christians do not resist this holy rule, nor do they resist the Holy Spirit, but allow themselves to be led, encouraged, guided, and are confident that they will be safely guided here in time and hereafter in eternity. O blessed guidance! Happy are all who have God Himself for their guide!

PRAYER

Lord, You have searched me and known me. You know well all my ways. You see and know full well, O Lord, that I have a heartfelt desire to walk in Your ways and to live as You have commanded Your children to live and as Jesus has taught us to live by His example. But, sadly, I find that I am led astray from the good way and from my purpose by temptations now on this side and now on that side. Sometimes it is my own heart that leads me astray by wicked desires; at other times it is the world that entices me with its bad example. Following either, I stir Your anger, O my God and my Lord, and wound my own conscience. The nearer I approach to the world, the further I stray from You.

So I pray You, lead me and guide me by Your counsel. You have said,

"I will counsel you with My eyes upon you" (Psalm 32:8). Here I am, Lord; let Your good Spirit lead me in the land of uprightness. I yield myself entirely to You, my God. You once led Your people dry-shod through the Red Sea. You brought them through the wilderness to the Promised Land. Lead me through the dangers of this life, through the wilderness and temptations of this world, with a good and unsullied conscience, into the life that never ends. I commit my heart, my mouth, my body, and my entire life to You. Govern my heart and fill it always with holy thoughts. Govern my body, that my hands may not reach out after forbidden things and that my feet may not walk in the paths of sin that lead to hell. Govern my life and my tongue, that I may not utter curses or shameful, unfitting, and unchristian words. Govern my entire life, that from now on I may not sin against You, but may be called and in truth actually be a genuine believer in Jesus Christ.

Do not forsake me if in weakness I should resist You, and do not leave me to my own guidance. For if I lead myself, I will doubtless go astray. Give me a holy carefulness in all my actions, and write Your holy fear into my heart that I may regulate my life solely by Your Word and by the example of my Jesus. Amen.

HYMN

Oh, that the Lord would guide my ways
To keep His statues still!
Oh, that my God would grant me grace
To know and do His will!

Order my footsteps by Thy Word
And make my heart sincere.
Let sin have no dominion, Lord,
But keep my conscience clear.

Assist my soul, too apt to stray,
A stricter watch to keep;
And should I e'er forget Thy way,
Restore Thy wand'ring sheep.

Make me to walk in Thy commands—
'Tis a delightful road—
Nor let my head or heart or hands
Offend against my God. LSB 707:1–4

BELIEVING CHRISTIANS PRAY THAT TRUE LOVE OF GOD MAY BE KINDLED IN THEIR HEARTS

EXHORTATION

God is love, and whoever abides in love abides in God,
and God abides in him. . . . We love because He first loved us.
1 John 4:16, 19

God is love. Because God is love, He desires that all His believing children should also abide in true love. Love is a bond that unites God and our heart, and it also unites us with our neighbor's heart.

Accordingly, believing Christians ask God to fill their heart with His holy love. For this gift, too, is one of those good gifts that come down from above. Believing Christians must not despise the means by which the love of God may be awakened and increased in them—through the devout hearing of and meditation on the Word of God, and the worthy use of the Holy Supper. If Christians dwell in the love of God, they must manifest this love by holy Christian conduct, becoming speech, and God-pleasing works. Love is like a fire; it cannot hide its flames and smoke.

Believing Christians must be very careful not to relapse into a love of the world (2 Timothy 4:10); for if anyone loves the world, the love of the Father is not in him. Out of love to God, therefore, they must avoid the friendship and society of the world, because these draw away from the love of God. They must abide in this love until death and thus depart from this world with the love of God in their heart. This love of God is to increase in them as they increase in years. We ought to be ashamed to have spent twenty, thirty, yes, forty years in the lust and love of the world, and during all that time have forgotten to love God. For such wayward-ness, a Christian, when God has opened his eyes, should make amends by all the more fervent, ardent, and constant love, and abide in such love until death.

PRAYER

O loving and gracious God, You alone are worthy to be loved. You and You alone I ought to love with all my heart and with all my soul and with all my strength. I acknowledge and confess before You with exceedingly great sorrow in my soul that my love to You, my faithful Creator and loving Father; to Jesus, my Redeemer and Savior; and to the Holy Spirit, my teacher and guide, has not only been extinguished in me by original sin, but that I have not at all times yielded to the calling and operation of Your grace. I have denied the promptings of Your Holy Spirit by which true love of You might again have been kindled in my heart.

I pray You to change my heart. Pluck from it all love of this passing world and of sin. Let these words ring in my ears: "Do not love the world or the things in the world. If anyone loves the world, the love of the Father is not in him" (1 John 2:15). Destroy in me all love for the lust of the flesh, the lust of the eye, and the pride of life. You know how inclined I am to them by my fallen nature. Kindle in me by Your Holy Spirit a pure and true love for You, that I may love You as my highest good for Your own sake, and flee from the vanities of the world. I know that if I desire to be a child of God, then the love of sin, of the world, and of self, must be cast out of my heart, and I must love You above all things.

And so, my God, I come to You and pray You: grant me Your Holy Spirit to plant this noble, necessary, and Christian grace in my heart. In His strength I will constantly love You, my God, with all my heart. My soul will think of You. My lips will speak of You. You will be more precious to me than the entire world and its joys, dearer than all earthly fortune and its glory, yes, dearer than all people. From love of You I will cease to sin knowingly. From love of You I will shun the society of sinful persons. From love of You I will begin to become truly pious, and order my life according to Your Word and will. I will honor and fear You. I will serve, follow, and obey You.

O loving God, enkindle this love in my heart more and more, that I may not love You only for a few days, weeks, or years, but that my love for You be ever increasing and continue to my blessed end. Fill me with courage whenever I am called upon to suffer for love of You. Strengthen me in such times with Your mighty aid. Thus let me be united with You here in time and there in eternity. Amen.

HYMN

Thee will I love, my strength, my tower;
Thee will I love, my hope, my joy.
Thee will I love with all my power,
With ardor time shall ne'er destroy.
Thee will I love, O Light divine,
So long as life is mine.

Thee will I love, my life, my Savior,
Who art my best and truest friend.
Thee will I love and praise forever,
For never shall Thy kindness end.
Thee will I love with all my heart—
Thou my Redeemer art!

I thank Thee, Jesus, Sun from heaven,
Whose radiance hath brought light to me;
I thank Thee, who hast richly given
All that could make me glad and free;
I thank Thee that my soul is healed
By what Thy lips revealed.

O keep me watchful, then, and humble;
Permit me nevermore to stray.
Uphold me when my feet would stumble,
And keep me on the narrow way.
Fill all my nature with Thy light,
O Radiance strong and bright.

Thee will I love, my crown of gladness;
Thee will I love, my God and Lord,
Amid the darkest depths of sadness
And not for hope of high reward,
For Thine own sake, O Light divine,
So long as life is mine. LSB 694:1–5

BELIEVING CHRISTIANS PRAY GOD TO IMPLANT IN THE HEART LOVE FOR THE NEIGHBOR

EXHORTATION

*If anyone says, "I love God," and hates his brother, he is a liar;
for he who does not love his brother whom he has seen cannot
love God whom he has not seen. And this commandment we have
from Him: whoever loves God must also love his brother.*
1 John 4:20–21

"A new commandment I give to you, that you love one another: just as I have loved you, you also are to love one another. By this all people will know that you are My disciples, if you have love for one another" (John 13:34–35). With these words, Christ describes by what mark His true disciples will be known, namely, by the love that they show to their neighbor. No one should imagine that it is possible to dwell in the love of God and harbor hatred of the neighbor. This can never be.

However, we are to regard as our neighbors our friends, our benefactors, and relatives. When loving these persons, we indeed fulfill our duty, but this is not an exclusively Christian virtue. The unbelieving also love their friends, benefactors, and relatives, as long as these do nothing to hurt them. However, we are to regard as our neighbors the people living next door, our fellow-citizens, and strangers, yes, even persons who envy us, take advantage of us, and hate us.

It is especially toward this second class of neighbors that we are to manifest our love. We do this not only by not wishing them harm or reviling them or returning evil for evil, but rather by wishing them good, by showing them love and friendship, and by loving them as we love ourselves. As regards our enemies, we must banish from our heart all bitterness, revengefulness, hatred, and malice. We must show by word and deed that we bear them no grudge and hatred, but only cherish love for them in our hearts. We must do, really and truly, what Jesus says: "Love your enemies and pray for those who persecute you, so that you may be sons of your Father who is in heaven" (Matthew 5:44–45).

PRAYER

O loving and kind God, You love us fervently, and from such love You bless us in body and soul. But You have also commanded us to extend a similar love to our neighbor. Sadly, I confess to You that my heart is utterly unfit for such sincere and true love of my neighbor. According to Your commandment I should love my neighbor as myself. When You bless my neighbor with good fortune, health, and prosperity, I ought to rejoice as though I had received such blessings. I ought to cordially love my enemy, who hates, reviles, persecutes, and offends me. I ought to pray for my enemy and wish that person well. I ought to request from You many blessings, prosperity, and happiness in body and soul for those who hate me.

But, O all-knowing God, You see how far my heart is from fulfilling these duties. Sadly, when You bless my neighbor, granting him good fortune, honor, and benefits, and You do not grant the same blessings to me, I look on him with envy because You are so kind to him. O all-knowing God, You see how my prayers for my enemies are so weak and lifeless: I either forget entirely to pray for them, or whenever I do think of them—for Your Spirit reminds me of the duty I owe them—I mention only in a few words. O my God and Father, I perceive from these things the misery and depravity in which I still lie, and I see that I am not yet in the state of the true disciples of Jesus in which I ought to be, and which is known by this, that the followers of Jesus love one another and all people, even those who envy, hate, and persecute them.

I pray You, then, change my revengeful heart, which rebels against Your holy will, so that by Your grace I may love my neighbor as heartily and sincerely as myself. Grant me strength and power that I may rejoice when I see the blessings You shower on my neighbor, and that I may not be grieved when You do not at the same time cheer me with equal blessings. Preserve me from all deceitfulness, that I may not pretend to be friendly in word while being hostile in heart. Keep me from being like

Judas, who could kiss and then betray. Keep me honest in all my dealings with my neighbors. And if I am to suffer persecution, abuse, and wrong from my enemies, grant me strength to overcome these ills with meekness, not returning evil for evil, or reviling for reviling, but on the contrary, let me wish them blessing and all manner of good.

O Lord, my God, You see how hard it is for flesh and blood to fulfill this duty. By Your grace and with Your aid it will be possible for me. Grant, O heavenly Father, that I may always have my eyes fixed on the perfect love You showed us while we were still Your enemies. Grant me to keep constantly before my eyes the love of Jesus, who prayed for His enemies and did good to them. Write into my heart the merciful love of Your Spirit, who never wearies of working on my rebellious heart and knocking at its door. Grant that these reflections may move me to true love of my neighbor, and that I may thus receive the witness that I am a true disciple of Jesus.

Love in Christ is strong and living, Binding faithful hearts in one; Love in Christ is true and giving. May His will in us be done. Amen.

LSB 706:1

HYMN

Lord, Thee I love with all my heart;
I pray Thee, ne'er from me depart,
With tender mercy cheer me.
Earth has no pleasure I would share.
Yea, heav'n itself were void and bare
If Thou, Lord, wert not near me.
And should my heart for sorrow break,
My trust in Thee can nothing shake.
Thou art the portion I have sought;
Thy precious blood my soul hath bought.
Lord Jesus Christ, my God and Lord, my God
and Lord,
Forsake me not! I trust Thy Word.

Yea, Lord, 'twas Thy rich bounty gave
My body, soul, and all I have
In this poor life of labor.
Lord, grant that I in ev'ry place
May glorify Thy lavish grace
And help and serve my neighbor.

Let no false doctrine me beguile;
Let Satan not my soul defile.
   Give strength and patience unto me
   To bear my cross and follow Thee.
Lord Jesus Christ, my God and Lord, my God and Lord,
In death Thy comfort still afford.

Lord, let at last Thine angels come,
To Abr'ham's bosom bear me home,
   That I may die unfearing;
And in its narrow chamber keep
My body safe in peaceful sleep
   Until Thy reappearing.
And then from death awaken me,
That these mine eyes with joy may see,
   O Son of God, Thy glorious face,
   My Savior and my fount of grace.
Lord Jesus Christ, my prayer attend, my prayer
   attend,
And I will praise Thee without end. LSB 708:1–3

BELIEVING CHRISTIANS RECOGNIZE THAT GOD ALONE IS THE HIGHEST GOOD

EXHORTATION

Whom have I in heaven but You? And there is nothing on
earth I desire besides You. My flesh and my heart may fail,
but God is the strength of my heart and my portion forever.
Psalm 73:25–26

People have always wanted to have and possess the highest good, but most have not obtained it because they are ignorant of what good is the highest and best of all. The very highest good must be a permanent and perfect one. It must be able to raise us up and comfort us in suffering and death, in fortune and misfortune.

According to this description, the very highest good cannot be wealth, which many people regard as their highest good. Wealth forsakes us in death, and offers us no comfort in that hour. Nor is honor and prosperity the highest good. How often does it happen that the honored person falls into contempt and disgrace! How often is prosperity changed into adversity and misery! Wisdom and skill have the advantage over other earthly possessions that we cannot be robbed of them during life, but they, too, nevertheless vanish at death.

In view of all this, believing Christians seek a true and permanent good. And that is found in God alone. Having God, a Christian has everything: the highest honor, the greatest wealth, the greatest wisdom, and not just in time but also for all eternity. God cheers us in the days of happiness, sustains us under the cross and in tribulation, refreshes us in death and remains united with us in eternity. People can attain this good only by hearing and reading the Word of God. By the working of the Holy Spirit they can learn from this Word to know that they are sinners and to believe in Christ as their Savior. Having received this Word, they must be careful not to drive God away from them by again choosing for their highest good the love of the world with its emptiness and sinful desires.

PRAYER

O God, rich in grace! How glorious and perfect You are! Whoever has You has all things, knows all things, and can do all things. Indeed, whoever has You has the very highest, best, and most excellent good. Write this truth deeply in my heart, that I may seek You alone and find You. Preserve my heart from the folly of worldly people who imagine that by enjoying great honor, great wealth, and great pleasure and glory in this world they have obtained the highest good. How widely they have missed the mark! These are all things that people leave when they die; they neither get to take them into eternity nor can they comfort them in their last hour. Such persons pass into eternity naked and bare, yes, without God. Grant me, then, to carefully distinguish the true good from all the things that pass away.

O triune God, You alone are my highest, dearest, truest, and very best good! You desire to give Yourself to me, to unite Yourself with me.

Therefore, unite with my soul in time and eternity. All earthly things are exposed to the ravages of the enemies. Moth and rust can consume them. My foes can rob me of them. Misfortune can destroy them. Yet God, my highest good, always remains my own. With Him I go out; with Him I enter in. He accompanies me in all my journeys. He is with me when I lie down to rest. And with Him I will at last enter the joys that never end. Therefore, my God, whom have I in heaven but You? And there is nothing on earth that I desire besides You. When I have You, I have true wealth, true glory, the very highest good. So dwell in me, live in me, abide with me. Then I will have a helper in my crosses and sufferings, a support in need, the greatest wealth in poverty, the strongest comfort in sickness, and the sweetest comfort in my last hour. When the children of this world are forsaken by their possessions, God will not forsake me. This highest good I still have when I leave this world. Yes, this good will then be given to me for my inexpressible delight in still more perfect, excellent, glorious, and abundant measure.

Hence, all earthly treasure! Jesus is my pleasure, Jesus is my choice. Hence, all empty glory! Naught to me thy story Told with tempting voice. Pain or loss, Or shame or cross, shall not from my Savior move me Since He deigns to love me. Amen.   *LSB 743:4*

HYMN

Beautiful Savior,
King of Creation,
Son of God and Son of Man!
Truly, I'd love Thee,
Truly, I'd serve Thee,
Light of my soul, my joy, my crown.

Fair are the meadows,
Fair are the woodlands,
Robed in flow'rs of blooming spring;
Jesus is fairer,
Jesus is purer,
He makes our sorr'wing spirit sing.

Fair is the sunshine,
Fair is the moonlight,
Bright the sparkling stars on high;
Jesus shines brighter,

Jesus shines purer
Than all the angels in the sky.

Beautiful Savior,
Lord of the nations,
Son of God and Son of Man!
Glory and honor,
Praise, adoration,
Now and forevermore be Thine! LSB 537:1-4

BELIEVING CHRISTIANS ASK GOD TO PRESERVE AND INCREASE THE FAITH HE HAS KINDLED IN THEM

EXHORTATION

If you confess with your mouth that Jesus is Lord and believe in your heart that God raised Him from the dead, you will be saved. Romans 10:9

The apostles said to the Lord, "Increase our faith!" Luke 17:5

As great as the unhappiness of unbelievers, so great the happiness of soul of believers who abide in the true knowledge of God, of Jesus Christ and His salvation. For unbelievers are like a room that is not lighted, which is gloomy and dreary. But believing souls are like a room in which a bright light is shining. That light is faith. No human being can give faith to himself. It is God who kindles faith in us, either through Holy Baptism, in which the Holy Spirit is poured on us abundantly, or through the Word of God, by which a person obtains knowledge and understanding of salvation, gives assent to the Word of God by God's power, regards it with the whole heart as divinely true, apprehends God with firm confidence, and appropriates Jesus Christ and His holy merit.

Believing Christians, then, should thank God for bringing them to faith and to the knowledge of Jesus Christ, and thus granting them a happiness that non-Christians do not know. They should remember their baptismal covenant and the glory that they have obtained by it, and should not willfully break the covenant they have made with God. They should diligently and reverently hear God's Word, in order that they may become ever more enlightened and attain to greater knowledge. They should put into practice whatever they hear and read, and thus manifest their faith by their works. Therefore, true Christians will not be content saying, "I believe," but they will also cause the fruits of faith—godliness, love, chastity, patience, meekness, and the like—to shine forth in their entire life. They must believe not only for a time, but must remain faithful to God until death. Then they may comfort themselves with the assurance that they will receive the end of their faith, the salvation of their souls.

PRAYER

O gracious God, what great mercy You have shown me! You have brought me to the true knowledge of my salvation, which is Jesus Christ with His merit, blood, and death. I know the means of my salvation: the Word of God and the Holy Sacraments. And not only do I know these things, but I give assent to them all. Indeed, I place all my hope and confidence in them. Now I know the true way to heaven; for whoever wants to come to God must believe in Christ. By this faith and knowledge I am set apart from the unbelievers and the heathen.

O gracious God, grant me Your Holy Spirit, that He may produce this knowledge in me. Grant that my faith may not be a sham, dead and unfruitful, but that it may be a living faith. Because I know Jesus Christ as my Savior, I will also love Him, obey Him, and hold Him more precious than all the world. I will serve Him and will not do what my flesh and blood and the evil world would prompt me to do. Nothing, whatever it may be, will become more precious to me than Jesus.

Because I know the means of salvation, I will, with Your aid, apply them for my salvation. I will devoutly hear Your Word and live according to it. I will flee and forsake what Your Word forbids. And on the other hand, by Your strength, with the aid of the Holy Spirit, I will strive to fulfill the duties and practice the virtues Your Word commands. The Holy

FOR USE IN HEALTH

Supper will sanctify me wholly. For the strengthening of my faith and for my salvation, I will partake often and devoutly as the food of sanctification, and will ever strive to grow in holiness.

O my God, increase in me faith, holiness, and obedience, that with each day I may become more pious, devout, and God-fearing, ever growing in conformity to the image of my Savior. Keep me in this grace to my blessed end, that I may live as a true and pious Christian, and also die in peace at Your appointed time.

How firm a foundation, O saints of the Lord, Is laid for your faith in His excellent Word! What more can He say than to you He has said Who unto the Savior for refuge have fled? Amen. *LSB 728:1*

HYMN

O God, forsake me not!
    Your gracious presence lend me;
Lord, lead Your helpless child;
    Your Holy Spirit send me
That I my course may run.
    O be my light, my lot,
My staff, my rock, my shield—
    O God, forsake me not!

O God, forsake me not!
    Take not Your Spirit from me;
Do not permit the might
    Of sin to overcome me.
Increase my feeble faith,
    Which You alone have wrought.
O be my strength and pow'r—
    O God, forsake me not!

O God, forsake me not!
    Lord, hear my supplication!
In ev'ry evil hour
    Help me resist temptation;
And when the prince of hell
    My conscience seeks to blot,
Be then not far from me—
    O God, forsake me not!

O God, forsake me not!
    Lord, I am Yours forever.
O keep me strong in faith
    That I may leave You never.
Grant me a blessed end
    When my good fight is fought;
Help me in life and death—
    O God, forsake me not!

LSB 731:1–4

139

BELIEVING CHRISTIANS PRAY FOR HUMILITY

EXHORTATION

Clothe yourselves, all of you, with humility toward one an-
other, for "God opposes the proud but gives grace to the humble."
Humble yourselves, therefore, under the mighty hand of God so
that at the proper time He may exalt you. 1 Peter 5:5–6

Among the sins that a believing Christian must contend against is pride and haughtiness dwelling in the heart and breaking forth into actions. Since the fall into sin we are proud by nature, but we must become humble by grace. Whoever does not become humble cannot please God or be a disciple of Christ.

When believing Christians reflect on this fact, they pray God for a heart that is humble toward God. For "He has told you, O man, what is good; and what does the Lord require of you but to do justice, and to love kindness, and to walk humbly with your God?" (Micah 6:8). However, Christians will become humble toward God when they consider the greatness, majesty, glory, and holiness of God; when they bear in mind that all the angels, cherubim, seraphim, and the elect worship and praise Him; and when they reflect, on the other hand, on what wretched worms they are in themselves, remembering that they are nothing but miserable beings that God can wipe out in a minute.

Believing Christians will become humble toward their fellow human beings when they hold themselves in low esteem over against their neighbor and consider that their neighbor may be much more humble, believing, pious, and devout and therefore more acceptable to God than they are. Believing Christians are also kept in humility when they remember that they share with their neighbor one Word, one Baptism, one Holy Supper, one heaven. And they also remember that like the poorest beggar they will also decay in the grave and turn to dust and ashes.

Believing Christians will become humble in their estimate of themselves when they reflect that all they have, all their gifts, skills, blessings, life, prosperity, and success did not come from themselves but from God. Further, God can quickly take all these things away; and so they must not boast of them or exalt themselves because of them or listen to the praise of flatterers. In order that they may not become proud in any way, let them diligently place before themselves the example of the humble Christ. He humbled Himself beneath God and all creatures, and admonishes us: "Learn from Me, for I am meek and humble of heart."

PRAYER

O great, holy, and merciful God, You are the high and exalted One, and before Your throne cherubim and seraphim and all Your elect cover their faces in humility. I confess that by nature I am inclined to seek my own honor, to take pride in myself, and to exalt myself above all else. Through the fall into sin Satan has poisoned my heart with pride, with which sin began, so that I often forget that I am earth, dust, and ashes.

O my God, give me a humble heart, that I may become profoundly aware of the fact that I have life and breath, prosperity and all things from You. Let me humble myself under Your mighty hand, that I might not presume to offend You by thoughts, words, or deeds. Teach me to know my wretchedness and Your great majesty; to know from myself I am nothing but sin, death, and damnation, and that whatever good there is found in me I have received it all from Your gracious hand. Keep me from boasting, then, and let me regard all things as Your gracious gifts that You can quickly take from me again if in the multitude of Your mercies I should forget You. Plant in my heart true humility, that I may obey, fear, honor, serve, worship, praise, and magnify You alone.

Plant in my heart true humility also toward my fellow human beings, that I may never indulge in odious comparisons with others, nor prefer myself over them. Help me to reflect that the proud have never yet been pleasing to You, but that You have made Your light, Your comfort, Your grace, and Your goodness to flow abundantly into humble hearts. Turn from me proud thoughts. Grant that I may beware of proud words. Preserve me from ambition and boastfulness, from which nothing but contempt of my neighbor will spring. Impress on my heart the image of my lowly Savior. He humbled Himself below angels and all people, and

He calls to me also: "Learn from Me, for I am meek and humble of heart." Let this call of my Savior echo in my heart whenever my heart would become lifted up in sinful pride. If my fellow human being is a lowly person, keep me from looking down on him. If he is exalted, rich, or honored, let me view these advantages as Your work, and acknowledge that You have made him what he is, have lifted him up and put him into this position, so that I may not grumble before You on account of these things, nor envy Your gifts to him, but rather rejoice in them.

O my God, help me to become converted and be as a little child who thinks nothing of himself. Let me become nothing in my own eyes. Give me Your Holy Spirit, that I may daily die to the sin of pride, regard myself worthy of no honor from anyone, and ascribe all honor and glory to You alone. Grant me to know with true humility of heart that all I am and all I have is by Your grace; that I may not boast except in my weakness.

Teach me, by means of such humility, to live in peace and concord with all people. Let my heart always be a dwelling place of the humble Christ; then I shall never exalt myself. Pride and haughtiness were the sin of Satan; from such preserve me by Your grace! And if it should please You, O my God, to let me fall into contempt and ridicule, to permit my enemy to revile me, and the haughty to trample me under foot, give me strength and ability to bear all with humility, patience, and trust in You, and to make even these things serve me as aids to humility and to a greater carefulness in my conduct. O Lord, grant me strength and ability to do all these things by Your mighty aid.

O keep me watchful, then, and humble; Permit me nevermore to stray. Uphold me when my feet would stumble, And keep me on the narrow way. Fill all my nature with Thy light, O Radiance strong and bright! Amen.

LSB 694:4

HYMN

Chief of sinners though I be,
Jesus shed His blood for me,
Died that I might live on high,
Lives that I might never die.
As the branch is to the vine,
I am His, and He is mine.

Oh, the height of Jesus' love,
Higher than the heav'ns above,
Deeper than the depths of sea,
Lasting as eternity!
Love that found me—wondrous
thought!
Found me when I sought Him not.

Only Jesus can impart
Balm to heal the wounded heart,
Peace that flows from sins forgiv'n,
Joy that lifts the soul to heav'n,
Faith and hope to walk with God
In the way that Enoch trod.

Chief of sinners though I be,
Christ is all in all to me;
All my wants to Him are known,
All my sorrows are His own.
He sustains the hidden life
Safe with Him from earthly strife.

O my Savior, help afford
By Your Spirit and Your Word!
When my wayward heart would
* stray*
Keep me in the narrow way;
Grace in time of need supply
While I live and when I die.

LSB 611:1–5

BELIEVING CHRISTIANS PRAY FOR MEEKNESS

EXHORTATION

Christ also suffered for you, leaving you an example, so that you might follow in His steps. He committed no sin, neither was deceit found in His mouth. When He was reviled, He did not revile in return; when He suffered, He did not threaten, but continued entrusting Himself to Him who judges justly. 1 Peter 2:21–23

After people have made a good beginning in the Christian life and in their renewal, they must always strive to become more perfect. They must not only seek to rid themselves outwardly of gross sins, such as contempt for God's Word, cursing, depravity, lewdness, unrighteousness, sinful games, and worldly ways; they must also be concerned to become pure inwardly. They seek to be free from pride, envy, wrath, hatred, and vengefulness, and must prayerfully exercise all diligence to become meek.

Meekness consists in not returning evil for evil, not reviling when we are reviled, not uttering threats against our neighbor from a hateful, angry, and vengeful heart. We shall know whether we are meek and possess this noble virtue when we are attacked by an enemy who would rob us of our honor, property, or good name. If we become worked up and enraged at such times, utter curses and threats, then the meek spirit of Christ is not dwelling in us. However, it is not contrary to meekness to seek protection against an enemy at the hands of the government. We remember how Paul, when his life was threatened, appealed to Caesar (Acts 25:11). It is not fitting for the children of God to bite like dogs, to tear into one another with rage and bitterness as though we were wild animals. In such persecutions, when we are oppressed by enemies, God desires to see a proof of our faith, and to lead us to a knowledge of our former sins, that we may ascertain whether we have not perhaps caused others to groan in sorrow over our own unjust procedures. The marks of meekness are these: forgiving from the heart and praying for our enemies (Matthew 5:44), wishing them well, doing good to them wherever we can, rejoicing in their prosperity, not paying attention to every word of reviling, not returning a reply to every word that is uttered against us, and being ready to be reconciled with our enemies.

PRAYER

O loving God, You are love itself, and You want to pour out Your love into our hearts by the Holy Spirit. I confess with heartfelt sorrow that my heart is often quite rebellious and unmanageable. On occasions when my enemy gets under my skin, persecutes, and hates me, I ought to harbor humility, love, meekness, and gentleness. But sadly I find in me stubbornness, hatred, anger, vengefulness, and enmity, by which I am driven to speak harshly to those who wrong me, and to take revenge on those who have attacked me unjustly.

But, O God, when I learn from Your Holy Word that those who do such things will never enter the kingdom of God, and that such behavior in the presence of enemies is not a trait of Your children, Your true Christians, then I am terrified. I still have these evil traits of the devil about me, who is vengeful, malicious, and will never be reconciled. And so I pray You, O my gracious God, have mercy on me and give me Your Holy Spirit, that He may sanctify my heart and cleanse it from all malice and vengefulness. Help me always to behold the example of my Jesus, who refused to revile in return when He was reviled, and when He suffered, did not threaten His enemies that He would one day take revenge on them, but committed all affairs to You, the God who judges with justice.

Grant me, O Lord, such a quiet, meek, and peaceful mind, so that I may not retain any grudge or hatred in my heart. Grant me grace never to let the sun set on my wrath, but that I seek my rest to forgive my adversaries before night falls. Grant me strength, so that when my enemies revile me, I may be like a deaf person, who hears not, and like a dumb person, who opens not his mouth. On the other hand, grant me grace, that I may be able to rejoice when my enemies prosper; that I may wish them all possible good, and be pleased when they obtain it. Yes, help me to assist them gladly and do them good whenever they run into trouble.

Protect me from betraying any ill will in words, gestures, or deeds. Let me with all my heart be as merciful toward my enemies as toward everyone else. Let me speak kindly, be sincere, pleasant in address, and also kind in actions, lest by my unforgiving spirit my prayer be hindered and all my worship and devotion be rejected by You. Grant that I may heartily forgive those who trespass against me, even as I desire that You would forgive me all my faults and iniquities, lest I daily pray against myself. Let Your blessings descend on me that You have promised to the meek: "Blessed are the meek, for they shall inherit the earth. Blessed are the peacemakers, for they shall be called sons of God" (Matthew 5:5, 9). Arrest by Your Spirit the evil lust that rises up in me to war against this virtue, so that I may live and die as Your believing child, and at last by Your grace may be transferred to the home of peace. Amen.

HYMN

I am trusting Thee to guide me;
Thou alone shalt lead,
Ev'ry day and hour supplying
All my need.

I am trusting Thee for power;
Thine can never fail.
Words which Thou Thyself shalt give me
Must prevail.

I am trusting Thee, Lord Jesus;
Never let me fall.
I am trusting Thee forever
And for all. LSB 729:4–6

BELIEVING CHRISTIANS ACKNOWLEDGE THE CONSTANT GOODNESS OF GOD

EXHORTATION

The steadfast love of the LORD never ceases; His mercies never come to an end; they are new every morning; great is Your faithfulness. Lamentations 3:22–23

For everything there is a season; the goodness and mercy of God, however, are everlasting. In Psalm 136, David repeats "His steadfast love endures forever" at the close of each verse. The goodness of God is like that of a mother who takes her child when it is born into her arms, cares for it, nurtures it, and rears it. That is how God treats us human beings.

Now, believing Christians acknowledge this as an unmerited kindness. We have in no way deserved such treatment from God. If He were to deal with us by what we have deserved, destruction would overwhelm us in body and soul. It is a goodness that we need. If God were not so kind and merciful, we would waste away and perish, and could not live a day, not even an hour. Just as no creature can live without air, so people cannot exist without the goodness of God. Yes—and this is vital—it is a constant goodness. When believing Christians look back on their entire life, from birth through childhood, youth and ripening years, they see nothing other than God's goodness. Whatever good there is in us, God has wrought it. All that we possess in earthly things, God's goodness has given to us. Yes, what is even more wonderful, it is a goodness even the ungrateful and the wicked share. On them also God makes His sun shine; He clothes and feeds them. It is only of the indwelling of the Holy Spirit that they are not partakers—and that is because they shut their heart to Him.

However, believing Christians allow the goodness of God to lead them to repentance, to the love and fear of God, and are assured that they will enjoy God's goodness even to death, and indeed through all eternity.

PRAYER

How excellent is Your loving-kindness, O God! Therefore, the children of men put their trust under the shadow of Your wings. They shall be abundantly satisfied with the rich treasures of Your house, and You will make them drink from the river of Your pleasures. Goodness like this I, too, have experienced, O my God. It has been renewed to me every day, every hour, every week, yes, every year. When I was born, Your goodness, like a nurse and mother, took me into its arms and reared me. Your goodness led me by the hand in my youth and accompanied me everywhere. In my mature life Your goodness has provided for me, supported me, sustained me, and bestowed many blessings on me. Yes, till this day and this hour in which I am standing before You, Your goodness has hovered over me, Your light shone on me, and You have filled me with blessing, grace, and comfort. This goodness of Yours has often preserved me from misfortune and injury. Your goodness and faithfulness have kept me in all my ways and attended my going out and coming in, lest any harm befall me. This goodness of Yours has also made my soul bright with heavenly light, illumined me by Your Word, sanctified me by Your Holy Spirit, and brought me to a true and living knowledge of You.

O my God, let Your goodness continue to be over me. Do not forsake me in old age when I become gray! Let Your goodness and faithfulness be my guides until death, until they have brought my soul to its comfort in Your bosom and my body to its rest in the earth. Moreover, let Your goodness lead me to repentance, that, contemplating the blessings I have received, I may yield my heart to You for a dwelling place and my soul for Your possession. According to all Your goodness, have mercy on me if I happen to err and sin in my weakness. Bring me back by Your mercy to the way of repentance and peace, and let me relish Your grace here in time and hereafter in eternity. For all Your goodness given to me I thank and praise You from my inmost heart. Not only do I praise You here while I live, but I will also praise You, O good and merciful God, there through all eternity. Amen.

HYMN

My soul, now praise your Maker!
 Let all within me bless His
 name
Who makes you full partaker
 Of mercies more than you dare
 claim.
Forget Him not whose meekness
 Still bears with all your sin,
Who heals your ev'ry weakness,
 Renews your life within;
Whose grace and care are endless
 And saved you through the
 past;
Who leaves no suff'rer friendless
 But rights the wronged at last.

He offers all His treasure
 Of justice, truth, and righ-
 teousness,
His love beyond all measure,
 His yearning pity o'er distress;
Nor treats us as we merit
 But sets His anger by.
The poor and contrite spirit
 Finds His compassion nigh;
And high as heav'n above us,
 As dawn from close of day,
So far, since He has loved us,
 He puts our sins away.

For as a tender father
 Has pity on His children here,
God in His arms will gather
 All who are His in childlike
 fear.
He knows how frail our powers,
 Who but from dust are made.
We flourish like the flowers,
 And even so we fade;
The wind but through them passes,
 And all their bloom is o'er.
We wither like the grasses;
 Our place knows us no more.

His grace remains forever,
 And children's children yet
 shall prove
That God forsakes them never
 Who in true fear shall seek His
 love.
In heav'n is fixed His dwelling,
 His rule is over all;
O hosts with might excelling,
 With praise before Him fall.
Praise Him forever reigning,
 All you who hear His Word—
Our life and all sustaining.
 My soul, O praise the Lord!

LSB 820:1–4

Believing Christians Ponder the Future Glory of the Children of God

EXHORTATION

Beloved, we are God's children now, and what we will be has not yet appeared; but we know that when He appears we shall be like Him, because we shall see Him as He is. And everyone who thus hopes in Him purifies himself as He is pure. 1 John 3:2–3

All true Christians should daily, yes, hourly, ponder three things: who they are, namely, children of God; what God is to them, namely, a Father, a benefactor, and the very best of friends; and what they have yet to expect from God, namely, heavenly joy and glory. This reflection will kindle and strengthen in them love of God, and rouse hatred and contempt for the world and every sinful way of life.

For even in the present life the believers possess great glories. They have the forgiveness of sins, divine sonship, peace with God, a comforter in every affliction, an advocate and intercessor, joy of soul, and rest in God. Compared with this glory, silver, gold, money, and even a king's crown must be esteemed as nothing. Great glories also are awaiting them after this life. They will enter into heaven and have the unspeakable privilege of beholding the triune God. They will have holy angels and the saints as their companions. They will be delivered from all suffering and enjoy everlasting happiness and finally a glad and blessed resurrection of the body.

Believing Christians should rejoice at this prospect, comfort themselves with it whenever they run into troubles, and be assured that all their suffering will at last be turned into endless rejoicing. In particular, however, they must not trifle away these glories by a sinful, worldly life, but remember that they have been destined for something more glorious. To this end they abide in faith and holiness of life, look on earthly things as things that pass away and that they must leave behind, while on the other hand, they often direct their heart yonder where they long to be forever.

PRAYER

O how gracious, kind, and merciful You are, O eternal and mighty God! Not only did You create man in great glory, but when we had fallen, You did once more promise great glory to all who will accept Your grace and obey the promptings of Your Holy Spirit by faith and a holy life. For such regenerate and sanctified souls may comfort themselves with the reflection that they possess great glory even here in time: sonship with God, the righteousness of Christ, the indwelling of the Holy Spirit, peace with You, Your favor, grace, and love to which they may always claim, a fearless access by prayer, and from which they can obtain help and mercy in their troubles.

To this glory a still greater glory will be added after this life. When the soul departs from the body, it is promised admission to the vision of Your countenance, the fellowship of Your saints, and abundance of heavenly joy. This glory will also be shared by the body after the resurrection, in which it will be transfigured and shine like the sun.

O my God, grant me grace always to have this glory before my eyes, and to consider that, dying, I shall really begin to live, that in death my misery, but not my life, shall have an end, and that I shall then pass from unrest to rest, from tribulation to joy, from anguish to supreme delight, from sadness and this valley of sorrow to consolation.

O keep me in faith and godliness, and when the world would lead me astray, let me call to mind who I am—Your child—and what I have to expect at Your hands—everlasting glory and bliss—so that I may not love the world anymore and miss the glory of heaven on account of it. Grant me to walk cautiously, not unwisely, but as the wise, being careful of every step as were those who ran in a race in order that they might obtain the prize. At the end of my life may I be able to say truthfully: I have fought the good fight, I have finished the course, I have kept the faith; now there is laid up for me a crown of righteousness the righteous Judge will give me at that day, and not to me only, but to all who have loved His appearing. Amen.

HYMN

Jerusalem the golden,
 With milk and honey blest—
The promise of salvation,
 The place of peace and rest—
We know not, oh, we know not
 What joys await us there:
The radiancy of glory,
 The bliss beyond compare!

Within those walls of Zion
 Sounds forth the joyful song,
As saints join with the angels
 And all the martyr throng.
The Prince is ever with them;
 The daylight is serene;
The city of the blessed
 Shines bright with glorious
sheen.

Around the throne of David,
 The saints, from care released,
Raise loud their songs of triumph
 To celebrate the feast.
They sing to Christ their leader,
 Who conquered in the fight,
Who won for them forever
 Their gleaming robes of white.

O sweet and blessed country,
 The home of God's elect!
O sweet and blessed country
 That faithful hearts expect!
In mercy, Jesus, bring us
 To that eternal rest
With You and God the Father
 And Spirit, ever blest.

LSB 672:1–4

BELIEVING CHRISTIANS MAKE CONFESSION AND PRAY TO GOD FOR FORGIVENESS OF SINS

EXHORTATION

Have mercy on me, O God, according to Your steadfast love; according to Your abundant mercy blot out my transgressions. Wash me thoroughly from my iniquity, and cleanse me from my sin! Psalm 51:1–2

The state of true Christians—having a gracious God—is truly the happiest. True, the world imagines that possessing riches, being honored, feasting royally, that these things constitute happiness. But the world deceives itself. All these things must pass away and very often they lead to a bad conscience, a heavy responsibility, and an unhappy death.

Accordingly, believing Christians examine their consciences every

151

day, whether they are still in the grace of God. When they go to confession, they not only remember their sins, but heartily pray God to forgive them. They repent of them, mourn over them, seek refuge in the mercy of God and in the blessed Passion of Jesus, and humbly cry out for mercy.

And when by the mouth of His servant God grants them the forgiveness of their sins, they take comfort in it, and they strive to keep a gracious God by letting the Holy Spirit rule them. They are eager to lead a Christian life and show it by their speech, words, and works. They flee vice and their former sinful habits, and then they know that, living and dying, they will have a gracious God.

PRAYER

Holy, triune God, Father, Son, and Holy Spirit, I, a poor sinner, have come before Your most holy countenance and pray You heartily and humbly to forgive all my sins. O my God, I observe, sadly, that in many ways I have provoked You to anger by many evil thoughts, words, and deeds. Lord, I am grieved over this and truly sorry for it. Through Holy Baptism You have made me a sheep of Your pasture and a member of Your body, so I ought to hear Your voice and be obedient to You alone. Yes, being Your own, I ought to present my members as a living sacrifice, holy and acceptable to You. But what can I say? I have more often listened to the voice of the world and my own flesh than to Your voice, and have done what is displeasing to You in many ways. Oh, the blindness of my heart! Oh, the folly of my youthful years! If now You enter into judgment with me and deal with me according to Your justice, I am lost forever. My conscience bears witness against me and my sins are more than the sands on the seashore.

Take pity on me according to Your great mercy. O my Father, do not charge against me what evil I have done during the time of my life, but credit me with what Jesus Christ, my Savior, has done for me. I lay hold in true faith on the blood He shed for me. I make His merit my own. I say: For Jesus' sake be merciful to me, a poor sinner. From now on I shall begin to lead a new and godly life, and will no longer sin wantonly and willfully against You, O triune God.

Since Christ has full atonement made And brought to us salvation,

Each Christian therefore may be glad And build on this foundation. Your grace alone, dear Lord, I plead, Your death is now my life indeed, For You have paid my ransom. Amen.

LSB 555:6

HYMN

Jesus sinners doth receive;
Oh, may all this saying ponder
Who in sin's delusions live
And from God and heaven wander!
Here is hope for all who grieve:
Jesus sinners doth receive!

We deserve but grief and shame,
Yet His words, rich grace revealing,
Pardon, peace, and life proclaim;
Here our ills have perfect healing.
Firmly in these words believe:
Jesus sinners doth receive.

Sheep that from the fold did stray
No true shepherd e'er forsaketh;
Weary souls that lost their way
Christ, the Shepherd, gently taketh
In His arms that they may live:
Jesus sinners doth receive.

I, a sinner, come to Thee
With a penitent confession.
Savior, mercy show to me;
Grant for all my sins remission.

Let these words my soul relieve:
Jesus sinners doth receive.

Oh, how blest it is to know:
Were as scarlet my transgression,
It shall be as white as snow
By Thy blood and bitter passion;
For these words I now believe:
Jesus sinners doth receive.

Now my conscience is at peace;
From the Law I stand acquitted.
Christ hath purchased my release
And my ev'ry sin remitted.
Naught remains my soul to grieve:
Jesus sinners doth receive.

Jesus sinners doth receive;
Also I have been forgiven;
And when I this earth must leave,
I shall find an open heaven.
Dying, still to Him I cleave:
Jesus sinners doth receive.

LSB 609:1–7

ANOTHER PRAYER OF CONFESSION

O Lord, You are all knowing, and from You nothing is hid. You see all that we do and hear all that we speak. When I think of this, I am grieved, for I have surely spoken, thought, and done much evil in Your sight. In view of this, You would have just cause to turn Your back forever on me as Your disobedient child, and to abandon me utterly into hell. But behold, I come before You in this season of grace. I am ashamed to lift up my eyes before You and say: God, be merciful to me, a sinner. Oh, do not discipline me in Your hot anger as I have deserved. Do not remember the sins of my youth or my transgressions. According to Your great mercy, remember me for Your goodness' sake. Yes, for the sake of the blood and death of Jesus, have mercy on me.

Lord, Lord, gracious and full of compassion, slow to anger and full of great love, You will not keep Your anger forever, but will again have mercy on me. Do not deal with me according to my sins or reward me according to my iniquity. O God, You have said that You have no pleasure in the death of the sinner, but that the sinner turn to You and live. Have mercy also on me, O God, though I have provoked You to anger. Behold me not in my sins but in Jesus, Your Son, my only Savior, Mediator, and Redeemer. For the sake of the blood that He shed, have mercy on me. For the sake of His perfect righteousness, which I grasp by faith, have mercy on me. Let me know in my heart the consolation that my sins are forgiven me, that I am reconciled to You by Jesus, my Savior. By the power of Your Holy Spirit I will amend my life. I will contemplate Your most holy presence and reflect that whether I am moving or standing still, or whatever I do, You are present and watching me. Let such thoughts never leave my heart.

Thy love and grace alone avail To blot out my transgression; The best and holiest deeds must fail To break sin's dread oppression. Before Thee none can boasting stand, But all must fear Thy strict demand And live alone by mercy. Amen.   *LSB 607:2*

HYMN

Baptismal waters cover me
As I approach on bended knee;
My Father's mercy here I plead,
For grievous sins of thought and deed.

I look to Christ upon the tree,
His body broken there for me;
I lay before Him all my sin,
My darkest secrets from within.

Lord, may Your wounded hand impart
Your healing to my broken heart;
Your love alone can form in me
A heart that serves You joyfully.

From Your own mouth comes forth a word;
Your shepherd speaks, but You are heard;
Through him Your hand now stretches out,
Forgiving sin, destroying doubt.

Baptismal waters cover me;
Christ's wounded hand has set me free.
Held in my Father's strong embrace,
With joy I praise Him for His grace. LSB 616:1–4

BELIEVING CHRISTIANS PRAY WHEN RECEIVING THE LORD'S SUPPER

EXHORTATION

For as often as you eat this bread and drink the cup, you pro-
claim the Lord's death until He comes. 1 Corinthians 11:26

The Holy Supper of our Lord is the means for strengthening faith and love toward God and our fellow human beings. By this meal Jesus desires to unite with our souls, dwell in them, rule, sanctify, and preserve them in godliness. Believing Christians do not despise or neglect this Holy Supper as nominal Christians are in the sad habit of doing—so distracted are they with vanity, worldly pleasures, revenge, pride, and luxurious living that they do not regard this pledge of God to the soul. Believing Christians do not go to the Lord's Supper out of mere habit, but they approach it with humble, devout, and believing hearts, filled with the good resolve to continue steadfastly in the love and fear of God. And they also have resolved, after taking the Holy Supper of the Lord, to yield themselves entirely to God, to become more godly, devout, and zealous each day in their Christian conduct and in the exercise of Christian virtues by the power of this food for the soul. Yes, by its strength they intend to remain loyal to God even unto death in true faith and godliness.

PRAYER

My Jesus, how can I ever sufficiently praise Your great love? You have not only given Yourself into death for me, a poor sinner, but also have ordained Your holy body and Your precious blood as the food for my soul in the Holy Supper. O Love, Your death brings me life. Your body and Your blood strengthen and refresh me unto the life that never ends. By this means I abide in You and You in me; You live in me and I obtain righteousness and strength in You. Therefore, my sin cannot frighten me, and Satan cannot condemn me. In this gracious feast I receive the ransom for my sins. Here, I receive the body that was given into death for me. Here, I receive the blood that was shed for me for the forgiveness of sin. This is the blood of atonement by which my sins and the sins of all people have been canceled. Now, as surely as I receive it, so surely God is merciful to me, and I have the forgiveness of all my sins. In Holy Baptism, the first sacrament I received, You gave me a new life in the Holy Spirit, thus assuring me that I am Your child and heir. In the Holy Supper, the ongoing sacrament, You give me the pledge of Your body and blood to preserve and strengthen in me the new life.

O my God, sanctify my soul, strengthen my faith, that I may receive this feast of love worthily and for my salvation. Grant that my thoughts may always be with You. Drive from my heart all sinful suggestions, desires, and anything that might hinder my devotion, that You may abide in me, and that I may be and abide in You to all eternity.

Jesus, bread of life, I pray You, Let me gladly here obey You. By Your love I am invited, Be Your love with love requited; By this Supper let me measure, Lord, how vast and deep love's treasure. Through the gift of grace You give me As Your guest in heav'n receive me. Amen.   *LSB 636:8*

HYMN

O living Bread from heaven,
 How well You feed Your guest!
The gifts that You have given
 Have filled my heart with rest.

Oh, wondrous food of blessing,
 Oh, cup that heals our woes!
My heart, this gift possessing,
 With praises overflows.

My Lord, You here have led me
To this most holy place,
And with Yourself have fed me
The treasures of Your grace;
For You have freely given
What earth could never buy,
The bread of life from heaven,
That now I shall not die.

You gave me all I wanted;
This food can death destroy.
And You have freely granted
The cup of endless joy.
My Lord, I do not merit
The favor You have shown,

And all my soul and spirit,
Bow down before Your throne.

Lord, grant me then, thus
strengthened
With heav'nly food, while here
My course on earth is lengthened,
To serve with holy fear.
And when You call my spirit
To leave the world below,
I enter, through Your merit,
Where joys unmingled flow.

LSB 642:1–4

ANOTHER PRAYER WHEN GOING TO THE LORD'S SUPPER

O Jesus, now that I am to partake of Your holy feast of love, I receive it also in remembrance of You. I remember Your love, how for my sake You came into the world to make me an heir of life everlasting. I remember Your anguish, pain, and wounds by which my sins and punishments have been removed from me and Your righteousness bestowed on me. I remember Your death and Your resurrection by which life and salvation have been imparted to me. I know, O Jesus, that for Your sake I obtain grace, sonship, peace, and heaven's joy. I shall not be lost if I abide in You, O Jesus, and You abide in me.

O abide, then, in my heart. Dwell in my heart, live and run in it. Let me be Yours now and for eternity. Let Your holy body be my food, Your holy blood my drink, and refresh me unto life everlasting. Grant that I may never lose this treasure, but that You, my Jesus, henceforth may live, rule, and dwell in me. Israel's manna had to be gathered in a clean vessel. Oh, that You would then purify my heart by true faith, genuine repentance, love, and humility, so that I may worthily receive this pledge of Your love and constantly keep it for the strengthening of my faith, the sanctification of my life, and the assurance of my salvation. O precious Holy Spirit, preserve me in this grace unto my blessed end. Guard me, lest I again sin wantonly and fall from grace, and my last condition be worse than the first. Until death let me continue in faith in the triune God, in love toward my neighbor, and in godliness, that I may obtain the end of faith, the salvation of my soul.

Grant that we worthily receive Your supper, Lord, our Savior, And, truly grieving for our sins, May prove by our behavior That we are thankful for Your grace And day by day may run our race, In holiness increasing. Amen. *LSB 622:7*

HYMN

Let all mortal flesh keep silence
And with fear and trembling stand;
Ponder nothing earthly minded,
For with blessing in His hand
Christ our God to earth descending
Comes our homage to demand.

King of kings yet born of Mary,
As of old on earth He stood,
Lord of lords in human vesture,
In the body and the blood,
He will give to all the faithful
His own self for heav'nly food.

Rank on rank the hosts of heaven
Spreads its vanguard on the way
As the Light of Light, descending
From the realms of endless day,
Comes the pow'rs of hell to vanquish
As the darkness clears away.

At His feet the six-winged seraph,
Cherubim with sleepless eye,
Veil their faces to the presence
As with ceaseless voice they cry:
"Alleluia, Alleluia!
Alleluia, Lord Most High!" *LSB 621:1-4*

BELIEVING CHRISTIANS PRAY GOD TO GIVE THEM STRENGTH TO RESIST SIN

EXHORTATION

Let not sin therefore reign in your mortal body, to make you obey its passions. Do not present your members to sin as instruments for unrighteousness, but present yourselves to God as those who have been brought from death to life, and your members to God as instruments for righteousness. Romans 6:12–13

Sin is a departure from God, a transgression of the divine Law. Sin is the opposite of what is right. Christians neither willingly depart from God nor transgress His commandments nor commit unrighteousness. Their desire is that Jesus would live in them and that the Holy Spirit would rule them. However, because they cannot at all times perfectly achieve this, they must fight against sin.

This fight consists in the following: believing Christians know that whoever is born of God does not commit sin, that is, not intentionally and willfully; and so they are careful not to offend their God knowingly and intentionally. But because they are not satisfied with this, but would gladly consecrate, surrender, and devote their entire heart and soul, spirit and body, to God, they are grieved over a single sinful word spoken; a wicked and sinful thought arising in them will sadden them; and they groan when they have by any act offended God or their fellow human beings.

In this fight they seek refuge in Jesus Christ and pray for power and strength, that Jesus would aid them to overcome sin and the world. They must not only increase the fervor of their prayer, but pay ever stricter attention to the lusts and thoughts that arise in them, and also shun the places and opportunities that might lead them into sin. In this way they can rest assured, because they are in a state of sanctification and have a desire to serve God with all their heart and soul and strength, that God, who has worked in them to will and to do, will also grant them the power to accomplish God's will. Yes, Jesus will cover their defects and faults with His blood, and will be well pleased with their heartfelt desire.

PRAYER

Strong and almighty God, You know what is in man. You see, sadly, the violent struggle I am engaged in against sin. I would gladly be and remain godly with all my heart, no longer provoke Your anger, order my life according to Your Holy Word, and perform Your holy will alone. But I feel another law in my members at war with the law of my mind. When I think I have at last planted my feet firmly upon a good resolution, I often feel that pride, self-will, self-esteem, envy, and prejudice against my fellow human beings manifest themselves in me. Sinful thoughts are found in my heart, and I am also guilty of sinning by thoughtless words and actions unfit for one of Your children.

I am grieved over being full of so much uncleanness. Cleanse me, O Lord, and I shall be clean. In Your light and by Your grace I perceive that to sin is a great evil, my ruin and my plague, from which I would gladly be delivered. I struggle against it in Your strength, and still sometimes in my weakness I am overcome. However, it is just this miserable condition that grieves me. What is to finally become of me if I am now godly, now wicked, and my godliness has no permanency?

You see, my God, how I am shocked at myself but unable to help myself by my own strength. So I come to You and pray You to forgive me all my past sins and imperfections and to give me strength to fight against sin. Let Your Holy Spirit dwell in me and cleanse my heart. When I am about to become angry, vindictive, proud, let Him admonish me, calling to me in such moments and saying: Remember, you are a Christian. Remember, you are a child of God! Let Him do this that I might become meek, humble, and godly. Lord, You have wrought in me to will; give me also the grace to do. Strengthen me in the inner man, that in Your might I may lay aside one sin after another and rule over them. Increase my strength, that I may overcome the world outside and inside me. I can do all things through Him who strengthens me, Jesus Christ.

Lord, be our light when worldly darkness veils us; Lord, be our shield,

when earthly armor fails us; And in the day when hell itself assaults us,
Grant us Your peace, Lord. Amen. *LSB 659:3*

HYMN

Fight the good fight with all your might;
Christ is your strength, and Christ your right.
Lay hold on life, and it shall be
Your joy and crown eternally.

Run the straight race through God's good grace;
Lift up your eyes, and seek His face.
Life with its way before us lies;
Christ is the path, and Christ the prize.

Cast care aside, lean on your guide;
His boundless mercy will provide.
Trust, and enduring faith shall prove
Christ is your life and Christ your love.

Faint not nor fear, His arms are near;
He changes not who holds you dear;
Only believe, and you will see
That Christ is all eternally. LSB 664:1–4

BELIEVING CHRISTIANS DESIRE TO OFFER THEM- SELVES AS A SACRIFICE TO GOD

EXHORTATION

I appeal to you therefore, brothers, by the mercies of God, to
present your bodies as a living sacrifice, holy and acceptable to
God, which is your spiritual worship. Romans 12:1

As Christians, we remind ourselves continually that we belong to
God. This should encourage us to give ourselves and all that we possess
back to God as a sacrifice.

The sacrifices of the Old Testament that God accepted had to be voluntary offerings. People are not to lead a godly life in this world out of

fear of punishment or hell, but out of love of God; otherwise, their offering is a forced offering. No, even if there were no hell, Christians out of love would still yield themselves to God as His own. The sacrifices had to be offered to God entirely, with head, entrails, and limbs, and could not be offered by half. Accordingly, we should not give half our heart to the world and half to God, but should love Him and give ourselves to Him with all our heart, with all our soul, with all our strength. A half-hearted, divided service God rejects. The sacrifices had to be entirely without blemish; hence nothing lame or blind could be offered to God. Accordingly, we must be careful not to pollute our soul and body with sin, but strive to place both entirely at His service. God took a particular pleasure in sacrifices that were still young, in lambs a year or two old, thus indicating to us that we are not to wait with our conversion till we are old and gray, but are to yield ourselves even in our budding years of youth as a sacrifice to Him. What had once been offered to God could not be exchanged or withdrawn. Thus we must be steadfast in good resolve to yield ourselves to God as His own.

PRAYER

O Lord God, You commanded the people of Israel to bring You daily offerings that had to be entirely consecrated and surrendered to You. Behold, I bring to You my believing and penitent heart—a heart You will not despise.

Heavenly Father, You have created me that I should be Your own. Dear Jesus, You have redeemed me with Your blood, that I should live in Your kingdom and serve You in holiness and righteousness. O precious Holy Spirit, You have sanctified me that I should be Your dwelling place and that Christ should live in me. I shall in turn make an offering of my entire self and dedicate myself to You. I offer up to You my will; no longer do I want to accomplish what I want, but what You desire. I offer up to You my mouth, that I may praise and magnify You, and not use it for filthiness and foolish talk. I offer up to You my heart; fill it with a living faith, with Your grace, with Your love, with true godliness.

Of every sacrifice the fat portions in particular had to be offered to You; without these no offering was accepted. Be pleased, then, to receive my offering. If this is a heart unclean by nature and unfit for an offering, wash it with the blood of Jesus Christ that I accept in true faith. Cleanse it with Your Holy Spirit. Hallow it and make it a dwelling place for You, that You may govern and reign in it. I offer to You my life; I shall order it according to Your Holy Word and the prompting of Your Holy Spirit. I offer up to You my members; grant that they may become instruments of righteousness, that I may not misuse them for sin and shame, but that they remain consecrated to You.

As that which was offered had to be kept apart from all else, so I will gladly separate myself from this sinful world and stay away from its society. Yes, I will offer myself up to You while I am still living and in good health, and will not wait until I am lying on a bed of sickness; then it might be too late. O Lord, You did accept offerings at all times, in the morning, at noon, and in the evening. Graciously look also upon my offering. I may be bringing it at the noontide of my life, or it may be that my life's evening has already arrived. If I delayed my offering during life's morning and in my youth, You will not on that account despise it. I am bringing it to You like Abel, in faith. Look upon it according to Your mercy. For the remainder of my life I will remain Your own.

Hold me ever in Your keeping; Comfort me in pain and strife. In my laughter and my weeping Be with me throughout my life. Give me greater love for You, And my faith and hope renew In Your birth, Your life, and passion, In Your death and resurrection. Amen. *LSB 692:2*

HYMN

Take my life and let it be
Consecrated, Lord, to Thee;
Take my moments and my days,
Let them flow in ceaseless praise.

Take my hands and let them move
At the impulse of Thy love;
Take my feet and let them be
Swift and beautiful for Thee.

Take my voice and let me sing
Always, only for my King;
Take my lips and let them be
Filled with messages from Thee.

Take my silver and my gold,
Not a mite would I withhold;
Take my intellect and use
Ev'ry pow'r as Thou shalt choose.

Take my will and make it Thine,
It shall be no longer mine;
Take my heart, it is Thine own,
It shall be Thy royal throne.

Take my love, my Lord, I pour
At Thy feet its treasure store;
Take myself, and I will be
Ever, only, all for Thee. LSB 783:1–6

BELIEVING CHRISTIANS PRAY FOR GODLINESS

EXHORTATION

Mark the blameless and behold the upright, for there is a future for the man of peace. Psalm 37:37

Godliness is an ornament to the young and becoming to the old. God Himself exhorts Abraham when journeying to a strange land: "Walk before Me, and be blameless" (Genesis 17:1). However, to be godly outward morality is not sufficient, for that is found even among pagans. Godliness springs from faith, from the love of God, and from the inmost soul. Such godliness embraces, first, sincerity and uprightness of heart toward God and our fellow human beings; next, blamelessness of life, abstaining from indecent talk and unchristian works; for when these things are still found in a person, we cannot say that he is godly. Moreover, this godliness is to continue until death. It is not sufficient to be godly two or three days when we want to go to the Lord's Supper, but we must make our own the resolution of Job, who declared, "Till I die I will not put away my integrity from me" (Job 27:5). Now, because the Holy Spirit works in us this godliness, it has the most glorious and beautiful promises, namely, of the life that now is and of that which is to come.

PRAYER

Holy God, I hardly know whether I dare appear before Your holy countenance when I reflect on my natural unholiness and my sinful nature. Still, to me You are calling: "Walk before Me, and be blameless," and "If you do well, will you not be accepted?" Yes, You say also to me: "Mark the blameless and behold the upright, for there is a future for the man of peace." But, sadly, my godliness has not yet proceeded far. I have been still enmeshed in the world—its ways, its habits, and its vanities. But wherever the world and its sinful ways intrude themselves, Christ and the love of Him cannot be properly formed in us.

However, because this is displeasing to You, and because, on the contrary, You say to Your children: "Do not be conformed to this world," grant me grace utterly to renounce the world and its ways. Give me a true godly heart. Help me to be godly with all my heart, so that my Christian confession would be sincere and upright, not eye-service and hypocrisy. Grant me grace that I may be zealous for genuine godliness, not only outwardly for the sake of appearance but also inwardly, that I may love You above all else, serve You, and accomplish what is well-pleasing to You. Yes, as a godly child, before beginning anything, looks at his parents to read permission in their eyes, so let me look first into Your Holy Word and commandments to ascertain whether what I want to do is fitting for me as a godly Christian. Then, if my heart is godly, my mouth, too, will become godly, so that I speak nothing that is indecent. Yes, then, also my works and actions will please You.

Now that I have formed this resolution in Your name, my God, give me grace, ability, strength, and mercy to carry it out. If in the years past I have not always worked hard for this prize, forgive me for Christ's sake. Whatever I have neglected to do from ignorance or blindness, I will now supply with all the greater zeal, and from now on will live not according to the lusts of fallen humanity but according to Your will. Thus, I intend, my God, to become and remain godly with all my heart and throughout my life, so that at the appointed time as a godly Christian I may die a blessed death. To this end, grant me from on high the power of Your Holy Spirit, for Jesus Christ's sake.

Create in me a new heart, Lord, That gladly I obey Your Word. Let what You will be my desire, And with new life my soul inspire. Grant that I only You may love And seek those things which are above Till I behold You face to face, O Light eternal, through Your grace. Amen. *LSB 704:3–4*

HYMN

How can I thank You, Lord,
For all Your loving-kindness,
That You have patiently
Borne with me in my blindness!
When dead in many sins
And trespasses I lay,

I kindled, holy God,
Your anger ev'ry day.
It is Your work alone
That I am now converted;
O'er Satan's work in me
You have Your pow'r asserted.

Your mercy and Your grace
That rise afresh each morn
Have turned my stony heart
Into a heart newborn.

Lord, You have raised me up
To joy and exultation
And clearly shown the way
That leads me to salvation.
My sins are washed away;
For this I thank You, Lord.
Now with my heart and soul
All evil I abhor.

Grant that Your Spirit's help
To me be always given
Lest I should fall again
And lose the way to heaven.

Grant that He give me strength
In my infirmity;
May He renew my heart
To serve You willingly.

O Father, God of love,
Now hear my supplication;
O Savior, Son of God,
Accept my adoration;
O Holy Spirit, be
My ever faithful guide
That I may serve You here
And there with You abide.

LSB 703:1–5

BELIEVING CHRISTIANS PRAY FOR AN UNSTAINED CONSCIENCE

EXHORTATION

For our boast is this, the testimony of our conscience, that we behaved in the world with simplicity and godly sincerity, not by earthly wisdom but by the grace of God, and supremely so toward you. 2 Corinthians 1:12

Most people are concerned with keeping their body in good health. They also exert themselves greatly to acquire or to keep their possessions. If only they would put forth such great efforts to keep their conscience pure and unspotted!

The conscience is like the eye, which cannot endure a speck of dust. To wicked people, it is their accuser, witness, and judge. Yes, the remembrance of sin remains in the conscience likes scars on the face. On the Last Day, God and the conscience will be witnesses whom nobody will be able to argue with. Accordingly, the judgment will not take a long time because these witnesses cannot be contradicted.

Believing Christians will retain an unstained conscience if they hear and read God's Word and order their life accordingly, considering in all that they propose to say or do whether God in His Holy Word permits it; if they avoid sinful associations and occasions; for as a person handling fire or water is easily burned or becomes wet, so the conscience is easily violated in persons who walk carelessly. In particular, the conscience is guarded by devout, earnest prayer to God, that He would lead and guide us, by His power and grace keep us on the right course, by the reflection that God is everywhere present, and that we are always walking in His sight.

PRAYER

O Lord, my God, how great is Your goodness and love that You manifest toward us! You give us life and health, and prosper us according to Your mercy. O my God, all these things are presents and gifts from You, but they will become bitter like wormwood to us if in our healthy body, and joined to all our gifts and possessions, there is not an unstained conscience.

O my God, have mercy on me and keep me in Your fear, lest I violate my conscience. The conscience is like the eye, which becomes irritated, moist, and inflamed, and cannot readily be opened if the least little speck of dust enters it. The same thing happens to our conscience: If we have done anything contrary to it, it becomes restless; it accuses and condemns us. And when it is thoroughly aroused, we do not have the courage to lift our eyes to heaven.

O my God, I desire greatly to bring before Your holy face an inviolate soul and a pure conscience. Rule in me by Your Holy Spirit that I may be as careful with my conscience as with my eyes. What a precious treasure is a good conscience! Help me that I may never consent to a sin in word or wicked deed by which a grievous burden would be placed on my soul that would weigh me down either throughout my life or on my dying bed, or rouse Your anger and vengeance against me.

Preserve me from remorse of conscience and its anguish, and lest I should undergo these, grant me the grace that I may everywhere conduct myself in a cautious and Christian manner. Grant that I may always reflect on Your most holy presence, be afraid to do evil in Your sight, and remember that You are a discerner of hearts from whom nothing is hidden. Because I cannot hide myself from my conscience, but have to feel its smiting the moment I do evil, let me reflect that I shall be able still less to hide from You, O all-seeing and all-knowing God.

Grant that I may look to Jesus, my Savior, and walk in His footsteps. Grant that I may never allow Your Word, my rule of faith, to depart from my mouth, lest by denying my faith I wound my conscience. Let Your Word also be my rule of life, so that I may not purposely sin against it. O Lord Jesus, cleanse my conscience with Your holy blood, forgive me all my sins, and bestow on me the quiet, true rest of heart and conscience. Let Your Holy Spirit ever lead me in a plain path, and my conscience will remain inviolate and Your dwelling place in my heart be undisturbed.

O God, my faithful God, True fountain ever flowing, Without whom nothing is, All perfect gifts bestowing: Give me a healthy frame, And may I have within A conscience free from blame, A soul unstained by sin. Amen.

LSB 696:1

HYMN

Jesus, Thy boundless love to me
No thought can reach, no tongue declare;
Unite my thankful heart to Thee,
And reign without a rival there!
Thine wholly, Thine alone I am;
Be Thou alone my constant flame.

O grant that nothing in my soul
May dwell, but Thy pure love alone;
Oh, may Thy love possess me whole,
My joy, my treasure, and my crown!
All coldness from my heart remove;
My ev'ry act, word, thought be love.

This love unwearied I pursue
And dauntlessly to Thee aspire.
Oh, may Thy love my hope renew,
Burn in my soul like heav'nly fire!
And day and night, be all my care
To guard this sacred treasure there.

In suff'ring be Thy love my peace,
In weakness be Thy love my pow'r;
And when the storms of life shall cease,
O Jesus, in that final hour,
Be Thou my rod and staff and guide,
And draw me safely to Thy side! LSB 683:1–4

BELIEVING PARENTS COMMEND THEIR CHILDREN TO GOD IN PRAYER

EXHORTATION

Fathers, do not provoke your children to anger, but bring
them up in the discipline and instruction of the Lord. Ephesians 6:4

If there is any concern that lies close to the heart of godly parents, it is their children. And rightly so, for children are precious pledges that God will demand at the hands of parents.

Now, if godly parents ponder this fact, they will earnestly commend their children to God in prayer before they are born, and later they will bring their children with them when they come before God. Godly parents pray in particular that God would give their children pious hearts and the Holy Spirit, who will sanctify, govern, and guide them. This is the true foundation of their happiness; compared with this, wealth, skill, and prudence are to be deemed nothing.

Parents, however, should not only pray for their children but also should bring them up in the fear of God. This makes it necessary that they do not let them have their own way. The children's will is by nature perverse, and their imagination and desire are evil from their youth. Parents must instruct their children in the knowledge of God, train them to prayer and a Christian conduct, and not give them permission to go into the society of evil and vain people. If they permit this, their prayer is in vain; indeed, they mock God with their prayer.

Neglect in the training of their children entails upon the parents a heavy responsibility before God because He will require the blood of their neglected children at their hands. Such neglect also brings shame and disgrace upon the parents because their children shall not be an honor but a reproach to them, sometimes already in this life, but at any rate after their death. Neglect in the training of children also brings the anger of God upon the parents, as may be seen from 1 Samuel 2:29; 4:18. Negligent parents bring themselves and their children into hell, and thus have done them no kindness by their indulgence.

PRAYER

Lord, almighty God, Father of mercies, among other gifts of Your grace You have given me my children, and for such a blessing I heartily praise and magnify You. Yet I regard these children of mine as precious pledges, and I know You have entrusted them to me and will require them at my hand. I regard them as souls that Jesus has purchased with His holy blood, the Holy Spirit has sanctified in Holy Baptism, and You have adopted as Your own children. I am, then, concerned, lest any of them be lost through my own fault. You tell me and all parents: take care of this child; if he is missed, your soul shall answer for his soul.

And so, O Father of all grace, I come to You and in heartfelt prayer commend to You my children. I will do what I can. I will bring them up for Your honor, admonish them, correct them, instruct them, and pray for them. But, O Lord, You must perform the most important part. Immediately after their natural birth I placed them into the arms of Your mercy in Holy Baptism. Behold, I now do the same in my prayer. Bless my children. Attend them at their going out and their coming in. Keep them in Your holy fear, that they may never burden their conscience with sins or offend You, or worst of all, fall from Your grace. Give them believing, humble, obedient, and godly hearts, that, like the child Jesus, they may increase in stature, wisdom, and favor with God and men. Imprint on their hearts the image of Jesus in order that they may always keep, until their blessed end, a gracious God and an unstained conscience.

Let my children be devout in their prayers, well-grounded in their Christian faith, steadfast and zealous in worship, chaste in their living, godly in their conversation, so that by their words and actions they may give offense to no one and thus bring upon themselves a fearful judgment. Preserve them from temptations and evil company. By Your Holy Spirit keep them constantly in mind of Your most holy presence, that they remember that You are with them at home and away, in their room, by day and by night, in company with others and when they are alone. Let Your holy angels be with them when they go out and when they come in. Let Your angels guard them when they travel. Give them Your holy angels as their companions. By their aid rescue them from dangers, as You did with Lot. Let them, like Jacob, live under the angels' watchful care.

But if it should please You to make my children a cross to me, either by their sickness, or death, or any other calamity that I might have to see them suffer, grant me patience in such affliction, and remind me that nothing happens without Your divine direction, that my children were Yours before they were mine, and that You have sovereign power to take them again to Yourself. But if it is Your design by the suffering, misfortune, and death of my children to draw me to You, in order that I may recognize also in them that Your visible gifts are perishable, to stir me up to love You alone, the true and perfect God, keep me while traveling this thorny path in firm confidence and hope in Your almighty power, which can end and mend all things, even the crosses of my children.

Impart Your blessing to them also in their temporal affairs. Care for them, provide for them, give them food and clothing, and deal with them as their mighty heavenly Father. Be their helper in dangers and calamities, their physician in sickness, and their counselor whenever they are in need of good advice. Give to my children a pious soul, a healthy body, and a sound mind, and let them live in Your sight, in order that they may at all times honor and praise You. Implant in their hearts true godliness, and continue Your blessing on them that I may have comfort and joy in them.

O God, hear my prayer, and remember that they are Your children as well as mine. Therefore, be pleased to hear my supplication on their behalf at the throne of Your grace. Preserve me, O God, from being brought into shame by my children, either during my lifetime or after my death. On the last day let me stand at Your right hand with all my children and say to the praise of Your holy name: "Behold, here I am, my God, and the children which You have given to me; I have lost none of them." Yes, my God, grant me Your divine favor to this end, that none of my children may be lost, but that they may all enter with me, and I with them, into Your glory.

Shine in our hearts, O Spirit, precious light; Teach us Jesus Christ to know aright That we may abide in the Lord who bought us, Till to our true home He has brought us. Lord, have mercy! Amen.   *LSB 768:4*

HYMN

Oh, blest the house, whate'er befall,
Where Jesus Christ is all in all!
A home that is not wholly His—
How sad and poor and dark it is!

Oh, blest that house where faith is found
And all in hope and love abound;
They trust their God and serve Him still
And do in all His holy will!

Oh, blest the parents who give heed
Unto their children's foremost need
And weary not of care or cost.
May none to them and heav'n be lost!

Oh, blest that house; it prospers well.
In peace and joy the parents dwell,
And in their children's lives is shown
How richly God can bless His own.

Then here will I and mine today
A solemn promise make and say:
Though all the world forsake His Word,
I and my house will serve the Lord! *LSB 862:1–5*

GODLY CHILDREN PRAY FOR THEIR PARENTS

EXHORTATION

Children, obey your parents in the Lord, for this is right. "Honor your father and mother" (this is the first commandment with a promise), "that it may go well with you and that you may live long in the land." Ephesians 6:1–3

With other grievous sins that bring down on someone a curse, we must also count the treatment of adult children toward their parents. Although parents, from the first hour of their children's birth, endure care, trouble, and vexation on their account, yet their keenest grief is when the children are obstinate, domineering, perverse, and malicious toward them in their later years, while, on the contrary, they ought to cause their parents nothing but joy and delight.

Pious children, therefore, should pray diligently for their parents, and in their prayers ask God to grant them health, prosperity, long life, blessings without number, and keep them from every misfortune. Pious children should love their parents, gladly do everything they can for them, be willing and prompt to give them what they need, and care for them and nurse them when they are sick. Pious children should obey their parents, submit to their training with a good will, and neither contradict them nor argue with their orders and commands. Moreover, when they wish to get married, they should not become engaged secretly, without their parents' knowledge and consent, because that would bring nothing but curse and misfortune on them. Pious children should honor their parents in their hearts, namely, by recognizing them as occupying God's place, as God gives everything to children through their parents. They should also conduct themselves reverently in their presence both in speech and action, not hurl unkind and harsh words at them, and defend their honor and good name. Pious children should bear in mind that they can never repay all that their parents have done for them. Remember what anguish you have caused your mother, and with what toil and labor your father had to bring you up and support you. Ungrateful and obstinate children are veritable children of Belial, and it can never be well with them if they do not mourn with heartfelt genuine repentance and tears over their sins and acts of malice they have committed against their parents.

PRAYER

O gracious and merciful God, I praise You from my inmost heart for the grace given me when I was born of pious, Christian parents. That is the first divine favor You have shown me. If my parents had been non-Christians, I would perhaps still be hardened, unbelieving, and without knowledge of You. As it was my parents' first concern after my natural birth that I be placed in Your arms, my heavenly Father, through Holy Baptism in which You have given me the Holy Spirit as a pledge that I am Your child and an heir of heaven, so let this good Spirit ever lead and guide me that I may diligently fulfill my duties toward You and my parents.

I prostrate myself in prayer before Your most holy countenance and beg You: Keep my parents in good health, preserve them from misfortune, bless their business, their labor, and their profession. Grant them long life, reward them with spiritual and heavenly blessings for the faithfulness they have shown me and for which I can never recount or pay back.

Give me an obedient heart, O heavenly Father, that I may not offend my parents or knowingly and willingly grieve them. Grant that I may at all times place before my eyes the example of my Jesus, who not only was obedient to You, His heavenly Father, but also to His earthly father, Joseph, and to His mother, Mary, in order that by my obedience I may at all times and especially in their old age bring joy and delight to my parents. Guard me, lest by disobedience and obstinacy I bring on myself the curse and unhappiness with which wicked children have been threatened, but let it be well with me here in time and there in eternity.

Give me a heart that is respectful toward my parents, so I do not provoke them to anger by either words or actions, but conduct myself toward them in humility, cheerfully heeding their commands and submitting to their correction without contradiction. Keep me from becoming like the perverse, wicked children who insult and despise their parents, causing them nothing but grief and vexation, and bringing down a curse on themselves, depriving themselves of the blessing You have promised all good and pious children. Grant me grace not to sin against my parents, but to ponder diligently what care I have caused my mother, and with what toil I have been brought up, so that I may acknowledge this throughout my life with a grateful heart and mind. Let me cause my parents no disgrace, but on the contrary, nothing but joy.

If in the years of my childhood I have done anything against my parents, I humbly ask pardon now, O God, of You and of them, and I promise that by Your grace I will strive to rejoice their heart with my obedience and Christian conduct. Grant me Your Holy Spirit, that I may walk as is fitting for a child of God, in faith, godliness, chastity, and the fear of God, so that on the last day I may with my parents stand at Your right hand and enter with them into Your glory.

You are honor and obey Your father, mother, ev'ry day, Serve them each way that comes to hand; You'll then live long in the land. Have mercy, Lord! Amen.

LSB 581:5

HYMN

Our Father, by whose name
  All fatherhood is known,
Who dost in love proclaim
  Each family Thine own,
Bless Thou all parents, guarding
  well,
With constant love as sentinel,
The homes in which Thy people
  dwell.

O Christ, Thyself a child
  Within an earthly home,
With heart still undefiled,
  Thou didst to manhood come;

Our children bless in ev'ry place
That they may all behold Thy face,
And knowing Thee may grow in
  grace.

O Spirit, who dost bind
  Our hearts in unity,
Who teachest us to find
  The love from self set free,
In all our hearts such love increase
That ev'ry home by this release
May be the dwelling place of peace.

LSB 863:1–3

BOOK II

FOR THE USE OF THOSE AFFLICTED

AFFLICTED PERSONS TAKE COMFORT IN THE OMNIPOTENCE OF GOD

EXHORTATION

Fear not, for I am with you; be not dismayed, for I am your God; I will strengthen you, I will help you, I will uphold you with My righteous right hand. Isaiah 41:10

If anything can lift up afflicted souls, it is certainly the omnipotence of our gracious God. This is the afflicted people's anchor to which they cling by reflecting that with God nothing is impossible: No misery is so big that God cannot deliver from it. No burden is so heavy that He cannot remove it. No misfortune so severe that He cannot change it. Afflicted persons should consider that others have borne much heavier burdens, and that God has delivered them nevertheless. They should thus say with joy: "O God, You are as strong today as You have ever been. My trust is entirely in You."

The afflicted should remind themselves that God's almighty power is boundless. Therefore, they should not become disheartened, even though they do not see how and by what means and in what manner they can be helped. All this they should leave to the wisdom, goodness, and faithfulness of God. "My thoughts are not your thoughts, neither are your ways My ways, declares the LORD" (Isaiah 55:8). This reflection should strengthen the confidence and hope of the afflicted because they know that God is able and willing to help them. They should then be still, hope, pray, trust in God, patiently bear their affliction, and cheerfully lift up their eyes to heaven, saying: "My help comes from the LORD, who made heaven and earth" (Psalm 121:2).

PRAYER

O good and kind God, You know my heart is afflicted. There lies on it a heavy stone that I cannot roll away, a hard load that I can scarcely bear. I come to You, almighty God, to pour out my soul before You, for You are my confidence. I cast my burden from myself to You, and pray You to provide for me, to deliver me, and to assist me. The little boat tossed by the waves clings to the anchor, and so I cling to You, O living and mighty God. The hunted animal flees to the mountains, and I lift up my eyes to You, my rock, my deliverer, and mighty defender. I will not lose heart; I know that You are an almighty God. Nothing is impossible for You. O Lord, help me, and I shall be helped. Speak but one word and my affliction will pass away.

O my God, I know that You are merciful. Have mercy on me in my misery. You know my pain and my heart. Because You have laid this burden on me, help me to bear it. I know that You are a wise God. You will find ways and means that I know nothing of. Show me some well of comfort as You did for weeping Hagar of old. Help me as You did forsaken Elijah. Manifest Your great goodness toward me as You did to Peter in prison. Let the bonds of my misery and distress drop from my heart. Let the light of Your joy arise in me, bringing me Your assurance: "I will never leave you nor forsake you" (Hebrews 13:5). "For a small moment I deserted you, but with great compassion I will gather you" (Isaiah 54:7).

I know that You are a faithful God. You have never forsaken anyone who called on You, and so I know You will not forsake me. O Lord, my God, behold a wretched and helpless soul, lying here before Your throne of grace. Send me help from the sanctuary and strengthen me out of

Zion. Lord, I will not let You go unless You bless me. My God and Father, if You do not help me, who will? I was cast on You from the womb, and You took me into the arms of Your unwearied mercy and carried me up till now. Oh, then, let me find help now. I will cry out after You until You say: "Let it be done as you desire."

If God Himself be for me, I may a host defy; For when I pray, before me My foes, confounded, fly. If Christ, my head and master, Befriend me from above, What foe or what disaster Can drive me from His love? Amen.

LSB 724:1

HYMN

*In God, my faithful God,
I trust when dark my road;
Great woes may overtake me,
Yet He will not forsake me.
My troubles He can alter;
His hand lets nothing falter.*

*My sins fill me with care,
Yet I will not despair.
I build on Christ, who loves me;
From this rock nothing moves me.
To Him I will surrender,
To Him, my soul's defender.*

*If death my portion be,
It brings great gain to me;
It speeds my life's endeavor
To live with Christ forever.*

*He gives me joy in sorrow,
Come death now or tomorrow.*

*O Jesus Christ, my Lord,
So meek in deed and word,
You suffered death to save us
Because Your love would have us
Be heirs of heav'nly gladness
When ends this life of sadness.*

*"So be it," then, I say
With all my heart each day.
Dear Lord, we all adore You,
We sing for joy before You.
Guide us while here we wander
Until we praise You yonder.*

LSB 745:1–5

AFFLICTED PERSONS TAKE COMFORT IN THE LOVE OF GOD

EXHORTATION

"For a brief moment I deserted you, but with great compassion I will gather you. In overflowing anger for a moment I hid My face from you, but with everlasting love I will have compassion on you," says the LORD, your Redeemer. Isaiah 54:7–8

To afflicted souls in their sadness, trials, and sufferings, nothing more cheering can happen or be said than this: for Christ's sake God loves them nevertheless.

Under a grievous cross, the first thought suggested to us by Satan and our flesh is this: God is your enemy. He has ceased loving you. If He loved you, He would never have let this happen to you. He would never have hidden His gracious face from you. To such a thought, then, the afflicted person should not lend an ear but should set up against it the everlasting love of God, who does not forsake His children. The afflicted should remember that living in tribulations and sorrows and yet being a child of God is quite compatible. Christ, the beloved Son of God, suffered tribulations and yet remained the Son of God. The afflicted should ponder that God still loves those whom He allows to be subjected to great sorrow, trials, and crosses. A father remains a father whether he compliments his little one or chastises the child with the rod.

Add to this that such a cross is not sent to the afflicted soul out of anger, or for its ruin or harm, but that the soul may learn all the more God's goodness, almighty power, faithfulness, and wisdom. This love of God is very busy even while the cross endures: it supports the afflicted, preserves them, strengthens them, and blesses them. God's love refreshes and gladdens them in a wondrous way, and their burdens are thus lightened—a proof of His love.

PRAYER

The Lord is on my side, therefore I will not be afraid. You are my shelter, my rock, my fortress, and my deliverance—thus I sigh, my God, in my present affliction and anguish of soul. O Lord, You know full well how sad my heart is and how full of suffering and pain I am. But I also know that this distress will not be able to crush me if You are with me. Do not hide Your face from me any longer. I am full of anxiety; give me relief! You have shown me much love and goodness from the days of my youth. Embrace me with Your love now in the present distress of my soul. A sheep, when pursued, flees to the shepherd; a child, when terrified, to its father. So I now come to You, my shepherd and my Father.

O great God, You have promised me Your aid. You have said: "I am with you in your distress; I will rescue you. Do not fear, for I am with you! Do not discouraged, for I am your God! I will strengthen you. I will uphold you with My righteous right hand. I will never leave you nor forsake you." Now, then, O great God, I am in need of help. Be at my side. Do not leave me.

I know that I am not forsaken. Your love is so tender that You have to have mercy on me. You have loved me with an everlasting love, and with loving-kindness You have drawn me. Embrace me now with the arms of Your love. Hold me, lest I sink. Refresh me in my suffering. Make me to hear joy and gladness that the bones You have broken may rejoice. Give me beauty for sackcloth and ashes, and turn my sorrow into joy. Manifest also in me Your love and goodness that others have extolled in so many ways, so that with them I may praise Your great name. O God of love, seal in my heart the assurance that, as little as a father can forget his child, so little could You ever forget me. Faithful Father, behold, Your child is in sorrow. Gladden me. I am full of anxiety. Have mercy on me and help me for Jesus' sake.

Be still, my soul; the Lord is on your side; Bear patiently the cross of grief or pain; Leave to your God to order and provide; In ev'ry change He faithful will remain. Be still, my soul; your best, your heav'nly Friend Through thorny ways leads to a joyful end. Amen.   *LSB 752:1*

HYMN

Jesus Christ, my sure defense
And my Savior, now is living!
Knowing this, my confidence
Rests upon the hope here given,
Though the night of death be fraught
Still with many an anxious thought.

Jesus, my Redeemer, lives;
Likewise I to life shall waken.
He will bring me where He is;
Shall my courage then be shaken?
Shall I fear, or could the Head
Rise and leave His members dead?

No, too closely I am bound
By my hope to Christ forever;
Faith's strong hand the Rock has found,
Grasped it, and will leave it never;
Even death now cannot part
From its Lord the trusting heart. LSB 741:1–3

AFFLICTED PERSONS TAKE COMFORT IN GOD'S HELP

EXHORTATION

I lift up my eyes to the hills. From where does my help come?
My help comes from the LORD, who made heaven and earth.
Psalm 121:1–2

To be without help in times of suffering and distress is harder to bear than the suffering itself. On the other hand, hoping for help and final deliverance can lighten even the heaviest load.

Afflicted souls should sustain themselves with the reflection that God can help, for with God nothing is impossible; nothing is too difficult or too great for Him. He can help in every need. Afflicted persons should re-member that God is willing to help them because of His glorious prom-ises that He will be with them in their distress, that He will pluck them out of the net, that He will never leave or forsake them. Afflicted persons should ponder the examples of others whom God has helped already. Indeed, others may have been more wretched, sadder, more forsaken and miserable than they; yet the Lord helped them. Why then should we cast off hope?

Afflicted persons should watch with prayer and supplication for God's help, hoping and trusting that His help will not fail them; for what the Lord promises, He surely fulfills. Let His Word be more certain to you than anything. Though your heart should say no to your every hope, even then, do not despair. Afflicted persons, indeed, may not see how they can be helped, but they should bear in mind that God can do abundantly more than anything we ask or think, and that He Himself will be their helper, Father, comforter, deliverer, and friend. Having Him, they have everything. Yes, they should allow time to lighten their sorrow; this also is a blessing from God, that He alleviates our sufferings by making us forget them in the course of time.

PRAYER

When I am afflicted, I think of God. Where else can I turn, whom else should I think of in sorrow and grief of heart than of You alone, my God? You have never yet allowed me to go away sorrowful from Your most holy presence. And so, hear now my prayer for Christ's sake. Give ear to my crying, my King and my God. When I call, do not be silent, but answer me speedily.

Your hand sent me the affliction I suffer; You can deliver me from it according to Your mercy. Lord, You kill and make alive; You bring down to hell and raise up again. Lord, You make poor and make rich; You humble and lift up. You raise up the poor out of the dust and lift the beggar from his hovel. So I say in faith, Lord, help me. You can help, for You are the almighty God. You are willing to help, for You have promised to do so. Father, will You forsake Your child? My Father, can You endure the cries of Your child and not come to my aid? You have said: "Before they call I will answer; while they are yet speaking I will hear" (Isaiah 65:24). "My heart is moved for you, I will surely have mercy on you." Oh, hear me also at this time. Hear the cry of my heart and the sigh of my lips.

Yet I know, my Father, that You hear me at all times. And so I will not instruct You on the day and hour You are to help me. I will cheerfully wait for Your hour of helping me. Meanwhile, strengthen my faith, my hope, my confidence. Give me patience and strength to bear my affliction, and at last let me see the day when You will gladden me with Your mercy. O my Father, You have never yet forsaken anyone; do not forsake me either. You have at all times gladdened the afflicted; gladden me also. You have helped the distressed; help me also. When, where, and how You are going to do this, I leave entirely to Your wisdom, love, goodness, and mercy. Be content, then, my soul. Why are you cast down within me? Hope in God, for I shall yet praise Him who is the help of my countenance and my God.

Well He knows what best to grant me; All the longing hopes that haunt me, Joy and sorrow, have their day. I shall doubt His wisdom never; As God wills, so be it ever; I commit to Him my way. Amen.   *LSB 732:5*

HYMN

I trust, O Lord, Your holy name;
O let me not be put to shame
    Nor let me be confounded.
    My faith, O Lord,
Be in Your Word
    Forever firmly grounded.

Bow down Your gracious ear to me
And hear my cry, my prayer,
    my plea;
    Make haste for my protection,
    For woes and fear
Surround me here.
    Help me in my affliction.

You are my strength, my shield,
    my rock,
My fortress that withstands each
    shock,
    My help, my life, my tower,
My battle sword,
Almighty Lord—
    Who can resist Your power?

With You, O Lord, I cast my lot;
O faithful God, forsake me not,
    To You my soul commending.
Lord, be my stay,
And lead the way
    Now and when life is ending.

All honor, praise, and majesty
To Father, Son, and Spirit be,
    Our God forever glorious,
In whose rich grace
We run our race
    Till we depart victorious.
             LSB 734:1–5

THE AFFLICTED TAKE COMFORT IN THE MERCY OF GOD

EXHORTATION

The LORD is merciful and gracious, slow to anger and abounding in steadfast love. He will not always chide, nor will He keep His anger forever. . . . As a father shows compassion to his children, so the LORD shows compassion to those who fear Him.
Psalm 103:8–9, 13

While in misery and distress, how sad it is to have to deal with hardhearted and unkind people! However, afflicted children of God should rest assured that their faithful God knows all their suffering, distress, and trials—how great and grievous they are, how long they will last, and how keenly they are felt by the soul. Not only does God know these things, but He also takes pity on the afflicted. We see this in the instance of the grief-stricken widow of Nain and of all the sick and distressed whom Jesus went to meet of His own accord, and whom He freely helped. Thus He spoke concerning the multitude: "I have compassion on the crowd" (Matthew 15:32). And concerning Zion, we read: "My heart yearns for him; I will surely have mercy on him" (Jeremiah 31:20). Reflecting on this fact that God is so merciful and exercises compassion, afflicted people should not lose heart but seek refuge with the merciful God, for they that mourn shall be comforted.

God manifests His mercy toward the afflicted, partly by giving them cheerfulness and resolute courage, party by sustaining them in their suffering and giving them strength to endure and bear it, partly by removing it from them altogether. If a father takes pity on his child, God will not allow the afflicted to perish in their distress.

PRAYER

All-loving God, Your mercy has no end, and Your kindness is new each morning. See, I, an afflicted and sorrowful soul, come before Your holy face to pour out the great grief of my heavy heart. My distressful condition and the great misery that has overtaken me are well known to You. My soul is sorrowful; my spirit is in anguish; numberless afflictions surround me. I look around me for helpers, but find none. Some people refuse to give me comfort; others do not know my distress and I do not reveal it to them. But to You, O God, I make complaint with a heart full of grief. I know that You are merciful and moved to pity by our distress. You took pity on the stricken widow weeping for her son. You were moved to compassion when You saw the people who had gathered to hear You and had nothing to eat, and Your compassion went hand in hand with Your mercy and comfort.

And so I come to You and plead: have mercy on me! O God, I am Your creature; do not forsake the work of Your hands. Yes, I am even more: I am also Your child whom You have taken into the arms of Your mercy in Holy Baptism. And so I say to You: O my Father, have compassion on Your poor and forsaken child. My Jesus, I have been bought with Your holy blood; I am Your portion and inheritance, purchased with Your precious blood! I know You will have compassion on Your own. O precious Holy Spirit, bear witness with my spirit that despite all my suffering I am still a child of God. And when I am faint in praying and can hardly put words together any more, You Yourself cry within me: "Abba! Father!"

Behold, I am sinking; reach out Your hand for me! Lord, help me and be at my side! Lord, let Your mercy spread over me and give me cheerfulness of heart! Yes, write upon my heart and constantly cry out to my soul these words: "You are not forsaken. I will have compassion on you. I am with you in your distress. I will deliver you and honor you." O Lord, according to Your great mercy strengthen my faith, sustain me in my distress, give me each day new strength and fresh ability, so that my faith may not cease, my hope may not sink, and my confidence in You may not grow weak.

You say: "Is Ephraim my dear son? Is he my darling child? For as often as I speak against him, I do earnestly remember him still. Therefore my heart yearns for him; I will surely have mercy on him" (Jeremiah 31:20). Remember me also: You have promised mercy also to me. You have never yet forsaken me. Do not forsake me now! Help Your child who seeks refuge only in Your mercy.

The King of love my shepherd is, Whose goodness faileth never; I
nothing lack if I am His And He is mine forever. Amen.   *LSB 709:1*

HYMN

Oh, how great is Your compassion,
  Faithful Father, God of grace,
  That with all our fallen race
In our depth of degradation
  You had mercy so that we
  Might be saved eternally!

Your great love for this has striven
That we may, from sin made
  free,
  Live with You eternally.
Your dear Son Himself has given
  And extends His gracious call,
  To His supper leads us all.

Firmly to our soul's salvation
  Witnesses Your Spirit, Lord,
  In Your Sacraments and Word.
There He sends true consolation,
  Giving us the gift of faith
  That we fear not hell nor death.

Lord, Your mercy will not leave
  me;
  Ever will Your truth abide.
  Then in You I will confide.
Since Your Word cannot deceive
  me,
  My salvation is to me
  Safe and sure eternally.

I will praise Your great compas-
  sion,
  Faithful Father, God of grace,
That with all our fallen race
In our depth of degradation
  You had mercy so that we
  Might be saved eternally.
            LSB 559:1–5

THE AFFLICTED PONDER THE DIVINE PROMISES

EXHORTATION

*Because he holds fast to Me in love, I will deliver him; I will
protect him, because he knows My name. When he calls to Me, I
will answer him; I will be with him in trouble; I will rescue him
and honor him. With long life I will satisfy him and show him My
salvation.* Psalm 91:14–16

As greatly as trials, misfortune, and distress depress us, so gloriously do the divine promises of mercy cheer us. And so afflicted persons
should reflect that all the divine promises concern them also. We are not

to imagine that the promises were given only to Moses, David, and those living at that time. No, they were intended also for us. As Paul says in Romans 15:4: "For whatever was written in former days was written for our instruction, that through endurance and through the encouragement of the Scriptures we might have hope." The afflicted should further consider that all divine promises are fulfilled at the time God has appointed. Therefore, afflicted persons should not prescribe to God the time and season when He is to help, but wait for His help in meekness and faith.

Afflicted persons should reflect that God's promises to help, redeem, save, and deliver us from all external ills are sometimes fulfilled in this life, as when the sick recover, mourners are made to rejoice, people in distress are delivered, and afflicted persons are comforted. Yet, sometimes God does not fulfill these promises until we reach the life everlasting, when all the promises of God reach their perfect fulfillment. Reflecting on this fact, the afflicted should be still and hope in the goodness of God, who has already fulfilled His promises to so many thousands of people.

PRAYER

Lord, when You said, "Seek My face," my heart said to You, "Your face, Lord, will I seek." In my grief I do not know where to find consolation and counsel except with You. With You my heart has found at all times comfort, help, and counsel.

I especially seek consolation in Your glorious promises. In them I find the true and living fountain to refresh my anguished soul. I come into Your sanctuary. In Your Holy Word I seek strengthening manna for my famished soul and living water for my faint heart. You have said: "Call upon Me in the day of trouble; I will deliver you" (Psalm 51:15). O Lord, the troubles of my soul have increased, bring me out of my distress. You have said, "Fear not, for I am with you; be not dismayed, for I am your God; I will strengthen you, I will help you, I will uphold you with my righteous right hand" (Isaiah 41:10). You have said: "The mountains may depart and the hills be removed, but My steadfast love shall not depart from you" (Isaiah 54:10). O Lord, have mercy on me; do not depart from me. Cast me not away from Your presence; uphold me with Your free Spirit.

FOR THE USE OF THOSE AFFLICTED

O my Lord and God, I know that You will faithfully keep Your promises and truths to me in heaven. If Your Word is not to be my comfort, I will have to be lost in my distress. But though my heart is filled with grief, Your consolations refresh my soul. Your Holy Word places You before me as my mighty God, a loving Father, a strong helper, a gracious comforter, a sure deliverer. In this I trust and take my comfort. My heart is content and not dismayed as I wait for the Lord.

And so return to your peace, O my soul. The Lord will not cast away forever. He afflicts indeed, but He has compassion on you according to His great goodness. Why are you cast down, O my soul, and why are you so disturbed within me? Hope in God. My soul waits for the Lord more than the watchmen for the dawn, until He shows us His mercy. Gladden my afflicted soul, raise up my downcast soul, comfort my sorrowful soul. Take me into Your arms and comfort me. Do not leave me or withdraw Your hand from me, O God of my salvation. I yearn for You. My soul long and sighs, "When will You comfort me?"

Whom shall we trust but Thee, O Lord? Where rest but on Thy faithful Word? None ever called on Thee in vain: Give peace, O God, give peace again! Amen. *LSB 751:3*

HYMN

*Entrust your days and burdens
To God's most loving hand;
He cares for you while ruling
The sky, the sea, the land.
For He who guides the tempests
Along their thund'rous ways
Will find for you a pathway
And guide you all your days.*

*Rely on God your Savior
And find your life secure.
Make His work your foundation
That your work may endure.
No anxious thought, no worry,
No self-tormenting care
Can win your Father's favor;
His heart is moved by prayer.*

Take heart, have hope, my spirit,

*And do not be dismayed;
God helps in ev'ry trial
And makes you unafraid.
Await His time with patience
Through darkest hours of night
Until the sun you hoped for
Delights your eager sight.*

*Leave all to His direction;
His wisdom rules for you
In ways to rouse your wonder
At all His love can do.
Soon He, His promise keeping,
With wonder-working pow'rs
Will banish from your spirit
What gave you troubled hours.*

*O blessèd heir of heaven,
You'll hear the song resound*

Of endless jubilation
 When you with life are crowned.
In your right hand your maker
 Will place the victor's palm,
And you will thank Him gladly
 With heaven's joyful psalm.

Our hands and feet, Lord, strengthen;
 With joy our spirits bless
Until we see the ending
 Of all our life's distress.
And so throughout our lifetime
 Keep us within Your care
And at our end then bring us
 To heav'n to praise You there. LSB 754:1–6

THE AFFLICTED PONDER GOD'S DESIGN IN SENDING THE CROSS

EXHORTATION

For the moment all discipline seems painful rather than pleasant, but later it yields the peaceful fruit of righteousness to those who have been trained by it. Hebrews 12:11

When children are chastened by their father, they weep and think themselves greatly afflicted. Is it a wonder, then, if afflicted persons do not know how to conduct themselves under the cross?

The afflicted should reflect that by sending us a cross God does not mean to lead us into destruction, but to save us from it. When a surgeon cuts into a wound, the surgeon intends to heal and purify. By means of tribulation, God intends to draw us away from this world and to Himself. When God sees that we have fallen in love with earthly things and creatures, He takes them from us in order that we may love Him alone and find our joy in Him. Yes, when He sees that because of our constant happiness, ease, and ongoing prosperity we are becoming sluggish in our prayers and negligent in our Christian faith, He sends us a little grief and sorrow, in order that we may long for Him again and seek to grow in love and knowledge of Him. All the while, however, He remains a gracious, almighty, wise, and kind God, who loves us deeply.

PRAYER

My God, You have plunged me into such great sadness and grief that my heart is now in anguish, my mouth is filled with sighing, and my eyes are filled with tears. I do not know where to turn. Was I not happy? Was I not enjoying peace? Did I not have rest? Where, then, does this unrest come from?

My distress is great, but I will not on that account flee from you, my shepherd. You have struck me down with this grievous blow. Raise me up again with Your powerful Word, that I may ponder why this distress was sent my way. I know for certain that this cross has afflicted me not for my perdition or to injure my soul. No, my Father, lover of my life, it is not Your purpose to destroy me and bring Your anger crashing down on my head. Instead, by placing me in this mournful condition it is Your purpose to test me, whether I will love You in evil as well as in good days.

You would test my faith, whether I believe that You are an almighty, wise, and merciful God who is able to deliver me from this distress and to sustain me in it. You would test my patience, whether I will gladly bear this cross to Your glory. You would test my confidence, whether I trust in You above all things and rely on You, on Your grace, love, and mercy. You would test my hope, whether I will hope when there seems to be nothing to hope for, and would rely on Your Word and promise.

Yes, my gracious God and Father, You would by means of the cross draw me away from the world, its desires, sins, and habits, that I may turn to You alone and cling to You. You take from me what gives me gladness so that I may learn to find my joy in You alone. You take from me what I delight in so that I may count You as my highest and dearest treasure. Well and good, my gracious God. I wish to become as You want me to be. I wish to bear whatever You lay on me.

Give me Your Holy Spirit, that He may furnish me with the strength and ability to do this. Without You it is impossible for me to maintain myself in such troubles, but by Your Spirit and gracious comfort I can be more than a conqueror. I am also willing and glad to be patient and hold still while You are at work, no matter how long it may last. I will also renounce the world and its pleasures and cling to You alone, that I may become one spirit with You. Thus this cross will purify me and greatly benefit my soul. You will send me help at the proper time.

His wisdom never plans in vain Nor falters nor mistakes. All that His counsels may ordain A blessed ending makes. Amen. *LSB 737:6*

HYMN

If thou but trust in God to guide thee
And hope in Him through all thy ways,
He'll give thee strength, whate'er betide thee,
And bear thee through the evil days.
Who trusts in God's unchanging love
Builds on the rock that naught can move.

What can these anxious cares avail thee,
These never-ceasing moans and sighs?
What can it help if thou bewail thee
O'er each dark moment as it flies?
Our cross and trials do but press
The heavier for our bitterness.

Be patient and await His leisure
In cheerful hope, with heart content
To take whate'er thy Father's pleasure
And His discerning love hath sent,
Nor doubt our inmost wants are known
To Him who chose us for His own.

God knows full well when times of gladness
Shall be the needful thing for thee.
When He has tried thy soul with sadness
And from all guile has found thee free,
He comes to thee all unaware
And makes thee own His loving care.

Nor think amid the fiery trial
That God hath cast thee off unheard,
That he whose hopes meet no denial
Must surely be of God preferred.
Time passes and much change doth bring
And sets a bound to ev'rything.

All are alike before the Highest;
'Tis easy for our God, we know,
To raise thee up, though low thou liest,
To make the rich man poor and low.
True wonders still by Him are wrought
Who setteth up and brings to naught.

Sing, pray, and keep His ways unswerving,
Perform thy duties faithfully,
And trust His Word; though undeserving,
Thou yet shalt find it true for thee.
God never yet forsook in need
The soul that trusted Him indeed. LSB 750:1–7

THE AFFLICTED PRAY FOR PATIENCE AND STRENGTH

EXHORTATION

Therefore do not throw away your confidence, which has a
great reward. For you have need of endurance, so that when you
have done the will of God you may receive what is promised.
Hebrews 10:35–36

Patience is a fruit of the Spirit; it comes from God, and to obtain it we must call upon Him. The afflicted must pray more fervently and earnestly, the harder their tribulations assail them, as it is written concerning Christ: "And being in an agony He prayed more earnestly" (Luke 22:44).

Accordingly, the afflicted should reflect that this is patience: to remain quiet in our trials and submit to God's will. They know that their affliction comes from God, who can remove it again. They know that God loves them dearly, despite the fact that He has laid the cross on them, and that He has not ceased to be their Father. And so the afflicted do not murmur against God, though their trial is long and grievous, but they say: "I will hold my peace and not open my mouth; You will do all things well."

If they should nevertheless become discouraged on account of violent pains and manifold suffering, they must call on God for strength. God strengthens the afflicted by letting them know in their hearts that the trial will soon cease, by assuring them He will not forsake them, or by affording them some help and relief. By these means the afflicted become strong again in the Lord and in the power of His might. People should by all means beware of becoming impatient, for God has promised that He will help us bear our cross. Patience brings true quietness of heart and mind.

PRAYER

Lord, all my desire is before You, and my groaning is not hidden from You. O my God, You know well my distress and misery. This is my consolation, that I know it comes from Your loving hands. I have not chosen it for myself, but You have laid it on me. Help me, then, to bear it. And since patience, too, belongs to the good gifts that come down from above, from the Father of lights, grant me this gift according to Your mercy. When You strengthen me, when You help and comfort me, I can do all things, and the cross will not be too heavy for me. "I can do all things through [Christ] who strengthens me" (Philippians 4:13).

Do not assail me too harshly or I may not be able to stand it. Have patience with my weakness, strengthen my weary hands, support my tottering knees. Say to my fainting heart: Your God is King. Your Jesus is with you. Your King comes to you. He is just and having salvation. Yes, when You help me, then I am helped indeed. Therefore, help me, O my salvation, for Your name's sake. I seek refuge in You.

Impress on my soul that it is Your holy will that I should suffer like this and bear my cross so that I may cheerfully resolve to say: Father, not my will, but Yours be done. Place before me Your love, namely, that under the cross and in the midst of great afflictions You still love me, that my suffering lasts only a little while, and that the sufferings of this present time are not worthy to be compared with the glory that will be revealed to us. Help me to bear in mind that You are my gracious God and loving Father, that this cross is not a sign of Your anger but of Your grace. Convince me that it will be for my benefit because by it I am drawn to You. Hold before my soul the example of my dear Savior Jesus Christ, who patiently endured all things and like a lamb did not open His mouth. Grant that with such quiet and resignation I may follow Him by Your grace. Grant me to endure and to suffer with Him, that I also may be crowned and lifted up to glory with Him. Let not my cross pluck Your Word from my heart, but give me new strength and new courage when I must weather a storm or have just passed through one. Yes, remind me that I shall soon be gladdened by Your help, and that Your powerful comfort will refresh me.

Be still, my soul; your God will undertake To guide the future as He has the past. Your hope, your confidence let nothing shake; All now mysterious shall be bright at last. Be still, my soul; the waves and wind still know His voice who ruled them while He dwelt below. Amen.   *LSB 752:2*

HYMN

Why should cross and trial grieve me?
  Christ is near
  With His cheer;
Never will He leave me.
Who can rob me of the heaven
  That God's Son
  For me won
When His life was given?

When life's troubles rise to meet me,
  Though their weight
  May be great,
They will not defeat me.
God, my loving Savior, sends them;
  He who knows
  All my woes
Knows how best to end them.

God gives me my days of gladness,
  And I will
  Trust Him still
When He sends me sadness.

God is good; His love attends me
  Day by day,
  Come what may,
Guides me and defends me.

From God's joy can nothing sever,
  For I am
  His dear lamb,
He, my Shepherd ever.
I am His because He gave me
  His own blood
  For my good,
By His death to save me.

Now in Christ, death cannot slay me,
  Though it might,
  Day and night,
Trouble and dismay me.
Christ has made my death a portal
  From the strife
  Of this life
To His joy immortal! *LSB 756:1–5*

THE AFFLICTED PRAY GOD TO REMOVE THEIR AFFLICTIONS

EXHORTATION

Like a swallow or a crane I chirp; I moan like a dove. My eyes are weary with looking upward. O Lord, I am oppressed; be my pledge of safety! . . . Behold, it was for my welfare that I had great bitterness; but in love You have delivered my life from the pit of destruction, for You have cast all my sins behind Your back.
Isaiah 38:14, 17

God has promised His children alleviation and comfort in their sufferings, either in this life or in that which is to come. Afflicted persons, therefore, are not forbidden to ask God that He would grant them these things in this life, provided they submit themselves at the same time entirely to the will of God.

And so, when they experience the severity, bitterness, and tediousness of their cross, they may pray indeed that He would remove it. That is what Christ, our Savior, did Himself when He asked His heavenly Father that the bitter cup might be taken away from Him. In this way afflicted persons manifest their trust and confidence in God's almighty power. However, this prayer for the removal of the cross must be combined with a humble submission to God's will. It is better that we bear willingly the cross that God has sent us than that He remove it from us on account of our murmuring, and then, in anger, send us an even more grievous one!

This prayer for the removal of our affliction should flow from the good intention that we may be able to serve God more cheerfully and with less hindrance, since affliction frequently distracts us, zaps our zeal, and makes us unfit for holy exercises. But if impatience were to prompt the desire to be rid of the cross, or the wish to indulge again in the pleasures and joys of the world, it is easily seen that God would not grant such a prayer. If the heart is still carnal, vain, and earthly minded, He many times lets the cross remain till, like a holy fire, it has consumed this dross and all impurities.

PRAYER

O God, abundant in mercy, You behold the afflicted and distressed, and Your tender mercies are over all the works of Your hands. Behold, I, a poor, afflicted soul, am standing here at the door of Your grace and begging You to help me. You know how You have afflicted me. You know what You have laid on me. You also know that none other but You can remove it from me. Your fatherly hand that has wounded me must heal me. He that struck me down must restore me to life. He that brought me to Sheol must bring me up again.

O God, abundant in mercy, I come to You and say: Lord, help me. Have compassion on me. Your wrath endures but a moment, and You take pleasure in life. However, what is but a moment to You seems much too long to me. Merciful God, You have given Your children such kind permission in Your Word to pray to You, saying: "Ask, and it will be given to you; seek, and you will find; knock, and it will be opened to you" (Matthew 7:7). Let my asking, seeking, and knocking find favor with You. Remove my affliction from me; however, not my will but Yours be done. I will not instruct You as to the time and season, the manner and method of helping me, but will patiently await Your help.

Let me experience some refreshing. If You will not take my distress away from me entirely, remove but a part of it. You hide from Your believers only for a moment in order to gather them again with great mercies. O God, how long will You forget me entirely? How long will You hide Your face from me? Is Your mercy gone forever? Has Your promise failed? Let me realize that You are still my Father, and that You will have compassion on me. Let me become persuaded that my eager prayer has been acceptable to You. Long my heart has panted, until it had almost fainted, thirsting after You. With You nothing is impossible. Lord of hosts is Your name, great in wisdom and mighty in power. You are the consolation of Israel, the helper of those in need. Do not forsake me, but save me and be gracious to me for Your name's sake.

Enliven me again after You have afflicted me for so long, after I have endured my suffering, and do not withdraw Your hand from me, O God of my salvation. But if Your hour for helping has not arrived, give me such strength that I can bear my cross to Your glory. For if You, dear Father, bear it with me, or lighten the burden while I walk in Your strength, I will also consider that You have removed it, rejoice in this, and thank You for it. However, if You will not remove my cross at all in the present life, but if it is Your holy design that I should bear it until death, let Your will be done also in this. Only do not allow me to be tempted beyond what I can bear, and sweeten all my bitterness and affliction with the enjoyment of Your love, with Your mighty comfort, and with a refreshing foretaste of heaven.

Rock of Ages, cleft for me, Let me hide myself in Thee; Let the water and the blood, From Thy riven side which flowed, Be of sin the double cure: Cleanse me from its guilt and pow'r. Amen. *LSB 761:1*

HYMN

The will of God is always best
And shall be done forever;
And they who trust in Him are blest;
He will forsake them never.
He helps indeed
In time of need;
He chastens with forbearing.
They who depend
On God, their friend,
Shall not be left despairing.

God is my comfort and my trust,
My hope and life abiding;
And to His counsel, wise and just,
I yield, in Him confiding.
The very hairs,
His Word declares,
Upon my head He numbers.
By night and day
God is my stay;
He never sleeps nor slumbers.

Lord, this I ask, O hear my plea,
Deny me not this favor:
When Satan sorely troubles me,
Then do not let me waver.
O guard me well,
My fear dispel,
Fulfill Your faithful saying:
All who believe
By grace receive
An answer to their praying.

When life's brief course on earth
is run
And I this world am leaving,
Grant me to say, "Your will be
done,"
Your faithful Word believing.
My dearest Friend,
I now commend
My soul into Your keeping;
From sin and hell,
And death as well,
By You the vict'ry reaping.
LSB 758:1–4

THE AFFLICTED REFLECT ON THE HAPPY OUTCOME OF BEARING THE CROSS

EXHORTATION

For the Lord will not cast off forever, but, though He cause grief, He will have compassion according to the abundance of His steadfast love; for He does not willingly afflict or grieve the children of men. Lamentations 3:31–33

Every affliction becomes light when there is hope that there will be a change for the better soon. A difficult journey becomes short when it is quickly accomplished. Similarly, the afflicted should bear in mind that their misery will certainly have an end, maybe even in this lifetime. It can happen with them just as God turned to their advantage David's flight, Hezekiah's sickness, Job's distress, the widow's tears, and the paralyzed man's pains. Most certainly, however, God will end the cross of the godly and turn it to their advantage at death, for then they shall obtain the crown, the white robe, and the joy of heaven, and He will wipe away tears from all eyes.

The afflicted should bear in mind, when they are saddened by affliction, that their soul is being edified by suffering, for by that means they are led to know the omnipotence, wisdom, love, and mercy of God. By means of their sufferings and their happy outcome, their confidence has been established and their faith strengthened. And if the love of the world has been extinguished in them by the cross, so that they now become more godly, more devout, more Christlike, more humble, and more meek, they have certainly derived a huge benefit from their cross. Thus the outcome of the cross remains a happy and blessed one, whether the cross is brought to an end here in time or hereafter in eternity.

PRAYER

O mighty God, how grievous and great is my affliction! You know that every day has its peculiar burden, and nearly every hour its special pain. Yet my confidence shall not cease on that account, but in the midst of tribulations I will lift up my eyes to the hills from which comes my help, namely, to You, the almighty, good, and merciful God. I know that You will gladden me at last after my tribulation. After the storm, You will surely make the sun shine on me. You have promised to refresh those who labor and are burdened. I await then the fulfillment of Your gracious promise.

If it contributes to Your glory and my salvation, grant me the desire of my heart and the petition of my lips, for in You, O Lord, have I trusted since my youth. I know that Your right hand can change all things. If it be Your holy will, change my condition. Refresh me, gladden me, hear me! By this I will know Your great omnipotence, that You are able to deliver me from the most grievous and greatest afflictions. By this I shall know Your great goodness, by which You have had pity on me like a father. Without this affliction, I would perhaps not have learned the Christian faith as well as I have by my afflictions. Now I see Your holy design. You wanted to make me humble, meek, and godly, to draw me to Yourself so that at all times I might find my joy in You and rest my hope on You alone. Now that these things have been accomplished, may You remove my affliction and make my mind, which was quite restless before, once more quiet, resigned, and content.

O what a glorious fruit this bitter root has borne! What a great benefit has come out of my affliction! David's persecutions furnished him the occasion for composing the most excellent hymns of praise and thanksgiving. My tears, too, shall become a seed from which good fruits shall grow. The thorns that prick me shall bear roses. After my battle shall come the victory, after the conflict the crown, after the suffering the deliverance, after the sad and mournful night the joyful morning. For this I thank You, for this I praise You. Bless the Lord, O my soul, and forget not all His benefits. How glorious will be my future deliverance on the Last Day, when freed from every evil I will enter into the joyful life of heaven!

Then shall I end my sad complaints And weary, sinful days And join with the triumphant saints Who sing my Savior's praise. Amen. *LSB 757:5*

HYMN

What God ordains is always good:
   His will is just and holy.
As He directs my life for me,
   I follow meek and lowly.
My God indeed
In ev'ry need
Knows well how He will shield me;
To Him, then, I will yield me.

What God ordains is always good:
   He never will deceive me;
He leads me in His righteous way,
   And never will He leave me.
I take content
What He has sent;
His hand that sends me sadness
Will turn my tears to gladness.

What God ordains is always good:
   His loving thought attends me;
No poison can be in the cup
   That my physician sends me.
My God is true;
Each morning new
I trust His grace unending,
My life to Him commending.

What God ordains is always good:
   He is my friend and Father;
He suffers naught to do me harm
   Though many storms may gather.
Now I may know
Both joy and woe;
Someday I shall see clearly
That He has loved me dearly.

What God ordains is always good:
   Though I the cup am drinking
Which savors now of bitterness,
   I take it without shrinking.
For after grief
God gives relief,
My heart with comfort filling
And all my sorrow stilling.

What God ordains is always good:
   This truth remains unshaken.
Though sorrow, need, or death be mine,
   I shall not be forsaken.
I fear no harm,
For with His arm
He shall embrace and shield me;
So to my God I yield me. LSB 760:1–6

AFFLICTED WIDOWS POUR OUT THEIR HEARTS BEFORE GOD

EXHORTATION

You shall not mistreat any widow or fatherless child. If you do mistreat them, and they cry out to Me, I will surely hear their cry.
Exodus 22:22–23

"Alas, I am a widow; my husband is dead," says the wise woman of Tekoa (2 Samuel 14:5). Widowhood is a state of mourning because a woman must be without her husband's help, counsel, comfort, presence, and kindness. Even wealthy widows feel this loss keenly, while to a poor widow it is even more painful, because death has deprived her of the person who supported her and her children, and under the blessing of God, provided for them. Widowhood is an afflicted state because unchristian persons frequently do violence to widows, rob them of their possessions, oppress, despise, and do them wrong.

However, widowhood is a state God protects. God has commanded all people not to harm widows and orphans, and has threatened to avenge any wrong that may done to them. God has promised to be the widow's husband, helper, and judge. He will take care of widows, manage their affairs, and prosper their interests. Yes, He has promised them His special blessing and comfort, as well as His particular help and mercy.

Reflecting on these facts, godly widows will not despair of God; even though their husbands have died, their God is not dead. They will accept their lot as a trial of their trust and hope in God. No one should cling to or put confidence in a creature. Now, if some widows imagine that no one will support them and their children except their husbands, they are making idols of their husbands. Hence God desires to free them from this sin and show them that He is able to sustain and support them and their children also without their husbands. And so Christian widows will persevere in prayer, zealously serve God, lead a quiet, Christian life, not grow distrustful, and God will abundantly provide for them, support and sustain them.

PRAYER

O merciful and gracious God, You are the refuge of all the afflicted, desolate, and distressed. It has pleased You in Your holy and inscrutable counsel to bring upon me the sad state of widowhood. My sun is gone down at noontide, and the crown of my house is gone. I am a woman in mourning; my husband is dead. Where will I turn now? Where will I seek counsel and active aid? O my God, I come to You. When You said, "Seek My face," my heart said to You, "Your face, Lord, will I seek." You have promised in Your Holy Word to be the Judge of widows and the

Father of orphans. Oh, then, be now my husband, my judge, my helper, my deliverer, my refuge, and the Father of my children. Behold the tears flowing down my cheeks, and let them rise to heaven to receive a gracious hearing. Behold my sighing, and have compassion on me. Make me to understand truly that You have not forsaken me, though I have to live without a husband, and that You, O eternal and immortal God, are not dead but live forever, though my husband is in the grave.

It seems that by this affliction You would draw me away from all creatures in order that I may trust only in You and rest all my hope on You. My God and Father, I believe from my heart that You are able to protect me and my children and to provide for all our needs. Strengthen my faith according to Your grace and mercy. Show me a sign of Your goodness. Guide me as You guided Naomi. Provide for me as You provided for Ruth. Bless my jar of oil as You did for the widow of Israel. Let my jar of flour and of oil not fail, as You provided for the widow of Zarephath. Wipe away my tears and say to me, "Weep not!" as You spoke to the widow of Nain. O Lord, give me what I need from day to day. Bless my going out and my coming in. Preserve me from misfortune, and provide for me and my family according to Your promise.

I place all my trust in You, O living God; I rely on You with all my heart and all my soul. You are wise enough to sustain me. You are powerful enough to protect me. You are rich enough to support me and provide for me. You are merciful enough to give me all that I need. You are present everywhere to help me in every need and to deliver me. If a traveler trusts the road signs to point out the right way; if a patient commits body and life to the physician; why should I not trust You and rely on You, O almighty and wise God? Help me, O God of my salvation, for Your name's sake. Father and mother may forsake me, but You, O Lord, will take me up. In love for my soul You have delivered it from the pit of corruption. My heart is filled with sorrows, but Your consolations and gracious promises delight my soul.

Grant that I may in this lonely state conduct myself as a believer and a godly person, that I may find my joy in You, delight myself in You, and give no one offense. I know it is true that those who serve God are comforted after their trials, delivered from their afflictions, and find favor after chastisement. So then, my God, let me also find favor with You after my suffering, help after my affliction, joy after my weeping, consolation after my sadness. Make all my enemies my friends, and grant that I may find favor and grace with all people. Hear my prayer, give me Your blessing, guide me by Your hand, provide for me and my family according to Your gracious promise. I was cast on You from the womb, and so You will be my shield and shelter also at this time. You will keep me and do good to me, until You will bring me to that glory where I will praise You with joyful lips forever.

When peace, like a river, attendeth my way; When sorrows, like sea billows, roll; Whatever my lot, Thou has taught me to say, It is well, it is well with my soul. Though Satan should buffet, though trials should come, Let this blest assurance control, That Christ hath regarded my helpless estate And hath shed His own blood for my soul. Amen.

LSB 763:1–2

HYMN

In the very midst of life
 Snares of death surround us;
Who shall help us in the strife
 Lest the foe confound us?
Thou only, Lord, Thou only!
We mourn that we have greatly
 erred,
That our sins Thy wrath have
 stirred.
 Holy and righteous God!
 Holy and mighty God!
 Holy and all-merciful Savior!
 Eternal Lord God!
Save us lest we perish
In the bitter pangs of death.
 Have mercy, O Lord!

In the midst of death's dark vale
 Pow'rs of hell o'ertake us.
Who will help when they assail,
 Who secure will make us?
Thou only, Lord, Thou only!

Thy heart is moved with tenderness,
Pities us in our distress.
 Holy and righteous God!
 Holy and mighty God!
 Holy and all-merciful Savior!
 Eternal Lord God!
Save us from the terror
Of the fiery pit of hell.
 Have mercy, O Lord!

In the midst of utter woe
 When our sins oppress us,
Where shall we for refuge go,
 Where for grace to bless us?
To Thee, Lord Jesus, only!
Thy precious blood was shed to win
Full atonement for our sin.
 Holy and righteous God!
 Holy and mighty God!
 Holy and all-merciful Savior!
 Eternal Lord God!
Lord, preserve and keep us
In the peace that faith can give.
 Have mercy, O Lord! *LSB 755:1–3*

FORSAKEN ORPHANS TELL THEIR TROUBLES TO GOD

EXHORTATION

For my father and my mother have forsaken me, but the
Lord will take me in. Psalm 27:10

If ever there were a sad state, surely it is that of being an orphan—that state when children, bereft of father and mother, must live among strangers, become servants, labor, and spend their days among them. Sad though this state is, nevertheless it produces many good results in the souls of those orphans who fear God. For children whom father and mother have forsaken should bear in mind that, though they have no parents on earth, they have a rich Father in heaven, who has become their Father in Holy Baptism. This heavenly Father does not die. He is rich. He has all that we need. He is mighty and can give everything. He is a wise God who knows wonderful and glorious ways for accomplishing everything.

Godly orphans should reflect that God often deprives children of their parents intentionally, in order to show them that He is able, even without father and mother, to sustain, support, and provide for poor and forsaken children, yes, to raise them to honor and to bless them abundantly. To teach us this He has placed before our eyes numerous instances of persons who declare, as did Jacob with joyful lips: "With only my staff I crossed this Jordan" (Genesis 32:10). From home I took with me my staff and poverty and my bare life, so all I now possess is what God has given to me.

However, orphans should also persevere in their trust in God, be humble toward all, diligent at their work, devout at their prayers, eager in their church attendance, attentive listeners, chaste in life, godly in conduct, faithful in the performance of their duties, upright in all their dealings. Above all, however, they should have God before their eyes and in their hearts, not consent to any sin, nor act contrary to God's commandment. If they keep within these bounds, God will surely not forsake them. He will guide them in strange but glorious ways, so that they will have cause to praise the almighty power and goodness of God all the days of their lives.

PRAYER

O gracious and merciful God and Father, I, a poor, forsaken child, prostrate myself before your exalted throne and pray You humbly and from my heart: take me into Your fatherly care. It has pleased You in Your wise counsel to deprive me of the care of my parents. Where shall I go now? I have become an orphan. Who will take care of me now that I no longer have my parents? O loving and kind God and Father, I come to You: take me into Your care and have compassion on me. I was cast on You from the womb; You have been my trust from my youth. Behold, my father and my mother have forsaken me, but You, O Lord, take me in.

O my God, You give food to the birds roving over the wide fields. You clothe the flowers. You provide for the wild animals in the forest. You will likewise provide for me as a faithful father. You will take pity on me and be gracious to me. My eyes are longing for You. I lift up my eyes to the hills. Where does my help come from? My help comes from the Lord, the maker of heaven and earth. I know that You have not forsaken me, though I am forsaken by my loved ones. How many examples do I see before me of children whose parents You permitted to die, and yet whom You gloriously guided, provided for, and supported. O God, You drew Moses out of the water, look on me now that the waves of affliction are about to engulf me. O Lord Jesus, You have taken faithful care of children and blessed them; bless me also. Take me into the arms of Your mercy, bear me up, preserve me from misfortune. O precious Holy Spirit, You guide believers like children; guide me also. Show me Your way, O Lord. Lead me into Your truth. Unite my heart to fear Your name. O triune God, be my keeper who protects me; my helper who comforts me, my companion wherever I go.

Bless me with good friends wherever I journey. Raise up for me patrons and benefactors who will take pity on me in my distress. Let my foster parents and guardians be filled with love toward me. Do good to them in return according to Your mercy. Preserve them from misfortune and reward them with temporal, spiritual, and heavenly blessings for all the good they do to me.

Give me a humble and obedient heart that I may not forfeit the favor and kindness of my patrons through stubbornness, evil living, or sinful practices. Guard me against temptations that I may not deny You because of my poverty or fall away from faith, but help me to grow more and more in knowledge and love of You. Let Your good Spirit always guide, sanctify, rule, and keep me, that I may not be led to intentional sins by evil companions. Let me not fall into wild partying and unchastity, and protect me from a perverse heart. O gracious God and Father, frighten me away from the paths of the wicked! Warn me when I am about to commit sin. Admonish me when I would indulge any evil desire. Hold me when I fall. Bring me back to Your fold when I am going astray. Strengthen me when I am weak. Restore me to health when I am ill.

O faithful God and Father, I commit myself entirely to You. Let my going out and my coming in be commended to You. How I will thank You and sing Your praises, for having done so much good to me! My tongue will say: This is what God has done. He has blessed, sustained, accompanied, guided, and provided for me. Yes, I will tell all my fellow human beings how You have shown Yourself a gracious Father to me. O Lord, hear the prayer of the forsaken orphan. Hear the voice of Your child. You became my Father in Holy Baptism, and so be merciful to Your child. I know You can help me and are willing to help me. O Lord, help me for Your goodness' sake, that I may be able to say in days to come: The Lord has done great things for me, and I am glad!

Jesus, lead Thou on Till our rest is won; And although the way be cheerless, We will follow calm and fearless. Guide us by Thy hand to our fatherland. Amen. *LSB 718:1*

HYMN

O God, forsake me not!
Your gracious presence lend
me;
Lord, lead Your helpless child;
Your Holy Spirit send me
That I my course may run.
O be my light, my lot,
My staff, my rock, my shield—
O God, forsake me not!

O God, forsake me not!
Take not Your Spirit from me;
Do not permit the might
Of sin to overcome me.
Increase my feeble faith,
Which You alone have
wrought.
O be my strength and pow'r—
O God, forsake me not!

O God, forsake me not!
Lord, hear my supplication!
In ev'ry evil hour
Help me resist temptation;
And when the prince of hell
My conscience seeks to blot,
Be then not far from me—
O God, forsake me not!

O God, forsake me not!
Lord, I am Yours forever.
O keep me strong in faith
That I may leave You never.
Grant me a blessèd end
When my good fight is fought;
Help me in life and death—
O God, forsake me not!
LSB 731:1–4

THE AFFLICTED COMPLAIN OF WEAKNESS OF FAITH

EXHORTATION

A bruised reed He will not break, and a faintly burning wick He will not quench. Isaiah 42:3

Increase our faith! Luke 17:5

If there is anything that can frighten believing souls, it is this: that believers imagine they are not praying aright, that they have no faith at all, or that their faith is not genuine, living faith. Thence arises the doubt whether they are going to be saved.

Such anxious souls may derive comfort from the following reflections: A prayer addressed to God in the name of Jesus and in reliance on His merit and blood is a true prayer, and a weak faith is a genuine and saving faith as much as a strong faith is. Is not a little child a human be-ing as well as a grown strong man? When people would like to believe, they are already believers, because such a desire is a work of the Holy Spirit. A godless person has no such desire. A weak faith apprehends Je-sus, His holy merit and His wounds, just as well as a strong faith. If a gold coin is placed into the hand of a child and a robust man, the one has as much as the other. Satan cannot extinguish the light of faith in the heart because he cannot even extinguish a lamp at night. Although the joy of faith is not always felt during prayer, faith is nevertheless present, just as an ember or spark hidden beneath the ashes is present, though it is not seen. The certain test that a person has faith is his hatred of and striv-ing against unbelief and sin. Then spring the fruits of faith: "love, joy, peace, patience, kindness, goodness, faithfulness" (Galatians 5:22). For such anxious souls are afraid to speak or do anything wicked. But where these traits are found in a person, there faith exists and the Holy Spirit; for these are not the fruits of the flesh (Galatians 5:19), but of faith and the Holy Spirit. For faith and the Holy Spirit cannot be separated.

Prayer, reading the Holy Scriptures, patience, waiting upon God—these things strengthen faith. Faith is a gift of God. Now God is not going to ask of you more than He has given you. Christ has died also for those weak in faith, and prays for them that their faith may not fail. And even if you cannot believe this, it is nevertheless true, because Scripture says so.

PRAYER

O God, plenteous in mercy, I know from Your Holy Word that faith alone saves, and that without faith no one is acceptable to You. However, desiring to please You and to be saved, I am alarmed at myself when at times I find so little faith in my heart. So kindle in my spirit the light of faith so that I can rightly know You, the one true God, as You have revealed Yourself in Your Word, that I may with my heart believe Your revealed Word, and with firm confidence and unwavering trust may ac-cept the promises of Your grace and of the forgiveness of sins which my Jesus has won for me. For it seems to me at times that I am not praying aright, that I am not at all a believer, or that I shall not persevere in faith to the end.

I bring these complaints before You, my God, because I know that every good and every perfect gift comes down from above. Now, since faith is not anyone's achievement, but Your gift, I pray You: Strengthen my weak faith! The bruised reed You will not break, not quench the smoldering wick. My God, engrave in my heart this comforting truth, that a prayer which rests on the merit, blood, and death of Jesus is a true prayer. And that faith, no matter how strong or weak, that holds to You, O triune God, is also a faith that is acceptable to You and that saves.

If it is Your will, grant me also that I may perceive my faith by an inward joy during prayer, by strong consolations, and by a joyful hope. O my Jesus, pray also for me, as You prayed for Peter, that my faith may not fail! Seal in me the comfort that I have been purchased with Your holy blood and have become Your child in Holy Baptism, that my prayer is pleasing to God because of Your intercession for me; that Your blood was shed also for me that I might be made righteous and saved by it. And You, O gracious Holy Spirit, work in me the true fruits of faith. Impel me, sanctify me, yes, dwell in me and witness to my spirit that I am truly a child of God.

Blessed be Your holy name, because You have made me to abhor unbelief and sin, to mourn over it, to fight against it by prayer, and You have given me a heartfelt desire to live for You alone, to serve and obey You. From these things I see that You are still dwelling in me. Increase and preserve in me these fruits of faith, and make them sweeter and more refreshing to me from day to day. If You will grant me this request, I will gladly be content with my weak faith.

O Holy Spirit, grant us grace That we our Lord and Savior In faith and fervent love embrace And truly serve Him ever. The hour of death cannot bring loss When we are sheltered by the cross That cancelled our transgressions. Amen. *LSB 693:1*

HYMN

*Through Jesus' blood and merit
I am at peace with God.
What, then, can daunt my spirit,
However dark my road?
My courage shall not fail me,*

*For God is on my side;
Though hell itself assail me,
Its rage I may deride.*

*There's nothing that can sever
From this great love of God;*

No want, no pain whatever,
　No famine, peril, flood.
Though thousand foes surround
me,
　For slaughter mark His sheep,
They never shall confound me,
　The vict'ry I shall reap.

For neither life's temptation
　Nor death's most trying hour
Nor angels of high station
　Nor any other pow'r

Nor things that now are present
　Nor things that are to come
Nor height, however pleasant,
　Nor darkest depths of gloom

Nor any creature ever
　Shall from the love of God
This ransomed sinner sever;
　For in my Savior's blood
This love has its foundation;
　God hears my faithful prayer
And long before creation
　Named me His child and heir.

LSB 746:1–4

꧂

THE AFFLICTED COMPLAIN OF SINFUL, WICKED, AND BLASPHEMOUS THOUGHTS

EXHORTATION

So to keep me from becoming conceited because of the surpassing greatness of the revelations, a thorn was given me in the flesh, a messenger of Satan to harass me, to keep me from becoming conceited. Three times I pleaded with the Lord about this, that it should leave me. But He said to me, "My grace is sufficient for you, for My power is made perfect in weakness."
2 Corinthians 12:7–9

It is sad when the sick complain of pains in every part of the body, but sadder still is the state of the soul when the afflicted complain of sinful, wicked, and blasphemous thoughts.

For the comfort of such afflicted souls the following reflections may serve: Spiritual trials, despondency, terrors, and anxiety of the soul come from God, by whose will the afflicted must suffer these things. Without the will of God not a hair can fall from their heads; how much less, then, could such anxiety of soul come on them? Pious Christians and children of God perceive these wicked and abominable thoughts and are alarmed.

The wicked also have these thoughts, but laugh about them. But the fact that the godly are shocked at such thoughts is a sign that they heartily love God, that they are in a state of divine grace and faith, and so cannot endure such evil things to arise in their hearts. The alarm, this anxiety because of these blasphemous thoughts, is a sign that Jesus and the Holy Spirit are still dwelling in the hearts of these persons. If Satan were in their hearts—as the afflicted imagine he is—they would never be alarmed at these thoughts.

Such blasphemous thoughts God does not charge against the souls of the godly because they arise against their will; they mourn over them; they have no pleasure in them. For when these thoughts approach, the godly feel as if they were perspiring in an agony of fear; and they resist these thoughts. Trials are not a sign of anger, but of the grace of God. Persons thus afflicted nevertheless have a gracious God, as may be seen in the case of Job. God has not departed from them. He is still in their hearts, but He hides Himself from them.

When these thoughts come, the soul, like a house in which bombs are thrown, makes its stand by suffering and not by acting. Accordingly, let the afflicted but keep silent and not utter their evil thoughts in words, nor readily tell them to unbelievers lest they give anyone offense. They must continue to contradict these thoughts and say: It is not so. I am not damned; Satan is damned. I am redeemed. The wicked word in me is not mine; I do not approve of it. Away with it from my heart! I belong to God. God is mine. Who shall separate us?

By blasphemous thoughts we must not suffer ourselves to be kept from prayer and the reading of God's Word, but should rather pray and read more often. Because persons thus afflicted declare that they would prefer walking on thorns and suffering pains in their body to these thoughts, yes, because they are also on their guard against sin and evil works, it is incontrovertible proof that faith, Jesus, the Holy Spirit, indeed, the entire Holy Trinity is still in their hearts. Even if we can neither pray nor think of God on account of these evil thoughts, still their very complaint is a prayer and their sighing a certain sign of the presence of God in their hearts. For this yearning arises from indwelling grace. Yes, in their sighing and moaning they pray most vigorously, zealously, and effectually.

Although they imagine that whatever they do will provoke God's anger, God does not regard this badly. He regards their will and desire. They imagine that they are farthest removed from God, but they are closest to Him. They imagine that they are the most wicked people, but they are the most faithful. They imagine themselves cast away, but they are God's beloved. They should patiently endure, for there is no instance of God forsaking such afflicted souls. He rather gladdens, refreshes, and comforts them again. But they must wait for the proper time, just as a disease must be permitted to run its course. Bye and bye it will disappear, abate, and finally cease. That has been the experience of the godly in such circumstances in times past.

These trials make a person humble, devout, cautious, and pious, so that he does not readily do or speak evil. Yes, this affliction will purify the heart from evil habits and practices, from lukewarmness in prayer and in hearing the divine Word. Is not that a glorious benefit derived from it? These reasons we should consider point by point, or have friends of God explain them to us, and at the same time we should use medicines for our body, work diligently, and go out walking with Christians in the open air, in the gardens and fields, but always have Christian people about us all the time except when we wish to engage in prayer. To join in singing a hymn with those present is also edifying. Additionally, Romans 8, Psalm 28, and Psalm 88 should be read diligently.

PRAYER

O holy God, You inhabit the praises of Israel, and all the holy angels and the elect praise and exalt You without ceasing. I, an afflicted soul, confess to You with truly sorrowful heart that I am violently hindered in the praise of Your holy name by wicked and blasphemous thoughts. These thoughts arise often, yes, each day in my heart. All-knowing God, You know that they fall on me like flying arrows, that they distress and frighten me. But You also know that I am alarmed at this and shed bitter tears because I have to endure these fiery darts.

O my God, do not charge against me what is done against my will! You see how I fight and wrestle, how I sigh, how I abhor these thoughts, and how gladly I would drive them from my heart. O Lord, do not let

Your hand become too heavy on me, lest I perish! I will cheerfully drink the cup that You, my dear Father, have poured out for me. Only let it be a cup of Your grace, not of Your wrath. Be merciful to me, for I am weak. How I am terrified when I perceive that the evil hour is about to commence! Do not cast me away on this account, for I cannot change this condition, but have to endure it.

Yet Your right hand, O Most High, can alter everything. Enliven me, O triune God, and when the evil hour and my anguish are past, let me experience again Your holy presence and Your rich consolation. Yes, in the midst of my distress whisper in my heart a comforting passage to which I may cling, and by means of which I may raise myself up and gallantly defend myself. If my misery is to last a long time, then give me also great patience, along with much power and strength to endure it. Do not let my faith fail, but bear witness with my spirit that I am Your child and an heir of life eternal.

O my God, I will gladly endure this trial also because I know that You have sent it not for my destruction but for my awakening to whatever is good, for my purification from sin, evil practices, and worldly behavior, and for the sanctification of my life. Shall I not drink the cup the Father gives me to drink? Does it not come from loving hands? This fire is to consume the evil lusts and the old Adam in my heart, and consecrate it for You, O great God, a temple and a dwelling. And so I say in the midst of my anguish: You are still my Father, my deliverer, my helper, and my faithful defender. Send into my heart the power of Your Holy Spirit, that He may help me fight and overcome. You have said: "None that wait on Me shall be put to shame." Lord, I trust in You; let me never be put to shame. Deliver me by Your righteousness. Hasten to my help. Be my strong rock, a house of defense to save me. For Your name's sake lead me and guide me.

You have said that Your kindness shall not depart from me, and that mercy shall be built up for me forever. O Lord, let this light arise also for me that I may behold my delight in Your grace. O my Father, let the hour come when You will remove from me the anxiety of my soul. Strengthen me. Help me. Guard my heart as with a wall. Surround it like the house of Job, that the evil thoughts at last no longer enter it, yes, that by Your power I may learn to despise them. You, O faithful God, will not allow me to be tempted beyond what I am able. Alleviate my anguish, and I will also accept that as help until You are pleased to finally deliver me from it entirely at the right time. O Jesus, fountain of all grace, You cast away no one who comes to You burdened with infirmity, but You give comfort to all. Although their faith is as small as a mustard seed, You will count them worthy to move great mountains.

I trust, O Lord, Your holy name; O let me not be put to shame Nor let me be confounded. My faith, O Lord, Be in Your Word Forever firmly grounded. Amen. *LSB 734:1*

HYMN

God moves in a mysterious way
His wonders to perform;
He plants His footsteps in the sea
And rides upon the storm.

Judge not the Lord by feeble sense,
But trust Him for His grace;
Behind a frowning providence
Faith sees a smiling face.

His purposes will ripen fast,
Unfolding ev'ry hour;
The bud may have a bitter taste,
But sweet will be the flow'r.

Blind unbelief is sure to err
And scan His work in vain;
God is His own interpreter,
And He will make it plain.

You fearful saints, fresh courage take;
The clouds you so much dread
Are big with mercy and will break
In blessings on your head. LSB 765:1–4

BOOK III

FOR THE USE OF THE SICK

MORNING PRAYER OF A SICK PERSON

EXHORTATION

But I call to God, and the LORD will save me. Evening and morning and at noon I utter my complaint and moan, and He hears my voice. Psalm 55:16–17

Although God permits people to become sick, He does not want them to cease praying. In fact, He wants the sick to pray more eagerly. Yes, as the sickness grows more severe, prayer is to become more fervent. We see an example of this in our Lord Jesus Christ, where Luke records: "and being in an agony He prayed more earnestly" (Luke 22:44).

When God permits people to become sick, they should at the dawn of the day promptly lift up their heart to God and praise Him for the protection He provided during the night. If the night was sad and restless, the sick should call upon God for relief; if the night was quiet and tolerable, the sick should thank God for it. Having thus directed the heart to God in the morning, the sick should bring before Him their petitions and commend themselves for the day to the protection and guardian care of God, diligently think of Him, and patiently endure whatever He sends them.

At the same time, the sick should bear in mind that Jesus is with them—even in their sickness—there to comfort and sustain them, yes, to teach and instruct them. Perhaps the sick, while healthy, were not diligent in attending church or devout in prayer. God wishes to remind them of this fault, in order that they may pray more fervently now. Perhaps they lack comfort and edification because they have not gathered a supply of comforting passages and prayer in their days of prosperity. But if they have been lovers of God and of His Word, God wishes to show them by means of their sickness how they are to put into practice what they have heard regarding patience, trust, and resignation and submission to His will.

PRAYER

O holy triune God—Father, Son, and Holy Spirit—at the break of day I come before Your most holy throne with thanks that You have once more allowed me to live to see this day. You know, Lord, how I have passed the night on my sickbed. I cannot praise Your goodness enough for again allowing me to see the light of the sun. You have made all pain and discomfort to pass away. O God of love, I thank You for Your protection and help. Your eyes have watched over me this night. Your hand has covered me. Your grace has sustained me. O my God, the sun is rising again. Let Your grace also rise anew on me. Give me this day new strength, new grace, and new patience to bear my affliction willingly.

O Lord, my God, it has pleased You to visit me with this sickness. So be it; I will endure it as long as it pleases You. Perhaps it is Your design to separate me from my habitual sins and my ordinary labor, in order that You may speak with me in private, and teach and instruct me how to care for my soul. Now I have time to examine my past life and to see whether I have served You, honored You, and obeyed You. May I mourn over it, feel ashamed in Your presence, and sincerely repent, that I may enter into a covenant with You and thus work out my salvation with fear and trembling.

Grant, O Jesus, that throughout this day my heart may stay close to You, pray fervently, reflect on Your wounds, Your blood, and Your death, and consider the true salvation and eternal happiness of my soul. O my

God, whisper into my heart one beautiful Bible passage after another that can bring me comfort, assure me of Your fatherly love, seal Your grace to me, and convince me of Your speedy help.

Preserve me this day from sudden accidents, new pains, hours of sadness, and all sorts of suffering. Refresh me when I am faint. Strengthen me by Your Holy Spirit in my weakness. But if it is Your will that I should endure pain and suffering this day, then abide with me and do not leave me. Help me to close this day in a happy and blessed state of mind, and to accept whatever You may lay on me with resignation and quiet courage. Behold, my God, here I am; do with me as it pleases You. You are my Father, and I am Your child. You can preserve my life and gladden me with Your help. When evening comes, I will thank You for Your goodness and with all my heart praise Your mercy for all that You have done for me.

When life's troubles rise to meet me, Though their weight May be great, They will not defeat me. God, my loving Savior, sends them; He who knows All my woes, Knows how best to end them. Amen. *LSB 756:2*

HYMN

What a friend we have in Jesus,
All our sins and griefs to bear!
What a privilege to carry
Ev'rything to God in prayer!
Oh, what peace we often forfeit;
Oh, what needless pain we
bear—
All because we do not carry
Ev'rything to God in prayer!

Have we trials and temptations?
Is there trouble anywhere?
We should never be discouraged—
Take it to the Lord in prayer.
Can we find a friend so faithful
Who will all our sorrows share?

Jesus knows our ev'ry weakness—
Take it to the Lord in prayer.

Are we weak and heavy laden,
Cumbered with a load of care?
Precious Savior, still our refuge—
Take it to the Lord in prayer.
Do thy friends despise, forsake
thee?
Take it to the Lord in prayer.
In His arms He'll take and shield
thee;
Thou wilt find a solace there.
LSB 770:1–3

EVENING PRAYER OF A SICK PERSON

EXHORTATION

I cry aloud to God, aloud to God, and He will hear me. In the day of my trouble I seek the Lord; in the night my hand is stretched out without wearying; my soul refuses to be comforted. When I remember God, I moan; when I meditate, my spirit faints. Psalm 77:1–3

When we ponder the numerous accidents that may befall us at any time, we surely ought never to get up or go to bed without commending ourselves—body and soul—to the mighty protection of our gracious God. The sick in particular should do this. If God has helped them in their sickness through the day, they should thank God for His gracious aid. If God has blessed the medicine, if He has made the suffering tolerable through the day, the sick should heartily thank God for this. They should also ask forgiveness if they have sinned against God by murmuring and impatience. When night approaches, which the sick in particular dread, they should come before God again with prayer and beg Him graciously to ward off every calamity, danger, and accident.

Having thus commended themselves, body and soul, to God, they should not doubt that the triune God will be their light and the strength of their life also during this night. He will stand guard at their bedside, tend and keep them, and for the sake of Jesus' suffering and death forgive them all their sins and be gracious to them. Even if it is appointed for them to die during the night, the triune God will enfold them in His gracious presence and cause their souls to be conducted to heaven by the holy angels. With such good thoughts, the sick should consign themselves entirely to divine wisdom, love, and grace.

PRAYER

O merciful God, I have lived through another day. According to Your goodness You have spared my life until this hour. My heart shall praise and thank You for Your fatherly faithfulness. Especially I praise Your name because You have helped me to bear my pain and sickness this day. O Lord, You lay burdens on us, but You also help us to bear them. You are our God, the God of salvation, and to You, Lord, belong the escapes from death. "Though He cause grief, He will have compassion according to the abundance of His steadfast love" (Lamentations 3:32). You, O Lord, are gracious, good, and kind to all who call on You. You delivers the needy when they cry and do not hide Yourself from their prayer.

O mighty God, the evening is at hand. So I turn to You in prayer, saying: O my Father, abide with me! Do not depart from me this night! Yes, give Your angel charge that he come and keep guard over Your own. Send us the heavenly watchmen that we may be kept safe from Satan. Thus we shall sleep in Your name while the angels are with us. We will bless You, O Holy Trinity, forever and ever.

Ward off from me this night all dangerous and sudden accidents, soothe my pains, guard me against terror, fright, and calamity. O heavenly Father, remain with Your sick child. If You grant me Your gracious presence, I will not be afraid. The Lord is my light and my salvation, whom shall I fear? The Lord is the strength of my life, of whom should I be afraid? O Jesus, the sun is setting and departing, but You are the Sun of Righteousness who never departs. O my Jesus, fold me in Your arms this night. Let Your left hand be under my head and Your right hand cover me. Grant that I may fall asleep thinking of You and even while I am asleep delight myself in the blood that You shed for me. Let me rejoice in Your wounds and find in them consolation, forgiveness of sins, and refreshment for my soul. O precious Holy Spirit, all, except a few, are leaving me. Remain with me, O comfort of the afflicted and consolation of the distressed! Strengthen me in true faith and Christian patience. O Holy Trinity, grant me Your protection. The Lord bless me and keep me; the Lord make His face shine on me and be gracious to me; The Lord lift up His countenance upon me and give me peace.

Lord Jesus, since You love me, Now spread Your wings above me And shield me from alarm. Though Satan would devour me, Let angel guards sing o'er me: This child of God shall meet no harm. Amen. *LSB 880:4*

HYMN

The royal banners forward go;
The cross shows forth redemption's flow,
Where He, by whom our flesh was made,
Our ransom in His flesh has paid:

Where deep for us the spear was dyed,
Life's torrent rushing from His side,
To wash us in the precious flood
Where flowed the water and the blood.

Fulfilled is all that David told
In sure prophetic song of old,
That God the nations' king should be
And reign in triumph from the tree,

On whose hard arms, so widely flung,
The weight of this world's ransom hung,
The price of humankind to pay
And spoil the spoiler of his prey.

O tree of beauty, tree most fair,
Ordained those holy limbs to bear:
Gone is thy shame, each crimsoned bough
Proclaims the King of Glory now.

To Thee, eternal Three in One,
Let homage meet by all be done;
As by the cross Thou dost restore,
So guide and keep us evermore.
Amen. LSB 455:1–6

THE SICK PRAY
FOR PATIENCE

EXHORTATION

Why are you cast down, O my soul, and why are you in turmoil within me? Hope in God; for I shall again praise Him, my salvation and my God. Psalm 42:11

"For you have need of endurance, so that when you have done the will of God you may receive what is promised" (Hebrews 10:36). Surely, whoever would do the will of God must not be obstinate and self-willed, but patient and resigned. A sick person should be especially moved to patience by the example of Christ, who in the greatest pains did not open His mouth, but was like a lamb. If we would be like Him in glory, we must also suffer patiently as He did.

The sick should consider that their sickness is sent in accordance with God's will; for without the will of God not a sparrow can fall to the earth, nor a hair fall from the head; how much less can such a heavy burden and sickness be laid on us without God! The sick should also be moved to patience by God's love and omnipotence. What God lays on us, He can also remove; if He speaks one word, the sick become well again. The sick should consider that by their sins they have deserved even worse afflictions and greater pains. Accordingly, instead of yielding to impatience, they should humble themselves in true repentance before God, and beg His mercy. The sick should reflect that impatience does not lighten the cross but makes it press all the heavier. But God has promised that He will help us bear the cross that He has laid on us.

PRAYER

Merciful God, gracious Father, behold me, a poor human being, lying here on my sickbed and unable to rise from it. But I come to You and appear before Your lofty throne. It has pleased You in Your fatherly goodness to afflict me with this suffering and to send me this sickness in place of the health I had enjoyed up till now. And so now, my God and Father, let Your will be done. Give me patience that I may bear all without murmuring and without rebelling. "God gives me my days of gladness, And I will Trust Him still When He sends me sadness. God is good; His love attends me Day by day, Come what may, Guides me and defends me" *(LSB 756:3)*. Since I have received good at Your hands, since I have been refreshed and gladdened by You in days of health, I will also by Your power accept in patience these days of sickness and suffering, and will humbly call to mind how many happy hours of health I have enjoyed in my life, in comparison with these few hours of suffering that are to be counted as little, yes, as nothing.

I know, my God, that You are kind and gracious. You will not lay on me more than I can bear. I cling to Your Word, which says: "God is faithful, and He will not let you be tempted beyond your ability, but with the temptation He will also provide the way of escape, that you may be able to endure it" (1 Corinthians 10:13). My God, You know full well my ability and my weakness. You will adjust my suffering to my strength. Behold Your weak and sick child, and deal with me according to Your fatherly love. I do not refuse to suffer—I know that You do not harbor thoughts of evil against me. I know that my suffering is to serve for my sanctification. My God, here I am; do with me as You please. Give me to understand Your holy counsel rightly: that this sickness is to be fire to consume the impurities that are still in my soul, to purify me. It is a bell rousing me to repentance, that I may think of my sins and feel heartily sorry for them; a bell calling me to prayer, that I may seek forgiveness of all my transgressions for Jesus' sake, for the sake of His suffering and death. Yes, it is Your voice summoning me: Set your house in order! Think of your death and grave! Prepare for eternity!

So be it. Make me ready, then, and prepared, as You would have me be there in eternity. I know that after the sufferings of this present time there will follow eternal and exceedingly great glory. And so, be still, my soul; why are you in turmoil within me? Hope in God; for I shall again praise Him, my salvation and my God.

The will of God is always best And shall be done forever; And they who trust in Him are blest; He will forsake them never. He helps indeed In time of need; He chastens with forbearing. They who depend On God their friend, Shall not be left despairing. Amen. *LSB 758:1*

HYMN

I'm but a stranger here,
Heav'n is my home;
Earth is a desert drear,
Heav'n is my home.
Danger and sorrow stand
Round me on ev'ry hand;
Heav'n is my fatherland,
Heav'n is my home.

What though the tempest rage,
Heav'n is my home;
Short is my pilgrimage,
Heav'n is my home;
And time's wild wintry blast
Soon shall be overpast;
I shall reach home at last,
Heav'n is my home.

Therefore I murmur not,
Heav'n is my home;
Whate'er my earthly lot,
Heav'n is my home;
And I shall surely stand
There at my Lord's right hand;
Heav'n is my fatherland,
Heav'n is my home. LSB 748:1–3

THE SICK PRAY
FOR GOD'S ASSISTANCE

EXHORTATION

Behold, God is my helper; the Lord is the upholder of my life.
Psalm 54:4

In times of suffering and in misfortune, it is a great comfort to have help from a good friend. Unfortunately, sometimes we have no one who bothers to check on us. However, we Christians know with certainty that God will come to the assistance of all who are in distress, for He has promised help and grace to all His children. So the sick should not lose heart if they see all people forsake them or that no one is concerned about them, but should firmly believe that God will not forsake them but send them help and deliverance at the right time.

When the sick have good friends and are not without means, but find that these accomplish nothing, they should not lose courage or doubt the divine promises, but be assured that in all their gloomy hours of grief, God will be near to aid them. The sick will become aware of the divine help when their life is spared or if their pains become endurable or when they receive strength from God to endure even the most severe suffering. Yes, God is faithful. He is often near us when we imagine Him most distant.

PRAYER

O faithful God, You behold me now in a wretched and sad condition. My strength is failing. My body is wasting away, and the burden of my cross weighs ever more heavily on me. Lord, my God, You hear my supplications and know my afflictions. I ask You fervently, abide with me and do not forsake me! I appeal to Your promises, for You have said: "Fear not, for I am with you; be not dismayed, for I am your God; I will strengthen you, I will help you, I will uphold you with My righteous right hand" (Isaiah 41:10). And again: "I will not leave you or forsake you" (Joshua 1:5). O my God, on this word I rely!

I need Your help greatly. I cannot endure my affliction unless You remain with me and help me bear it. Unless Your hand sustains me, I will soon be crushed and choked by this sickness. Remember that I am formed from the dust—how soon this earthly frame of mine will be broken, how quickly I am sinking, and how fast my life ebbs away. How soon all will be over for me unless Your divine power and fatherly hand support me, and You will come to my aid according to Your gracious promise! Your comfort is a great joy to me, for if You are with me, O my God, I will not be afraid. If I am comforted when some of my good friends are with me during the day, and even watch with me during the night, how much more comforting is Your presence, my God! People may pity me and sympathize with me, but if You are with me, I have the best helper, deliverer, and physician at my side. Your most holy presence will refresh and sustain me, soothe my pains, and quiet my anguish.

Do not forsake me or withdraw Your hand from me, O God of my salvation. If a loving mother does not leave her sick child, neither will You, O God, leave me. Let me feel Your gracious presence by an inward joy, by some comforting passage of Scripture that strengthens me, by some sweet thought. Comfort me in my suffering as a mother comforts her child. O my God, make my faith firm. Sustain my strength. Help me to fight and overcome. By Your help I become strong in weakness. "I can do all things through [Christ] who strengthens me" (Philippians 4:13).

Lord, Thee I love with all my heart; I pray Thee, ne'er from me depart, With tender mercy cheer me. Earth has no pleasure I would share. Yea, heav'n itself were void and bare If Thou, Lord, wert not near me.

And should my heart for sorrow break, My trust in Thee can nothing shake. Thou art the portion I have sought; Thy precious blood my soul has bought. Lord Jesus Christ, my God and Lord, my God and Lord, Forsake me not! I trust Thy Word. Amen. *LSB 708:1*

HYMN

Who trusts in God
A strong abode
In heav'n and earth possesses;
Who looks in love
To Christ above,
No fear that heart oppresses.
In You alone,
Dear Lord, we own
Sweet hope and consolation,
Our shield from foes,
Our balm for woes,
Our great and sure salvation.

Though Satan's wrath
Beset our path
And worldly scorn assail us,
While You are near,
We shall not fear;
Your strength will never fail us.
Your rod and staff
Will keep us safe

And guide our steps forever;
Nor shades of death
Nor hell beneath
Our lives from You will sever.

In all the strife
Of mortal life
Our feet will stand securely;
Temptation's hour
Will lose its pow'r,
For You will guard us surely.
O God, renew
With heav'nly dew
Our body, soul, and spirit
Until we stand
At Your right hand
Through Jesus' saving merit.
LSB 714:1–3

THE SICK REMEMBER
THAT THEY ARE HUMAN
AND MORTAL

EXHORTATION

Man who is born of a woman is few of days and full of trou-
ble. He comes out like a flower and withers; he flees like a shadow
and continues not. Job 14:1–2

Although all people are mortal, though people die and are buried every day, the majority of them never reflect on their mortality, especially in days of health and prosperity. And so God must remind them occasionally that they will have to die. He does this by means of sickness. For when He causes the healthy to grow weak, the beautiful roses to wilt, the strong to become faint by sickness, it is then that they become aware of their transitory condition.

Accordingly, sincere Christians should reflect upon their mortality every night when they undress and put on their nightclothes. They should say in their heart: thus I will also be undressed and wrapped in my shroud when I have died. However, when God afflicts people with sickness, they should again call to mind their approaching death. When people imagine that they will not die if they do not think about death, it is a delusion of Satan. Whether we think about it or not, our end comes whenever it pleases God. But those who prepare for dying in peace have a more blessed departure. People should remind themselves of their mortality by thinking of their ancestors and friends who have died, and should believe that sometime their turn, too, will come. Therefore, blessed are they who apprehend Jesus Christ by faith while reflecting upon mortality, and who continue until death in a Christian and godly life. Those who die in Christ will not be separated from Him when they die, but will reach the end of their faith, namely, the salvation of their souls.

PRAYER

My God, it has pleased You in accordance with Your holy counsel to lay upon me this sickness, and thus not only to draw me away from my business, my sins, and sinful habits, and to call me to sincere repentance but also to remind me that I am mortal and must die. Behold, You have made my days as a handbreadth; my age is as nothing before You. Indeed, every person at his or her best is only vanity.

My God, because sickness is a forerunner of death, I am strongly reminded that I am human and mortal. I am dust, and to dust I will return. And so I look upon my open grave as upon my mother's lap in which You will let me calmly rest and sleep. I know also that it is appointed for us to die once, but after that the Judgment. For this reason I have prayed in my days of health: O Lord, make me to know my end and the measure of my days, that I may know how frail I am. I know also that I must leave everything, my property and estate, my honor and fortune, and all that I possess in this world. I have here no continuing city, but I seek one that is to come.

If it is Your intention now by this sickness to remind me of my end, as You reminded King Hezekiah, and to call to me as to him: "Set your house in order, for you shall die; you shall not recover" (2 Kings 20:1), oh, then grant that I may reflect cheerfully upon my mortality and my end. Let me dwell on earth with such thoughts as these: Perhaps I will not leave this bed, and this may be the last year of my life. Perhaps this sickness is to indicate to me that the days of my life, which You have written in Your book, are past, in order that I may prepare to die in peace by prayer, repentance, faith, and an honest inquiry into the life I have lived up till now. Yes, make me understand, O my God, that I do not have to fear dying because I have prepared for dying in peace, but that I am to be drawn away from the world and from sin by such preparation, and that my life, spirit, and soul become consecrated to You by it. Yes, for this very purpose You sent me this sickness, that I may thus test and examine myself, turn from sin, prepare myself to die to the world, and live in You. Behold, my God, here I am. Receive my soul, but first prepare me well here in time, that at my dying I may be found in Your grace and die in peace.

For me to live is Jesus, To die is gain for me; So when my Savior pleases, I meet death willingly. Amen. *LSB 742:1*

HYMN

In peace and joy I now depart
Since God so wills it.
Serene and confident my heart;
Stillness fills it.
For the Lord has promised me
That death is but a slumber.

Christ Jesus brought this gift to me,
My faithful Savior,
Whom You have made my eyes to see
By Your favor.
Now I know He is my life,

My friend when I am dying.

You sent the people of the earth
 Their great salvation;
Your invitation summons forth
 Ev'ry nation
By Your holy, precious Word,
In ev'ry place resounding.

Christ is the hope and saving light
 Of those in blindness;
He guides and comforts those in night
 By His kindness.
For Your people Israel
In Him find joy and glory. LSB 938:1–4

THE SICK RESIGN THEMSELVES TO THE WILL OF GOD, TO LIVE OR TO DIE

EXHORTATION

And going a little farther He fell on His face and prayed, saying, "My Father, if it be possible, let this cup pass from Me; nevertheless, not as I will, but as You will." Matthew 26:39

"God's will is always best," we are in the habit of saying. However, when we are to submit to God's will solely and to be satisfied with what is contrary to our own will, we often feel a great repugnance to this. Accordingly, those whom God has afflicted with severe sickness should reflect that it is by God's will that they are in such a condition. They should beware of impatience; otherwise they would show that they are not satisfied with God's will. They should look at the example of Jesus Christ, who said, despite His greatest sufferings and agony that forced from Him His sweat like drops of blood: "Father . . . not as I will, but as You will." Such resignation and submission to His will is pleasing to God and a mark of His children.

Yes, even if a person were to persist in resisting God's will constantly, still nothing apart from His will would be achieved. If God has decreed that we shall not be healed of this sickness, then we shall not prevent this by our stubbornness. The counsel and will of God will befall us nevertheless. And so it is best of all for the sick to say: Behold, Lord, here I am; do to me as it seems good to You. I am willing to live longer, if that is Your pleasure. I am also glad to die, if that is Your will.

PRAYER

O gracious, kind, and merciful God, I come now before Your most holy throne with my prayer and sighing, though my body is confined to this bed. I see, O my God, that it is Your will that I should lie sick and be deprived for a time of the precious gift of health. So be it. If such is Your will, it shall be mine also. If it pleases You, I shall be pleased. Your will and mine shall be but one will. I was born according to Your will; I am also willing to die whenever it pleases You. According to Your will I have enjoyed good health a long time. According to Your good pleasure I am not willing to be sick as long as You deem it profitable and good for my soul. Yes, my God, even if I could regain my health contrary to Your will, I would not choose that, but would rather fulfill Your gracious counsel as I lie here in my sickness.

In my present condition, therefore, I will say with my Jesus: Father, not my will but Yours be done. If I am to live longer in this world, I shall continue praising You. Yes, the years that You will add to my life I will spend to Your glory and in true godliness. But if it is Your pleasure that I will not rise from this bed but will die of this sickness, prepare me to die in peace. I know that my earthly house of this tabernacle must be destroyed sometime, but I also know that You have prepared for those who believe in You a house not made with hands, eternal in the heavens. In heaven is my heritage, my fatherland, my citizenship. Shall I not be glad to enter upon my inheritance, to hasten to my fatherland, to enjoy the glory of the children of God? Though I have reason to pray that my life may be prolonged and preserved, still I am brought up short by this other question: Whether it would be better to depart and be with Christ, to behold my Jesus, whom I loved when I had not yet seen Him. And so, my God, I leave all to You. You know what is best and most salutary for me.

Behold, here I am. Do with me, Lord, according to Your good pleasure.

If death my portion be, It brings great gain to me; It speeds my life's endeavor To live with Christ forever. He gives me joy in sorrow, Come death now or tomorrow. Amen.   *LSB 745:3*

HYMN

Lord, it belongs not to my care
Whether I die or live;
To love and serve Thee is my share,
And this Thy grace must give.

If life be long, I will be glad
That I may long obey;
If short, yet why should I be sad
To soar to endless day?

Christ leads me through no darker rooms
Than He went through before;
He that unto God's kingdom comes
Must enter by this door.

Come, Lord, when grace has made me meet
Thy blessèd face to see;
For if Thy work on earth be sweet,
What will Thy glory be!

Then shall I end my sad complaints
And weary, sinful days
And join with the triumphant saints
Who sing my Savior's praise.

My knowledge of that life is small,
The eye of faith is dim;
But 'tis enough that Christ knows all,
And I shall be with Him. *LSB 757:1–6*

THE SICK REALIZE THAT THE CROSS AND AFFLICTION COME FROM GOD

EXHORTATION

The LORD kills and brings to life; He brings down to Sheol and raises up. 1 Samuel 2:6

God is love. He loves people fervently. Every day believing Christians receive proof of His love by the gracious help and the blessings that come from His hand. They also behold it in His great works of love: creation, redemption, and sanctification. Because God is love, He affords a great comfort to the sick when they say to themselves: My affliction does not come from an enemy who hates me, but from a God who loves me. It comes from a Father who since the days of my youth has furnished me help in many dangers and accidents.

If this fact is firmly established in the soul, then there follows from it a glorious comfort: the Father never intends evil for His child. The Lover of human beings has retained a heart abounding in love even in the afflictions that He sends to His children. In view of these facts, the sick should take heart in reliance upon God. They should diligently call on God in prayer. They should lay their weary head in God's lap, look up to heaven with joy and cheerful courage, and say to themselves: "When life's troubles rise to meet me, Though their weight May be great, They will not defeat me. God, my loving Savior, sends them; He who knows All my woes Knows how best to end them" *(LSB 756:2)*. Especially should they not permit themselves to be led astray by the severity of their sickness, their great pains, and their seeming danger. Here again this comforting reflection is well grounded: God lays upon us our crosses, but He daily bears our burdens. "Our God is a God of salvation, and to GOD, the Lord, belong deliverances from death" (Psalm 68:20).

PRAYER

O Lord God, You are merciful, patient, and abundant in goodness and truth. You forgive iniquity, transgression, and sin. You do not keep Your anger forever, but look on the afflicted and raise up those who are bowed down. Behold, I, a poor mortal, lie here before You and ask You to look on me from Your exalted throne and hear me! I know and believe that my affliction and tribulation come from You. Your hand wounds, but it also heals; it makes sore, but it also binds up.

Because my sickness is sent me from heaven, I, in turn, rightly look to heaven for help. I lift up my eyes to the hills. Where does my help come from? My help comes from the Lord, the maker of heaven and earth. I have received health, life, and prosperity from Your hands. When, then, should I not accept sickness also? Shall we receive good from the hand of God and not evil also? The trees in the field in their season are in full bloom, gloriously adorned with foliage and fruit, basking in the sun and warmed by its rays. But in winter they look desolate and dead; they have to endure storms and frost. All this comes from You, O God. And so I, too, will bear in mind that this is the time of my suffering and affliction You have decreed and appointed for me. Yes, just as You know the place of every star, whether it is high or low in the heavens, so You know my present condition. You know how heavy my burden is. You know how long I have been afflicted. You also know how much strength I have to endure all this.

Lay upon me, my kind God, as much as You will, but give me power and strength that I may be able to bear it. I know that without Your will not a hair can fall from my head—how much less can I become sick without Your will? If not even a sparrow falls to the ground without Your will, how much less can I become subject to pains, discomfort, and sickness, yes, how much less can I die without Your counsel and will! If my affliction comes from You, it comes from my Father. If it comes from my Father, it comes from loving hands and a loving heart, not for my destruction, but for the welfare of my soul.

Correct me, my Father. But do it with moderation, lest I be utterly consumed. Send me grief, but make me also to rejoice in turn. When You hide Your face from me, make it shine again. Let Your face shine on me, and I will recover. I will gladly fall into the hands of my Father when I have deserved punishment, for His anger endures but for a moment while His favor is for life. He will have compassion on Zion, and be gracious to His child.

Come, holy Light, guide divine, Now cause the Word of life to shine. Teach us to know our God aright And call Him Father with delight. From ev'ry error keep us free; Let none but Christ our master be That we in living faith abide, In Him, our Lord, with all our might confide. Alleluia, alleluia! Amen.   *LSB 497:2*

HYMN

Hear us, Father, when we pray,
   Through Your Son and in Your Spirit.
By Your Spirit's Word convey
   All that we through Christ inherit,
That as baptized heirs we may
Truly pray.

When we know not what to say
   And our wounded souls are pleading,
May Your Spirit, night and day,
   Groan within us interceding;
By His sighs, too deep for words,
We are heard.

Jesus, advocate on high,
   Sacrificed on Calv'ry's altar,
Through Your priestly blood we cry:
   Hear our prayers, though they may falter;
Place them on Your Father's throne
As Your own.

By Your Spirit now attend
   To our prayers and supplications,
As like incense they ascend
   To Your heav'nly habitations.
May their fragrance waft above,
God of love. LSB 773:1–4

THE SICK REALIZE THE USEFULNESS OF THEIR SICKNESS

EXHORTATION

This illness does not lead to death. It is for the glory of God, so that the Son of God may be glorified through it. John 11:4

The unregenerate refuse to believe that sickness can be of great usefulness. They say, "Not only is the body made weak and in peril of death, but its powers also are weakened—not to mention other discomforts and the expense connected with sickness." Still, notwithstanding all this, sickness has its uses, sometimes even for the body, and a person after sickness seems to be healthier and stronger than before.

Sickness, however, is of glorious profit especially to the soul. By means of it God brings many a person back from sinful ways. How many sinners live unconcerned in their waywardness, regarding neither God nor His Word, and heaping up sin upon sin! But by sickness, pain, and suffering, God stops many such people by force, recalling them to their senses so that they are delivered from the snares of Satan. Sickness, additionally, is of use to the godly. By it they learn to know the almighty power, goodness, wisdom, love, and mercy of God, all of which they indeed knew well enough before and believed, but now progress deeper in that knowledge.

Additionally, after sickness a greater love toward God, greater fervor in prayer, and greater sincerity in Christian conduct can be observed among the godly. They learn to submit themselves to God, to reflect on death, to prepare for a departure in peace, to think much of heaven, and to commend their souls into God's hands. If the sick bear these things in mind, they will be content in God, even in sickness.

PRAYER

Dear God and Father, I perceive quite plainly Your holy counsel concerning me. This is to be my year of suffering, my season of suffering, when the sun of my prosperity is to be clouded for a season, my health enfeebled, my physical strength diminished. I thank You, my God, that before visiting me in this way, You have made me to understand Your ways, so that I see that the cross is also a way to heaven and that You are doing good to our souls in sickness. I see plainly, my God, that You would draw me away from the world. You would make the world bitter and heaven sweet to me, so that I may deny ungodliness and worldly lusts, and live soberly, righteously, and godly in this present world, that I may test and examine my life and turn to You in sincere repentance. Indeed, when we are in prosperity and know of no tribulation, we imagine that we are in the world only to collect riches or to have fun, give parties, keep company the world, and conform to its customs, ways, and manners. But since that would ruin our soul and lead to eternal damnation, You are accustomed, in accordance with Your faithfulness, occasionally to take us aside from the multitude in order to speak to us alone.

O my God, it seems that You would now speak with me alone and tell me that I must beware of the sins, temptations, wickedness, and customs of the world. You would persuade me to repent of the sins I have committed. You want me to not be conformed to the world but to be transformed by the renewing of my mind, that I may know what is the good and acceptable and perfect will of God. Well, then, my God, I will do this. If You will restore my health, I will become more godly, will pray more zealously, shun evil, renounce my former evil habits, avoid the places and opportunities for sin, and become a new person. If anyone loves the world, the love of the Father is not in him. If You have seen, my God, that I have also been lazy in my Christian conduct, negligent in prayer, willing to sin and enjoy the pleasures of the world, You would rouse me by this sickness to think of my salvation and to rise from the sleep of sin. "Awake, O sleeper, and arise from the dead, and Christ will shine on you" (Ephesians 5:14).

Lord, I see that You would make this sickness remind me of my death and make me know my end, in order that upon recovery I may learn to know and praise Your almighty power, love, and goodness, all of which would not be done if You had not thus visited me. O Lord, perform the good work You have begun in me for Your glory and the salvation of my soul. Restore my soul to health by means of this bitter medicine. By these sharp cuts and pains heal the wounds of sin. With this sharp lotion wash away my sinfulness, and grant that I may humble myself before You in genuine repentance and living faith, and seek and find help, counsel, comfort, and forgiveness of sin in the wounds of Jesus.

O sweet and blessed country, The home of God's elect! O sweet and blessed country That faithful hearts expect! In mercy, Jesus, bring us To that eternal rest With You and God the Father And Spirit, ever blest. Amen.   *LSB 672:4*

HYMN

Sing with all the saints in glory,
   Sing the resurrection song!
Death and sorrow, earth's dark story,
   To the former days belong.
All around the clouds are breaking;
   Soon the storms of time shall cease;
In God's likeness we awaken,
   Knowing everlasting peace.

Oh, what glory, far exceeding
   All that eye has yet perceived!
Holiest hearts for ages pleading
   Never that full joy conceived.
God has promised, Christ prepares it;
   There on high our welcome waits.
Ev'ry humble spirit shares it,
   Christ has passed the eternal gates.

Life eternal! Heav'n rejoices:
   Jesus lives who once was dead.
Shout with joy, O deathless voices!
   Child of God, lift up your head!
Life eternal! Oh, what wonders
   Crowd on faith; what joy unknown,
When, amid earth's closing thunders,
   Saints shall stand before the throne! LSB 671:1–3

THE SICK REST THEIR CONFIDENCE ON THE ALMIGHTY POWER OF GOD

EXHORTATION

O Lord my God, I cried to you for help, and you have helped me. O Lord, you have brought up my soul from Sheol; you restored me to life from among those who go down to the pit.
Psalm 30:2–3

In dangerous situations, nothing is more cheering and comforting than to know you have a good friend who can and will help you. The sick may not be able to say this of any human being, but they can be assured that God is such a friend.

The sick may see the almighty power of God in the examples of others. When they hear, read, or recall that God has raised the dead and has restored those who were sick to the point of death, they can confidently conclude that the almighty God, who gave help in those instances, is living still. The sick may reflect on the unlimited power of our great God, greater than the power of all the rulers of the world, yes, than of all people. Accordingly, what is impossible for human beings is possible with God. What we find too difficult, He finds quite easy! The sick should consider that God does not lack means to help them. At His command, sickness must yield. He can so bless even the most minor herb or medicine so that it must remove the evil in our sickness and promote our recovery.

When the sick ponder these things, they should be at peace with God, persevere in prayer, and wait for the hour of God's deliverance. However, they should also use medicines and remedies that the physicians prescribe for them, but should be on their guard against all superstitious practices, and be assured that the Almighty will surely help them when the right time comes.

PRAYER

O my Lord and God, You see me overwhelmed with pain and suffering. My misery is renewed each morning. My sickness does not yield, and it may well be that I shall die of this sickness. I commit this to Your holy will. I am willing to live or to die whenever it pleases You. You have made my days as a handbreadth. The number of my years is with You. You have appointed to me boundaries that I cannot pass. You have recorded in Your book the number of my days, when as yet there were none of them. Still, I do not lose courage on that account, but lift up my eyes to the hills. Where does my help come from? My help comes from the Lord. I know that You are an almighty God, that life and death are in Your hands; but I know also that You can raise the dead by Your almighty power, restore people from the most dangerous sicknesses, and alleviate and remove the greatest misery and suffering. Indeed, the Lord's hand is not shortened. The Helper of Israel can reverse every anguish, yes, He is able to do exceedingly more than we ask or think. He can deliver all who come to Him.

Therefore, in this present sickness I do not look about me for puny human help or for inner strength, for I am sick and miserable. But I look above, to You, my God and Lord. I say now with the believing centurion: "Lord . . . only say the word, and [Your] servant will be healed" (Matthew 8:8). Yes, speak the word only and I will live. I will be delivered from all my suffering. I know that with the Lord nothing is impossible. Lord, Your almighty power is without limit. Where is there a god like You? My God, You restored sick Hezekiah to health, You delivered the woman from her afflicted condition, You healed the paralyzed, You raised the young man. Graciously look also on me, O mighty protector of all who trust in You! Help me also. Have compassion on me, show me a sign for good. You are my helper and deliverer. My God, do not tarry. However, do all as it pleases You. I know You are able by Your almighty power, and willing by Your goodness, to do it, if it is good for my soul. Meanwhile, I pray to You in faith:

In God, my faithful God, I trust when dark my road; Great woes may overtake me, Yet He will not forsake me. My troubles He can alter; His hand lets nothing falter. Amen.   *LSB 745:1*

HYMN

O bless the Lord, my soul!
　Let all within me join
And aid my tongue to bless His
　name
　　Whose favors are divine.

O bless the Lord, my soul,
　Nor let His mercies lie
Forgotten in unthankfulness
　And without praises die!

'Tis He forgives thy sins;
　'Tis He relieves thy pain;
'Tis He that heals thy sicknesses
　And makes thee young again.

He crowns thy life with love
　When ransomed from the
　grave;
He that redeemed my soul from
　hell
　　Hath sov'reign pow'r to save.

He fills the poor with good;
　He gives the suff'rers rest.
The Lord hath judgments for the
proud
　　And justice for the oppressed.

His wondrous works and ways
　He made by Moses known,
But sent the world His truth and
grace
　　By His belovèd Son. LSB 814:1–6

THE SICK REMEMBER THEIR BAPTISMAL COVENANT

EXHORTATION

Baptism, which corresponds to this, now saves you, not as a removal of dirt from the body but as an appeal to God for a good conscience. 1 Peter 3:21

If any name by which we refer to God is comforting, it is certainly the name *Father*. And if any glory that we can discover in humanity is great, it is certainly this: to be a child of God. Now, just as we can be cheered by this reflection all our life, we can also derive comfort from it in sickness. The sick should not let this comfort slip from their heart.

They should reflect: God is an almighty God, with whom nothing is impossible. God is a faithful God, who means well for His children. God is a wise Father, who can turn the bitterest cross into a wholesome medicine for His children. God is a kind and loving Father, who may afflict

His children, but will have compassion on them again. When the sick ponder all these things, they can derive a heartfelt joy.

Now Christians who are sick remember that they have attained this glory of being children of God by Holy Baptism, in which they entered into a covenant with the triune God. This thought, now, should raise them up and cheer them. However, they should also as children leave all that happens to them to the disposition of their heavenly Father's will and counsel, and not murmur against the Father, but have the confidence that God will prove Himself faithful. If they have provoked the Father in heaven to anger in their days of health, and have at times lived like a child of this world, they should heartily pray God to forgive them during this sickness, resolve upon a genuine change of life, and firmly believe that God will have compassion also on His sick children.

PRAYER

Lord God, Father, Son, and Holy Spirit, behold, I, Your child, find myself in a condition where I know of no further help in all the world. I look everywhere for help, but no one comes to my aid. I shall not lose heart on that account, but rather go to You, my heavenly Father, and pour out my grief before You. If a sheep in distress hurries to the shepherd, or a child to his father, or a subject to his king, O my king, O my Father, O my shepherd, I, too, come to You.

O triune God, in Baptism I entered into a covenant with You. In this covenant You promised to be my Father—to provide for me, to help me, and to love me. Jesus has washed me with His holy blood and bestowed on me the garment of His perfect righteousness. The Holy Spirit has been poured on me abundantly and is still crying in my heart, "Abba, Father!" He gives witness with my spirit that I am a child of God.

O triune God, behold, here a poor child is coming to You. My father and my mother have forsaken me; my relatives and friends cannot help me. Therefore, O my heavenly Father, take me up. If the centurion had compassion on his servant who lay sick unto death, if he was at pains to help him, O my Father, also have compassion on me and help me. As the father whose daughter lay at the point of death followed Jesus and said: "My daughter has just died, but come and lay Your hand on her, and she will live" (Matthew 9:18), I, too, my God and Father, follow You and say:

If it is Your will, if it is good for me, restore me to health and preserve my life. I know that You are an almighty Father, a wise Father, a gracious and loving Father. Where will the child go when in trouble but to the Father? Lord God, Father in heaven, have compassion on me. Lord God, the Son, the Savior of the world, have compassion on me. Lord God, the Holy Spirit, have compassion on me. Just as a father pities his children, so the Lord pities those that fear Him. Have pity on me also!

If I have been a disobedient child, I am sorry for it. Thought I have forsaken You, still I come back. As the father did not deny help to his prodigal son, so may You receive me again into Your grace; for I come to You penitent and believing and say: Have mercy, have mercy on me, O God, my Redeemer. "If You, O LORD, should mark iniquities, O Lord, who could stand?" (Psalm 130:3).

Thus trusting in You, my Father, I am waiting for Your help. I have already realized that I can truly be a child of God and at the same time be sick, miserable, and burdened with many a cross. Accordingly, Satan shall not easily shake my childlike confidence. Only let me soon behold Your fatherly heart and know that You have not forgotten me. Let me feel the touch of Your fatherly hand.

Be still, my soul; the Lord is on your side; Bear patiently the cross of grief or pain; Leave to your God to order and provide; In ev'ry change He faithful will remain. Be still, my soul; your best, your heav'nly Friend Through thorny ways leads to a joyful end. Amen. *LSB 752:1*

HYMN

I am trusting Thee, Lord Jesus,
Trusting only Thee;
Trusting Thee for full salvation,
Great and free.

I am trusting Thee for pardon;
At Thy feet I bow,
For Thy grace and tender mercy
Trusting now.

I am trusting Thee for cleansing
In the crimson flood;
Trusting Thee to make me holy
By Thy blood.

I am trusting Thee to guide me;
Thou alone shalt lead,
Ev'ry day and hour supplying
All my need.

I am trusting Thee for power;
Thine can never fail.
Words which Thou Thyself shalt give me
Must prevail.

I am trusting Thee, Lord Jesus;
Never let me fall.
I am trusting Thee forever
And for all. *LSB 729:1–6*

THE SICK TAKE THEIR STAND ON THE BLESSINGS OF THE TRIUNE GOD

EXHORTATION

The Lord will rescue me from every evil deed and bring me safely into His heavenly kingdom. To Him be the glory forever and ever. Amen. 2 Timothy 4:18

Godly Christians never lack comfort in their affliction and sickness if they but reflect who they are, and with whom they have to deal. They are God's children. And so they should believe that the triune God will not forsake them in their misery and suffering. Their Creator will not forsake them. He has guided them in their youth, provided for them in the years that followed, and like a father, preserved them up till now. Should God forsake His creatures, the work of His hands? He may hide Himself, but He will not forsake His creatures. Their redeemer, Jesus, will not forsake them. He suffered tortures, anguish, and death for them. Should He who shed His holy blood for them leave them without help in their sickness? No. He loves them too fervently. Their sanctifier, the precious Holy Spirit, will not forsake them. He will comfort, refresh, gladden them, and witness to them that they are the children of God, even though their sickness, suffering, and pains continue.

When the sick have this threefold comfort in their heart, they will patiently bear their grievous affliction, and firmly believe that their help is not far off. However, they must also pray for the forgiveness of everything that they have done contrary to the triune God while in their health. And in such trustful confidence, they must with patience and trust await God's help.

PRAYER

O holy triune God, though I am now feeble in health, I will not become weak in my faith. I will trust in You, for those who trust in the Lord are like Mount Zion, which cannot be moved. As my sickness lingers and grows heavy on me, my heart is indeed inclined to feel down at times, but I rouse myself again by Your Holy Spirit and especially by reviewing Your past blessings.

Can You forsake me, O my Creator? You made me out of nothing and preserved me till this hour! Is the Lord's hand shortened? No! The hand that has led, guided, strengthened, and sustained me up till now will also sustain me in my sickness. You have wooed me with an everlasting love, and guided me by Your goodness. It is Your love that has granted me so many days of health. It is Your love that has turned away from me misfortune, great sufferings, and dangerous situations. It is Your love that till this day You have shown me grace, yes, so much grace and mercy. And so I commit myself to You also in my sickness. Can you forsake me, my Redeemer? You purchased me with Your holy blood from sin, death, and the devil! Since You have delivered my soul from the pit of corruption by Your great love, You will grant help also to my poor, sick, body. Since Your love has redeemed from the curse of death, yes, from hell, it can speedily help me also in my sickness. O Lamb of God, You take away the sin of the world, have mercy on me in my present suffering. Can You forsake me, O my Sanctifier? You have sanctified my soul and body and consecrated them in Holy Baptism to be Your temple, and You have dwelt with me ever since. You will surely remain my helper and my comforter also in my sickness and will witness with my spirit that I am a child of God, even though I am now surrounded by so much suffering and tribulation.

And so I shall be of good cheer in my pain and suffering, and will say to my soul: The heavenly Father has embraced you in His everlasting love; the Son of God has chosen you for His own, His brother and coheir; the Holy Spirit has assured you of His sweet consolation and of His gracious indwelling. And so all is yours, my soul: the grace of God is yours; yours the merit and righteousness of Christ; yours the consolations of the Holy Spirit; heaven itself is yours with all its glory. Since this is so, I will not worry about my sick body, but will cast my burden on the Lord, and trust in God who has shown me so many favors.

O my Father, I trust in You. O Jesus, I flee to You. O Holy Spirit, I commit myself to You. Lord God Father, what You have created; Lord God Son, what You have redeemed; Lord God Holy Spirit, what You have sanctified, I commend into Your hands. Praise, honor, and glory to Your holy name forever and ever! Amen.

HYMN

O God, our help in ages past,
　Our hope for years to come,
Our shelter from the stormy blast,
　And our eternal home:

Under the shadow of Thy throne
　Thy saints have dwelt secure;
Sufficient is Thine arm alone,
　And our defense is sure.

Before the hills in order stood
　Or earth received her frame,
From everlasting Thou art God,
　To endless years the same.

A thousand ages in Thy sight
　Are like an evening gone,
Short as the watch that ends the
　night
　Before the rising sun.

Time, like an ever-rolling stream,
　Soon bears us all away;
We fly forgotten as a dream
　Dies at the op'ning day.

O God, our help in ages past,
　Our hope for years to come,
Be Thou our guard while troubles
　last
　And our eternal home!

LSB 733:1–6

THE SICK RESOLVE
TO BEAR THEIR SUFFERINGS
WITHOUT COMPLAINING

EXHORTATION

I am mute; I do not open my mouth, for it is You who have done it. Psalm 39:9

How long will You forget me, O Lord? Forever? How long will You hide Your face from me? That is how pious Christians on their sickbeds often sigh in the words of Psalm 13. They often think that God's hour for helping them is delayed too long. When it does not arrive for days, weeks, and months, many do not refrain from murmuring.

The godly, however, must not permit matters to come to such a pass within themselves. They should bear in mind that God does not forget or forsake His children in their suffering, sickness, and affliction, for that would be contrary to His promise. Though He delays, wait for His help nevertheless. Even His delay is for the good of the soul. Even if the cross should grow heavier during the long delay of God's help, no murmuring should arise on that account, but we should remind ourselves of God's almighty power, love, and mercy. As the medicine is measured to the patient, and the bitter drops are numbered, even so we are to believe that our crosses are weighed and measured for us. God is faithful. He will not permit us to be tempted beyond what we are able to bear. Accordingly, if our suffering is severe and of many kinds, if it lasts a long time, we should not even then surrender our confidence, but wait for the hour of help with persistent sighing, prayer, faith, hope, and trust.

PRAYER

O holy and wise God, I now perceive Your counsel and will with respect to me, that I am to spend these days and weeks, as long as it pleases You, confined to my bed and my house. So be it. I do not oppose Your holy will. I will not murmur against You. Instead, I will say: Here I am, Lord. Do with me as seems good to You. The cup my Father has given I will not refuse to drink. My Father will not pour out poison for me instead of medicine. I will bear the Lord's anger, for I have sinned against Him. Even this bitter suffering cannot but prove salutary to my soul, though my flesh and blood detest it. You have been my Father and my God from my youth; You will remain as You ever were even though now I am sick.

If I am to lie here and suffer a long time, my God, do not draw out my sufferings too long, but give me an occasional hour of relief in which I am rid of my pains and my sufferings are lightened. If I am to suffer much, give me also much strength, for You know how weak I am, and that I cannot endure much more. Do not lay hold of me too violently, lest I perish. You know well how much I can endure and how frail my life is. I am neither of steel or stone; the wind passes over me, and I sink and die. Do with me as a mother does with her little child. Help me bear my burden.

Yes, bear it with me and take me into Your arms and embrace me. If my suffering is to grow still more severe than it is now, do not leave me. Stay with Your gracious help and support. If I am to pass still more sad nights, let me experience Your comfort and the assurance that You are my God, my Father, and my friend despite it all.

I truly know that when You send affliction to Your children, it is not Your intention to destroy them but to draw them to You. Draw me, then, my God, by this sickness away from evil habits and the lusts of the world, to You, to holiness, to godliness, to heaven, and to everlasting salvation. Yes, my God, though You make me to suffer in this way, I will not flee from You on that account. My shepherd, though You lead me on a path through thorns that wound my body and soul, I follow You willingly. I loved You when You gave me health, happiness, and prosperity; and so I will love You also in sickness, suffering, and pain. I know that You can and will help me.

God gives me my days of gladness, And I will Trust Him still When He sends me sadness. God is good; His love attends me Day by day, Come what may, Guides me and defends me. Amen. *LSB 756:3*

HYMN

What God ordains is always good:
His will is just and holy.
As He directs my life for me,
I follow meek and lowly.
My God indeed
In ev'ry need
Knows well how He will shield me;
To Him, then, I will yield me.

What God ordains is always good:
He never will deceive me;
He leads me in His righteous way,
And never will He leave me.
I take content
What He has sent;
His hand that sends me sadness
Will turn my tears to gladness.

What God ordains is always good:
His loving thought attends me;
No poison can be in the cup
That my physician sends me.
My God is true;
Each morning new
I trust His grace unending,
My life to Him commending.

What God ordains is always good:
He is my friend and Father;
He suffers naught to do me harm
Though many storms may gather.
Now I may know
Both joy and woe;
Someday I shall see clearly
That He has loved me dearly.

What God ordains is always good:
  Though I the cup am drinking
Which savors now of bitterness,
  I take it without shrinking.
For after grief
God gives relief,
My heart with comfort filling
And all my sorrow stilling.

What God ordains is always good:
  This truth remains unshaken.
Though sorrow, need, or death be
  mine,
  I shall not be forsaken.
I fear no harm,
For with His arm
He shall embrace and shield me;
So to my God I yield me. LSB 760:1–6

THE SICK PREPARE TO RECEIVE THE LORD'S SUPPER

EXHORTATION

Let a person examine himself, then, and so eat of the bread and drink of the cup. 1 Corinthians 11:28

Every Christian should live in such a way as to be able to die in peace any moment. Now, if a person in health should conduct themselves that way, how much more the sick! Accordingly, the sick do well when at the first attack of sickness they think of their sins and say: "I do remember my faults this day." Because sickness and suffering come on account of sin, and whoever sins against the Creator is often punished by sickness, the sick must be concerned about becoming reconciled with God.

This reconciliation takes place when the sick, with tears and in faith, beg God to forgive their sins, and with true repentance receive the Lord's Supper. For we must not imagine that we have to die when we receive the Lord's Supper when we are sick; it is not a food unto death, but unto life and salvation! But we are to be reminded that repentance and partaking of the Lord's Supper must not be delayed until we are in the throes of death and our reason and strength are gone. We should take these steps earlier, while we are still in possession of our senses, while we are able to pray and become reconciled with God. If people thus turn to God with their inmost heart, they will live in Him and obtain grace for Christ's sake.

PRAYER

Lord God, merciful, kind, and of great faithfulness, I, a poor sinner, have resolved to seek reconciliation with You, and to pray You from my heart to forgive the sins that I have committed in my lifetime. I will seek Your grace and pardon for my sins in the wounds of Jesus, and thus prepare for a peaceful departure from this world. It has pleased You, my God, to send me this sickness; but since I do not know whether I will rise again restored to health or if I am to die, I will above all care for my soul and commend everything else to You, my kind and merciful God. I will seek to be at peace with You while I have my reason and can remember when I sinned, how often I've sinned, and how grievously I've sinned. I will ask You to forgive while I am still able to pray, for my sickness may increase, and my reason and the powers of my mind leave me, and then I may not be able to pray to You or to think of You.

I know, indeed, that those who prepare to die do not on that account die sooner, but they obtain for themselves the greatest benefit by such preparation. If they are restored to health, they will shun the sins of which they were reminded and of which they repented in their sickness. If they die, they have the assurance of dying happy and well prepared. These are my thoughts, my God. In order to obtain and be assured of the forgiveness of my sins, I desire to partake of the Holy Supper, and then await patiently, cheerfully, and believingly how You will deal with me. Accordingly, I prostrate myself before You in the anguish of my heart and say: Be merciful to Your child. Do not charge against me the sins of my youth and the follies of my early years. O Lord, for Jesus', my Savior's, sake pardon my iniquity, for it is great. O my God, bless my holy purpose with Your grace. Graciously grant that I may receive the Holy Supper unto the assurance that You forgive me all my sins.

I lay my sins on Jesus, The spotless Lamb of God; He bears them all and frees us From the accursed load. I bring my guilt to Jesus To wash my crimson stains Clean in His blood most precious Till not a spot remains. Amen.
LSB 606:1

HYMN

Lord Jesus Christ, we humbly pray
That we may feast on You today;
Beneath these forms of bread and wine
Enrich us with Your grace divine.

Give us, who share this wondrous food,
Your body broken and Your blood,
The grateful peace of sins forgiv'n,
The certain joys of heirs of heav'n.

By faith Your Word has made us bold
To seize the gift of love retold;
All that You are we here receive,
And all we are to You we give.

One bread, one cup, one body, we,
Rejoicing in our unity,
Proclaim Your love until You come
To bring Your scattered loved ones home.

Lord Jesus Christ, we humbly pray:
O keep us steadfast till that day
When each will be Your welcomed guest
In heaven's high and holy feast. LSB 623:1–5

THE SICK PRAY TO GOD FOR THE FORGIVENESS OF SINS

EXHORTATION

Therefore I despise myself, and repent in dust and ashes. Job 42:6

It is a fine and praiseworthy custom of true Christians to appear before God every evening and reflect on what they have spoken, thought, and done during the day, and to call on Him for the forgiveness of the sins they have committed, and thus to be at peace with God before they lie down to rest. Now, if this is to be done every day, how much more careful should the sick be not to neglect this practice!

They should institute an examination covering not one day, or one week, or one month, but their entire life. They should ask themselves how they have spent their days of health, whether they have used them for the glory of God and the good of their fellow human beings. They should inquire where, how often, and how grievously they have sinned in their days of health. Since the sick have ample time to think of their sickness, this inquiry should be all the more earnest. After such investigation, the sick should call on God from the heart to forgive them all their sins, especially since they do not know how near or far the moment will be when they will be called to the judgment seat of God.

If the sick in their sickness come to a knowledge of their sin, they should thank God for the sickness by which their eyes were opened, so that they learned to know their misery and were given an opportunity to ask for God's forgiveness, which might not have happened if they had not been taken ill. However, the sick must also keep faithfully in days of health what they promised in days of sickness, lest they bring a greater evil on themselves because of their faithlessness.

PRAYER

O gracious and loving Father, in Your name I have resolved to become reconciled to You, to pray for grace and the forgiveness of my sins, and then to receive Holy Communion in my sickness. I want to do this now, while I still have my full reason. I live, but I know not how long. I must die, and I know not when. And so I come before Your throne of grace, and humbly pray You to forgive me all sins that I committed during my entire life.

My God, I must confess that I have provoked You to anger in many ways in the past. It is sad but true that I have not always used my days of health for Your glory, for attending divine services, for my growth in Christian faith and godliness. And so You had reason to visit this sickness on me, so that I may examine myself and repent of the misuse of my health and of all my other sins. Forgive me that I have not loved You more fervently, and have not lived a more godly life. O Lord, remember not the sins of my youth. According to Your mercy remember me for Your goodness' sake. How I tremble when I hear that at Your judgment seat I shall have to give account for every idle word that I have spoken! How shall I be able to stand before You with the record of my thoughts, since You will also judge the secrets of our hearts? And because I am to give an account of my entire life, of all my works and actions, O Lord, who can stand before You?

And so I come before Your throne of grace, trusting wholly in Jesus Christ, my Lord and Savior. Have mercy on me for the sake of His wounds. For the sake of the blood that He shed, forgive me all my sins. For the sake of His agony and bloody sweat, help me, O Lord my God! I am ashamed, my God, to lift up my eyes to You. I am ashamed of my former years and the sins that I have committed. Oh, that I had led a more godly and Christian life! Therefore, I vow to You, O God, that I will begin a new life. If You will restore me to health, I will spend the years that You permit me yet to live on earth for Your glory, in faith and true godliness, and receive them as a gift, as an addition to my life. All my life I shall remember this sickness and the anguish of my soul, but also Your mighty power. O Lord, have mercy on Your child, and according to Your great mercy blot out all my sin, for Your goodness' sake.

O Jesus Christ, do not delay, But hasten our salvation; We often tremble on our way In fear and tribulation O hear and grant our fervent plea: Come, mighty judge, and set us free From death and ev'ry evil. Amen.
LSB 508:7

HYMN

A multitude comes from the east and the west
   To sit at the feast of salvation
With Abraham, Isaac, and Jacob, the blest,
   Obeying the Lord's invitation.
   Have mercy upon us, O Jesus!

O God, let us hear when our Shepherd shall call
   In accents persuasive and tender,
That while there is time we make haste, one and all,
   And find Him, our mighty defender.
   Have mercy upon us, O Jesus!

All trials shall be like a dream that is past,
   Forgotten all trouble and mourning.
All questions and doubts have been answered at last,
   When rises the light of that morning.
   Have mercy upon us, O Jesus!

The heavens shall ring with an anthem more grand
Than ever on earth was recorded.
The blest of the Lord shall receive at His hand
The crown to the victors awarded.
Have mercy upon us, O Jesus! LSB 510:1–4

THE SICK PRAY BEFORE RECEIVING THE LORD'S SUPPER

EXHORTATION

The cup of blessing that we bless, is it not a participation in the blood of Christ? The bread that we break, is it not a participation in the body of Christ? 1 Corinthians 10:16

True Christians should always exercise diligent care to receive the Lord's Supper reverently and worthily. The sick, in particular, can do this when they examine themselves before communing. For they are then free from all those distractions that at public communion with the congregation sometimes disturb devotion. They can continue in their devotion without hindrance, if God keeps them free from pain and the discomforts of their sickness.

No one should hesitate to receive communion privately because we know that Jesus has promised to be with His believers by His gracious presence everywhere and always. At the time of their communion, the sick should also reflect that this may be the last time they receive the Lord's Supper. Therefore, they should with a firmer resolve decide that they will abide in faith and godliness. Godly persons have expressed the wish that their last word might be Jesus, their last food the Lord's Supper, and that their last thought might be of Jesus as He hung bleeding on the cross. Ought not the sick, then, rejoice when one of these wishes is to be realized? And should they doubt that by God's grace the other two will be granted them? But if the sick were to desire the Holy Communion to be administered to them in their sickness so that it may restore them to health, that would be very wrong and superstitious.

PRAYER

Dearest Jesus, I desire to receive now, while lying in my sickness, the love-feast You instituted, since I do not know when I shall depart from this world. However, in order not to appear before the judgment seat of God without You, I desire, while I am still living, to be united afresh with You, in order that You may remain in me and I in You. I desire now to receive private communion, and I am certain that You will gladden and refresh me with Your grace also in my house.

O dearest Friend of the soul, You are near to the afflicted. You gladden those that mourn. You are a helper to those who are oppressed in spirit. Oh, let my heart now be made glad and my soul refreshed by this heavenly food, this heavenly drink. I have, indeed, also received it with the congregation when I was well, but not always—sadly—with such reverence and prayerful attention as would have been proper. I was in many ways distracted by the multitude of people, by vanity, by the lust of the eyes. But now nothing will disturb my devotion. In my solitude I will betroth myself to You and unite with You.

O dearest Jesus, since I am about to partake in holy devotion of Your heavenly feast of joy here on earth, and there is no other hindrance to disturb me, I pray that You would subdue my pains in this sickness and give me relief during this hour, that I may carry out my purpose without hindrance or disturbance. I now show forth Your death, and remind myself of Your suffering and dying, Your wounds and pains, Your agony and anguish, Your death on the cross, and all that You have done for me. I think of these things and I thank You for them, and say: "Then, for all that wrought my pardon, For Thy sorrows deep and sore, For Thine anguish in the Garden, I will thank Thee evermore, Thank Thee for Thy groaning, sighing, For Thy bleeding and Thy dying, For that last triumphant cry, And shall praise Thee, Lord, on high" *(LSB 420:7)*.

I also remind myself of the institution of Your Holy Supper in which You give me food and drink for eternal life. I believe Your words, and accept them as the words of an all-knowing, almighty, and truthful God. I believe that in Holy Communion I receive Your true body and Your true blood. When I receive the bread that has been blessed, I receive in an invisible manner Your true body, O Jesus, and when I receive the cup that has been blessed, I receive in an invisible manner Your true blood. This heavenly food and drink will strengthen me in the faith that I am reconciled to God. This heavenly food and drink will comfort me with the assurance that I am not lost but have eternal life. This heavenly and food drink will guarantee to me that I stand in grace, that I have forgiveness of sins and am united with You, the very propitiation of our sins, yes, for the sins of the whole world. This heavenly food and drink will remind me of the heavenly banquet of joy, the joy and glory everlasting to which You will bring me at my death.

O Jesus, O Bridegroom of my soul, sanctify and cleanse me that as Your bride I may pledge myself to You forever. O Shepherd of my soul, lead Your sheep to green pastures. Feed me with the bread of life. Refresh me with Your holy blood. Then Satan cannot harm me and sin cannot raise charges against me or condemn me. Here I have a perfect ransom for my sins, which You have paid for me on the cross, and by which I am justified and saved.

Jesus, sun of life, my splendor, Jesus, friend of friends, most tender, Jesus, joy of my desiring, Fount of life, my soul inspiring: At Your feet I cry, my maker, Let me be a fit partaker Of this blessed food from heaven, For our good, Your glory, given. Amen. *LSB 636:6*

HYMN

Draw near and take the body of the Lord,
And drink the holy blood for you outpoured;
Offered was He for greatest and for least,
Himself the victim and Himself the priest.

He who His saints in this world rules and shields,
To all believers life eternal yields;
With heav'nly bread He makes the hungry whole,
Gives living waters to the thirsting soul.

Come forward then with faithful hearts sincere,
And take the pledges of salvation here.
O Lord, our hearts with grateful thanks endow
As in this feast of love You bless us now. LSB 637:1–3

THE SICK PRAY AFTER RECEIVING THE LORD'S SUPPER

EXHORTATION

It is not longer I who live, but Christ who lives in me. And the life I now live in the flesh I live by faith in the Son of God, who loved me and gave Himself for me. Galatians 2:20

True Christians always have reason for heartfelt gratitude to God when they have received the Lord's Supper. How much more should the sick thank God from their inmost heart when they had been able to receive the Lord's Supper in sound mind! However, in this connection we are to be reminded that we must not imagine that a turn for the better must occur after the sick has communed. A turn for the better has, indeed, taken place if the sick received the Sacrament worthily, for then they have obtained the forgiveness of sins and peace with God and entered into the most intimate communion with Jesus Christ. But the Lord's Supper was not instituted to bring a change in a person's sickness; we have no promise to that effect.

Accordingly, the sick should not receive Communion to see whether they will get well or die. That would be a misuse of the Sacrament. They should instead use it to strengthen their faith, to assure themselves of the forgiveness of their sins, of the grace of God, and of the salvation of their souls. When they have thus received it in the way Christ instituted it, they should praise God for it, and with a quiet heart and believing soul commit themselves to God. In war, when people have put away their most valuable goods, they are content. Our soul is our greatest treasure. When in sincere repentance and union with Jesus Christ we have commended our soul into God's hands, we are assured that God will deal kindly also with the body.

PRAYER

My Jesus, I have heartily desired to receive Holy Communion before I die. This desire has now been fulfilled and stilled. You have fed me with Your holy body and given me Your holy blood to drink. For this I praise You from my inmost heart. I am lying here on my sickbed, from which I may rise again by Your almighty power, but on which I also may die if that is Your holy will. And so I have prepared myself. My soul is now restored, for I have been united with Jesus. Yes, I will gladly die now that I have entered into the most intimate communion with You, O Jesus. Praise the Lord, O my soul, and do not forget all His benefits. Lord, now let Your servant depart in peace, for my eyes have seen Your salvation.

O Jesus, live in me. Give me a calm mind, Christian contentment, and a soul that is completely yielded to You. Grant me grace constantly to have holy and pious thoughts, and let the lovely and sweet remembrance of You live always in my heart. If it is Your will, O God, to call me out of this life by death, then Your will be done. I know that my sin has been forgiven me, and so I am not afraid to come to You. For where there is forgiveness, there is also life and salvation. I know that Jesus has given me His righteousness. When I appear before You, O God, in this beautiful and glorious garment, You will on its account pronounce me free from guilt and exempt from the Judgment. Now that I am justified by faith, I have peace with God through our Lord Jesus Christ. Heaven and the access to the throne of grace have been opened for me. I know that Jesus is my advocate with God. I die in the grace of God, in peace with God. I am assured of the comfort of the Holy Spirit. Thus I am saved. I die saved. I depart saved from this world, and shall be saved in eternity.

This is a great favor that You have bestowed on my soul, O God, that in a sound mind I have been permitted to keep this heavenly feast of love with Jesus. May this heavenly food strengthen and keep me in true faith unto life everlasting! Thus, then, my wish, too, has been fulfilled that the Lord's Supper might be my last food before I die. Grant me also that the last word I shall speak in this world may be Jesus, and my last thoughts may be directed to the blood, death, suffering, and dying of Jesus, and to His holy merit. Then I know that I shall live and die happy and blessed. If God is for us, who can be against us? Yes, who will separate us from the love of Christ? I will not let Him go until He brings me to the assembly of saints and the elect.

Lord, I believe what You have said; Help me when doubts assail me. Remember that I am but dust, And let my faith not fail me. Your supper in this vale of tears Refreshes me and stills my fears And is my priceless treasure. Amen. *LSB 622:6*

HYMN

The King of love my shepherd is,
Whose goodness faileth never;
I nothing lack if I am His
And He is mine forever.

Where streams of living water flow,
My ransomed soul He leadeth
And, where the verdant pastures grow,
With food celestial feedeth.

Perverse and foolish oft I strayed,
But yet in love He sought me
And on His shoulder gently laid
And home rejoicing brought me.

In death's dark vale I fear no ill
With Thee, dear Lord, beside me,
Thy rod and staff my comfort still,
Thy cross before to guide me.

Thou spreadst a table in my sight;
Thine unction grace bestoweth;
And, oh, what transport of delight
From Thy pure chalice floweth!

And so through all the length of days
Thy goodness faileth never;
Good Shepherd, may I sing Thy praise
Within Thy house forever! LSB 709:1–6

THE SICK PRAY WHEN TAKING MEDICINE

EXHORTATION

Is anyone among you sick? Let him call for the elders of the church, and let them pray over him, anointing him with oil in the name of the Lord . . . and the Lord will raise him up. And if he has committed sins, he will be forgiven. James 5:14–15

Devout prayer is a must in days of health, so why should a sick person forget to pray, especially when taking medicine? As regards medicine and its use, the sick should not despise physicians and medicines, and should not think: if I am to get well again, God can restore my health without medicine; and if I am to die, medicine will not help me. No. We are not to think that way, for that would be to tempt God. God has not promised to help us without means. What God has not promised us we cannot ask of Him. Those who despise medicine and die from refusing to use it are murderers of their own bodies.

Still, we must not put our trust in physicians and medicines, but in God. Thus among the sins of King Asa this, too, is charged against him, that in his sickness he did not seek the Lord, but the physicians, and put more trust in them than in God (2 Chronicles 16:12). And so the sick should choose the middle way—they should pray with their lips and heart, and in firm confidence in God's help take their medicine and thus use it. In this way they know it will be a blessing to them.

PRAYER

O great God, You see my condition, for nothing is hidden from Your all-seeing eyes. You see into the most private places, and You look also on my sickbed and know how I feel at this very moment. O my God, I will use the medicine prescribed for me in Your name, but my only hope is in You, for You are the Lord who heals us. Still, since You allow herbs to grow out of the earth and have Yourself created healing medicines to serve for our health, I now take such medicine, praying and calling on Your holy name from my heart: put Your blessing upon it!

I know, indeed, that You are able without medicine to help and make well again, for if You speak the word only, the sick are restored to health, and at Your word sickness must yield. Yet, since You have commanded to use these means also, I will use them in obedience to Your direction. I pray You, O great God, bless the medicine that, firmly trusting in You, I now take in Your name. Let it be blessed to me for the recovery of my health, for the alleviation of my pains, and for the refreshing of my feeble condition. If You pronounce Your blessing on it, even the smallest herb can help me. Yes, any medicine can heal when Your blessing accompanies it. I do not take this medicine to compel my health to return, but as a means which You have allowed me to use for the purpose of recovering my health at Your hand. I lift up my eyes to heaven when taking it. I sigh to You before using it, and after as well. If You will let it take effect in me, I shall recover, for my days are in Your hands. Nothing can and may prosper without Your blessing. And so, O dispenser of blessings, I cry for Your blessing. What You, Lord, have blessed, that shall be blessed indeed. If You will help me by means of medicine, I will indeed return heartfelt thanks to You and will bear in mind that it was not the medicine in itself but Your hands that healed me. With Hezekiah I will spread Your praise among all people.

I leave all things to God's direction; He loves me both in joy and woe. His will is good, sure His affection; His tender love is true, I know. My fortress and my rock is He: What pleases God, that pleases me. Amen.
LSB 719:1

HYMN

Who trusts in God
A strong abode
In heav'n and earth possesses;
Who looks in love
To Christ above,
No fear that heart oppresses.
In You alone,
Dear Lord, we own

Sweet hope and consolation,
Our shield from foes,
Our balm for woes,
Our great and sure salvation.

Though Satan's wrath
Beset our path
And worldly scorn assail us,
While You are near,
We shall not fear;

Your strength will never fail us.
    Your rod and staff
    Will keep us safe
And guide our steps forever;
    Nor shades of death
    Nor hell beneath
Our lives from You will sever.

In all the strife
    Of mortal life

Our feet will stand securely;
    Temptation's hour
    Will lose its pow'r,
For You will guard us surely.
    O God, renew
    With heav'nly dew
Our body, soul, and spirit
    Until we stand
    At Your right hand
Through Jesus' saving merit.

LSB 714:1–3

THE SICK PRAY FOR THE ALLEVIATION OF THEIR PAINS

EXHORTATION

If I speak, my pain is not assuaged, and if I forbear, how much of it leaves me? Job 16:6

Sickness and bodily ailments that God sends people are not all of one kind, as we learn from experience. To some, God sends a sickness that causes them no pain in any member, no, not in their little finger; on others, He visits strong pains. This should remind us that if we can pray, learn to know God, and wish to be reconciled to Him, we must do this at present and not wait until we become sick.

But when the sick are seized with pain, they should not murmur against God on that account, but accept whatever comes calmly and patiently. Still they may ask to have their condition eased, as also our Lord did in His suffering. Children tell their troubles to their earthly parents, and we may certainly do the same with our heavenly Father.

However, when in great pain, the sick should remember the great sins that they committed during their lifetime, and should acknowledge such sufferings are well deserved, but remember also God's great mercy and power, which can deliver them from these pains. If they are not able to pray much or long because of the pains, let them sigh to God and know that such groaning of the heart does not go unheard. Impatience, however, does not lessen our pains, but increases them.

PRAYER

Lord, hear my prayer and give ear to my supplication, my King and my God, for to You will I pray. I ask and beg You graciously to look on me in my bodily weakness, and to lessen my pains and my great suffering. You have certainly promised that You will not let us be tempted beyond what we can bear, but with the temptation will make a way of escape so that we can bear it. Behold, my God, the burden is fast becoming too heavy for me to bear. My pains are becoming intolerable, my body is weak, my strength reduced, my tongue sticks to the roof of my mouth, my bones are consumed as with fire, my eyes fail me, because I must wait such a long time for my God. How long, O Lord, shall my soul be in anguish and long for You? Do not delay, my God! You see my great need.

You know that I have lived through many days and nights. You have heard my moans and my sighs, my complaints and cries. Where shall I turn in my misery and my pains? Where shall I go? Where but to You alone, my Lord and my God? If I were to tell my troubles to other people, they might feel sorry for me, but they could not deliver me. And so I come to You. I know You can help me. It lies with You to do so. Speak the word only and I shall live. O dearest Jesus, You commanded the raging sea to be calm. Command also my pains to abate! You healed the paralyzed man with a word. Magnify Your mercy also in me! Refresh me again, after I have suffered so long and endured so much. Come to me with Your help, before my pains consume me altogether. And if according to Your counsel I am to suffer pain still longer, let me nevertheless be pastured as Your sheep in Your mercy, so that I may believingly and patiently wait for the favor of my Father to quiet my pains. Lay Your gracious hand on me, and I shall be made whole and free from pain.

Out of the depths I cry to You, O Lord! Let Your ear be attentive to the voice of my supplication. My soul waits for the Lord more than watchmen await the dawn. I know that with the Lord there is help. Help me, O God of my salvation, for Your name's sake. However, not as I will, but as You will. If I am to endure pain still longer, let Your will be done. Only give me strength to bear it. Grant me an occasional day, or at least an hour, of rest, O God, that I may be refreshed and strengthened. Our affliction is light and but for a moment, and so make my pains less severe and finally deliver me from them.

As a mother stills her child, Thou canst hush the ocean wild; Boist'rous waves obey Thy will When Thou say'st to them, "Be still!" Wondrous Sov'reign of the sea, Jesus, Savior, pilot me. Amen. *LSB 715:2*

HYMN

When in the hour of deepest need
We know not where to look for aid;
When days and nights of anxious thought
No help or counsel yet have brought,

Then is our comfort this alone
That we may meet before Your throne;
To You, O faithful God, we cry
For rescue in our misery.

For You have promised, Lord, to heed
Your children's cries in time of need
Through Him whose name alone is great,
Our Savior and our advocate.

And so we come, O God, today
And all our woes before You lay;
For sorely tried, cast down, we stand,
Perplexed by fears on ev'ry hand.

O from our sins, Lord, turn Your face;
Absolve us through Your boundless grace.
Be with us in our anguish still;
Free us at last from ev'ry ill.

So we with all our hearts each day
To You our glad thanksgiving pay,
Then walk obedient to Your Word,
And now and ever praise You, Lord. *LSB 615:1–6*

THE SICK SIGH TO GOD NOT TO FORSAKE THEM

EXHORTATION

But Zion said, "The LORD has forsaken me; my Lord has forgotten me." "Can a woman forget her nursing child, that she should have no compassion on the son of her womb? Even these may forget, yet I will not forget you. Behold, I have engraved you on the palms of My hands." Isaiah 49:14–16

A great joy is caused when a poor person finds a rich benefactor, or when a forsaken person obtains strong aid. The sick can have much cheer in their sickness and suffering because they have the promise that God will not forsake them. They should bear in mind, however, that delaying help does not mean forsaking a person. Many sick persons cry and say that God has forsaken them because He does not help them right away, or as speedily as they expect. But we are not to think this way. God will not deny His aid, though He may take His time; His help will surely come.

The sick should reflect that God has His appointed hour for help, and they should wait for it patiently. They should reflect whether in days of health they had not forsaken God, and whether they should be surprised that God now makes them aware of their unfaithfulness. God would remind the sick person of this by delaying His help. And so, let the sick persist in saying with faith: God cannot forsake me. I am His child. God will not forsake me, for He has often helped in times past. If the sick will thus take courage in God, they will patiently bear the delay of divine help and will ultimately obtain the glorious proof that God had not forsaken them at all.

PRAYER

O dearest God and Father, You have loved me with an everlasting love, and drawn me with tender mercies. I, a poor sufferer, come to You and humbly pray You not to forsake me in my bodily infirmity. You know, God, that without You there is no help for me. You are the mighty

God of Jacob, the defender of Israel, the refuge of the afflicted, the helper of sufferers, and their comfort in time of need. The Lord is on my side; I will not fear. He will arise and have pity on Zion. He will in mercy look on me. People say they cannot help me, and thus I am forsaken by all of them. But I know I am not forsaken by You—You never forsake the person who trusts in You. You are faithful to all who put their firm confidence in You. You may lead me by strange ways, but I will not be terrified; for with rejoicing I will behold Your wonderful counsel at the end.

O my God, do not forsake me! You know how long this suffering has already lasted. In the evening I think it will be better in the morning. At noon I long for the evening to come. Yes, during the night I often cry: Watchmen, what of the night? My soul waits for You more than they who watch for the morning. O my God, do not forsake me. Behold how my suffering is becoming ever more grievous. Do not let this burden crush me. Remove the stone that oppresses me, the rod that is coming down on me, the pains that afflict me. You know my feeble strength and how much I am able to endure. My God, do not forsake me. Behold how my sufferings have multiplied. My sorrows do not seem to grow less, but more. Where shall I go if You are forsaking me? If You will not help me, no creature can help me. If You are forsaking me, I shall be left without help.

But I know that You do not forsake me. I appeal to Your promise. For You have said: "I will not leave you or forsake you." Those who trust in the Lord are like Mount Zion, which cannot be moved, but abides forever. The strength of Israel has promised to give strength to His people and to deliver the needy when they cry, the poor also, and the one who has no helper. I trust in Your Word, and my hope is that You will establish Your faithfulness in the very heavens. You cannot forsake me, for I am Your child. Am I not Your purchased possession, bought with Your precious blood? I am Your own; therefore, You will not and cannot forsake Your own child. I am confident that You will not forsake me; You have never yet forsaken me in any afflictions and tribulations, though sufferings without number took hold of me, and the waves of sorrow closed around my head. You will not forsake me this time either. In this thought I rest content and am of good cheer.

And though it tarry through the night And till the morning waken, My heart shall never doubt His might Nor count itself forsaken. O Israel, trust in God your Lord. Born of the Spirit and the Word, Now wait for His appearing. Amen.

LSB 607:4

HYMN

O God, forsake me not!
    Your gracious presence lend me;
Lord, lead Your helpless child;
    Your Holy Spirit send me
That I my course may run.
    O be my light, my lot,
My staff, my rock, my shield—
    O God, forsake me not!

O God, forsake me not!
    Take not Your Spirit from me;
Do not permit the might
    Of sin to overcome me.
Increase my feeble faith,
    Which You alone have wrought.
O be my strength and pow'r—
    O God, forsake me not!

O God, forsake me not!
    Lord, hear my supplication!
In ev'ry evil hour
    Help me resist temptation;
And when the prince of hell
    My conscience seeks to blot,
Be then not far from me—
    O God, forsake me not!

O God, forsake me not!
    Lord, I am Yours forever.
O keep me strong in faith
    That I may leave You never.
Grant me a blessèd end
    When my good fight is fought;
Help me in life and death—
    O God, forsake me not! LSB 731:1–4

THE SICK CONTEMPLATE THEIR DEATH

EXHORTATION

For I am already being poured out as a drink offering, and the time of my departure has come. I have fought the good fight, I have finished the race, I have kept the faith. Henceforth there is laid up for me the crown of righteousness, which the Lord, the righteous judge, will award me on that Day, and not only to me but also to all who have loved His appearing. 2 Timothy 4:6–8

Reflecting on our death is a useful occupation. By so doing we withdraw our hearts from vanity and sins. We regard all that is earthly as things that we cannot take with us to heaven, which we cannot keep, and from which we can derive no comfort in the hour of death. To remind ourselves of our death is also a necessary matter, for those who imagine that death is still a long way off can become bold, reckless, and vicious; they plunge into worldliness and let the world squeeze them into its mold. Now if such persons are suddenly overtaken by death, they are certainly lost. Reflecting on our death is very salutary, for the person who dies before he dies, that is, who considers his end, does not die when he dies. For such people death has no terrors, for the death of believers is nothing but a sweet slumber and going to their Father. And who is afraid of going to the Father or of going to bed?

However, we are not to think that it is a sign of death when a sick person talks a lot about dying, arranges for the funeral, makes a last will and testament, and readies self to die in peace. Not at all. No one dies a moment sooner than when God has determined. Nor should we picture our dying hour to ourselves as something cruel and terrible, as some sick persons do who are afraid to die and to think of their heart stopping. The heathen think that of all the terrible things, death is the worst. Christians, though, die in the grace of God, in the arms of Jesus, in the fellowship of the Holy Spirit. What is terrible in that? Is it not rather a comfort, a pleasure, and a joy?

PRAYER

It is enough. Now, Lord, take my life. I sigh to You, my God, because in my great weakness, which is constantly increasing, I perceive plainly that the end of my life is at hand. I desire to be unclothed and be with Christ. I am not afraid of death and dying. I have often thought of it while I was well, and so it does not seem terrible to me now. As Noah's dove gladly returned to the ark, as a stranger hastens with longing to his fatherland, so I regard my death as my being received into rest out of unrest, as a happy arrival after my pilgrimage to the heavenly land of joy, where my heartfelt longings will be stilled in the heavenly embrace of my Jesus.

I know that the death of believers is a sweet slumber and a passage into the life everlasting. Wicked people and the children of this world may be afraid of death, for they know nothing about our gracious God. They are not in communion with Jesus Christ, and they have not yielded their hearts to the Holy Spirit to dwell in them. But I am not afraid to die because I am assured of all these facts. The Lord is my light and my salvation, whom shall I fear? The Lord is the strength of my life, of whom shall I be afraid? God is my Father. Jesus is my Guide and Comforter. I am going to Him. I shall be with Him, why should I fear? The Bridegroom of my soul will welcome me, His bride.

When my Jesus spoke of His impending death, He said: I go to the Father. Yes, dearest Jesus, I shall repeat these words after You: When I die, I go to the Father, to heaven, to joy, to eternal life. Why should I be afraid to die? Jesus is mine. His righteousness is mine. His merit is mine. Heaven is mine. How could I not be glad? My body returns to the earth, but my soul ascends to God. It passes from this world to heaven, from vanity into bliss, from mourning into rejoicing, from suffering into happiness, from weeping into glory. Is not this a blessed transition? I go to rest, to joy, to gladness, to light, to everlasting pleasures. Do I not see the angels even now standing about my bed to conduct my soul yonder to glory? Do I not see Jesus extending His arms to receive me, His child? Do I not see many thousands of saints ready to welcome me?

Therefore, I am without fear. I forget those things that are behind, earth and all things earthly that I possessed here, and reach for those things that are before me, the heavenly treasure that is reserved for me on high. I have fought the good fight. I have finished the race. I have kept the faith. Henceforth, there is laid up for me the crown of righteousness that the Lord, the righteous judge, will award me on that Day, and not only to me but also to all who have loved His appearing. How pleased I will be when I am unclothed! What happiness will be mine when I am in the arms of Jesus! What delight will seize me when I have passed through death to the life that never ends!

From me this is not hidden, Yet I am not afraid; I leave my cares, as bidden, To whom my vows were paid. Though life from me be taken And ev'rything I own, I trust in You unshaken And cleave to You alone. No danger, thirst, or hunger, No pain or poverty, No earthly tyrant's anger Shall ever vanquish me. Though earth should break asunder, My fortress You shall be; No fire or sword or thunder Shall sever You from me. Amen. *LSB 724:7–8*

HYMN

Jerusalem the golden,
  With milk and honey blest—
The promise of salvation,
  The place of peace and rest—
We know not, oh, we know not
  What joys await us there:
The radiancy of glory,
  The bliss beyond compare!

Within those walls of Zion
  Sounds forth the joyful song,
As saints join with the angels
  And all the martyr throng.
The Prince is ever with them;
  The daylight is serene;
The city of the blessèd
  Shines bright with glorious
  sheen.

Around the throne of David,
  The saints, from care released,
Raise loud their songs of triumph
  To celebrate the feast.
They sing to Christ their leader,
  Who conquered in the fight,
Who won for them forever
  Their gleaming robes of white.

O sweet and blessèd country,
  The home of God's elect!
O sweet and blessèd country
  That faithful hearts expect!
In mercy, Jesus, bring us
  To that eternal rest
With You and God the Father
  And Spirit, ever blest.
  LSB 672:1–4

THE SICK CONTEMPLATE THEIR GRAVE AND RESURRECTION

EXHORTATION

Jesus said to her, "I am the resurrection and the life. Whoever believes in Me, though he die, yet shall he live, and everyone who lives and believes in Me shall never die." John 11:25–26

No matter how dark the grave may look, a person viewing it as a Christian will not be terrified. For it is a chamber of rest, where we are relieved of all misery, grief, and heartache. However, while the believer's body will sleep and rest free from pain, the believer's soul will enjoy heavenly and endless joy, for the souls of the righteous are in the hands of God. No sorrow can touch them; consolations, joy, and gladness always surround them. Nor shall the body remain in the grave. When the bones and weary members have rested, they will rise again in glory on the Last Day, shine like the sun, and be reunited with the soul.

If anyone should raise the objection: "But it pains me to leave my loved ones and my possessions," that person should be reminded that in heaven there will be a general reunion. If our dear ones will remain faithful and God-fearing, they will follow us and never be separated from us. As to our earthly possessions, God will give us, instead, heavenly treasures. If the sick ponder these facts, the contemplation of the grave cannot seem horrible to them.

PRAYER

Gracious and merciful God, behold, I am ready according to Your holy will either to live or to die. I am not afraid to die because I know that death will bring me rest after so many trials and afflictions. For departing from this life I leave all my sufferings, tribulations, crosses, and unrest behind me. I enter into rest and joy. You will delight, refresh, and make me glad after I have spent gloomy nights and sorrowful days in this world. Nor am I afraid of the grave. Behold, it will be my chamber of rest. My misery, sickness, and suffering do not go into the grave with me, but must remain behind. O quiet retreat! O pleasant place of repose! When shall you enfold my weary members and my feeble body?

Jesus has hallowed the grave for me. When He was laid in the grave after He had endured all His suffering, His pain and His sorrow ceased. And so the Lord has prepared also for my body a chamber of rest in the earth, and for the soul a place of refreshment in heaven. People seek beautiful houses and soft beds for their rest, but these cannot compare with my grave. We may be driven from a beautiful house by fire, war, or other disaster, but in my grave no one will disturb me. Jesus will guard my bones that not one of them shall be lost; yes, He will gather them again out of this world. Many a person must suffer pains and discomfort even on a soft bed, but no evil will come near me and no pain shall touch me in the grave. And so the grave is a bed free from all suffering and pain. As soon as a person is laid in it, the pains and discomfort cease.

Why should I be afraid of the grave when I am not to remain in it? I know that my Redeemer lives and that He will raise me from the dust at the last day. My Jesus says, "Whoever believes in Me has eternal life, and I will raise Him up on the last day." Hence my grave is to be a place where I will tarry but a short time, where my body will sleep till Jesus comes and says, "Arise, O dead, and appear before the Judge!" The hour is coming in which all that are in their graves will hear His voice and come forth. When I shall hear that voice, I, too, will come forth from my grave. My body will be reunited with my soul, made immortal and glorified, and I will shine like the sun. All the weakness that was in me and around me will have disappeared. A grain of wheat that seemed dead when buried in the ground begins to sprout again. Thus my bones will be gathered, be furnished with sinews and arteries, and clothed with skin. It is sown in corruption, but it is raised imperishable. It is sown in weakness, but it is raised in power. It is sown a natural body, but it is raised a spiritual body, endowed with heavenly characteristics.

Sing with all the saints in glory, Sing the resurrection song! Death and sorrow, earth's dark story, To the former days belong. All around the clouds are breaking; Soon the storms of time shall cease; In God's likeness we awaken, Knowing everlasting peace. Amen.   *LSB 671:1*

HYMN

Jesus lives! The vict'ry's won!
Death no longer can appall me;
Jesus lives! Death's reign is done!
From the grave will Christ
recall me.
Brighter scenes will then
commence;
This shall be my confidence.

Jesus lives! To Him the throne
High above all things is given.
I shall go where He is gone,
Live and reign with Him in
heaven.
God is faithful; doubtings, hence!
This shall be my confidence.

Jesus lives! For me He died,
Hence will I, to Jesus living,
Pure in heart and act abide,
Praise to Him and glory giving.
All I need God will dispense;
This shall be my confidence.

Jesus lives! I know full well
Nothing me from Him shall
sever.
Neither death nor pow'rs of hell
Part me now from Christ
forever.
God will be my sure defense;
This shall be my confidence.

Jesus lives! And now is death
But the gate of life immortal;
This shall calm my trembling
breath
When I pass its gloomy portal.
Faith shall cry, as fails each sense:
Jesus is my confidence! LSB 490:1–5

BELIEVING CHRISTIANS THANK GOD FOR RESTORED HEALTH

EXHORTATION

See, you are well! Sin no more, that nothing worse may happen to you. John 5:14

It is a fact that many sick persons make lots of promises to God with their lips that they will become new creatures, pious Christians, fervent in prayer, diligent in attending the divine services, and altogether different people in heart, manner, and conduct, if only God will let them get well. But, sadly, daily experience shows that many, after they have recovered their health, do not keep these promises, but become as proud, vicious, unruly, misbehaved, and as defiant as they were before, if they do not actually become worse.

And so, when true Christians have been healed, they should recognize the almighty power of God, and praise and glorify Him who cast them down and raised them and graciously delivered them from the peril of death. The sick who have been restored to health should pay the vows they made when they were ill, and keep their promises. They made promises to God, not human beings. It is better not to make any promise than to make a promise to God and break it. If, like Hezekiah, they have gained new strength, they should return thanks to their almighty helper and deliverer, and praise and glorify God also before other people, thus giving those others an opportunity to recognize the grace of God that has been shown in their lives. They should also remember the anguish of their soul, diligently reflect on the mortal danger from which they have escaped, and lead a pious and godly life to the glory of the blessed Trinity. Yes, they should continue in faith and in godly behavior, so that they will be ready whenever God determines for them to die in peace and leave this life with joy.

PRAYER

O almighty and gracious God, I now appear before Your most holy face, and thank You from my inmost soul, because You have raised me up from my sickbed. I still remember the anxious hours, the grievous suffering, the sorrowful nights, the great danger that hovered over me. But Your mighty hand has graciously lifted me from my couch. You have placed me on my feet again that I may go in and out. Your mercy has turned my mourning into dancing. You have put off my sackcloth and girded me with gladness. Lord, You have done great things for me, and I am glad. Your love and mercy have helped me up till now. For this I know to be true, that the one who serves You will be comforted after affliction, delivered from trials, and find grace after chastening. For You, O God, take no pleasure in our destruction. After the tempest, you make the sun to shine again. After our wailing and weeping, You overwhelm us with joy. I, too, have experienced this mercy and faithfulness of my Father in my sickness, and so as long as I live I will remember the anguish of my soul.

But I will also extol—in the presence of the great congregation—what You, O almighty One, have done for me. You have blessed my medicine. You have soothed my pain. You have given me strength to overcome my affliction, after nights of toil and suffering. You have granted me days of refreshing, and have had pity on me like a father. Oh, bless the Lord, O my soul, and all that is within me, bless His holy name! Bless the Lord, O my soul, and forget not all His benefits. I will bless the Lord at all times. His praise shall continually be in my mouth. My soul shall make her boast in the Lord; the humble and other sick persons shall hear of it and be glad. O magnify the Lord with me, all you, who like me, have ever been in trouble, sickness, affliction, and let us exalt His name together. For when we poor ones cried, the Lord heard us and saved us from all our troubles. Whoever in faith looks to the Lord in affliction and calls on Him in prayer, their face shall not be ashamed. He does not let them go away sorrowful from His throne, but has compassion on them according to His mercy.

O my God, let the grace and mercy You have shown me be always before my eyes and in my heart. Now I know and have proof that You are an almighty God. You can make the dead live, restore the sick to health, make the weak strong, and give joy to the sorrowful. I was closing in on death, but Your goodness has preserved my life at this time. And so, my God, I have firmly resolved by Your grace to use the health that You have granted me, the life that You have renewed to me, and the years that by Your counsel I am still to spend in this world, for Your glory and in true godliness. Oh, in my pains and sickness I have learned that silver and gold, worldly honor and glory, even good friends, could not take away from me the burden of my cross. If it were not for Your help, I would have perished in my affliction. And so I will give up seeking after vain things and find all my delight in You. I will shun the sinful society of the world. I will go about Your altar, O Lord, with the voice of thanksgiving, and tell of all Your wondrous works. Having had this special mercy revealed to me, I will deny all ungodliness and worldly lusts, and live soberly, godly, and with righteousness in this world, so that like the wise virgins I may be ready when You come to me with the summons of death to enter the marriage feast of the Lamb in His kingdom in everlasting joy and glory!

Savior, when Your love shall call us From our struggling pilgrim way, Let not fear of death appall us, Glad Your summons to obey. May we ever, may we ever Reign with You in endless day. Amen.   *LSB 924:1–3*

HYMN

How can I thank You, Lord,
  For all Your loving-kindness,
That You have patiently
  Borne with me in my blindness!
When dead in many sins
  And trespasses I lay,
I kindled, holy God,
  Your anger ev'ry day.

It is Your work alone
  That I am now converted;
O'er Satan's work in me
  You have Your pow'r asserted.
Your mercy and Your grace
  That rise afresh each morn
Have turned my stony heart
  Into a heart newborn.

Lord, You have raised me up
  To joy and exultation
And clearly shown the way
  That leads me to salvation.
My sins are washed away;
  For this I thank You, Lord.
Now with my heart and soul
  All evil I abhor.

Grant that Your Spirit's help
  To me be always given
Lest I should fall again
  And lose the way to heaven.
Grant that He give me strength
  In my infirmity;
May He renew my heart
  To serve You willingly.

O Father, God of love,
  Now hear my supplication;
O Savior, Son of God,
  Accept my adoration;
O Holy Spirit, be
  My ever faithful guide
That I may serve You here
  And there with You abide.
      LSB 703:1–5

SCRIPTURE AND PRAYERS FOR THOSE WHO HAVE BEEN RESTORED TO HEALTH

O LORD my God, I cried to You for help, and You have healed me. Psalm 30:2

Blessed be the Lord, who has shown to me His marvelous loving-kindness. Your vows are upon me, O God. I will renew praises to You, for You have delivered my soul from death and my feet from stumbling, that I may come before You in the light of the living.

We sought the Lord in our distress; O God, in mercy hear us. Our Savior saw our helplessness And came with peace to cheer us. For this we thank and praise the Lord, Who is by one and all adored: To God all praise and glory! Amen.   *LSB 819:3*

I am not worthy of the least of all the deeds of steadfast love and all the faithfulness that You have shown to Your servant. Genesis 32:10

My God, it is nothing but mercy and love on Your part that You have delivered me from all my pains and troubles. I am altogether unworthy of all such benefits. Your faithfulness has been truly glorified in me when You dealt with me in Your loving-kindness as You promised. Let this never pass from my mind. Let me always be stirred by this remembrance to show love and faithfulness to You as long as I live, so that I may render acceptable service to You as Your good and faithful servant, and finally receive Your cheering welcome: "Enter into the joy of Your master" (Matthew 25:21).

All who confess Christ's holy name, Give God the praise and glory. Let all who know His pow'r proclaim Aloud the wondrous story. Cast ev'ry idol from its throne, For God is God, and He alone: To God all praise and glory! Amen.   *LSB 819:5*

He has redeemed my soul from going down into the pit,
and my life shall look upon the light. Behold, God does all these
things, twice, three times, with a man, to bring back his soul from
the pit, that he may be lighted with the light of life. Job 33:28–30

Lord Jesus, You have shown Yourself to me a true redeemer and deliverer because You not only kept my soul but also preserved my body when there was only a step, yes a hair's breadth, between death and me. Deliver me still from spiritual and bodily destruction. Deliver me from the hand of all my enemies. Deliver me especially from the dominion of sin. Grant me grace, that I may become a light in the Lord and walk as a child of the light. Let me serve You without fear, in holiness and righteousness before You, all the days of my life. Give me strength to keep my faith and preserve a good conscience to the end. The rest of my time in the flesh let me live, not in the lusts of the flesh, but in doing Your will, that I may thus remain united to You forever.

In Thee is gladness Amid all sadness, Jesus, sunshine of my heart. By Thee are given The gifts of heaven, Thou the true Redeemer art. Our souls Thou wakest, Our bonds Thou breakest; Who trusts Thee surely Has built securely; He stands forever: Alleluia! Our hearts are pining To see Thy shining, Dying or living To Thee are cleaving; Naught can us sever: Alleluia! Amen. *LSB 818:1*

This illness does not lead to death. It is for the glory of God.
John 11:4

I have realized, my Savior, that in me has been done what once long ago You said concerning the sickness of Your friend Lazarus. My past sickness did not lead to death, for in a manner quite glorious You have delivered me from it. To You alone belongs the glory. Let my recovery also reflect Your glory. Give me a new heart and a new mind. Let me proclaim everywhere the great things You have done for me. Give me strength to live to Your glory alone, and to praise You without ceasing with my body and with my spirit.

He never shall forsake His flock, His chosen generation; He is their refuge and their rock, Their peace and their salvation. As with a mother's tender hand, He leads His own, His chosen band: To God all praise and glory! Amen. *LSB 819:4*

See, you are well! Sin no more, that nothing worse may happen to you. John 5:14

O Lord Jesus, let me always bear in mind this warning. One well-deserved chastisement for my sins You have taken from me by delivering me from the sickness through which I have just passed. Something worse than that can easily happen to me if I again consent to sin and act contrary to Your commandment. From this graciously keep me. Guard me that from now on I may not sin purposefully, but walk before You and remain godly. Give me an undivided heart to fear Your name.

All who confess Christ's holy name, Give God the praise and glory. Let all who know His pow'r proclaim Aloud the wondrous story. Cast ev'ry idol from its throne, For God is God, and He alone: To God all praise and glory! Amen.   *LSB 819:5*

A glad heart makes a cheerful face, but by sorrow of heart the spirit is crushed. . . . All the days of the afflicted are evil, but the cheerful of heart has a continual feast. Better is a little with the fear of the Lord than great treasure and trouble with it. Better is a dinner of herbs where love is than a fattened ox and hatred with it. Proverbs 15:13, 15–17

My God, You have taught me the truth of this by my recent sickness. I have learned what vain things are property, money, prosperity, and good fortune, and how useless they are when we are deprived of good health. Yes, I have learned that this valuable gift cannot be purchased with all that we possess. Thanks be to You for this wholesome lesson! Now enable me also to heed it. Keep me from falling in love with earthly things and from prizing them more than I should. Enable me to esteem health as a precious gift, to guard it with all diligence, and to avoid everything by which I might forfeit it.

O God, my faithful God, True fountain ever flowing, Without whom nothing is, All perfect gifts bestowing: Give me a healthy frame, And may I have within A conscience free from blame, A soul unstained by sin. Amen.   *LSB 696:1*

I have sworn an oath and confirmed it, to keep your righteous rules. Psalm 119:106

During my past sickness I have frequently thought of amending my life. Frequently, too, I vowed to You, O God, that I would do so. I now renew my promise. Remind me of it often, lest I forget to pay You my vows. Give me the strength of Your Spirit to fulfill them. Make me by Your Spirit a person who walks in Your ways, keeps Your commandments, and lives according to them. Let integrity and uprightness preserve me in all my ways. Let me to the end live soberly, uprightly, and godly in this present world, in order that I may realize that godliness is profitable for all things and has the promise of this life and of that yet to come.

May we Thy precepts, Lord, fulfill And do on earth our Father's will As angels do above; Still walk in Christ, the living way, With all Thy children and obey The law of Christian love. Amen. *LSB 698:1*

Mark the blameless and behold the upright, for there is a future for the man of peace. Psalm 37:37

Dear Father, let this faithful call of Yours always echo in my heart and ring in my ears; enable me to follow it faithfully. Make me truly godly. Teach me to do Your will, for You are my God. Your Spirit is good. Lead me in the land of uprightness. Grant me strength in ever-increasing measure to pursue holiness and to do Your will. Enable me to grow and increase in faith, in love, in godliness from day to day, and bless me with prosperity while I live here.

Let me be Thine forever, My faithful God and Lord; Let me forsake Thee never Nor wander from Thy Word. Lord, do not let me waver, But give me steadfastness, And for such grace forever Thy holy name I'll bless. Amen. *LSB 689:1*

Behold, blessed is the one whom God reproves; therefore despise not the discipline of the Almighty. For He wounds, but He binds up; He shatters, but His hands heal. He will deliver you from six troubles; in seven no evil shall touch you. Job 5:17–19

How true is Your Word, O my God, for I have experienced exactly what is written here. You wounded me, but You have also bound me up. You shattered me, but Your hand has also healed me. You have delivered me from many and various troubles. Blessed be Your holy name! Perhaps some new trouble awaits me; You alone know. If it should come, grant that I may be truly prepared and ready for it, and let me rely firmly on Your Word when it comes. Let me remember how often You have gloriously helped me. Let me look to You in childlike confidence and hope, and wait until You help me again. Let me taste and see, even beneath Your chastening rod, Your good purposes concerning me, and that all things work together for good to those who love You.

While life's dark maze I tread And griefs around me spread, Be Thou my guide; Bid darkness turn to day, Wipe sorrow's tears away, Nor let me ever stray From Thee aside. Amen.　　　　　　　　*LSB 702:3*

　　So you also must consider yourselves dead to sin and alive to God in Christ Jesus. Romans 6:11

My God, You have spared my life and given me a new opportunity to live. And so it belongs to You alone. Constantly remind me that I must consecrate my life to You alone. Let me daily die to sin and live for righteousness. Let me live to Your glory, and order all that I do or refrain from doing according to Your will. Let me always find favor in Your sight through Jesus Christ, my Lord. Renew me by Your grace from day to day, and make me to be a living sacrifice, holy and acceptable to You. Keep me in Your fellowship to the end that no one may pluck me out of Your hand.

Finish then Thy new creation, Pure and spotless let us be; Let us see Thy great salvation Perfectly restored in Thee, Changed from glory into glory, Till in heav'n we take our place, Till we cast our crowns before Thee, Lost in wonder, love, and praise! Amen.　　　　　　*LSB 700:4*

BOOK IV

FOR THE USE OF THE DYING AND THOSE ATTENDING THEM

THE DYING PERSON PLACES HIMSELF BEFORE THE JUDGMENT SEAT OF GOD

EXHORTATION

For we must all appear before the judgment seat of Christ, so that each one may receive what is due for what he has done in the body, whether good or evil. 2 Corinthians 5:10

"But if we judged ourselves truly, we would not be judged" says St. Paul (1 Corinthians 11:31). Indeed, if we examine our life of our own accord, charge ourselves with our wrongdoing, and pray for pardon for Christ's sake, God will not judge and condemn us, but He will be gracious to us. For whoever confesses their iniquities and quits them will obtain mercy.

Now the dying, too, should do this. They should reflect that they will have to appear before Christ's judgment seat, for it is appointed that we die once and after that comes the Judgment. Now this takes place immediately after death, when the soul must at once appear before God. If in this world you have been a believer and led a godly life, you will not be condemned; because your sins were forgiven you on earth for the sake of the blood of Jesus Christ, they are no longer remembered in heaven, but remain forgiven. But the ungodly must appear before the divine judgment seat because they died without being reconciled to God. The dying, then, do well to seek reconciliation now, to ask God for forgiveness for the sake of the blood of Christ, and in that way obtain mercy. Thus, the dying are assured that, no matter when and where they die, by a sudden or a slow death, God will graciously receive their souls and will on the Last Day raise their bodies to joy everlasting because they have been justified by the blood of Jesus.

PRAYER

I know, O God, that it is appointed unto men once to die, but after this comes the Judgment. And so I place myself now before Your judgment seat while I am yet living, and wish to be reconciled with You before I die. O righteous God, since I do not know how long it will be before I depart from this world, behold, I come before Your judgment and accuse myself. I acknowledge that I am a great sinner. I have transgressed all Your holy commandments, often and knowingly. I have not loved You with my whole heart, with all my soul, with all my strength. I have not always followed in the footsteps of my Jesus. I have not always allowed the Holy Spirit to lead me, as I should have done. I remember that I was made Your child in Holy Baptism, but I have not always lived as Your child. I have often made many promises to You at confession and Communion, but have kept few and have repeatedly been conformed to the world. O Lord, I have not done what is right. The load of my sins weighs me down. I have not walked in the way You appointed for me. My iniquities have gone over my head; as a heavy burden they are too much for me to bear.

O gracious God, You have promised that You have no pleasure in the death of the wicked, but that the wicked turn from his way and live. See, I come now, desiring to make my peace with You, while I am still sound in my mind and can recall my past life. Oh, I repent of all my sins. I prostrate myself before Your tribunal and say: Lord God, Father in heaven, have mercy on me! Lord God, Son, the Savior of the world, have mercy on me! Lord God, Holy Spirit, have mercy on me! O Father, I take refuge in Your mercy and confess that I have sinned in Your sight and am no longer worthy to be called Your child. Yet I pray You to be merciful to Your child and not to cast me away because of my transgressions. I flee to You, O Jesus, my advocate! Oh, intercede now for me, a poor sinner, in the hour of my death. For if anyone sins, we have an advocate with the Father, Jesus Christ, the Righteous One. He is the propitiation for the sins of the whole world. Oh, pardon my iniquities for the sake of Your blood, and let me find mercy at the bar of strict justice because of Your holy wounds. Have mercy on me, O God, according to Your loving-kindness. According to Your tender mercies blot out my transgressions. O blessed Holy Spirit, I flee to You! Create in me a clean heart. Bear witness to me that I am a child of God, and that I have received God's favor. Yes, work in me a sincere repentance, a living faith, and a holy resolve to live only to Your glory and to die in childlike obedience to You.

Yes, work in me holy thoughts, devout supplications, and sweet meditations on death. Grant me a refreshing contemplation of heaven and of the future glory. Let my heart hear the comforting words: "My child, be of good cheer; your sins are forgiven you." Then I shall not be afraid to die because I know that the sins that have been forgiven here are forgiven also in heaven. O Holy Trinity, have mercy on me. Let me find grace with You at my departure from this world, and do not charge against me anything that I have ever done amiss, but have compassion on me according to your love.

When life's brief course on earth is run And I this world am leaving, Grant me to say, "Your will be done," Your faithful Word believing. My dearest Friend, I now commend My soul into Your keeping; From sin and hell, and death as well, By You the vict'ry reaping. Amen.   *LSB 758:4*

HYMN

The day is surely drawing near
When Jesus, God's anointed,
In all His power shall appear
As judge whom God appointed.
Then fright shall banish idle mirth,
And flames on flames shall ravage earth
As Scripture long has warned us.

The final trumpet then shall sound
  And all the earth be shaken,
And all who rest beneath the ground
  Shall from their sleep awaken.
But all who live will in that hour,
By God's almighty, boundless pow'r,
  Be changed at His commanding.

The books are opened then to all,
  A record truly telling
What each has done, both great and small,
  When he on earth was dwelling,
And ev'ry heart be clearly seen,
And all be known as they have been
  In thoughts and words and actions.

Then woe to those who scorned the Lord
  And sought but carnal pleasures,
Who here despised His precious Word
  And loved their earthly treasures!
With shame and trembling they will stand
And at the judge's stern command
  To Satan be delivered.

My Savior paid the debt I owe
  And for my sin was smitten;
Within the Book of Life I know
  My name has now been written.
I will not doubt, for I am free,
And Satan cannot threaten me;
  There is no condemnation!

May Christ our intercessor be
  And through His blood and merit
Read from His book that we are free
  With all who life inherit.
Then we shall see Him face to face,
With all His saints in that blest place
  Which He has purchased for us.

O Jesus Christ, do not delay,
  But hasten our salvation;
We often tremble on our way
  In fear and tribulation.
O hear and grant our fervent plea:
Come, mighty judge, and set us free
  From death and ev'ry evil. LSB 508:1–7

THE DYING PERSON FORGIVES AND ASKS TO BE FORGIVEN

EXHORTATION

For if you forgive others their trespasses, your heavenly Father will also forgive you, but if you do not forgive others their trespasses, neither will your Father forgive your trespasses.
Matthew 6:14–15

It is a part of true preparation for dying in peace that we are to be reconciled with our fellow human beings. The dying should not delay this reconciliation but attend to it at once.

However, the dying should bear in mind that if others have done many things to spite them, they must not take any grudge against their enemies and offenders with them to the grave, but must heartily forgive them and, if possible, show them by kindness or through good friends that they have been forgiven. However, if the dying have caused others grief and offended them, they should not rest until they have been reconciled. Yes, they should not be ashamed to ask those they have offended to come to their dying bed so that they can ask forgiveness of them with heart, lips, and hands. Or, if they live far away, they must contact them and ask forgiveness. Or, if they are dead, they must implore forgiveness from God for the wrong done to them.

At the same time, the dying should also restore to their fellow neighbors or their heirs anything they have stolen, filched, or wrongfully taken, because sin cannot be forgiven if a person is unwilling to restore what can be restored or its equivalent. The dying should feel impelled to seek such reconciliation, not only by their duty as Christians but also by the divine command and threat in Matthew 6:15, and they should remember that if they are unwilling to forgive, neither will they ever obtain mercy from God. As we deal with our enemies, that is how God deals with us.

PRAYER

My God, I live, yet I do not know for how long. I must die, and I know not when. So I will seek reconciliation with my fellow human beings, that I may depart from this world with peace in my heart. Heaven is called the home of peace—no souls that are irreconcilable, revengeful, and filled with wrath and hatred will be admitted into it, but driven back. Therefore, I will purge my heart from all anger and animosity. I will gladly forgive and ask to be forgiven, so that God for Jesus' sake may graciously receive me as a person who wishes to be reconciled. I am still on the way to eternity, and so I will lay aside all enmity in the certain confidence that as I forgive from the heart, I will also be forgiven.

Therefore, I forgive right now from my inmost heart all my enemies, all who have opposed me, and all who have hurt me by words, deeds, or gestures. I pardon and forgive them not only with my lips but also in my heart in the presence of God. I will never again remember what they have done to me; I will forget it. To assure them that I am reconciled with them, I wish them everything good and will seek to do them good wherever and whenever I am able. Yes, I ask God to bless them and let it be well with them and their children now and in eternity.

And as I now from my heart pardon and have forgiven all who have ever angered me, or ever hurt or grieved me, so I also ask forgiveness now of all those whom I have ever offended, or in any way injured or grieved. O my dear friends, forgive me all for the love of Jesus; do not bear a grudge. I admit that I have wronged you; I ask your forgiveness with my heart, mouth, and hand. Would to God I could see you all here at my deathbed, I would ask you each personally to forgive me.

Yes, graciously forgive me, O merciful God, all the grief I have caused my fellow human beings while I lived, no matter who they may be, no matter whether I did it maliciously or in weakness, intentionally or not. Oh, forgive me for Your mercy's sake. From now on I cast out of my heart all enmity. I will not avenge myself or think of any wrong that I have suffered. Oh, remember not my sins and iniquities. O my heavenly Father, have mercy on me. O my Jesus, wash me clean from sins and intercede for me. O Holy Spirit, sanctify my heart and cleanse it from all unrighteousness. Thus I die cheerfully and at peace.

And thus I live in God contented And die without a thought of fear; My soul has to God's plans consented, For through His Son my faith is clear. O God, for Jesus' sake I pray Your peace may bless my dying day.

LSB 598:3

HYMN

I am trusting Thee, Lord Jesus,
  Trusting only Thee;
Trusting Thee for full salvation,
  Great and free.

I am trusting Thee for pardon;
  At Thy feet I bow,
For Thy grace and tender mercy
  Trusting now.

I am trusting Thee for cleansing
  In the crimson flood;
Trusting Thee to make me holy
  By Thy blood.

I am trusting Thee to guide me;
  Thou alone shalt lead,
Ev'ry day and hour supplying
  All my need.

I am trusting Thee for power;
  Thine can never fail.
Words which Thou Thyself shalt give me
  Must prevail.

I am trusting Thee, Lord Jesus;
  Never let me fall.
I am trusting Thee forever
  And for all. LSB 729:1–6

THE DYING BIDS DEAR ONES FAREWELL WITH A BLESSING

EXHORTATION

And now I commend you to God and to the word of His grace, which is able to build you up and to give you the inheritance among all those who are sanctified. Acts 20:32

It often is recorded in Holy Scripture that persons close to death bid farewell to their loved ones and friends, and that they give their children, if they have any, their blessing. In the cases of Moses, Isaac, Jacob, our Lord Jesus Christ, and others this is clearly seen. Now, this blessing is not pointless. Because it is a farewell prayer of a dying person offered in faith to God in the name of Christ it will not remain unanswered.

Survivors have had these dying words impressed deeply on them. The admonition of a dying father, departing mother, or a friend is not soon forgotten, but remains fastened in the mind to spur proper conduct.

While it is praiseworthy that a dying person bids farewell to the world with prayers, blessings, and good wishes, the dying should be careful not to wish evil to anyone, for such a desire for revenge is utterly unfitting for a child of God. Children should be admonished not to grieve or cause heartache to their parents in days of their health, and thus make it impossible for their parents to leave them with their blessing. The parents' curse has often changed a child's fortune to misfortune. However, godly Christian parents give even to the children that disappoint them a blessing rather than a curse.

PRAYER

O eternal, kind, and great God, I do not know how near my end may be, when You will issue Your command and summon me out of this world. Therefore, I wish to prepare for my death in time, and especially turn to You with prayer and singing, because this is the best means to delight and strengthen me in my weakness. Whenever I sing or pray in my grief, I experience new courage arising in me, and Your Spirit witnesses to me that this is the foretaste of eternal bliss.

I will now prepare myself for the life to come and attend to those things I have left. And so I bid farewell to all my relatives, acquaintances, benefactors, and friends. O great God, I commend them to Your protection, love, and grace. For all the love and favors that they have shown me, richly reward them for me, as I cannot repay them. I leave my friends, family, and acquaintances, but, O God, do not forsake them. Keep them in Your fear, in faith, and in godliness, so that we may see each other in the life everlasting.

I go the way of all flesh; I go ahead, but in heaven all the believers and children of God will meet again. O faithful God, shower Your abundant blessing on those I leave behind who will be in sadness and pain over my departure from this world. The Lord bless you, my loved and dear ones. May He bless you in body and soul! May He always be your Father, provider, and sustainer. May He take you into His protection. May His fatherly mercy take care of all that you need and protect you always from all evil. Fear God and do right at all times. Put your trust in Him and know that He will be gracious to you and will have compassion on you. Do not turn from Him by unbelief, wickedness, and unchristian conduct, but be faithful to Him unto death, and He will give you a crown of life. Do not forsake God, and He will not forsake you. Honor Him, serve Him, love Him, and obey Him. Yes, the God of all grace and mercy bless your going out and your coming in, that you may be and remain blessed of the Lord.

O great God, I have blessed them; let them be blessed. And now I lay myself in Your arms, O Blessed Trinity. Take my soul and receive it to everlasting joy. I desire to depart and to be with Christ. Lord Jesus, I live to You and to You I die; living and dying I am Yours.

For me to live is Jesus, To die is gain for me; So when my Savior pleases, I meet death willingly. Amen. *LSB 742:1*

HYMN

For all the saints who from their labors rest,
Who Thee by faith before the world confessed,
Thy name, O Jesus, be forever blest.
    Alleluia! Alleluia!

Thou wast their rock, their fortress, and their might;
Thou, Lord, their captain in the well-fought fight;
Thou, in the darkness drear, their one true light.
    Alleluia! Alleluia!

Oh, may Thy soldiers, faithful, true, and bold,
Fight as the saints who nobly fought of old
And win with them the victor's crown of gold!
    Alleluia! Alleluia!

Oh, blest communion, fellowship divine!
We feebly struggle, they in glory shine;
Yet all are one in Thee, for all are Thine.
    Alleluia! Alleluia!

And when the fight is fierce, the warfare long,
Steals on the ear the distant triumph song,
And hearts are brave again, and arms are strong.
    Alleluia! Alleluia!

The golden evening brightens in the west;
Soon, soon to faithful warriors cometh rest;
Sweet is the calm of paradise the blest.
  Alleluia! Alleluia!

But, lo, there breaks a yet more glorious day:
The saints triumphant rise in bright array;
The King of Glory passes on His way.
  Alleluia! Alleluia!

From earth's wide bounds, from ocean's farthest coast,
Through gates of pearl streams in the countless host,
Singing to Father, Son, and Holy Ghost:
  Alleluia! Alleluia! LSB 677:1–8

THE DYING PERSON
COMMENDS THE
SOUL TO GOD

EXHORTATION

Into Your hand I commit my spirit; You have redeemed me, O LORD, *faithful God.* Psalm 31:5

Often dying persons have many things to set in order and arrange before their death. They want to set their houses in order, and, while doing so, may be tempted to forget what is most valuable: their souls! But to act thus is very unwise and just plain wrong. Sincere Christians should rather commend their souls as well as their bodies each night when they go to bed and each morning when they rise to the protection of God because they do not know what God will decree concerning them during that day or night.

But if godly Christians are doing this every day, dying persons should do this even more so. They have before them the example of their Savior. When He was about to die, He said "Father, into Your hands I commit My spirit" (Luke 23:46). Stephen did the same. While being stoned, he cried: "Lord Jesus, receive my spirit" (Acts 7:59). Such care for the soul is pleasing to God; and by it a person manifests faith and trust in God. However, this is also highly necessary. We witness many changes and accidents in dying persons. How wise it is then to commend the soul to God while the person is still of sound mind, and thus to put the best treasure of all (the soul) into safekeeping, while, as regards all other things, the dying simply resign themselves to God's will for life or death. When all things have been thus put in order, a person dies in peace.

PRAYER

Merciful and loving God, You turn men to destruction and say, Return, you children of men. You take Your beloved ones to Yourself through death and make them partakers of the glory that our Lord Jesus purchased for us by His bitter suffering and death. I see that my weakness is a voice calling to me: "Here is the bridegroom! Come out to meet him" (Matthew 25:6). "Stay dressed for action and keep your lamps burning" (Luke 12:35). "Blessed are those servants whom the master finds awake when he comes" (Luke 12:37). "Set your house in order, for you shall die" (2 Kings 20:1).

Now, as I do not know when my hour will be at hand, I will yield myself to You in time and commit my soul with all its powers into Your keeping. Let my heart be emptied of all worldly, sinful, and wicked thoughts, that I may speak of You, picture to myself Your glory, and unceasingly contemplate the joy of the elect, which also awaits me. Fill my heart with Your Holy Spirit, that He may create good impulses in me. Help me to remember Jesus Christ, and always to keep before my eyes the blood that He shed and His death.

When my last hour is at hand, preserve me, according to Your holy will, from temptations, from thoughts that weigh heavy on the soul, from great pains and unbecoming behavior. Let me keep my sound mind till the end, until I expire, so that my heart, lips, and spirit may sing, speak, and pray to You. And if I should lose my speech, make me enjoy Your sweetness in my heart and feel Your most holy presence.

Give me by Your grace cheerfulness to die. Let me in my dying moment glimpse the pleasures of the blessed, and then let me taste a few drops of heaven's sweetness, that I may go from here in full joy and consolation. When my soul quits my body, I commend it to You; receive it into Your hands, O Father. Into your hands I commend my soul. Yes, Lord Jesus, receive my spirit. Cover it with Your perfect righteousness and conduct it to the marriage feast, like a child to its inheritance, until it shall be reunited with my body on the Last Day. Yes, I also commit to You my body in the cool earth. Grant it undisturbed rest until the last trumpet sounds and you call: "Awake, O sleeper, and arise from the dead, and Christ will shine on you" (Ephesians 5:14). And then let me gladly and happily arise to the life that never ends, for Jesus' sake.

Lord, let at last Thine angels come, To Abr'ham's bosom bear me home, That I may die unfearing; And in its narrow chamber keep My body safe in peaceful sleep Until Thy reappearing. And then from death awaken me, That these mine eyes with joy may see, O Son of God, Thy glorious face, My Savior and my fount of grace. Lord Jesus Christ, my prayer attend, my prayer attend, And I will praise Thee without end. Amen.

LSB 708:3

HYMN

Abide with me, fast falls the eventide.
The darkness deepens; Lord, with me abide.
When other helpers fail and comforts flee,
Help of the helpless, O abide with me.

I need Thy presence ev'ry passing hour;
What but Thy grace can foil the tempter's pow'r?
Who like Thyself my guide and stay can be?
Through cloud and sunshine, O abide with me.

Come not in terrors, as the King of kings,
But kind and good, with healing in Thy wings;
Tears for all woes, a heart for ev'ry plea.
Come, Friend of sinners, thus abide with me.

Swift to its close ebbs out life's little day;
Earth's joys grow dim, its glories pass away;
Change and decay in all around I see;
O Thou who changest not, abide with me.

I fear no foe with Thee at hand to bless;
Ills have no weight and tears no bitterness.
Where is death's sting? Where, grave, thy victory?
I triumph still if Thou abide with me!

Hold Thou Thy cross before my closing eyes;
Shine through the gloom, and point me to the skies.
Heav'n's morning breaks, and earth's vain shadows flee;
In life, in death, O Lord, abide with me. LSB 878:1–6

THE DYING CONTEMPLATE HEAVEN

EXHORTATION

But he, full of the Holy Spirit, gazed into heaven and saw the
glory of God, and Jesus standing at the right hand of God. And
he said, "Behold, I see the heavens opened, and the Son of Man
standing at the right hand of God." Acts 7:55–56

Nothing is sweeter or more pleasant to believers than to think of God and of heaven. In heaven is our home, our fatherland, our consolation, our heritage, our crown, our glory, our desire, our joy. Our body is on earth, but our soul is with God; our work is here, but our thoughts are there.

If that is the state of believers, what should the dying do? The dying will experience many sad things: the gathering darkness, the farewell from loved ones, the tears of bystanders, the last agony, and the like. Yet all this can be sweetened for them if they fix their heart beyond the skies to which they are headed. As opposed to the earth that is growing dim around them, they place the glory of heaven, where all is bathed in a light that does not fade. During the painful leave-taking, they can think of the holy angels and the company of the saints in heaven, whose companionship they will enjoy forever. There are no good-byes there. When they see their dear ones weeping, let them remind themselves of the everlasting joy, gladness, and bliss that awaits them in the life eternal, where there are no more sighing, sorrows, or tears.

Yes, even agony should cause no fright because they die in the arms of Jesus and in the fellowship of the Holy Spirit. To those who occupy their mind with such heavenly thoughts—picturing the crown, the white robe, the glory of heaven—to them even their dying bed becomes a paradise.

PRAYER

O gracious God, how great is Your love and mercy toward us mortals! Not only do You do us good, sending us help, hearing our prayers, having mercy on us, and overwhelming us with many blessings during our life, but You have reserved even more and glorious treasures in heaven for us. For in heaven, O God, what great gifts will be ours!

By faith, then, I picture to myself even now Your great majesty and glory, the splendor in which You dwell, the many thousands of seraphim, all the angels and the elect, that is, all godly persons who have ever lived on earth, standing around Your throne, praising and magnifying You, and shouting Holy, holy, holy, to the glory of Your name. Yes, I picture to myself that it will not be long till I shall be among them, after I have fallen asleep calmly and peacefully. I call to mind the glorious crown that I shall wear on my head, and the white robe with which I shall be clothed, yes, and that I myself will shine like the sun.

O the glory! O the bliss! O the gladness that the Father of all grace and mercy will bestow on me for Jesus' sake! And so I am not frightened by death because it will open the door for me to all this glory. If an earthly king can decorate his palace with so much glory that people are amazed and do not become weary in admiring it, how great and glorious will be the magnificence of the heavenly King and the splendor of the infinite God! Therefore I will gladly die and leave this earth. I behold heaven with joy; for there is my eternal home.

Here I have no lasting city anyway. The home that Jesus, my Savior, has purchased for me by His suffering and death is the only home that lasts. I will enter it by faith in Him. When I look to heaven, I am reminded that is where my fatherland is, where all godly Christians and believers are assembled. While I am in the world, I am a pilgrim and a stranger journeying continuously, but when I have arrived in heaven through a happy death, I enter into rest, peace, and eternal happiness. I look up to heaven with joy and say to myself: There is my heritage. If I have a great heritage here on earth, in heaven there is laid up for me an inheritance undefiled that does not fade away. I reflect that heaven is the

paradise where God will delight the believers, and that in comparison
with it the paradise on earth is a mere shadow. My God, when I will see
Your glory in heaven, I will say to You, as the Queen of Sheba once said
to Solomon: O my God, O my Jesus, the half of Your glory was not told
me in my earthly life. Your glory and Your prosperity exceed anything
that I have heard.

Come, O Christ, and loose the chains that bind us; Lead us forth and
cast this world behind us. With You, the Anointed, Finds the soul its joy
and rest appointed. Amen.

LSB 679:5

HYMN

Jerusalem the golden,
  With milk and honey blest—
The promise of salvation,
  The place of peace and rest—
We know not, oh, we know not
  What joys await us there:
The radiancy of glory,
  The bliss beyond compare!

Within those walls of Zion
  Sounds forth the joyful song,
As saints join with the angels
  And all the martyr throng.
The Prince is ever with them;
  The daylight is serene;
The city of the blessèd
  Shines bright with glorious
  sheen.

Around the throne of David,
  The saints, from care released,
Raise loud their songs of triumph
  To celebrate the feast.
They sing to Christ their leader,
  Who conquered in the fight,
Who won for them forever
  Their gleaming robes of white.

O sweet and blessèd country,
  The home of God's elect!
O sweet and blessèd country
  That faithful hearts expect!
In mercy, Jesus, bring us
  To that eternal rest
With You and God the Father
  And Spirit, ever blest.

LSB 672:1–4

THE DYING MEDITATE ON GOD'S PROMISES

EXHORTATION

Come, you who are blessed by My Father, inherit the kingdom prepared for you from the foundation of the world. Matthew 25:34

Dying persons need relief and refreshing for the soul as well as for the body. But what can refresh the soul? Not gold or silver, not honor or earthly splendor, but the Word of God. David says of this Word: "Your Word is the joy of my heart" (see Psalm 119:111). For this reason we should, while we are well, gather and store in our heart beautiful passages of comfort, that we may have an abundant supply in the agony of death.

Dying persons, however, should especially remind themselves, or be reminded, of the divine promises that we find in the Holy Scriptures regarding God's help, assistance, presence, and grace. They should, moreover, appropriate these comforting passages and promises as if God was speaking directly to them and was giving these promises to them personally. For in the Holy Scriptures God speaks to all in general and to each person specifically.

Having these promises before their eyes, they should put their trust in them and not doubt that God will fulfill them also in their case. If God does not do so this very minute or in an hour, if He delays the fulfillment, He will nevertheless gloriously redeem His promises in His own time.

PRAYER

O God, rich in mercy, how sweet are the promises You have made me in Your Word. I am assured You will be with me in trouble and that You will deliver me, for You say: "Fear not, for I am with you" (Isaiah 43:5). "Do not be dismayed, for the Lord your God is with you" (Joshua 1:9). My Jesus has said: "Where I am, there will My servant be also" (John 12:26). And, "In my Father's house are many rooms. . . . And if I go and prepare a place for you, I will come again and will take you to Myself, that where

I am you may be also" (John 14:2–3). Yes, what a sweet consolation when I am assured that Jesus intercedes for me and is my advocate, and that the Holy Spirit also prays for me with groans too deep for words.

O gracious God, fulfill all these promises in me now! My distress is continually becoming greater. Be with me and abide with me in my last agony. Let me enter glory and occupy the place that You have prepared for me. O Jesus, be now my advocate. Plead for me, a poor sinner, that I may obtain grace and mercy. O blessed Holy Spirit, assist me in my weakness, and give me power and strength. If a severe struggle is before me, help me to conquer and overcome. If I have to climb a steep mountain, give me strength. If there is a critical hour before me, help me pass through it. When my lips can no longer pray, make intercession for me before God with groans that cannot be uttered; yes, carry my feeble sighs up to God.

O God, rich in grace, I cling to Your promises and believe that You will fulfill them in me, a poor, wretched sinner, according to Your mercy. I believe Your Word; I trust in Your Word. When You said, seek My face, my heart said to you: Your face, Lord, I will seek. Your Word has always been the consolation and joy of my life; let it be my comfort and refreshment now in the hour of death. When the time comes that for peace I have great bitterness, in love deliver my soul from the pit of corruption. Refresh me when the sweat of death begins. Cheer me when my lips grow pallid. Comfort me when hearing and sight fail me. O Blessed Trinity, let me hear in my heart joy and gladness, the voice of jubilation and rejoicing, as a prelude and foretaste of heavenly glory.

Then let us praise the Father And worship God the Son And sing to God the Spirit, Eternal Three in One, Till all the ransomed number Fall down before the throne, Ascribing pow'r and glory And praise to God alone. Amen. *LSB 517:3*

HYMN

Lord, dismiss us with Your blessing,
    Fill our hearts with joy and peace;
Let us each, Your love possessing,
    Triumph in redeeming grace.
O refresh us, O refresh us,
Trav'ling through this wilderness.

Thanks we give and adoration
For Your Gospel's joyful sound.
May the fruits of Your salvation
In our hearts and lives abound.
Ever faithful, ever faithful
To Your truth may we be found.

Savior, when Your love shall call us
From our struggling pilgrim way,
Let not fear of death appall us,
Glad Your summons to obey.
May we ever, may we ever
Reign with You in endless day. LSB 924:1–3

THE DYING CONTEMPLATE THE JOY AND FELLOWSHIP OF HEAVEN

EXHORTATION

After this I looked, and behold, a great multitude that no one
could number, from every nation, from all tribes and peoples
and languages, standing before the throne and before the Lamb,
clothed in white robes, with palm branches in their hands, and
crying out with a loud voice, "Salvation belongs to our God who
sits on the throne, and to the Lamb!" Revelation 7:9–10

Could the dying picture anything sweeter and more pleasant than the joy and fellowship of heaven—a thought that often delights the godly person on earth? Indeed, the dying should regard everything that they behold on earth as things that they must leave soon and will never see again. They should meditate on heaven and eagerly think of the future joy of heaven, how after departing from this life they will be translated to the joys and splendor of that heavenly homeland, where there is nothing but light, peace, joy, consolation, and glory, where everlasting raptures will delight them in place of their former sufferings and pains.

The dying should also engage in meditations on the heavenly fellowship, how they will soon behold the face of the Blessed Trinity and meet so many thousands of angels and the chosen people of God. When the dying thus picture to themselves this heavenly fellowship and their future bliss, their suffering will be sweetened and the time of it shortened for them; yes, on account of it, they will feel their soul stirred with holy emotions.

PRAYER

How lovely is Your dwelling place, O Lord of hosts. My soul longs, yes, faints for the courts of the Lord. Oh, when shall I come where I shall see Your face and stand before Your throne with all the angels and Your chosen people? What great glory and bliss will I meet when I shall have departed from this body and died in peace, because I will be translated into the home of peace, crowned with glory and honor, and be made a partaker of the splendor of heaven! What glory and joy await me! I shall behold the Blessed Trinity face-to-face. What I have believed here, I shall see there. What I could not comprehend here, I will perfectly know and perceive there. There I shall be completely suffused with light, illumined and filled with the light of heaven. What joy it will be to look upon the great, majestic God in His glory!

And so I sigh and pray with longing: As the deer pants for the streams, so my soul pants for You, O God. My soul thirsts for the living God. When shall I come and appear before Him? The highest joy is to see God, in whom we have believed here, though we have never seen Him. This vision will constitute my highest delight, my greatest sweetness, and my most perfect bliss. My sorrow will be changed into joy, my weeping into shouts of triumph, my tribulation into rapture, my misery into delight, my afflictions into consolation, my heart's anguish into abundant glory.

In heaven I will also live in a joyful and blessed fellowship. Here I am among human beings—yes, I have had to pass my life among friends and foes—but in glory I shall meet so many thousands of holy angels, hovering in great splendor and light around the throne of God and singing: "Holy, holy, holy, Lord God of Sabaoth!" I shall there meet all the godly and elect who have ever lived since the beginning of the world. I shall meet my dear ones and friends who have died in faith before me, and shall live in sweetest communion with them. How satisfied my soul will be then! Then my longing will become embracing. I shall be with the Lord, and no sorrow will touch me. And this shall last not only an hour or a year, but forever and ever, without end.

O sweet and blessed country, The home of God's elect! O sweet and blessed country That faithful hearts expect! In mercy, Jesus, bring us To that eternal rest With You and God the Father And Spirit, ever blest. Amen. *LSB 672:4*

HYMN

Oh, what their joy and their glory must be,
Those endless Sabbaths the blessèd ones see!
Crowns for the valiant, to weary ones rest;
God shall be all, and in all ever blest.

In new Jerusalem joy shall be found,
Blessings of peace shall forever abound;
Wish and fulfillment are not severed there,
Nor the things prayed for come short of the prayer.

We, where no trouble distraction can bring,
Safely the anthems of Zion shall sing;
While for Your grace, Lord, their voices of praise
Your blessèd people shall evermore raise.

Now let us worship our Lord and our King,
Joyfully raising our voices to sing:
Praise to the Father, and praise to the Son,
Praise to the Spirit, to God, Three in One.

LSB 675:1–4

THE DYING TAKE COMFORT IN THE PROMISED ASSISTANCE OF THE BLESSED TRINITY

EXHORTATION

His left hand is under my head, and his right hand embraces me! Song of Solomon 2:6

The presence of God in our suffering cannot but be sweet and comforting to the soul. God, however, is not only present with all His creatures; to the believers He is near also with His special presence in life as in death, as He has promised: "Behold, I am with you always, to the end of the age" (Matthew 28:20). Oh, if God were to open the eyes of the godly—as He did to Elisha's servant—they would see gathered around their bed so many angels rejoicing that they may conduct another soul to glory! For frequently godly persons at the moment of their death have joyfully exclaimed and said, "How light it is around my bed! Do you not see that bright light there?" Surely that must have been a vision of God's holy angels.

However, believers should be assured especially of the assistance of the Blessed Trinity. The Father in heaven will remember His fatherly faithfulness and come to the aid of His child. Jesus will not forsake in their last agony the souls He has purchased at the price of His own blood. The Holy Spirit also will refresh them in that hour with His strong consolations. Let hearing and sight fail; let all the senses fail; still the dying know that God will be faithful to His promises even in their dying hour: "I will be with him in trouble." Blessed is the person whom God permits to experience all this at death!

PRAYER

Come, Lord Jesus! Thus I say now with the whole Church on earth; Yes, come and take my soul to Yourself. I have even now tasted Your sweetness, and I am longing and thirsting for the full stream. I do not regard dying as something terrible, for I die in the love of my heavenly Father. The Father has provided for me, nourished me, led me, and guided me all my life. Will He now leave me because the end of my life is at hand? Never. He loves me too dearly for that. If a father stays with his sick child and helps him as much as he can, how much more can I comfort myself with the almighty and powerful aid of my Father in heaven! My heavenly Father will not deny me the heritage that Jesus has acquired for me by His death. He will bid me enter the Kingdom He has prepared for me from the foundation of the world.

Dying does not seem terrible to me. I die united with Jesus Christ. This union has begun here by faith and will never be abolished. In this union I am a living member in the Body of which Christ is the Head. If the head knows well the condition of the members, my Jesus, too, knows my condition now. I am in Him, and He is in me, and in holy union with Him I am now ready to die. He has said: "I am with you always, to the end of the age" (Matthew 28:20). And so He will be with me also in my dying hour. As He loved His own until the end, when He gave Himself into death for them, He loves them also when they are about to die. If, then, I am in the arms of Jesus, death is not terrible to me because I have Him who by His death has taken away the bitterness of dying. Jesus has even here put on me the garments of salvation and clothed me with the robe of His righteousness. Yonder He will robe me in the white garment of honor and glory. The Bridegroom of my soul leads me to the marriage feast. The Lover of my soul makes me share His glory. My Lord fulfills for me now what He has said: "Where I am, there will My servant be also" (John 12:26).

Death is not terrible to me. I die in the fellowship of the Holy Spirit. During my present life, He has consecrated my heart to be a temple. He will remain united with me even in death. He who has so often comforted me in my affliction, gladdened me in my suffering, refreshed me in my misery, sustained me under my cross, He will not forsake me in the last hour, but will bear witness with my spirit that I am certainly God's child. If I should even lose my speech and no longer be able to pray aloud, He will make intercession for me with groans too deep for words. Yes, since He is the down payment of our inheritance, He assures me even now that I am an heir of heaven and shall enter into complete possession of it. The Father holds out to me the crown. Jesus leads me by the right hand into joy. The Holy Spirit adorns me with light and bliss. The holy angels rejoice over my entrance into the heavenly life of joy. All the elect and godly receive me with rejoicing.

All honor, praise, and majesty To Father, Son, and Spirit be, Our God forever glorious, In whose rich grace We run our race Till we depart victorious. *LSB 734:5*

HYMN

Father most holy, merciful, and tender;
Jesus, our Savior, with the Father reigning;
Spirit of comfort, advocate, defender,
*   Light never waning;*

Trinity blessèd, unity unshaken,
Goodness unbounded, very God of heaven,
Light of the angels, joy of those forsaken,
*   Hope of all living,*

Maker of all things, all Thy creatures praise Thee;
All for Thy worship were and are created;
Now, as we also worship Thee devoutly,
*   Hear Thou our voices.*

Lord God Almighty, unto Thee be glory,
One in three persons, over all exalted!
Glory we offer, praise Thee and adore Thee,
*   Now and forever. LSB 504:1–4*

THE DYING PERSON IS READY TO FALL ASLEEP IN JESUS

EXHORTATION

Lord Jesus, receive my spirit. Acts 7:59

Dying persons frequently complain that they are distracted with all sorts of thoughts that will not let up or go away. To dispel them, believers do well if by faith and in holy contemplation they picture to themselves Jesus upon the cross, and at the same time resolve in their heart these pious thoughts: The wounds of Jesus were inflicted for my sake; they shall be my only refuge in death. For me also the blood of Jesus was shed; I, too, am washed and sanctified with His blood. The extended arms of Jesus desire to embrace me also and to draw me to heaven. He dies on the cross so that my death may be sweetened for me, and that I may by death be led to everlasting life. These and similar reflections will dispel earthly thoughts and make the mind quite calm and still and the heart joyful.

While engaged in these reflections, believers should also put their entire trust in this Savior of the world. They should make the righteousness and merit of Christ their own, come before God with them, and say: For the sake of the righteousness, blood, death, and merit of my Jesus be merciful to me, O God. Trusting in these, I live and die and wish to enter the joy of heaven.

PRAYER

O Jesus, dearest Savior, if I am now to depart from this world—for the signs of my death are continually multiplying and announce to me that the end of my life is very near—I turn to You alone and say: Lord Jesus, receive my spirit. O my Redeemer, You have redeemed me by Your holy blood, with Your innocent suffering and death, from sin and from the power of the devil. Let Your blood avail for me now, that I may stand justified by it before Your judgment seat. If Satan would raise charges against me, I shall show him Your bleeding wounds. If my sins would condemn me, I shall grasp the ransom that was paid for my sins, Your holy blood. In my dying anguish I cling to Your all-sufficient merit. You are my Savior, oh, then, save me! Forgive me my sins. Give me Your perfect righteousness. Lead me to everlasting bliss.

You are the life; and so I shall not die, though my life ends because I live in You and You in me. This life will not become perfect, because I shall live with You forever, and because neither things present nor things to come shall separate me from You. You are the Way; lead me through the dark valley of the shadow of death into everlasting life. You are the Truth; You have always fulfilled Your gracious promises to me, so fulfill now what You have promised, saying: "Where I am, there will My servant be also. . . . And I, when I am lifted up from the earth, will draw all people to Myself" (John 12:26, 32). Take me now to You, and let me be with You where You dwell. Lord, let Your servant depart in peace, according to Your word. Draw me to Yourself, into the full enjoyment of Your heavenly treasures.

I picture to myself how You died for me on the cross, how You shed Your blood, how You laid down Your life for me. May Your holy wounds let me obtain grace and mercy. You are the Lamb of God. You permitted Yourself to be slain for me on the cross, and through Your blood I am reconciled to God. You are my High Priest, who makes intercession for me. You are the Hero who came to my help. You are the Prince of Peace, who welcomes me to the home of peace. O Jesus, I come to You. I grasp and hold You by faith and say: My dear Jesus, I will not leave the One who gave Himself for me. I will cleave to Him and not be driven from Him. You are the light of life, and I will not leave You.

Yes, I will now think of Jesus only: He will be the light and salvation of my soul, the strength of my life, my sun and delight, my wish and desire, my thinking and planning, my all. Away, vain thoughts! I will delight myself in the merit of Jesus and in the blood He shed for me. I will place before myself His holy wounds. I will take comfort in His bitter suffering, and my last word will be *Jesus*, yes, my last thought will be Jesus, Jesus.

Be Thou my consolation, My shield, when I must die; Remind me of Thy passion When my last hour draws nigh. Mine eyes shall then behold

Thee, Upon Thy cross shall dwell, My heart by faith enfold Thee. Who dieth thus dies well. Amen. *LSB 450:7*

HYMN

For me to live is Jesus,
　To die is gain for me;
So when my Savior pleases,
　I meet death willingly.

For Christ, my Lord, my brother,
　I leave this world so dim
And gladly seek another,
　Where I shall be with Him.

My woes are nearly over,
　Though long and dark the
　road;
My sin His merits cover,
　And I have peace with God.

Lord, when my pow'rs are failing,
　My breath comes heavily,
And words are unavailing,
　O hear my sighs to Thee.

In my last hour, O grant me
　A slumber soft and still,
No doubts to vex or haunt me,
　Safe anchored in Thy will;

And so to Thee still cleaving
　When death shall come to me,
I fall asleep believing
　And wake in heav'n with Thee!
　　　　LSB 742:1–6

THE DYING PERSON PRAYS FOR A BLESSED END

EXHORTATION

It is enough; now, O Lord, take away my life, for I am no better than my fathers. 1 Kings 19:4

In the Old Testament, when a person brought an offering to the Lord, it had to be voluntary, not a compulsory offering. This rule applies also to our dying: we must not die with displeasure or by constraint or with grumbling and disgust, but we should learn from God's Word, while still in good health, that there is glory prepared for us in the life to come, learn about the crown, the white robe, and the joy that we shall obtain after this life. We should also acquaint ourselves with the Way that leads to this glory, which is Jesus Christ, in order that we may persevere in faith until death.

On the approach of the hour that God has appointed for our departure from this world, we should lift up our eyes unto heaven with joy and beg God for a blessed end. This may be done in the following manner: We may commit our body and soul to God, continually think of our dear Savior, pray fervently, and thus await our last hour. At the same time we may call on God to grant us a quiet, gentle, rational, and blessed end. If unbecoming actions occur occasionally, those gathered at the bedside of a dying person need not worry too much about this, as the dying may be less sensible of it than they think, and meanwhile the dying remains in sweet communion with his beloved Redeemer.

PRAYER

Merciful and gracious God, I perceive that the time of my departure is near, that I shall depart in peace and lie down to rest. My sight fails me, my strength is leaving me, and it seems as if my change is at hand. So I come to You and offer my last prayer, which is this: I commend my spirit to You, O Lord, and ask for a blessed end through Jesus Christ! Amen.

Lord God, heavenly Father, You have created me and have always provided for me and sustained me. Now, mercifully receive my soul. O Jesus, You have redeemed and washed me with Your blood. Now let me die saved in true faith, trusting in Your merit and blood. O Lord Jesus, into your hands I commend my spirit. O precious Holy Spirit, my comforter and aid, do not forsake me now. Give me courage and the assurance that I am an heir of everlasting life. Pray in me and with me, and make intercession for me before God with groans too deep for words.

Behold, I am ready to leave this earth, and am longing only for You and to be with You, most Blessed Trinity! As the children of Israel had their Year of Jubilee, when every slave was liberated and all property was restored, so, O my God, my year of jubilee begins when I die, and delivered from the service of every sin and the burden of every cross, I attain to the perfect liberty of the children of God in the life everlasting.

O my Jesus, open to me the door of heaven, accompany and guide me to everlasting life, to the congregation of the saints in light. O my God, grant me a rational end, that I may keep my mind to the last moment of my life. Keep me in holy and good thoughts, that I may ever remember Jesus Christ. And if my eyes should grow dim, refresh my soul inwardly with Your heavenly comfort and light. Let Jesus ever stand before the eyes of my soul. Grant that I may rejoice in the blood that He shed for me, and that I may hide myself in His pierced side, take comfort in His merit, and by true faith lay hold of His righteousness.

If it pleases You, grant me a gentle death. Preserve me from impatient actions, temptations, and distracting thoughts. Let my heart, which has been Your dwelling here, gently throb its last. Let me die calmly in Your arms. Grant me a blessed end, that I may soon behold Your holy countenance with rejoicing.

O Blessed Trinity, bless my going out from this present mortality and my coming into happy eternity. The Lord bless me and keep me; the Lord make His face to shine upon me and be gracious to me; the Lord lift up His countenance upon me and give me peace! In the name of the triune God, the Father, Son, and Holy Spirit, I live and I die. In His name I close my eyes and commit myself to God and His mercy.

Let me depart this life Confiding in my Savior; By grace receive my soul That it may live forever; And let my body have A quiet resting place Within a Christian grave; And let it sleep in peace. Amen.   *LSB 696:5*

HYMN

I heard the voice of Jesus say,
  "Come unto Me and rest;
Lay down, thou weary one, lay down
  Thy head upon My breast."
I came to Jesus as I was,
  So weary, worn, and sad;
I found in Him a resting place,
  And He has made me glad.

I heard the voice of Jesus say,
  "Behold, I freely give
The living water; thirsty one,
  Stoop down and drink and live."
I came to Jesus, and I drank
  Of that life-giving stream;
My thirst was quenched, my soul revived,

And now I live in Him.
I heard the voice of Jesus say,
  "I am this dark world's light.
Look unto Me; thy morn shall rise
  And all thy day be bright."
I looked to Jesus, and I found
  In Him my star, my sun;
And in that light of life I'll walk
  Till trav'ling days are done.
    LSB 699:1–3

PRAYER OF THOSE PRESENT FOR THE DYING

O holy triune God, Father, Son, and Holy Spirit, You hear prayer, and so all flesh comes to You. Behold, we are coming now before You and offer up our prayer on behalf of this dying Christian.

Lord God, Father in heaven, have mercy on him/her. You have created him/her in Your image; He/she is Your creature and Your child whom You received by Holy Baptism into Your grace. Have mercy, O Lord! Your child is about to die. Let him/her now obtain a child's portion, the heritage in heaven, the salvation of his/her soul. Forgive him/her all sins that during his/her entire earthly life he/she has committed, and look upon him/her with favor.

O Son of God, the Savior of the world, have mercy on this dying Christian. You have redeemed him/her with Your holy blood. You died for him/her. Do not charge his/her sins against him/her, but impute to him/her Your righteousness and Your merit. Wash him/her with Your holy blood. Cover him/her with Your righteousness, and let him/her now appear before the throne of God, cleansed with Your blood.

Lord God, Holy Spirit, have mercy upon this dying Christian. Preserve him/her in faith; witness to his/her spirit that he/she truly is a child of God, and make intercession for him/her before God with groans that cannot be uttered. Sanctify, strengthen, and lead him/her into everlasting life.

O Holy Trinity, receive this dying Christian with favor. Remember not the sins of his/her youth, nor his/her transgressions. According to Your mercy, remember him/her for Your goodness' sake, O Lord. Receive his/her spirit into Your hands, and let it share eternal joy. On the last day grant to the body that is now dying a glad and glorious resurrection. Meanwhile, let it rest gently in the cool earth, until at the general resurrection body and soul will be reunited and enter into the bliss of heaven.

But, Lord, since his/her agony and anguish are increasing, let not the remembrance of Jesus and Him crucified slip from his/her mind.

When his/her eyes grow dim, let a bright light shine in his/her soul. Yes, O Jesus, O bright and morning star, enlighten him/her unto everlasting life. When he/she can no longer see us, grant him/her, O triune God, constantly to behold You by faith, until he/she will see You face-to-face. When his/her lips close and he/she can pray no longer, Lord Jesus, intercede for him/her and be his/her advocate with the Father in heaven. Help him/her to battle and to overcome, and let even the sighing of his/her heart be acceptable to You. When the death-sweat breaks out on him/her, strengthen him/her and be his/her support.

O triune God, abide with him/her, and keep him/her in faith until he/she has finished his/her course happily and joyfully. Lord God Father, what You have created; Lord God Son, what You have redeemed; Lord God Holy Spirit, what You have sanctified, we commend into Your hands. To Your name be praise, honor, and glory now and forevermore!

Hold Thou Thy cross before my closing eyes; Shine through the gloom, and point me to the skies. Heav'n's morning breaks, and earth's vain shadows flee; In life, in death, O Lord, abide with me. Amen.

LSB 878:6

ADDITIONAL SCRIPTURE VERSES AND PRAYERS

But Zion said, "The Lord has forsaken me; my Lord has forgotten me." "Can a woman forget her nursing child, that she should have no compassion on the son of her womb? Even these may forget, yet I will not forget you. Behold, I have engraved you on the palms of My hands; your walls are continually before Me."
Isaiah 49:14–16

If God Himself be for me, I may a host defy; For when I pray, before me My foes, confounded, fly. If Christ, my head and master, Befriend me from above, What foe or what disaster Can drive me from His love? My heart with joy is springing; I am no longer sad. My soul is filled with singing; Your sunshine makes me glad. The sun that cheers my spirit Is Jesus

Christ, my King; The heav'n I shall inherit Makes me rejoice and sing.

LSB 724:1, 10

O kind and merciful God, help me in my suffering and in my dying hour. O my God, You have always been my gracious God and my support; be with me now. O Jesus, abide with me; for it is toward evening, and the day is almost over. O precious Holy Spirit, strengthen me, keep me steadfast in the faith until my end. Enlighten me to everlasting life. I desire to die trusting in the blood and wounds of Jesus. Unto Him I live; unto Him I die; I trust in His merit. Amen.

As a deer pants for flowing streams, so pants my soul for you, O God. My soul thirsts for God, for the living God. When shall I come and appear before God? Psalm 42:1–2

The King shall come when morning dawns And light and beauty brings. Hail, Christ the Lord! Your people pray: Come quickly, King of kings!

LSB 348:5

Jesus, You are the light of my soul! When my eyes grow dim, let the brightness of heaven rise in my soul. Forsake me not when my eyes are closing in death. Show Yourself to me, and let me see Your image, bleeding, dying on the cross. Though I walk through the valley of the shadow of death, I will fear no evil; for my Jesus is with me. Yes, my Jesus, abide with me. Strengthen me in the faith, and let me be Your own here in time and hereafter in eternity. Amen.

As for me, I am poor and needy, but the Lord takes thought for me. You are my help and my deliverer; do not delay, O my God! Psalm 40:17

O Jesus, let Thy precious blood Be to my soul a cleansing flood. Turn not, O Lord, Thy guest away, But grant that justified I may Go to my house at peace with Thee: O God, be merciful to me!

LSB 613:3

Yes, my Jesus, I trust in You with all my heart. O come and release me! Bring rest to my weary body and receive my soul into the everlasting joy of heaven. O Jesus, hear my faint sighing; be my support in my anguish. O my

Savior and my Deliverer, deliver me, unloose me, and save me. Let Satan have no power over me. Open now the door of heaven and everlasting life to me. Come quickly, deliver me, refresh me, bless me, have mercy on me! Amen.

Fear not, for I am with you; be not dismayed, for I am your God; I will strengthen you, I will help you, I will uphold you with My righteous right hand. Isaiah 41:10

Only Jesus can impart Balm to heal the wounded heart, Peace that flows from sin forgiv'n, Joy that lifts the soul to heav'n, Faith and hope to walk with God In the way that Enoch trod. *LSB 611:3*

O Jesus, my only advocate with Your heavenly Father, You sit at His right hand and make intercession for us. Plead for me now in the hour of my death. I fear not, for You are with me. O Blessed Holy Spirit, comforter in every need, abide with me with Your consolations to the end. I have powerful help. My Father is with me, yes, the angels also are with me. And so I die rejoicing. Amen.

Nevertheless, I am continually with You; You hold my right hand. You guide me with Your counsel, and afterward You will receive me to glory. Psalm 73:23–24

O Lord, my God, to Thee I pray: O cast me not in wrath away! Let Thy good Spirit ne'er depart, But let Him draw to Thee my heart That truly penitent I be: O God, be merciful to me! *LSB 613:2*

By Your bitter agony and bloody sweat, help me, O Lord, my God! I will not leave You; do not depart from me! O Jesus, when my last struggle begins, help me to wrestle and to overcome! When the anguish of my heart becomes great, bring me out of my distresses. I am Your own; lead me through all my anguish to joy and bliss and glory. If You are with me, I am not afraid; I am happy, and I shall enter into the joy everlasting. Amen.

Well done, good and faithful servant. You have been faithful over a little; I will set you over much. Enter into the joy of your master. Matthew 25:23

Oh, that day when freed from sinning, I shall see Thy lovely face; Clothed then in the blood-washed linen, How I'll sing Thy wondrous grace! Come, my Lord, no longer tarry; Take my ransom'd soul away; Send Thine angels soon to carry Me to realms of endless day. *LSB 686:4*

O Jesus, by Your power and by the aid of the Holy Spirit I will remain faithful to You unto death. I will not forsake You, O friend of my soul. I do not flee from You, my shepherd. I leave You not, O my Bridegroom! Besides You there is nothing that can delight me. Lead me, O dearest friend, out of misery to joy, out of wretchedness to bliss! Amen.

For I know that my Redeemer lives, and at the last He will stand upon the earth. And after my skin has been thus destroyed, yet in my flesh I shall see God, whom I shall see for myself, and my eyes shall behold, and not another. My heart faints within me! Job 19:25–27

For me to live is Jesus, To die is gain for me; So when my Savior pleases, I meet death willingly. For Christ, my Lord, my brother, I leave this world so dim And gladly seek another, Where I shall be with Him.

LSB 742:1–2

Yes, to You, O triune God, I now commend myself for protection and mercy. I commit my dearly purchased soul to You. I die, and I shall rise again; I die, and I shall live forever in heavenly joy. O Blessed Trinity, bring me to my rest, to glory! Shorten my pains and sweeten my dying hour. Comfort me with the inward consolations of the Holy Spirit, and do not take Him from me. Let me soon behold Your glorious face in the everlasting joy of heaven. Amen.

As for me, I shall behold Your face in righteousness; when I awake, I shall be satisfied with Your likeness. Psalm 17:15

In that fair home shall never Be silent music's voice; With heart and lips forever We shall in God rejoice, While angel hosts are raising With saints from great to least A mighty hymn for praising The Giver of the feast. *LSB 514:4*

O my Jesus, my soul rejoices remembering Your glory and the joy that You have prepared for me. I leave this world gladly because I am coming to my Jesus, the Bridegroom of my soul. How glad, how happy I shall be when He will lead me, His bride, to the marriage feast, clothe me with the white robe, place the crown on my head, and after so many sufferings, pains, and afflictions at last comfort me without end! Amen.

The righteous man perishes, and no one lays it to heart; devout men are taken away, while no one understands. For the righteous man is taken away from calamity; he enters into peace; they rest in their beds who walk in their uprightness. Isaiah 57:1–2

Who so happy as I am, Even now the Shepherd's lamb? And when my short life is ended, By His angel host attended, He shall fold me to His breast, There within His arms to rest. *LSB 740:3*

I know that when I die, I go from misery to God, from burdens to delights, from anxiety to peace, from vanity to bliss, from worry to rest, from sorrow to joy. Therefore, my soul rejoices. O my God, here I am; receive my soul, glorify it, grant it everlasting life. My Jesus, I am Yours, and You are mine. In death and in life we shall be inseparable. Amen.

For we know that if the tent that is our earthly home is destroyed, we have a building from God, a house not made with hands, eternal in the heavens. 2 Corinthians 5:1

Oh, where shall joy be found? Where but on heav'nly ground? Where the angels singing With all His saints unite, Sweetest praises bringing In heav'nly joy and light. Oh, that we were there! Oh, that we were there! *LSB 386:4*

O dear Lord Jesus, seal in my heart this comfort, that when I quit this tabernacle and this dying-bed, I shall enter the glorious dwelling in heaven. What a glorious house, what a joyous place You have prepared for me, where there is no more anxiety, misery, and wretchedness, but joy, consolation, glory, bliss, and light! Oh, that we were there! Forsake me not; I will nevermore forsake You. I will cling to You, rely on Your mercy, and hide myself in Your wounds. I die trusting in Your death; make me righteous and save me by Your death. Amen.

And the ransomed of the Lord shall return and come to Zion with singing; everlasting joy shall be upon their heads; they shall obtain gladness and joy, and sorrow and sighing shall flee away.
Isaiah 35:10

Then let our songs abound, And ev'ry tear be dry; We're marching through Emmanuel's ground, We're marching through Emmanuel's ground To fairer worlds on high, To fairer worlds on high. We're marching to Zion, Beautiful, beautiful Zion; We're marching upward to Zion, The beautiful city of God. *LSB 669:4*

Remember, O Jesus, that I have been redeemed by Your blood, and let me soon enter Your heavenly Zion. Long enough I have eaten here the bread of sorrow; let me soon taste the sweet food of angels, the manna of heaven! Sighings and sorrows have been my daily occupation; let me hear joy and gladness. Let my soul catch a glimpse of Your glory. Gladden me after my suffering and refresh me in You and with You forever. Amen.

I have fought the good fight, I have finished the race, I have kept the faith. Henceforth there is laid up for me the crown of righteousness, which the Lord, the righteous judge, will award to me on that Day, and not only to me but also to all who have loved His appearing. 2 Timothy 4:7–8

Around the throne of David, The saints, from care released, Raise loud their songs of triumph To celebrate the feast. They sing to Christ their leader, Who conquered in the fight, Who won for them forever Their gleaming robes of white. *LSB 672:3*

O Jesus, help me to a happy victory when my last struggle begins! Be at my side, and all will become easy for me. Strengthen me when I am faint. O my Helper, support me in my anguish and weakness! Let Your grace strengthen me. Let Your blood refresh me. Let Your hand sustain me. Let Your holy merit cover my sins. Hold me, a wretched one, in Your arms, and revive me when I faint. Oh, how gloriously shall I be adorned and crowned by You after death! Show me the crown that You have laid up for me, and refresh my spirit with Your comforting presence. Amen.

Be faithful unto death, and I will give you the crown of life.
Revelation 2:10

The one who conquers will be clothed thus in white garments.
Revelation 3:5

Life eternal! Heav'n rejoices: Jesus lives who once was dead. Shout with joy, O deathless voices! Child of God, lift up your head! Life eternal! Oh, what wonders Crowd on faith; what joy unknown, When, amid earth's closing thunders, Saints shall stand before the throne.   *LSB 671:3*

The love of my Jesus I will never surrender. I have loved Him in the days of my health, and I will love Him unto death. O Jesus, for the sake of Your holy wounds, keep me in Your love. I will remain faithful to You unto death, and die faithful to You. With Jesus in my heart, with Christ in my mind, I die in Jesus' name. Amen.

For I am sure that neither death nor life, nor angels nor rulers, nor things present nor things to come, nor powers, nor height nor depth, nor anything else in all creation, will be able to separate us from the love of God in Christ Jesus our Lord. Romans 8:38–39

Jesus, priceless treasure, Fount of purest pleasure, Truest friend to me, Ah, how long in anguish Shall my spirit languish, Yearning, Lord, for Thee? Thou art mine, O Lamb divine! I will suffer naught to hide Thee; Naught I ask beside Thee.   *LSB 743:1*

Yes, this is the conclusion I have reached: I will never leave my Jesus! I abide in faith. I cling to Him. Death separates the soul from the body, but not my soul from Jesus. Jesus is mine, and I am His. I place myself in the arms of my Jesus, and there I will live and die in peace. How blessed, oh, how blessed I am! Amen.

Blessed is the man who remains steadfast under trial, for when he has stood the test he will receive the crown of life, which God has promised to those who love Him. James 1:12

Jerusalem, O city fair and high, Your tow'rs I yearn to see; My longing heart to you would gladly fly, It will not stay with me. Elijah's chariot take me Above the lower skies, To heaven's bliss awake me, Released from earthly ties. *LSB 674:1*

O yes, Lord Jesus, come to me. Come soon, come without delay, and take me away in peace. Give me patience and strength. I commit myself entirely, my body and soul, to You. Keep me in faith unto my blessed end. O Jesus, by Your great mercy and grace help me to attain eternal life and joy. Lord God, You have been our dwelling place in all generations; be my refuge now, my deliverer, my Savior, my God, my consolation, and my merciful Lord. Receive my soul, for it sighs for You. Oh, how I long to behold God face-to-face, to be with the angels and the elect, and to walk in heavenly splendor and brightness. Amen.

Into Your hand I commit my spirit; You have redeemed me, O LORD, faithful God. Psalm 31:5

O happy day, O yet far happier hour, When will you come at last, When by my gracious Father's love and pow'r I see that portal vast? From heaven's shining regions To greet me gladly come Your blessed angel legions To bid me welcome home. *LSB 674:2*

Now that I am dying, my only refuge, O triune God, is You. To the mercy of my heavenly Father, to the bloody wounds of Jesus Christ, to the loving-kindness of the Holy Spirit, I commend myself. O Blessed Trinity, to You I commend my body and soul. Oh, receive this little dove of Yours; I come flying on swift wing. Amen.

Lord Jesus, since You love me, Now spread Your wings above me And shield me from alarm. Though Satan would devour me, Let angel guards sing o'er me: This child of God shall meet no harm. *LSB 880:4*

But you have come to Mount Zion and to the city of the living God, the heavenly Jerusalem, and to innumerable angels in festal gathering, and to the assembly of the firstborn who are enrolled in heaven, and to God, the judge of all, and to the spirits of the righteous made perfect. Hebrew 12:22–23

The patriarchs' and prophets' noble train, With all Christ's foll'wers true, Who washed their robes and cleansed sin's guilty stain, Sing praises ever new! I see them shine forever, Resplendent as the sun, In light diminished never, Their glorious freedom won. *LSB 674:3*

My Jesus, how glorious will be the sight when I shall meet You in Your glory and all the angels and elect in heaven! I rejoice in expectation of that moment. I leave this earth and enter glory. I leave behind misery and receive joy. I leave fallen humanity and come into the presence of the holy angels and the redeemed in heaven. Amen.

Jesus Christ is the same yesterday and today and forever. Hebrews 13:8

Crown Him the Lord of life, Who triumphed o'er the grave And rose victorious in the strife For those He came to save. His glories now we sing, Who died and rose on high, Who died eternal life to bring, And lives that death may die. *LSB 525:4*

In this faith, O my Jesus, let me abide without wavering. Let my weary heart taste the sweetness of Your name, my Savior, and be refreshed. Let the power of Your death, which has fully atoned for all, avail for me in my dying hour and at the judgment seat of God, that I may here be righteous and pure and there be blessed forever in You. Amen.

My sheep hear My voice, and I know them, and they follow Me. I give them eternal life, and they will never perish, and no one will snatch them out of My hand. John 10:27–28

In death's dark vale I fear no ill With Thee, dear Lord, beside me, Thy rod and staff my comfort still, Thy cross before to guide me. *LSB 709:4*

O yes, Jesus, my shepherd, now bring me, Your poor sheep, to the joy of heaven. Let not Satan pluck me out of Your hand. You are mightier and stronger than Satan. Yours I am, and Yours I will remain. Satan has no claim and title to me, but You have purchased me to be Your own forever. Take my soul like a weary lamb into Your arms and bring it to the bliss of heaven. How happy and blessed I shall be when I shall be with my Jesus! Amen.

"Blessed are the dead who die in the Lord from now on." "Blessed indeed," says the Spirit, "that they may rest from their labors, for their deeds follow them!" Revelation 14:13

Goodness and mercy all my life Shall surely follow me; And in God's house forevermore My dwelling place shall be. *LSB 710:5*

Lord, instill into my soul this comfort, that I will die in You. O Jesus, You have lived in me and I have lived in You. I wish to die also in You, in Your love, in Your wounds, in Your grace. Cause my misery and grief, my pains and sufferings to cease, and bring me into the blessed life everlasting, where I shall rest from my labors, my sufferings, and my pain. O Jesus, hear me! Amen! Come, Lord Jesus!

The Lord will rescue me from every evil deed and bring me safely into His heavenly kingdom. To Him be the glory forever and ever. Amen. 2 Timothy 4:18

While I draw this fleeting breath, When mine eyelids close in death, When I soar to worlds unknown, See Thee on Thy judgment throne, Rock of Ages, cleft for me, Let me hide myself in Thee. *LSB 761:4*

O great God, remember me now in mercy and have compassion on me. Give me a rational, quiet, and peaceful end. My dying day is the day of my deliverance. My dying hour is the hour when I shall enter into joy everlasting. Keep me in a rational mind to the end of my life. Let me hear with joy the comfort that is promised me, and if it be Your holy will, grant that I may be able to bear witness of my faith and my hope to those surrounding my bed, and may thus be delivered by a peaceful end from all evil. Amen.

Come, you who are blessed by My Father, inherit the kingdom
prepared for you from the foundation of the world. Matthew 25:34

The soul forever lives with God, Who freely hath His grace bestowed
And through His Son redeemed it here From ev'ry sin, from ev'ry fear.

LSB 759:3

O my Jesus, let me, too, hear Your welcome when I part from this body.
Speak to my soul in that hour: "Come, you who are blessed by My Father."
Yes, let my soul and body be led to glory with these words. Meanwhile, I
cling to You by faith, and in You and through You I obtain the blessing and
the inheritance. Amen.

I will greatly rejoice in the LORD; my soul shall exult in my
God, for He has clothed me with the garments of salvation; He
has covered me with the robe of righteousness. Isaiah 61:10

Unnumbered choirs before the shining throne Their joyful anthems
raise Till heaven's arches echo with the tone Of that great hymn of praise.
And all its host rejoices, And all its blessed throng Unite their myriad
voices In one eternal song.   *LSB 674:4*

The joy of heaven, the white robe of glory, sweetens to me the bitterness
of death. Death is not bitter to me now. Jesus is with me. He comforts and
sustains me. O my God, You have clothed me with the robe of righteous-
ness. You have put on me the garment of heavenly joy. Your righteousness
is my righteousness, and now that I have been justified by faith I know that
I have peace with God through our Lord Jesus Christ. Yes, I may expect
life and salvation. How beautifully clothed shall I stand before You there!
Amen.

For God so loved the world, that He gave His only Son, that
whoever believes in Him should not perish but have eternal life.
John 3:16

In peace and joy I now depart Since God so wills it. Serene and confident my heart; Stillness fills it. For the Lord has promised me That death
is but a slumber.   *LSB 938:1*

O dearest God and Father, let me now depart quietly and in peace, trusting in Jesus Christ. I know that You have loved me also and have given me Your Son. I, too, have believed in Him, and wish to continue in this faith to the last moment of my life. Give me the assurance by Your Holy Spirit that I shall not be lost. Strengthen me in this faith, that I may soon behold in life everlasting what I have here believed. O Jesus, be at my side and do not forsake me! Amen.

Knowing that you were ransomed from the futile ways inherited from your forefathers, not with perishable things such as silver or gold, but with the precious blood of Christ, like that of a lamb without blemish or spot. 1 Peter 1:18–19

Jesus, Thy blood and righteousness My beauty are, my glorious dress; Midst flaming worlds, in these arrayed, With joy shall I lift up my head. Bold shall I stand in that great day, Cleansed and redeemed, no debt to pay; Fully absolved through these I am From sin and fear, from guilt and shame. *LSB 563:1–2*

I come before You, O great God, relying not on my righteousness but on the righteousness of Jesus Christ, which I make my own by faith. O Lamb of God, You take away the sin of the world! Have mercy on me. O righteous God, look not on my sin and uncleanness but upon the righteousness and holiness of Jesus. This I make my own. In His wounds I hide myself. Trusting in His merit I die. For His sake be gracious and merciful to me. Amen.

And there is salvation in no one else, for there is no other name under heaven given among men by which we must be saved. Acts 4:12

Thy works, not mine, O Christ, Speak gladness to this heart; They tell me all is done, They bid my fear depart. To whom save Thee, Who canst alone For sin atone, Lord, shall I flee? *LSB 565:1*

Jesus, my only Salvation and Refuge, I come to You in my dying hour. Oh, have compassion on me. Do not forsake me! The sweet name of Jesus, the remembrance of the blood that He shed, of His stripes, of His holy person shall now remain on my lips, in my heart, and in my thoughts. Lord

Jesus, unto You I live. Lord Jesus, unto You I die. Lord Jesus, living and dying I am Yours. Amen.

My little children, I am writing these things to you so that you may not sin. But if anyone does sin, we have an advocate with the Father, Jesus Christ the righteous. He is the propitiation for our sins, and not for ours only but also for the sins of the whole world.
1 John 2:1–2

Lord, Your mercy will not leave me; Ever will Your truth abide. Then in You I will confide. Since Your Word cannot deceive me, My salvation is to me Safe and sure eternally. *LSB 559:4*

O great God, the time is approaching when I must depart from this world and appear before Your judgment seat. O heavenly Father, have mercy on me and graciously receive me as Your child whom You have created and loved. O Jesus, plead for me! You are my mediator, advocate, and Savior. Take away my sins and clothe me with Your righteousness, and I am saved. O precious Holy Spirit, dwell and abide in my heart to bring me to my heavenly habitation. Amen.

Truly, truly, I say to you, whoever hears My word and believes Him who sent Me has eternal life. He does not come into judgment, but has passed from death to life. John 5:24

O Jesus Christ, my Lord, So meek in deed and word, You suffered death to save us Because Your love would have us Be heirs of heav'nly gladness When ends this life of sadness. *LSB 745:4*

My Savior, graciously fulfill this promise also to me. Let me come before Your judgment seat and there obtain mercy for Your sake. But let me not come into judgment or hear anything about the sentence of death. Keep me in faith to the end, that I, too, may receive the end of faith, the salvation of my soul. Amen.

Let us then with confidence draw near to the throne of grace, that we may receive mercy and find grace to help in time of need.
Hebrews 4:16

Jesus, Thy boundless love to me No thought can reach, no tongue declare; Unite my thankful heart to Thee, And reign without a rival there! Thine wholly, Thine alone I am; Be thou alone my constant flame. In suff'ring be Thy love my peace, In weakness be Thy love my pow'r; And when the storms of life shall cease, O Jesus, in that final hour, Be Thou my rod and staff and guide, And draw me safely to Thy side!   *LSB 683:1, 4*

Oh, yes, for Jesus' sake I shall obtain mercy. Lord God Father in heaven, have compassion on me. Lord God Son, Savior of the world, have compassion on me. Lord God, Holy Spirit, have compassion on me and be gracious and merciful to me. Amen.

For our sake He made Him to be sin who knew no sin, so that in Him we might become the righteousness of God. 2 Corinthians 5:21

Chief of sinners though I be, Jesus shed His blood for me, Died that I might live on high, Lives that I might never die. As the branch is to the vine, I am His, and He is mine!   *LSB 611:1*

Jesus, You have taken away my sins and have bestowed on me Your righteousness. What is mine, my sins and debts, has been laid on You. What is Yours, Your righteousness, has been given to me. I rejoice in this blessed exchange and comfort myself with it. Jesus, Thy blood and righteousness, my beauty are, my glorious dress; midst flaming worlds in these arrayed, with joy shall I lift up my head. In Jesus I am righteous; in Him I am saved. In my dying hour I wrap myself in His righteousness and can die cheerfully and find favor with God. Amen.

He will wipe away every tear from their eyes, and death shall be no more, neither shall there be mourning, nor crying, nor pain anymore, for the former things have passed away. Revelation 21:4

Oh, how blest are they whose toils are ended, Who through death have unto God ascended! They have arisen From the cares which keep us still in prison. Christ has wiped away their tears forever; They have that for which we still endeavor. By them are chanted Songs that ne'er to mortal ears were granted. Come, O Christ, and loose the chains that bind us; Lead us forth and cast this world behind us. With You, the Anointed, Finds the soul its joy and rest appointed.   *LSB 679:1, 4, 5*

O Jesus, I wait with joy for the hour when with glorified eyes I will see Your glad face. Then my body will shine like the sun, and my eyes will no longer be wet with tears, but filled with light and luster. With You I find joy and consolation. Here I am still sojourning as a stranger at an inn, but when I am with You, at last I will be in my true and eternal fatherland. Amen.

But if we walk in the light, as He is in the light, we have fellowship with one another, and the blood of Jesus His Son cleanses us from all sin. 1 John 1:7

Lord, when Your glory I shall see And taste Your kingdom's pleasure, Your blood my royal robe shall be, My joy beyond all measure! When I appear before Your throne, Your righteousness shall be my crown; With these I need not hide me. And there, in garments richly wrought, As Your own bride shall we be brought To stand in joy beside You.   *LSB 438:4*

I am in the fellowship of my Jesus. I live in it, and I die in it. O Jesus, You are in me, and I am in You. There is no condemnation for me because I am in Your fellowship. I am now entering into glory. The blood of Jesus sanctifies, clothes, adorns, and cleanses me. O heavenly Father, behold, it is in the righteousness of Your Son that I come to You. Amen.

Behold, the Lamb of God, who takes away the sin of the world! John 1:29

Lamb of God, pure and holy, Who on the cross didst suffer, Ever patient and lowly, Thyself to scorn didst offer. All sins Thou borest for us, Else had despair reigned o'er us: Thy peace be with us, O Jesus! O Jesus!
                    LSB 434:3

Lamb of God, You take away the sin of the world, have mercy on me! Lamb of God, You take away the sin of the world, have mercy on me! Lamb of God, You take away the sin of the world, grant me Your peace here and hereafter. Amen.

Lord, now You are letting Your servant depart in peace,
according to Your word; for my eyes have seen Your salvation.
Luke 2:29–30

In peace and joy I now depart Since God so wills it. Serene and confident my heart; Stillness fills it. For the Lord has promised me That death is but a slumber. Christ Jesus brought this gift to me, My faithful Savior, Whom You have made my eyes to see By Your favor. Now I know He is my life, My friend when I am dying. *LSB 938:1-2*

Yes, the peace of God, which surpasses all understanding, keep also my heart and mind in Christ Jesus unto life everlasting! There are the homes of peace; there they are shouting, "Victory!" There they are waving the palms before the Savior! Oh, how I wish I were there already. Amen.

Father, I desire that they also, whom you have given Me, may be with Me where I am, to see My glory that You have given Me because You loved Me before the foundation of the world. John 17:24

Jesus sat with His disciples On a mountainside one day; As the crowds of people gathered, He began to teach and say: "Blessed are the poor in spirit, Heaven's kingdom they will share. Blessed are the sad and mourning, Joy and comfort will be theirs." *LSB 932:1*

O Jesus, what a glad and happy meeting it will be when I shall come to You and see You face-to-face! Even here I have loved You before I have seen You; what unspeakable joy will thrill my heart when I come where You are, among all the saints and elect! Oh, how great is Your glory! In this life I have not heard the half of what I shall see with my eyes there. Draw me to You, and prepare me for a blessed entrance into Your glory. Amen.

For none of us lives to himself, and none of us dies to himself. For if we live, we live to the Lord, and if we die, we die to the Lord. So then, whether we live or whether we die, we are the Lord's. Romans 14:7–8

Lord, Thee I love with all my heart; I pray Thee ne'er from me depart, With tender mercy cheer me. Earth has no pleasure I would share. Yea, heav'n itself were void and bare If Thou, Lord, wert not near me. And should my heart for sorrow break, My trust in Thee can nothing shake. Thou art the portion I have sought; Thy precious blood my soul hath bought. Lord Jesus Christ, my God and Lord, my God and Lord, Forsake me not! I trust Thy Word. *LSB 708:1*

O great God, I have become Your own in Holy Baptism. I have remained Yours by faith. Let me be Yours also now that I am dying. O Jesus Christ, Son of God, You have atoned for me; enclose me in Your wounds. You alone are my consolation and my help. Amen.

Remember Jesus Christ, risen from the dead. 2 Timothy 2:8

Be Thou my consolation, My shield, when I must die; Remind me of Thy passion When my last hour draws nigh. Mine eyes shall then behold Thee, Upon Thy cross shall dwell, My heart by faith enfold Thee, Who dieth thus dies well. *LSB 450:7*

Jesus is graven in my heart. O yes, I now remember, O Jesus, Your anguish and pain, the blood You shed, and Your holy wounds. Jesus, I embrace You. I cling to You in my heart; do not depart from me. I am longing for You, O my Savior. How I wish I were with You! Amen.

"Jesus, remember me when You come into Your kingdom." And [Jesus] said to him, "Truly, I say to you, today you will be with Me in Paradise." Luke 23:42–43

Alas! And did my Savior bleed, And did my sov'reign die? Would He devote that sacred head For such a worm as I? Was it for crimes that I had done He groaned upon the tree? Amazing pity, grace unknown, and love beyond degree! Well might the sun in darkness hide And shut his glories in When God, the mighty maker, died, For His own creature's sin. *LSB 437:1–3*

O my Jesus, my only desire is for Your grace and mercy. Receive now my soul, purchased with Your precious blood, into Your holy hands! I commit it to You to be ushered into the joy of paradise. With the believing thief I pray: Lord, remember me. Remember me as Your child, purchased with Your blood to be Your own. Let me be with You in glory today. Amen.

FOR THE USE OF THE DYING AND THOSE ATTENDING THEM

The saying is trustworthy and deserving of full acceptance, that Christ Jesus came into the world to save sinners. 1 Timothy 1:15

Through Jesus' blood and merit I am at peace with God. What, then, can daunt my spirit, However dark my road? My courage shall not fail me, For God is on my side; Though hell itself assail me, Its rage I may deride. There's nothing that can sever From this great love of God; No want, no pain whatever, No famine, peril, flood, Though thousand foes surround me, For slaughter mark His sheep, They never shall confound me, The vict'ry I shall reap. For neither life's temptation Nor death's most trying hour Nor angels of high station Nor any other pow'r Nor things that now are present Nor things that are to come Nor height, however pleasant, Nor darkest depths of gloom Nor any creature ever Shall from the love of God This ransomed sinner sever; For in my Savior's blood This love has its foundation; God hears my faithful prayer And long before creation Named me His child and heir. *LSB 746:1–4*

Lord, I wait for Your salvation. Jesus saves sinners. He will save me also. Jesus receives sinners. He will receive me also. I belong to Jesus and remain His own. I lift up my eyes to heaven and see my Jesus summoning me to Him. Amen.

Whom have I in heaven but You? And there is nothing on earth that I desire besides You. My flesh and my heart may fail, but God is the strength of my heart and my portion forever. Psalm 73:25–26

My Savior, be Thou near me When death is at my door; Then let Thy presence cheer me, Forsake me nevermore! When soul and body languish, O leave me not alone, But take away mine anguish By virtue of Thine own! *LSB 450:6*

O Jesus, my life is closing. Take me to Yourself. My Shepherd, receive Your sheep. My Bridegroom, receive Your bride. My Father, receive Your child. My Jesus, take the soul that You purchased with Your blood to Yourself. This I pray, this I desire, and thus I close my eyes. Amen.

*After this I looked, and behold, a great multitude that no one
could number, from every nation, from all tribes and peoples
and languages, standing before the throne and before the Lamb,
clothed in white robes, with palm branches in their hands. . . .
And he said to me, "These are the ones coming out of the great
tribulation. They have washed their robes and made them white
in the blood of the Lamb."* Revelation 7:9, 14

Behold a host, arrayed in white, Like thousand snow-clad mountains bright! With palms they stand; Who is this band Before the throne of light? These are the saints of glorious fame, Who from the great affliction came And in the flood of Jesus' blood Are cleansed from guilt and shame. They now serve God both day and night; They sing their songs in endless light; Their anthems ring As they all sing With angels shining bright.

LSB 676:1

O my Jesus, I am waiting with joy for the white robe and the beautiful crown that You will give me. Meanwhile, wash my soul in Your blood. I claim it for myself. Receive me into the joyful life that never ends, for the sake of Your blood. Amen.

"Father, into Your hands I commit My spirit!" Luke 23:46

"Lord Jesus, receive my spirit." Acts 7:59

Jesus, all Your labor vast, All Your woe and conflict past, Yielding up Your soul at last: Hear us, holy Jesus. When the death shades round us low'r, Guard us from the tempter's pow'r, Keep us in that trial hour: Hear us, holy Jesus. May Your life and death supply Grace to live and grace to die, Grace to reach our home on high: Hear us, holy Jesus.   *LSB 447:19–21*

O my Jesus, thus I, too, pray to You now. Your last word on the cross shall be my last word in my life. Lord Jesus, I live to You. Lord Jesus, I die to You. Whether I live or whether I die, I am Yours. Would to God that I might meet my end like Jesus, committing my spirit into the hands and faithful keeping of the Father! O my refuge, let Your last word be my last word, and I shall leave this earth and go to the Father in the fullness of joy. Amen.

But according to His promise we are waiting for new heavens and a new earth in which righteousness dwells. 2 Peter 3:13

Jerusalem, O city fair and high, Your tow'rs I yearn to see; My longing heart to you would gladly fly, It will not stay with me. Elijah's chariot take me Above the lower skies, To heaven's bliss awake me, Released from earthly ties. *LSB 674:1*

O Holy and Blessed Trinity, receive my soul now into Your heavenly realm of joy! O come, Lord Jesus! I am waiting for You; lead me to Your joy! Lord God Father, what You have created; Lord God Son, what You have redeemed; Lord God Holy Spirit, what You have sanctified, I commit into Your hands. Praise and glory be to Your holy name, now and forever! Amen.

Behold, I am coming soon, bringing My recompense with Me. Revelation 22:12

Therefore I murmur not, Heav'n is my home; Whate'er my earthly lot, Heav'n is my home; And I shall surely stand There at my Lord's right hand; Heav'n is my fatherland, Heav'n is my home. *LSB 748:3*

SIGHINGS AND PRAYERS OF A DYING PERSON

BASED UPON THE POEM
SALVE CAPUT CRUENTATUM
BY BERNARD OF CLAIRVAUX

When my last hour is close at hand.

O my Jesus, You always know best. Perhaps my dying hour is now close at hand. Teach me that my age is as nothing before You, and that I must leave this world. Keep me in faith, that I may trust in the triune God in whom I have been baptized, and place all my hope in Your merit, blood, and wounds, O Jesus! Preserve me from temptation in my dying hour. Let Your left hand be under my head, and Your right hand embrace me. Refresh me in my last hour with the consolation of the Holy Spirit, and let me hear joy and gladness. Abide with me when my end comes.

And I must hence betake me.

O yes, my Jesus, I will journey the way of death, but if You, my Lord, are with me, then I will not be afraid. My death is my going to the Father. How I rejoice that I am coming to my heavenly Father, to You, my Jesus, where I shall find peace, joy, consolation, bliss, light, glorious garments, a beautiful crown! How happy I will be there! There all my misery and affliction will be at an end, and I will enter into rest, joy, and everlasting life. Be with me, O Jesus, on this way of death to eternal life; drive the enemies of my soul from me. Give me the boldness of faith and the sweetness of Your consolation, that with joy I may begin and complete my journey through the valley of death.

Lord Jesus Christ, beside me stand.

O yes, Lord Jesus, accompany me from this temporal life into the life unending. Though the way of death is gloomy, I shall nevertheless walk in the light, if You, O Jesus, are my light. Stand beside my deathbed and receive my soul when it leaves the body. When I close my physical eyes in death, let the eyes of my soul behold You. Accompany my soul until You have brought me into the holy habitation, to the holy angels, and to the company of Your chosen. Yes, accompany me as Your own to the throne of Your heavenly Father, in order that I may there obtain mercy and be received as an heir of salvation. Be at my side at my departure from this world.

Nor let Thy help forsake me.

You are the only one who can help me in my dying hour, O Jesus! Help me and strengthen my faith. Help me and witness to my spirit that I truly am God's child, and as such, shall now receive my eternal inheritance. Yes, do not forsake me when I grow pale and the pallor of death begins to spread over me. Do not forsake me when my eyes grow dim. Be and remain the light of my soul in that moment. Do not depart from me when I lose my hearing, but teach, comfort, and refresh me in my soul. Do not forsake me when I lose my speech and can no longer pray. O Jesus, in that moment, intercede for me, and You, O Holy Spirit, pray in me and make intercession to God with groans that cannot be spoken. Do not forsake me when I am passing away, but leave me to the joy of heaven.

Oh, receive my soul at this my earthly end.

Into Your merciful protection, O Jesus, I commend myself. You have bought my soul with Your holy blood. Wash it and cleanse it, that it may be found a clean vessel, pleasing to God. If the close of my natural life is now at hand, give me a rational end, if it is Your will, that I may direct my heart, eyes, and mind to You, and pray as long as my tongue can stammer, sigh as long as there is breath in me, yes, that I may receive with joy and for my comfort the encouraging words of those standing around me. If it pleases You, grant me a cheerful end, that dying I may enjoy Your fellowship, O Jesus, taste the sweetness of Your indwelling, and be refreshed with the comfort of the Holy Spirit. Grant me a blessed end, that I may quietly and happily fall asleep in faith, and remain united with You before dying, while dying, and after dying. I commend my soul to You that this may be done.

My soul to Thy blest hands I now commend.

How safe my soul is when it is in Your hands! Behold, I have commended myself to You every day, and this shall now be my last prayer: Lord Jesus, receive my spirit. My Jesus, You have redeemed my soul with Your holy blood from sin and from the power of the devil, and so I commend it to You. It is, and will forever remain, Your own. Receive it into the everlasting joy of heaven, to bliss, to glory. There I will be satisfied. Your hands are mighty and no one can snatch away from them—certainly not the world, for it has no claim on me; not Satan, for You have overcome him. Your hands are faithful hands. In them my soul is taken care of for eternity.

For Thou wilt safely keep it.

I entrust my soul to Your keeping until the Last Day, when You will unite it again with my glorified body, and make soul and body enjoy the bliss of heaven. Meanwhile, Lord Jesus, gladden, comfort, and refresh my soul with Your glory. Grant me to see forever what I have believed here in this life. Give me peace after unrest, joy after suffering, comfort after anguish, refreshing after misery. Let my soul behold, with the angels and Your chosen people, Your glory, the glory You have prepared for Your children.

My sins, dear Lord, disturb me sore.

O yes, my Jesus, I think of my sins today. I think of them and am heartily sorry that throughout my life I have provoked You to anger such a long time and in so many ways, by thoughts, deeds, and words. I mourn in my inmost soul that I have offended You, my creator, my redeemer, and my sanctifier. Oh, that I had not done so! If it were to be done again, I would not do it. But, O Jesus, with Your innocent blood, that beautiful ruby flood, wash away all my sins. Bind up my heart with the balm of Your consolations. Remember my sins no more, but cast them into the depths of the sea. O my Jesus, when my sins gather around me to frighten and accuse me, be at my side and show me Your holy wounds. Cancel with Your holy blood the record of my sins, and seal in my heart the forgiveness of my sins by Your Holy Spirit. This shall be my comfort.

My conscience cannot slumber.

Indeed, I feel what anguish and terror I must suffer on account of my sins. O sin, how bitter you are to a dying person! What fear and dread you cause! But, my Jesus, I implore You of mercy. Graciously forgive me what I have done against You throughout my days of pilgrimage. O Jesus, for the sake of the blood that You shed, forgive me all my trespasses. For the sake of Your wounds, have compassion on me. For the sake of Your everlasting love, receive me into Your grace. Have mercy on me, O God, according to Your loving-kindness. According to the multitude of Your compassions, blot out my iniquities. Wash me thoroughly from my iniquity and cleanse me from my sin. And so my conscience will be at peace and my heart quieted. Oh, I do not deny my iniquities and my sins; I confess before the all-knowing and holy God that there is a multitude of them.

Though they're as sands upon the shore.

If the sands on the shore are many, my sins are still more. I have sinned much by thoughts; much have I sinned by my words and vain talk; much have I sinned by my works and acts from my youth up till this hour. Now, if You, O Lord, should keep record of our sins, O Lord, who could stand? If You bring the thoughts of my heart before Your judgment, I will be ashamed. If I am to render an account for every idle word, I am lost. If You will judge and reward me according to my works, how will I fare? What shall a sinner do? What shall I attempt? My conscience accuses me.

I quail not at their number.

And why should I despair? My heavenly Father will not cast out His poor, repentant child. I will not despair. Jesus is my Savior, my mediator, and advocate with my Father in heaven. Who shall bring any charge against God's elect? It is God who justifies. Who is the one who condemns? It is Christ who died, yes, who is risen again, who is even at the right hand of God, and who makes intercession for us. I will not despair. The Holy Spirit will remain my support even in the anguish of death, and will bear witness to me that I am truly a child of God, that my sins have been forgiven me for Jesus' sake, and that in mercy God will enfold me in His arms. As often, then, as Satan, my sins, and my conscience terrify and smite me, You, O Jesus, will be the refuge of my soul and my consolation.

I call to mind that Thou hast died.

When dying, I will place You before me as You died for me on the cross and shed Your blood, and will say: Behold, the Lamb of God, who takes away the sin of the world! Lamb of God, pure and holy, Who on the cross didst suffer, Ever patient and lowly, Thyself to scorn didst offer. All sins Thou borest for us, Else had despair reigned o'er us: Have mercy on us, O Jesus! O Jesus! *(LSB 434:1)*. Your death brings me life. Because You died for me, I shall not die eternally or be condemned, but I will have life through You. God so loved the world that He gave His only-begotten Son, that whoever believes in Him should not perish, but have eternal life. Thus in my heart the memory of Your bitter sufferings, O Jesus, and of the blood You shed, will always remain.

Lord Jesus, and Thy riven side.

Let it be engraved on my heart, O Jesus. Your wounds were inflicted on You for my sake also, and I will take refuge in them. As a little bird, at the approach of a storm, when gusts of wind frighten both people and beasts, snugly hides in the hollow of a tree, so, Lord Jesus, the cavern of Your pierced side is my refuge, to which I hasten when sin and death terrify me. In Your holy wounds I hide, and will live and die happily in them. My soul is well sheltered in them. Because water and blood flowed from Your holy wounds, my cleansing from sin and my reconciliation with God is assured. The blood, wounds, and death of Jesus shall be my last thoughts and His holy name my last word. O Jesus Christ, Son of God, You have done so much for me. Hide me now in Your wounds. You are my only consolation and helper.

Shall rescue and preserve me.

For their sake I obtain grace with God, righteousness and everlasting salvation. While my body is enclosed in the coffin, my soul is enclosed in the wounds of Jesus. There it will be kept safely. Satan will not be able to carry it off; no enemy will drive it from its shelter. In these wounds my soul will rest and be brought to the assembly of the saints.

I have been grafted in the Vine.

Oh, what a great comfort it is in the hour of my death to know that I am a member of Your holy Body! In Holy Baptism I have been reborn and regenerated, and have been made a member of the Christian Church, whose head is Jesus. But if Jesus is my head, and I am His member, I know that I shall be where Jesus is. Now Jesus is in glory, and so that is where I am headed too. Could the Head leave His member without drawing it after Him? Yes, my Jesus will draw me after Him into His everlasting kingdom of joy. He has promised: "And I, when I am lifted up from the earth, will draw all people to Myself" (John 12:32). O Jesus, You have been exalted to the right hand of Your heavenly Father. Draw me after You; bring me to the everlasting joy of heaven. O yes, You will make me, Your child, share Your glory.

And hence I comfort borrow.

A glorious comfort! When the head wears the crown, all the members rejoice. Because my Jesus is crowned with glory and honor, I, too, shall obtain the victory after the battle, a glorious garment, and a beautiful crown from the hand of the Lord. That is a sure comfort. Because I am God's child, I am also an heir. Yes, an heir of God and a co-heir with Christ. I will be given heavenly treasures and be exalted to glory. This being so, should I not die gladly, gladly suffer and endure, so that I may live and reign with Him? This also will be my abiding comfort. Jesus, my head, will glorify me, His member. Jesus, my Savior, will give me everlasting life.

Yes, Thou wilt surely keep me Thine.

Though in this life a head may be severed from its body, still no one can separate me from Jesus. I am persuaded that neither death nor life nor angels nor principalities nor powers nor height nor depth shall be able to separate me from the love of God in Christ Jesus, my Lord. Yes, nothing, nothing can pull us apart: no cross and sickness, for I will firmly endure it; no struggle and agony of soul, for Jesus will be at my side and help me overcome; yes, not even death, for death will only serve to open the door for me, that I may go in and be with Jesus. I long to remain united with Jesus in life, suffering, and death. My body and soul may be separated, but Jesus and my soul will never be separated. I will have to part with the world and my friends, but never with Jesus. O Jesus, I have enclosed You in my heart and there I will hold tight to You in true faith, until You bring me to Your heavenly glory. Jesus is mine, and I am at all times Jesus' own.

In fear and pain and sorrow.

Though the anguish of death is a great sorrow, it is no sorrow to me, because Jesus is with me. Would Jesus leave me in my anguish? O faithful Friend of my soul, that is something I know You would never do. You have promised to be with me during times of trouble. Fulfill now this gracious promise to me. If the agony of death is the last sorrow, You, my Savior, will sweeten it to me by Your presence. "Be Thou my consolation, my shield, when I must die; Remind me of Thy passion When My last hour draws nigh. My eyes shall then behold Thee, Upon Thy cross shall dwell, My heart by faith enfold Thee" (LSB 449:4), and say: Lord Jesus, I will not leave You except You bless me. Lord Jesus I live to You; Lord Jesus I die to You; Lord Jesus, Yours I am, dead and living. Who dieth thus, dies well.

For though I die, I die to Thee.

Yes, my Jesus, I will gladly die because I know that I will come to You, into Your glory. I will die in faith, and trust in Your merit, blood, and death. I die glad and happy, for I die to You, longing for You. I die as Your child whom You have guided up till now. I die as Your sheep, that no one can pluck from Your hand. I die as Your heir, for whom the joy and bliss of heaven have been prepared.

Eternal life Thou hast for me.

You have prepared eternal life for me there in heaven. In heaven, with You, in joy everlasting, there will be no more sorrow and woe, no sickness and pain, no suffering and death, but gladness, consolation, peace, rest, sweetness, light, and glory. And this life in glory will last forever! It will never end! O Jesus, with what joy I look for that life, for that glory. My pleasant days here have been few, and toil and sorrow has been my daily bread; in heaven all my days shall be pleasant, days of joy, days of refreshing. There sorrow and weeping will have ceased forever. There my

Savior will wipe away all tears from my eyes. O happy hour when I reach that joy! And that I will reach it is a certainty; for this life of joy You have won for me.

Won for me with Thy dying.

O Lamb of God, You died for me. You are the propitiation for the sins of the whole world. For my sake You were mocked, crucified, and slain. Your death has sweetened my dying. It has all been for my benefit. Yes, Your deep humiliation leads to my exaltation. Thousand, thousand thanks shall be, dearest Jesus, unto Thee! You died for me. Your death has reconciled me to God and obtained peace, forgiveness of sins, righteousness, and the salvation of my soul. Because You live, I shall live also. Oh, therefore, do not be afraid, my soul. Look up to heaven with joy. Jesus has gained heaven for You, and has there prepared a place for you. He says: "I go to prepare a place for you." What if I have here no continuing city? When my heart breaks, when my body and soul are separated, I know where I go: to Jesus, to Jesus, my Savior. I know that if this earthly house is removed, I have a building from God, a dwelling place, a house eternal, not made with hands, in the heavens. And this building my Jesus acquired for me by His suffering and dying.

Since Thou from death didst rise again.

I receive from God's Word this glorious comfort: Though I die, I will rise again. Though my body be placed in the grave, cold and lifeless; though it turn to dust and ashes, it will not remain in the grave, but shine like the sun in the kingdom of the Father. It will be transfigured, glorified, and clothed in white garments. Is not this a great comfort? And the comfort grows out of the resurrection of Jesus from the dead. He died for me on the tree of the cross, as the innocent Lamb of God, and He was buried; but He rose again victoriously on the third day. Jesus is risen! I, too, shall rise. Jesus lives! I, too, shall live. O joy! O comfort! Though I die and my body is placed in the earth, I will come forth again, clothed with immortality and glory. Jesus did not remain in the grave, and neither will I.

In death He will not leave me.

Jesus will restore my life, and also my members; my body and soul, which were separated by death, will be reunited in the resurrection of life. Bury my body in the grave, then, without anxious concern; I shall not remain there. The grave is but my chamber of quiet rest, where I shall sleep quietly until Jesus wakes me. It is my bed of repose where I obtain rest after much waking, suffering, pain, and affliction. In my grave Jesus will cover me with the wings of His mercy. He will guard my bones until He will unite them again and restore to me the light of my eyes, my head, hands, and all my members. As little as the grave could hold Jesus, so little will it hold me when the trumpet's sound is heard, and the deep, cold grave is stirred. Thus I suffer no harm in the grave, since my body rests there from all care, from all toil, from all pain, and my soul is refreshed, and comforted by God in heavenly joy. Yes, my Savior, not only is Your resurrection my comfort, but Your ascension also!

Lord, Thy ascension soothes my pain.

When Jesus had risen from the dead, He ascended into heaven and entered into His glory. Behold, my Jesus has gone before me; I will follow Him. I, too, will have a glorious ascension. My soul will be with God immediately after its departure from this life, and in the blessed and glad resurrection of the dead we will be caught up in the clouds to meet the Lord; and then soul and body will enter together into the joy of their Lord. O my Jesus, remind me of this glorious ascension again and again, that I may comfort myself within the hour of death. Remind me that I cannot go to heaven until after I have laid aside this mortal body, and have been unclothed. This, now, will remain my greatest and most delightful comfort when I die: Jesus lives, and I will also live. Jesus ascended to heaven, and I will share His ascension when I enter heaven. Could there be anything sweeter and more delightful to me than the ascension of Jesus and my own future ascension? It drives the fear of death from me.

No fear of death shall grieve me.

I know that I will die, but I am not afraid. My soul will leave this frail, earthly tabernacle and enter into eternal glory. Is a child afraid to go to his father, or a bride to her bridegroom? By death I come to my heavenly

Father, to Jesus, the Bridegroom of my soul; why then should I be afraid to die? I enter into glory, into eternal light, eternal joy: I obtain the crown and the white robe. That does not make me fearful, but fills me with comfort and joy. I do not die; it is only my misery that dies. My soul drops its cross and receives the heavenly treasures; it leaves mortals and joins the holy angels and the elect. Yes, my Jesus, there is another thought still more powerful to drive away the fear of death: my holy union with You.

For Thou wilt have me where Thou art.

Oh, what a comfort that is! After my happy departure from this life I will ascend to heaven and be with my Jesus in His glory. The sheep is to be with the Shepherd; the disciple with the Master; the servant with the Lord. That is another thing He promised: "Where I am, there will My servant be also" (John 12:26). What joy when Jesus will clasp me in His arms and lead me to glory! O my Savior, when is the hour of blissful union and homecoming to arrive? You have not only acquired salvation for my soul; You have not only gone ahead to prepare a place for me, but You will also receive me to Yourself, as You promised to all Your children: "I will come again and will take you to Myself, that where I am you may be also" (John 14:3). It is well with me if I am where Jesus is, and this serves for my comfort.

To be with Thee, and ne'er to part.

He will receive me to Himself, so that I may live with Him in everlasting joy. I am now to inherit the mansion of my heavenly Father, and to share all heavenly treasures. My pilgrimage is at an end, and I have reached home. Yes, no separation will ever follow this union. I will stand before His throne and behold His face, and joys unspeakable will come to me through this vision. I will live with Him and be refreshed by Him forever and ever. And so I die with joy.

Therefore, I die rejoicing.

Why should I not die rejoicing? "In peace and joy I now depart Since God so wills it. Serene and confident my heart; Stillness fills it. For the Lord has promised me That death is but a slumber" *(LSB 938:1)*. I die rejoicing because my sins are forgiven for the sake of Jesus' blood and death. I die rejoicing because I will be raised from the grave to everlasting life. I die rejoicing because I will have a blessed ascension, and will come to my Jesus. Therefore, I leave this world rejoicing that I may soon be at Christ my brother's side, and with Him forever abide. I go rejoicing out of this world to heaven, from this valley of sorrow to the home of joy. For out of tribulation and great sorrow I will enter into a joy that no ear has heard, and which will endure forevermore.

Thus I go hence to Jesus Christ.

Because my Savior says: "I am ascending to My Father and your Father, to My God and your God" (John 20:17), I, too, say when dying: I ascend; I ascend to my heavenly Father, to my Jesus, to the Holy Spirit, and thus to the Blessed Trinity; to my Immanuel, to the lover of my soul, to my brother. Yes, my redeemed soul ascends to its Redeemer. I go to my Savior, who will lead me into heaven, and receive me into favor as a soul cleansed with His blood. Oh, how I long to behold Jesus in His glory and to embrace Him whom I have not seen, and yet whom I love!

My arms to Him extending.

I extend my arms to Jesus, to clasp Him to my heart, to hold Him, and never to let Him go. I embrace Jesus now by faith; I hold Him and will not let Him go, until He will lead me into His Father's house, to everlasting life. I extend my arms and cry, Yes, come, Lord Jesus! I now call to mind that my Jesus extended both His arms on the tree of the cross and died thus, as if He wished to embrace me. So I will also die with arms extended, to embrace Jesus. O Bridegroom of my soul, embrace me and present me transformed and glorified to Your Father. What a blessed entrance that will be when I enter heaven accompanied and conducted by Jesus! These things I will think about and so fall asleep in Jesus.

Thus quietly I start that sleep.

I rest gently, because I rest in the arms of Jesus. With Jesus in my heart, with Jesus in my mind, I fall asleep in God's name. O Jesus, let my death become a sweet and gentle sleep that I may quietly and peacefully breathe my last in faith and in Your love. Also let my body sleep gently in the cool earth until the Last Day. While my body is sleeping, my soul, too, rests in everlasting joy and bliss. What a sweet rest, a rest that no one can disturb! I rest from my crosses; I rest from my misery, from sorrow and grief; I rest from all pains. Oh, blessed, heavenly, glorious rest! If the child sleeps gently in its mother's arms, why should not I sleep gently and rest in the arms of my Jesus?

Which no man will be ending.

To raise the dead is a work of God. No mere human being, then, has of himself the power to raise the dead. But You, my Jesus, are true God, and can call the dead from their graves. Your voice shall resound through the earth and penetrate the graves, and the dead will arise. O Jesus, raise my body then to everlasting life on the glad day of Your coming, that this body which served You here may also be glorified. I know that my Redeemer lives, and that he will stand again upon the earth; and though my skin is destroyed, still in my flesh I shall see God, whom I shall see for myself and my own eyes shall behold and not another! What no mere human can do, my Savior will do.

But Jesus, God's Son glorified.

Before I die, then, I once more confess my faith in Jesus. He is Jesus, the Redeemer and Savior of the human race. He is also Christ, the promised Messiah. Yes, He is not only true man but also the very Son of God, yes, God Himself. Trusting in this Jesus Christ I wish now to die, glad and happy. The blood of Jesus Christ, the Son of God, cleanses me from all sin.

The gates of heaven will open wide.

O my Jesus, when the door of this life closes after me, open to me the door of heaven. During my life I have diligently meditated on heaven. I have also sought to attain heaven by faith, in holiness of living. And so, O Jesus, open wide to me the door of heaven when I close my pilgrimage. O Jesus, open to me the door of heaven and say: "Good and faithful soul, enter into the joy of your Lord." "Come, you who are blessed by My Father, inherit the kingdom prepared for you from the foundation of the world" (Matthew 25:34). Oh, how happy I will be with such a sweet welcome.

Lead me to life eternal.

As a bridegroom leads his bride to the marriage, so, O Jesus, lead me into everlasting life, into the life that never ends, into the glory that You won for me, into the joy that will never end. If you do this, I will die gladly. Now I am with Jesus; He is with me. I have been transferred from this miserable life on earth to the life of joy in heaven. Now I have passed from believing to seeing. I will behold face-to-face the God whom I love; of this I have no doubt. I will see Him in the everlasting joy and glory prepared for me. To You be praise and glory, now and ever, and unto the ages of ages!

THOSE PRESENT CALL TO THE DYING

Remember Jesus Christ. Remember His bitter suffering and death. Comfort yourself with the love of the Father in heaven, who has received you as His own child in Holy Baptism, and is now about to receive you as His child into everlasting glory. Comfort yourself with the bleeding wounds of Jesus Christ that He allowed to be inflicted on Him on account of your sins. Comfort yourself with His holy blood that He shed for your forgiveness. Comfort yourself with the support of the Holy Spirit who has sanctified you. Trusting in this triune God, live and die in peace. Amen.

BENEDICTION PRONOUNCED OVER A DYING PERSON

Depart, O soul, dearly bought by Jesus Christ. Depart to Your God and Father in Jesus Christ, who has created and loved you, whom you have feared, and in whom you have trusted as a child. Depart to the Lord Jesus, your dearest and most faithful shepherd and redeemer, who has bought you as His own sheep at the price of His blood, and to whom you have clung by faith. Depart to the comforter, the Holy Spirit, who has sanctified you and chosen you to be His temple and dwelling. Depart out of vanity into eternity. Depart into the heavenly fatherland, now that your pilgrimage has come to an end. Depart out of sorrow into joy. Depart out of all trouble to the living God. May He bless your going out and your coming in, and preserve you by His power unto salvation. Depart and enter the kingdom prepared for you from the foundation of the world. The Lord bless you and keep you; the Lord make His face shine on you and be gracious to you; the Lord lift up His countenance upon you and give you peace. Amen.

PRAYER OF THOSE PRESENT AFTER THE DYING PERSON HAS BREATHED THE LAST

O holy and righteous God, it has pleased You to call from this life the departed lying here before us by temporal death. Let us learn from this death that we, too, must die and leave this world, in order that we may prepare for it in time by repentance, a living faith, and avoiding the sins and vanities of the world. Refresh the soul that has now departed with heavenly consolation and joy, and fulfill for it all the gracious promises that in Your Holy Word You have made to those who believe in You. Grant to the body a soft and quiet rest in the earth until the Last Day, when You will reunite body and soul and lead them into glory, so that the entire person who served You here may be filled with heavenly joy there. Comfort all who are in grief over this death, and be and remain to the bereaved their father, provider, guardian, helper, and support. Do not forsake them, and do not withdraw Your hand from them, but let them abundantly experience Your goodness, grace, love, and help, until You will grant them also a happy and blessed end. Hear us for Your mercy's sake. Amen.

BOOK V

PRAYERS FOR SPECIAL OCCASIONS

BELIEVING CHRISTIANS PRAISE GOD ON THE RETURN OF THEIR BIRTHDAYS

EXHORTATION

What shall I render to the LORD for all His benefits to me?
Psalm 116:12

The return of the day when we first beheld the light of this world, our birthday, ought to be a day of praise and thanksgiving. We should spend it singing and praying, and with devotional exercises in thought and act. We should, in particular, reflect on the many and great blessings that we have received from the hand of our faithful God throughout the days of our life. He has carried us in His arms in childhood, in youth, to the present hour. Unbelievers do not consider these things. True, they remember the day and celebrate it, but how? Only with partying and such? A day thus spent does not deserve to be called a day of thanksgiving and praise, a day pleasing to God.

When the children of God live to see their birthday year after year, they praise the faithfulness and goodness of God. He had them to be born of Christian parents, who brought to them to the knowledge of salvation in Jesus Christ. He has given them a healthy body and sound mind, great blessings of God, though these gifts are rarely acknowledged. He has guarded them against misfortune, rescued them from dangers, and preserved them up to the present.

At the same time, children of God humbly ask for forgiveness of their sins, and promise God that they will spend the remaining days of their life in childlike obedience and godliness. They also comfort themselves with the thought that as they continue in faith and love, God will continue to spread the wings of His mercy over them. Finally, they reflect that the celebration of their birthday this year may be their last such celebration on earth.

PRAYER

Eternal, gracious, and merciful God, by Your favor I have again lived to see my birthday, the day on which You ushered me into the light of day, to receive me later by Holy Baptism as Your child. By the former favor I was made a human being and your creature, by the latter I become Your child and heir. And so this day will be a day of prayer, praise, and thanksgiving to me.

Bless the Lord, O my soul; all that is within me, bless His holy name! Bless the Lord, O my soul, and forget not all His benefits. O magnify the Lord with me, and let us exalt His name together. I will bless the Lord at all times; His praise will continually be in my mouth. Should I not praise and magnify You, my God, because You have let me be born not only with sound limbs and a well-formed body, which is a great favor, but also from Christian parents, who from my youth have taught me to know You, O triune God? Now I know and love You and have life and salvation of my soul in You.

Having been nurtured in Your arms, I have been guided and accompanied by You. You have given me food and clothing, and have graciously guarded me until this day. O my God, I am not worthy of the least of all of the mercies and of all the faithfulness that You have shown me. Come and hear; I will declare what the Lord has done for my body and soul. Unfortunately, I cannot recount everything! One could sooner number the stars in the sky than the gracious gifts I have received from You, O Lord. From how many dangers You have delivered me! How many calamities You have warded off from me! Your Spirit has taught, governed, guided, and when I was leaning toward sin, has inwardly warned and restrained me.

O my God, while my years increase and Your favors also become numerous, I am reminded today of the sins that I have committed throughout my life. Forgive them to me for Jesus' sake. Blot them out with His holy blood, and let me obtain mercy for His sake. Grant me grace to spend the remaining days of my life, which are written in Your book, in true fear of You and in sincere faith, that all my doings and my whole life may be pleasing to You. And since I do not know the number of my days on earth, while I know that You have fixed bounds for me which I cannot pass, keep me from shortening my own life by anger, intemperance, sins, recklessness, and crimes. Let me reach the limit of life appointed for me in health, under Your blessing and protection, until You will give me eternal and heavenly life for the sake of Jesus Christ. Until then I shall celebrate this day, as often as it recurs, with praise and thanksgiving, and shall now sing:

My soul, now praise your Maker! Let all within me bless His name Who makes you full partaker Of mercies more than you dare claim. Forget Him not whose meekness Still bears with all your sin, Who heals your ev'ry weakness, Renews your life within; Whose grace and care are endless And saved you through the past; Who leaves no suff'rer friendless But rights the wronged at last. Amen. *LSB 820:1*

HYMN

Oh, that I had a thousand voices
To praise my God with thousand tongues!
My heart, which in the Lord rejoices,
Would then proclaim in grateful songs
To all, wherever I might be,
What great things God has done for me.

O all you pow'rs that He implanted,
Arise, keep silence now no more;
Put forth the strength that God has granted!
Your noblest work is to adore.

O soul and body, join to raise
With heartfelt joy our Maker's praise.

You forest leaves so green and tender
*   That dance for joy in summer air,*
You meadow grasses, bright and slender,
*   You flow'rs so fragrant and so fair,*
You live to show God's praise alone.
Join me to make His glory known.

All creatures that have breath and motion,
*   That throng the earth, the sea, the sky,*
Come, share with me my heart's devotion,
*   Help me to sing God's praises high.*
My utmost pow'rs can never quite
Declare the wonders of His might.

Creator, humbly I implore You
*   To listen to my earthly song*
Until that day when I adore You,
*   Together with the angel throng*
And learn with choirs of heav'n to sing
Eternal anthems to my King. LSB 811:1–5

DEVOUT CHRISTIANS THANK GOD FOR THE INGATHERING OF THE HARVEST

EXHORTATION

And she did not know that it was I who gave her the grain, the wine, and the oil, and who lavished on her silver and gold, which they used for Baal. Therefore I will take back My grain in its time, and My wine in its season, and I will take away My wool and My flax, which were to cover her nakedness. Hosea 2:8–9

If we were to look for a glorious and great blessing apparent to all people, we would undoubtedly find it in our annual harvests. It is God who has protected our sowings in the earth during the winter, who caused them to sprout, grow, and bear fruit during the summer, averted hail, winds, and storms, and filled our barns and cellars with His blessings. On the other hand, if there is a favor that seems trifling and contemptible to the world, and for which God is thanked least of all, it is the annual harvest. Ungrateful humanity imagines that these things simply had to happen according to the laws of nature—things have to grow and God has nothing to do with it. Accordingly, God's anger is aroused, and by His just judgment He often causes the crops to fail, reminding everyone that the ground cannot produce anything apart from the Lord's will, and that without His blessing nothing can grow.

Believing Christians view the matter differently. When at harvest they see the full ears of grain and the vines loaded with clusters of grapes, they lift up their eyes to heaven, and praise the almighty Creator, giver, and preserver for the blessings received, and acknowledge that it is because of Him that so many grains come from one seed and such luscious fruit from an ordinary wood. They praise God's preserving providence, which provided throughout the year timely rain, and graciously averted thunderstorms, drought, hail, and floods, and guarded the crops. And when the time had arrived that they see the grains harvested and brought into the barns and the grapes crushed for wine, their heart is stirred and they receive all these gifts with grateful hands. They also make use of them and enjoy them with thanksgiving. They know that it is God who feeds them, provides for them, and keeps them.

Yes, they let God's goodness lead them to repentance. If we thank a benefactor who gives us a garment or something for our support, and are careful not to offend him, why should we not praise the greatest Benefactor who gives us all things?

PRAYER

O give thanks to the Lord, for He is good; His mercy endures forever. Thus I say, O my God, I have lived again to see the blessed time of harvest. O gracious God, how great is the goodness You have manifested toward us! You have laid the foundations of the earth that it should be established forever. But into this earth You have placed Your glorious treasures. You make it produce fruits for us in abundance, which serve for sustaining our life, for our food and health.

O living Father, You have especially crowned this year with Your blessing, and Your paths overflow with abundance. You have watered the hills from Your chambers. You have filled the earth with fruits of Your creation. You have caused the grass to grow for the cattle and vegetation for the service of humanity, that You might bring forth food from the earth. O faithful Father, this year again You have given food and drink to Your children, though they have been ungrateful. You have protected our harvest. Heaven has heard the cry of the earth, and the earth has yielded grain and wine. You have given us the early and latter rain in due season, causing our fields to bloom and giving us the bounties that spring from Your power. By Your grace our trees have yielded many kinds of beautiful and pleasant fruits, and the wine has made us glad. O loving God and Father, You have spread the wings of Your mercy over all our lands. You have caused the sun to shine in season, thus maturing all our crops. You have protected them from hail, blight, drought, and floods. While we slept, You were awake. You were the watchman and keeper of our fields.

O Lord, how great and manifold are Your works! In wisdom You have made them all, and the earth is full of Your riches. All creatures, human and animal, wait on You, that You may give them their food in due season. What You give them, they gather. You open Your hand, and they are filled with good. Yes, You have abundantly blessed us this year, O God, with the wealth of Your bounties.

For this we thank You with our inmost heart. O come, let us worship and bow down; let us kneel before the Lord, our maker. Let us enter His gates with thanksgiving and His courts with praise. Let us say with grateful hearts: The Lord has done great things for us, and indeed we are glad.

O Lord, let us not misuse the gifts and favors that You have bestowed on us, but let us learn from them Your love toward us and Your fatherly faithfulness. O God, if some who are ungrateful should show contempt for Your gifts by using them for gluttony or refusing to thank You for them, do not on that account withdraw Your blessing from us, but preserve them for us according to Your mercy.

O Father, You have loved us with an everlasting love, and You draw us to Yourself also by these earthly blessings, that we may know the giver by the gifts and the benefactor by His glorious presents, grant that Your goodness may lead us to repentance. Whenever we see Your gifts before us on the table, or receive them into our hands or mouth, let us always lift up our eyes to You, O fountain of every blessing! And as You sustain our bodies by Your bounties, let us through the Means of Grace that You have appointed increase also in the inner self, in faith, love, and godliness, that we may grow in all goodness, and be changed from glory to glory, until we are ushered into the enjoyment of Your heavenly blessings in everlasting life through Jesus Christ. Amen.

HYMN

Sing to the Lord of harvest,
  Sing songs of love and praise;
With joyful hearts and voices
  Your alleluias raise.
By Him the rolling seasons
  In fruitful order move;
Sing to the Lord of harvest
  A joyous song of love.

God makes the clouds rain goodness,
  The deserts bloom and spring,
The hills leap up in gladness,
  The valleys laugh and sing.

God fills them with His fullness,
  All things with large increase;
He crowns the year with blessing,
  With plenty and with peace.

Bring to this sacred altar
  The gifts His goodness gave,
The golden sheaves of harvest,
  The souls Christ died to save.
Your hearts lay down before Him
  When at His feet you fall,
And with your lives adore Him
  Who gave His life for all.

LSB 893:1–3

BELIEVING CHRISTIANS PRAY DURING A THUNDERSTORM

EXHORTATION

He makes darkness His covering, His canopy around Him, thick clouds dark with water. Out of the brightness before Him hailstones and coals of fire broke through His clouds. The LORD also thundered in the heavens, and the Most High uttered His voice, hailstones and coals of fire. Psalm 18:11–13

Among the external things by which ungodly children of this world, as a rule, are terrified and incited to pray, are thunderstorms. When God causes a severe tempest to arise with thunder and lightning, the lips of blasphemers at once begin to pray, not from love of God—for why did they not pray before?—but from fear of God's punishment.

Believing Christians know, indeed, that thunder and lightning are produced by natural causes; but they also know that they carry out the commands of God. Just as God can arm any other creature against humanity, He can easily frighten human beings and animals also by thunder, and set houses, villages, and towns on fire with His lightning. Accordingly, godly Christians should refrain from those hideous curse words in which thunder and lightning are invoked. They should not grow timid at the approach of a thunderstorm, become terrified, and ready to despair from fright. They should remember that God keeps thunder and lightning in His hands, and is well able to protect them, even if they should be out in the field and under the open sky.

However, in that case they should turn to God in prayer even more fervently, and recognize in the storm that they are nothing and God is all, that God is a mighty God, while we human beings are but poor worms, dust and ashes, which God could destroy with one nod or stroke. Accordingly, they should stand awed and reverent before the majesty of God, not only when it thunders but also when the sun is shining, and should be careful not to offend Him by words and deeds. Especially, however, should they live in such a manner as to be assured at all times of God's favor, even if He should take us out of this world in a thunderstorm.

PRAYER

Strong and almighty God, I hear Your voice in the clouds. I see Your lightning flash, and I listen to the roar and noise of Your thunder. Strong is Your arm and great is Your might. If You choose, You can, in the twinkling of an eye, dash me and all people, together with all creatures, to the ground. But, O Lord, remember Your tender mercies and Your lovingkindness, for they have always been of old. Remember not the sins of my youth or my many transgressions. According to Your mercy, remember me for Your goodness' sake. Rebuke me not in Your anger nor chasten me in Your hot displeasure.

With sincere humility of heart I acknowledge that I have abundantly deserved to be destroyed and dashed to pieces by You in Your just wrath. But, O long-suffering God, spare me in this thunderstorm. Have mercy on me, O God, according to Your loving-kindness; according to the multitude of Your tender mercies blot out my transgressions. I repent, and am heartily sorry that up till now I have offended You so often, and with my thoughts, words, and deeds have provoked You to anger. But I pray for mercy and forgiveness of all my sins and transgressions.

Consider, heavenly Father, that I am Your creature and also Your child. Where will children go in their troubles and anxieties but to their father? And so I come to You, O my Father, and pray You: be merciful to me, Your child! O Father, protect me, shelter me, guard me. My refuge is under the shadow of Your wings. Hide me in Your tender hand. Place an angel guard around me, that no calamity may touch me, no lightning harm me, no bolt strike me. O Lord Jesus, only Son of God, my mediator, advocate, and Savior, be not far from me, for trouble is near. Make haste to deliver me; be my strong defense. Do not leave me or take Your hand from me, O God of my salvation. Behold, I am forsaken by all creatures and human beings, but do not leave me. Have compassion on me and save me. I cling to You, O Jesus. I hide myself in Your holy wounds, and cry with Your disciples: Lord, save us! We perish! O precious Holy Spirit, stir up my heart to prayer and devotion, that I become roused through this thunderstorm and become godly. Henceforth, when Your Holy Word is knocking at my door, help me to heed the call, so that I may repent, turn, and cease from all sins, that I may then become a willing listener, and not conform to the world in its sinful ways.

O Holy Trinity, have mercy on me and all godly Christians! Shelter with Your almighty hand my body and my life, my house and my home. Preserve the fruits of the field. Do not let the lightning set my house on fire, nor Your thunderbolts strike me. Be my helper in trouble, for the help of mankind is useless. O mighty defender of Your children, look on me and let me dwell beneath Your sheltering protection. At the noise of Your thundering the mountains shake and the earth trembles. Must not a poor worm like me, then, quake before You? Let me now recognize that this world is passing away, that all I see will be one day consumed by fire, so that I will not become enticed with the lust of the flesh, the lust of the eyes, and the pride of life, and thus stir up Your anger. O Lord, preserve me from sudden and evil death. Let this thunderstorm pass by without harm. O Lord, who is like You, so majestic, almighty, and awe-inspiring, and yet so merciful and gracious, startling us and at the same time sheltering us? O spare me, and let me also this time find mercy and deliverance. Lord God, Father in heaven, have mercy upon us! Lord God Son, Savior of the world, have mercy upon us! Lord God Holy Spirit, comforter, have mercy upon us! Be gracious to us, and spare us, good Lord! Be gracious to us and help us, good Lord! From all calamity by fire and water, good Lord, deliver us! From sudden and evil death, good Lord, deliver us!

God moves in a mysterious way His wonders to perform; He plants His footsteps in the sea And rides upon the storm. Judge not the Lord by feeble sense, But trust Him for His grace; Behind a frowning providence Faith sees a smiling face. You fearful saints, fresh courage take; The clouds you so much dread Are big with mercy and will break In blessings on your head. Amen. *LSB 765:1, 2, 5*

HYMN

When in the hour of deepest need
We know not where to look for aid;
When days and nights of anxious thought
No help or counsel yet have brought,

Then is our comfort this alone
That we may meet before Your throne;
To You, O faithful God, we cry
For rescue in our misery.

For You have promised, Lord, to heed
Your children's cries in time of need
Through Him whose name alone is great,
Our Savior and our advocate.

And so we come, O God, today
And all our woes before You lay;
For sorely tried, cast down, we stand,
Perplexed by fears on ev'ry hand.

O from our sins, Lord, turn Your face;
Absolve us through Your boundless grace.

Be with us in our anguish still;
Free us at last from ev'ry ill.

So we with all our hearts each day
To You our glad thanksgiving pay,
Then walk obedient to Your Word,
And now and ever praise You, Lord. LSB 615:1–6

BELIEVING CHRISTIANS
THANK GOD AFTER THE
THUNDERSTORM HAS PASSED

EXHORTATION

God thunders wondrously with His voice; He does great things
that we cannot comprehend. Job 37:5

All the works that the Lord does in the sight of humanity are exceedingly great, and every one who observes them finds delight, joy, and pleasure in them. This applies especially to a thunderstorm when we consider it properly. Although it is produced by natural causes, it is nevertheless in God's hand. It is God who thunders. He governs the clouds that fill with vapor and fire. He guides them according to His pleasure. He uses them for His purpose, and sends them to accomplish His designs. Accordingly, His thunder is always awe-inspiring. It is terrible and fearful to behold and listen to. People are startled by it. The animals tremble and roar. All that has breath is moved to anxiety and fear. What else does God manifest by such an event than His great power and majesty, by which He can set all things into commotion, the moment He causes His voice to be heard on earth by the rumbling in the clouds?

But God accomplishes still more by a thunderstorm. He performs great things, which result sometimes in damage and sometimes in profit to humanity. In damage, when the lightning shatters sturdy trees, sets houses on fire, strikes and kills human beings and animals; in profit, because by the concussions of the thunder the atmosphere is purified and the fruitfulness of the soil increased. Is not this another proof that the God who can accomplish such great things in such an incomprehensible manner must be a great and glorious God?

It is but proper that all who view these acts of the Lord frequently should be roused to a living knowledge and humble adoration of Him. However, in numerous instances this lesson is disregarded. God does great things by means of His thunder, and yet is not known. Most people are scared and depressed as long as they hear the discharges of thunder, but as soon as the storm has passed, all impressions they received from it are also forgotten, just as if they had not heard the voice of the Lord, as if they had not heard what great things He has done for them. If the tempest has caused damage, they show a fleeting compassion and pity for those affected. But if it fortunately passed by without doing harm, no account of it is taken, and thus God continues to be unknown to them. O what hard hearts that will not permit themselves to be softened! O what criminal insensibility! O what shameful ingratitude!

True Christians guard against these things with all care. They behold and contemplate attentively the works of nature, and allow themselves to be guided by them to their Creator. They do this especially when the God of glory thunders in the heavens. When they behold a storm coming up, they marvel at the majesty, grandeur, and glory of Him who causes it to arise. When they hear the thunder roll overhead, and see the lightning flash around them, they commit themselves calmly and confidently into the hands of the Lord, where they always are, and in childlike trust expect from Him all good things. When the tempest has passed by harmlessly, they return thanks to God; they praise and glorify His goodness and faithfulness with heart, lip, and hands. And that leads them to God and brings them nothing but salvation and blessing. Of this, the mouth of truth Himself assures them when He says: "The one who offers thanksgiving as his sacrifice glorifies Me; to one who order his way rightly I will show the salvation of God!" (Psalm 50:23).

PRAYER

O God of my salvation, I, too, long for Your salvation. And so I now approach Your throne of grace to offer You the sacrifice of praise and thanks due to You because You have graciously delivered me from trouble, terror, and danger. I was full of anxiety when I heard Your mighty voice in the air because I did not know what You would perform by its means. I took refuge in You by prayer, and committed myself and all that is mine to Your fatherly care, and You did not cast me away. You showed me cordial concern, and proved by deed that You are glad to help.

How easily might Your lightning have set our houses and forests on fire! How easily might the storm have crushed the fruits of the field! How easily could the uproar have consumed and utterly destroyed our possessions and belongings! How easily could you have made us as Sodom, and dealt with us as You did with Gomorrah (Deuteronomy 29:23)! And all this You would have done justly if You intended to deal with us according to our sins and pay us back as we have deserved because of our iniquities. But You have not done this. You have remembered us in love. You have yielded Your right and given Your mercy sway. You have spared us punishment, and, instead, have showered Your blessings on us. It is because of Your goodness, O God, that we can put our trust under the shadow of Your wings, and that we may again dwell in safety. It is because of Your goodness that we are not consumed, and Your mercy is without end. This my soul knows very well.

Moved, humbled, and yet filled with gratitude, I come before You and say: You, Lord, have done great things for me, and for this I am glad. Give to the Lord glory and strength! Worship Him in the beauty of holiness. Tremble before Him all the earth. Make a joyful noise to the Lord, all the earth; make a loud noise and rejoice and sing praises. Let us come into His presence with thanksgiving. Let us make a joyful noise to Him with songs of praise. Let everything that has breath praise the Lord. Bless the Lord, O my soul, and forget not all His benefits toward you.

I have now seen, O strong and almighty God, how You have so soon, so graciously, turned aside the severe and terrible tempest, and have let it pass by without causing damage. Rouse me by this event that in all troubles that may yet befall me I may firmly trust in You and hope constantly in Your goodness. I behold again a serene sky; let me from now on taste and see that You are good. I have again seen Your greatness and glory; let this cheer me to face You always with childlike fear, cordial love, and humble reverence, and to walk before You so as to please You. I have again felt Your kindly hand; let me and mine and all people be committed to the same for the future.

If the tempest that passed us has caused damage and harm elsewhere, be gracious and have compassion on the injured. Guide them so that they may see that it is Your hand that has chastised them, so that they may humble themselves under it. Comfort and refresh them. Restore to them what they have lost by giving other blessings. Let them soon hear joy and gladness, that the bones You have broken may rejoice.

But let me also administer, employ, and use correctly and faithfully the gifts and possessions that You have preserved and, as it were, given to me anew. Let me receive my daily bread with thanksgiving. Let me manage my possessions as a faithful steward. Grant that I may not misuse them or abuse them in wastefulness and selfish indulgence, but always use them for Your glory, for my benefit, and for the welfare of my neighbor, in order that I may render a cheerful account to You at the end.

Take under Your gracious protection all that is mine also in the future, and guard it against destruction. If many more tempests are to arise, threatening ruin to me, let me be undismayed and trust in Your mercy and confidently hope in Your goodness. On such occasions let me experience that surely no one will be put to confusion who hopes in you. Yes, if it should be Your will to make me poor, in that case make me truly rich before You in spirit, in order that, while losing all, I may keep You and Your communion and heaven. If I only obtain heaven, I have all that I really need.

O my Father, O my Savior, O my Comforter, You who dwell in the heavens and have granted me Your protection and help during this storm that has now passed by, bring me also in heaven to You, that I may behold You face-to-face and give You praise and thanks forever. Teach me by Your Word to walk in the true way, and to do what is well pleasing to You. Lead me in the land of uprightness. Unite my heart to fear Your name. Let me remain loyal to You in my faith, in love, and in hope, and never cease from godliness until the end shall come, so that when the Lord Jesus is revealed on the Day of Judgment with flames of fire and with thunder and lightning to execute vengeance on those who do not know

God and are not obedient to the Gospel, I may not be terrified, but lift up
my head with joy, and enter with Him into life everlasting. Amen.

HYMN

I leave all things to God's direction;
He loves me both in joy and woe.
His will is good, sure His affection;
His tender love is true, I know.
My fortress and my rock is He:
What pleases God, that pleases me.

God knows what must be done to save me;
His love for me will never cease.
Upon His hands He did engrave me
With purest gold of loving grace.
His will supreme must ever be:
What pleases God, that pleases me.

My God desires the soul's salvation;
My soul He, too, desires to save.
Therefore with Christian resignation
All earthly troubles I will brave.
His will be done eternally:
What pleases God, that pleases me.

My God has all things in His keeping;
He is the ever faithful friend.
He gives me laughter after weeping,
And all His ways in blessings end.
His love endures eternally:
What pleases God, that pleases me. LSB 719:1–4

BELIEVING CHRISTIANS PRAY
TO GOD BEFORE TRAVELLING

EXHORTATION

The LORD is your keeper; the LORD is your shade on your
right hand. The sun shall not strike you by day, nor the moon by
night. The LORD will keep you from all evil; He will keep your life.

The LORD will keep your going out and your coming in from this time forth and forevermore. Psalm 121:5–8

There are many reasons that Christians leave home and travel: business trips, visiting others, health needs; for journeys for luxury and dissipation are not becoming to a true child of God. But if there is a compelling reason for believing Christians to leave their home and work for a time, they should start their journey with prayer and reflect when they leave home that God is with them in every foreign country to which they go, and that He hears and sees everything.

Accordingly, they must conduct themselves as being in God's presence, in an honorable, well-behaved, godly, Christian manner. At the beginning of their journey, believing Christians should commit themselves to God's gracious protection, praying that God would bring them home again in good health and with sound limbs—remembering that many have lost health and even life while traveling. They should also commend those whom they leave behind, as well as their house and possessions, to God, that He may through His holy angels take everything into His safekeeping, and guard it against fire, floods, or other calamities. They should pray God to let them find their possessions unharmed and their dear ones in good health upon their return.

PRAYER

Gracious and merciful God, in Your name I have resolved to be absent from my loved ones and from my home for a time, and so I come and pray to You. Bless my going out and my coming in. In Your name I begin my journey; let me accomplish it with You as my constant companion, and let me return to my home under Your protection. Let the host of angels surround and guard me like Jacob. Let Your angel stand by me in every danger as he stood by St. Paul. Let the company of Your angels travel with me going and coming, as with Joseph and Mary when they fled to Egypt with the young child Jesus, that I may remain safe from all misfortune, from thieves, murderers, and any other injury. O keeper of Israel, You never slumber or sleep; be a wall of fire around me by day and by night, as You were to Elisha, that no misfortune or disaster comes near me. Accompany me all along my path with Your angels' watch, as You guided the children of Israel through the desert with a pillar of cloud and of fire. Be my companion when I am traveling. Stay with me when I rest. Watch for me while I am sleeping. Yes, Lord, take care of me wherever I go and let me be commended to Your holy protection.

Grant that every hour there may be ringing in my ears the words You spoke to Abraham on his journey from home: "Walk before Me, and be blameless" (Genesis 17:1). Let me have before my eyes in foreign lands Your most holy presence. Keep me from desiring evil things while I am absent from home and traveling. Guard me against gluttony, dissipation, impudence, wickedness, conformity with worldly people, and committing sinful and shameful acts. Help me to return to my home with an untarnished conscience. Turn my eyes away from staring at wickedness; turn my mind away from evil desires when they arise in my heart. Keep me from contaminating either my body or soul on this journey. Grant that I may bear in mind that You hear all I speak, see all I do, and that You constantly observe me no matter what I am doing, so that I may not sin against You and draw down Your anger and disfavor on myself.

I commit to You all that belongs to me that I leave at home. Guard it against thieves, fire, and floods, and let me find everything as I left it upon my return. I commit to You also my loved ones whom I leave behind. O my God, I am going away from them, but You stay with them. Graciously turn from them every danger, every injury, every misfortune and sickness. Let me see them again in good health. Be their protector. Preserve, guide, and guard them, and let no sad message reach me. Let them live before You and enjoy Your protection and favor. In due time let me return safely to my home and find my loved ones safe and sound in Your protection.

O Lord Jesus, You journeyed with the two disciples in the guise of a traveler; be with me also when I am on my journey and fill my heart with good thoughts. Give me godly companions, that we may not by shameful words and wicked conversation sin against You on this journey, but may think about You and converse in Your most holy presence about Your goodness, Your wonderful works, Your faithfulness and truth. O my God, in Your name I have begun this journey; let me safely finish it in Your name, and I will with my loved ones heartily praise and glorify You for Your protection for as long as I live. Amen.

HYMN

Evening and morning,
Sunset and dawning,
Wealth, peace, and gladness,
Comfort in sadness:
These are Thy works; all the glory be Thine!
Times without number,
Awake or in slumber,
Thine eye observes us,
From danger preserves us,
Causing Thy mercy upon us to shine. LSB 726:1

PRAYER OF A PERSON LIVING IN A FOREIGN COUNTRY

Far from my friends and acquaintances I find myself in foreign areas, where I know very few people. But I know You, O Jesus, Son of the Most High, as my Immanuel, as my brother, as my best friend. And so I turn to You and humbly pray You to take care of me, and not to forsake me until I have returned to my home, indeed, until I have come to You in Your heavenly kingdom.

You have given the comforting promise to Your own: "Behold, I am with you always, to the end of the age" (Matthew 28:20). Fulfill this promise to me, and let me experience Your gracious presence at all times and in all places. You have hallowed all our travels when in Your youth You visited Jerusalem and other places, and when during Your ministry You traveled all around the land of the Jews, doing good and healing all who were oppressed by the devil. Let me always remember this, and following Your example, let me do nothing while I am away from home except what is good, what is praiseworthy, what is commendable. After Your resurrection, You joined Your disciples on the way to Emmaus, and at their request You stayed with them. Abide with me also, and do not leave me. Remain my companion, my protection, my comfort, my counselor, my guide, and my deliverer.

O Lord Jesus, let me experience Your closeness in every situation. Guard me against evil company, and if I should fall in with such, make me strong so that I may not sin and allow myself to be led astray. Give me strength to resist all allurements and temptations to sin, and to preserve a good conscience. Raise up for me faithful and good friends with whom I can be close and let me enjoy their company with profit and blessing to myself. Take me into Your protection, body and soul, and give me not only health of body but also this grace, that my body may shelter an uncontaminated soul and an unsullied conscience. Give me by Your Spirit the contentment of Moses, the chastity of Joseph, the godliness of Samuel, the temperance of Daniel. Fill my mind with wisdom that in all my doings I may act uprightly. Incline my will to virtue that I may exercise myself by doing what pleases You and so gain and keep a good reputation while I am away and bring home a good report and be able to enjoy Your favor. Bridle my passions, lest I become involved in strife and worry. Let me faithfully keep the unity of the Spirit in the bond of peace.

My Savior, strengthen me especially to the end that I may confess and glorify You before the world with lips and heart, with words and works. And if I should ever be attacked on account of my faith, grant me grace to be ready at all times to give a reason for the hope that is in me. Grant that I may in no way permit myself to be led astray into falling away from or denying Your teachings or into unfaithfulness toward You. Let Your Word be constantly a lamp to my feet and a light for my path. Then I shall be able to walk blamelessly and to stand before You at all times.

O my merciful God, keep me also in good health and preserve my life. Let me hear nothing but good tidings from my loved ones. Bless my business that brings me here, and let all my enterprises prosper. And when I have achieved my object, bring me safely and happily back to my loved ones, and I will pay You all my vows and praise and magnify You without ceasing for all the faithfulness and love You have shown me. On my return home let me ever bear in mind that I am both Your stranger and Your pilgrim, and that at all times I am to walk in such a way that I can complete my pilgrimage here on earth and happily enter my true fatherland in heaven and there live in communion with You forever. Amen.

HYMN

Guide me, O Thou great Redeemer,
Pilgrim through this barren land.
I am weak, but Thou art mighty;
Hold me with Thy pow'rful hand.
Bread of heaven, bread of heaven,
Feed me till I want no more;
Feed me till I want no more.

Open now the crystal fountain
Whence the healing stream doth flow;
Let the fiery, cloudy pillar
Lead me all my journey through.
Strong deliv'rer, strong deliv'rer,
Be Thou still my strength and shield;
Be Thou still my strength and shield.

When I tread the verge of Jordan,
Bid my anxious fears subside;
Death of death and hell's destruction,
Land me safe on Canaan's side.
Songs of praises, songs of praises
I will ever give to Thee;
I will ever give to Thee. LSB 918:1–3

PRAYER WHEN LYING SICK IN A FOREIGN COUNTRY

O infinitely good God, how very strange are the ways You lead us, how utterly incomprehensible are Your plans and Your guidance. This I confess, lying here sick. When I started my journey, I was well and healthy; now I am sick and miserable. While I was traveling, and until I arrived at this place, I was strong and robust; now I feel faint and weak. Thus the world that smiled at daybreak can change before the sun sets.

O my God, let this be to my benefit. Let me learn from it how vain and transitory is the life, happiness, and the prosperity of people here on earth, so that I may never place trust in these things, never set my affection on them, but strive and press forward to those things that are eternal and imperishable. Teach me to number my days, that I may apply my heart to wisdom. Teach me to see that, truly, man at his best is altogether vanity.

I must confess and acknowledge, indeed, that I am particularly grieved because I am so far from my loved ones and cannot enjoy their company and comforting conversation, and I do not know if I will ever see their faces again. But I will not lose heart on that account, but hope in You, my Father, who is with me also in these foreign areas, who cares for me even here, and surely will not fail to watch over me.

And so I calmly place myself into Your arms and say: Do with me as seems good in Your sight. Above all things, take loving care of my soul lest it perish. Turn me, and I shall be turned. Heal me, and I shall be healed. Graciously forgive me all sins with which I have ever offended and grieved You. Forgive them for the sake of Your Son, my reconciler, for Jesus Christ's sake. Strengthen my faith in His name, and let me always pray to You in His name and seek the help that I need. Work mightily in my heart by Your Spirit and fashion me here in time as You want me to be in eternity. Let Him bear witness to my spirit that I am a child of grace and an heir of everlasting life. Give me the patience I need, that I may not murmur or rebel against You, but accept in faith Your will and endure whatever You see fit to lay on me.

You, O Lord, are the one who gives power to the faint and strengthens those who have no might. Do this also to me according to Your great mercy. If I am to suffer much pain, let me consider that it is still less than my sins have deserved. If I am to suffer for a long time, let me nevertheless quietly submit to You and wait for the hour of my help and deliverance from morning to morning. And when it comes, let me be glad to see Your mercy. Do with me as seems best to You. Your will is best. Convince my heart that this is so. Teach me to pray with my Savior: "Father, if You are willing, remove this cup from Me. Nevertheless, not My will, but Yours, be done" (Luke 22:42).

If it is possible, if it pleases You, restore me to health. To that end, bless the medicine I take, and let me gain strength from day to day. Reward the faithfulness and care of those who are taking care of me, a stranger, and be their shield and their exceedingly great reward. But if it does not please You to let me rise again from this sickness; if it is Your will that I will find my grave in a foreign land, so be it. Only give me strength that I may surrender my will entirely to Your good and gracious will. In that event let me bear in mind that the whole earth is Yours, and You will be able to find and enliven my decayed bones here too. Take my absent friends and relatives into Your protection. Bless them with spiritual and temporal blessings. Let Your Spirit guide them in an even path, so that we may meet again yonder in the joy of heaven, and together praise and glorify You. Lord, I hope in You, and firmly believe that You will do all things well. My trust is in You alone! Amen.

HYMN

O God, forsake me not!
   Your gracious presence lend
  me;
Lord, lead Your helpless child;
   Your Holy Spirit send me
That I my course may run.
   O be my light, my lot,
My staff, my rock, my shield—
   O God, forsake me not!

O God, forsake me not!
   Take not Your Spirit from me;
Do not permit the might
   Of sin to overcome me.
Increase my feeble faith,
   Which You alone have
  wrought.
O be my strength and pow'r—
   O God, forsake me not!

O God, forsake me not!
   Lord, hear my supplication!
In ev'ry evil hour
   Help me resist temptation;
And when the prince of hell
   My conscience seeks to blot,
Be then not far from me—
   O God, forsake me not!

O God, forsake me not!
   Lord, I am Yours forever.
O keep me strong in faith
   That I may leave You never.
Grant me a blessèd end
   When my good fight is fought;
Help me in life and death—
   O God, forsake me not!
           LSB 731:1–4

PRAYER OF THANKSGIVING FOR A JOURNEY SAFELY COMPLETED

Lord God, merciful and gracious, patient and abundant in goodness and truth, You are able to do far more than all that we ask or think. You are rich in mercy and favor toward those who fear You and walk in Your ways. Today I come before Your most holy face for the first time in my own home since safely completing the journey I began in Your name and ended with Your aid. I vowed that I would give You thanks, and I now wish to pay my vow. Lift up my heart to You in fervent devotion and zeal and incline Your ears to my cry, my king and my God!

I cannot hide from You that my heart was anxious when I left home. I was mindful of the many dangers to which travelers are frequently exposed. How easily I might have met with disaster! How easily I might have fallen into the hands of those who might do me harm! How easily I might have met with an accident or sickness or something else that would have hindered my business! How easily my house and home and property might have suffered damage during my absence! But none of this has happened, and this I owe purely and alone to Your mighty protection, Your fatherly care, Your powerful aid, and Your faithful guidance. To You, to You alone, then, be blessing, praise, honor, and glory!

Not only did I enjoy Your protection, but You also showed me many mercies and much kindness as I traveled. You kept me in good health. You gave me faithful companions. You raised up friends for me. You blessed my business. You took all my possessions under Your protection so that I found them undamaged on my return. You kept my loved ones in good health, as I prayed for, and granted me a glad and joyful return to them. How great is Your mercy! How countless are Your blessings! How immeasurable are the riches of Your grace and love!

What shall I, what can I, render to You for all the goodness You have shown me? I am unable to do so. I am too weak and powerless for this task. I thank You with heart and voice and hands. With a heart filled with gratitude I say: Thousand, thousand thanks to You, O great King, for all these favors! Let this feeble thank-offering be acceptable to You because of Your mercy and the perfect atonement of Jesus. O Father, condescend to listen to my earthly hymns of praise and grant me also to raise in heaven with the angels loud "alleluias" to my King.

And now, my God, since I am again with my loved ones, let me continue to enjoy Your favor and grace with them. Stir me up to relate to them frequently the great things You have done for me on my journey, that they may be incited to praise and admiration of Your faithfulness and to have a childlike trust in You. Let me live with them in quiet, peace, and true contentment, and let me ever be mindful of this one thing, that I may serve You in righteousness and holiness all my days. Let me also well apply the blessing which You have bestowed on me through this journey, and always regard and use it with thanksgiving. In general, let me view the remainder of my life as a journey to eternity. Let me spend it in the power of Your good Spirit, in the fear of God, in piety, and in Your service. Let me pursue without wearying my pilgrimage to the heavenly fatherland, and successfully overcome all the obstacles in my path. And when I have finished my course, receive me into Your eternal, heavenly kingdom, and bring me to the rest which You have appointed and prepared for Your people in the age to come. There I will laud and praise You as You deserve. There I will glorify You. There I will extol You forever because of the faithfulness of Your love.

Praise and honor to the Father, Praise and honor to the Son, Praise and honor to the Spirit, Ever three and ever one: One in might and one in glory While unending ages run! Amen.   *LSB 909:4*

HYMN

All depends on our possessing
God's abundant grace and blessing,
    Though all earthly wealth depart.
They who trust with faith unshaken
By their God are not forsaken
    And will keep a dauntless heart.

He who to this day has fed me
And to many joys has led me
    Is and ever shall be mine.

He who ever gently schools me,
He who daily guides and rules me
 Will remain my help divine.

Many spend their lives in fretting
Over trifles and in getting
 Things that have no solid ground.
I shall strive to win a treasure
That will bring me lasting pleasure
 And that now is seldom found.

When with sorrow I am stricken,
Hope anew my heart will quicken;
 All my longing shall be stilled.
To His loving-kindness tender
Soul and body I surrender,
 For on God alone I build.

Well He knows what best to grant me;
All the longing hopes that haunt me,
 Joy and sorrow, have their day.
I shall doubt His wisdom never;
As God wills, so be it ever;
 I commit to Him my way.

If my days on earth He lengthen,
God my weary soul will strengthen;
 All my trust in Him I place.
Earthly wealth is not abiding,
Like a stream away is gliding;
 Safe I anchor in His grace. LSB 732:1–6

BELIEVING CHRISTIANS PRAY IN TIME OF WAR

EXHORTATION

Look, O Lord, for I am in distress; my stomach churns; my heart is wrung within me, because I have been very rebellious. In the street the sword bereaves; in the house it is like death. . . . He has bent His bow like an enemy, with His right hand set like a foe. . . . The Lord has become like an enemy. . . . In the dust of the streets lie the young and the old; my young women and my young men have fallen by the sword. Lamentations 1:20; 2:4, 5, 21

The three plagues with which God in His anger makes whole countries and cities waste and desolate are war, famine, and pestilence (Jeremiah 28:8). War is a severe punishment; for when God withdraws His protection from a country, its enemies soon make ready to attack it.

The reasons why God punishes a country with war and devastation are various: disobedience (Isaiah 1:19–20); living after the lusts of one's heart and setting aside the fear of God (Judges 4:1; 6:1); contempt of God's Word, either by not hearing it at all, or by failing to live according to it (Leviticus 26:14–17); and idolatry (Judges 2:12–14), whether it be obvious or hidden. Under this belongs dissipation, fornication, murder, the shedding of innocent blood, the oppression of strangers and widows, and the mistreatment of the poor. But when God calls to the sword and takes away peace (see Jeremiah 25:29), He also takes away the valor of the sword (see Psalm 89:43), so that a multitude of people and a great army obtain no victories, thus compelling them to flee before their enemies (Psalm 44:10) and bringing on destruction, sacking, and oppression of their country, and, finally, misery and wretchedness.

PRAYER

O God, we have provoked You to anger! We come before You in the anguish of our hearts and bend our knees before Your holy face. We bewail the great misery that our great sins and Your just anger have brought us. Lord, we dwelt in safety under Your protection. No sword frightened us because You were the foe of our foes and the enemy of our enemies. We went out and in at our gates in peace, and enjoyed the fruits of the land undisturbed. But now, O great God, You have withdrawn from us Your protection and our peace. The foe has started against us and unsheathed the sword. He threatens to burn, sack, and destroy our cities and to overrun our country.

What shall we say in our fright? We must confess that we have long ago deserved punishment and the rod of chastisement. Sadly, we have misused the times of peace and prosperity. When we ought to have been built up in You and walked in Your fear, serving and obeying You, we ended up treating Your Word with contempt, misusing Your holy name, practicing injustice and wickedness, and multiplying horrible vices among us. We are ashamed to speak of all our abominations before You, O God, whom we have provoked. They are crying to heaven anyway.

O merciful God, remember not our iniquities, for they are as many as the sands upon the shore, but according to Your mercy remember us for Your goodness' sake. We prostrate ourselves before You in supplication, relying not on our righteousness, but on Your grace and mercy. We have sinned and done evil; we have been wicked, we have apostatized and departed from Your commandments. O Lord, rebuke us not in Your anger, nor discipline us in Your hot displeasure. We flee to the Mercy Seat, to Jesus Christ, our only helper and advocate. Behold His blood and His wounds! O merciful God, have compassion on us! If You deal with us according to our sins and Your justice, the enemy will exterminate us, swallow us up, consume us with fire, and overwhelm us, and there will be no one to deliver us.

O mighty protector of the distressed, arise, lest we be overwhelmed. You can arm us with strength for the battle. You can cast down before us those who stand arrayed against us. In You is all our trust and all our hope in this great distress. Surely the wrath of man shall praise You. O God, how long will the adversary reproach? Will the enemy blaspheme Your name forever, as though none could deliver us from their hands? Deliver us, O God of our salvation, and forgive us our sins for Your name's sake. Take away from the enemies their courage; scatter them, and watch over our entire land, our houses and homes. Let peace spring up speedily, and turn from us the danger that threatens. Lord, to You belongs the honor of shattering swords, cutting spears in pieces, and burning chariots in the fire. O God of love, hear the cries of those who are now surrounded by dangers, and are in the hands of the enemy, and must endure many a disgraceful and merciless treatment. Have compassion on the poor, the widows, the aged and infirm, the children and the infants. Make a speedy end of this wasteful war, and hear our prayer for the sake of Your goodness and mercy.

God bless our native land; Firm may she ever stand Through storm and night. When the wild tempests rave, Ruler of wind and wave, Do

Thou our country save By Thy great might. So shall our prayers arise To God above the skies; On Him we wait. Thou who art ever nigh, Guarding with watchful eye, To Thee aloud we cry: God save the state! Amen.

LSB 965:1–2

HYMN

Eternal Father, strong to save,
Whose arm hath bound the restless wave,
Who bidd'st the mighty ocean deep
Its own appointed limits keep:
O hear us when we cry to Thee
For those in peril on the sea.

O Christ, whose voice the waters heard
And hushed their raging at Thy word,
Who walkedst on the foaming deep
And calm amid its rage didst sleep:
O hear us when we cry to Thee
For those in peril on the sea.

Most Holy Spirit, who didst brood
Upon the chaos dark and rude,
And bid its angry tumult cease,
And give, for wild confusion, peace:
O hear us when we cry to Thee
For those in peril on the sea.

O Trinity of love and pow'r,
Our people shield in danger's hour;
From rock and tempest, fire and foe,
Protect them wheresoe'er they go;
Thus evermore shall rise to Thee
Glad praise from air and land and sea. LSB 717:1–4

BELIEVING CHRISTIANS PRAISE AND THANK GOD FOR THE RESTORATION OF PEACE

EXHORTATION

Come, behold the works of the LORD, how He has brought desolations on the earth. He makes wars cease to the end of the earth; He breaks the bow and shatters the spear; He burns the chariots with fire. "Be still, and know that I am God. I will be exalted among the nations, I will be exalted in the earth!" The LORD of hosts is with us; the God of Jacob is our fortress. Psalm 46:8–11

No gladder tidings can ring out after a bloody and grievous war than this: "There is peace!" Then fugitives return to their homes; the banished have hope of regaining their own; the land recuperates and teams with joy because it is no longer trampled by the feet of the enemy.

Believing Christians regard such peace as a gift that comes down from above. Accordingly, with their heart and voice united, they praise God because He has made an end of the destruction, robbery, pillaging, slaughter, and burning, and because the inhabitants of the land have been delivered from the terror and violence of their foes. They return thanks because in the midst of the dangers of war, God protected them and their possessions and did not give them as spoil into the hands of their enemies.

They perceive that blessed peace is like the sun and the dew, which raises up and refreshes the drooping. They pray God to let the peace become permanent and to restrain all who would seek to disturb it. They employ the times of peace not for wild living and luxury, but for growth in their Christian faith and for serving their God without distraction.

PRAYER

Lord, You are gracious, merciful, and abundant in goodness. In Your justice You deprived our country of peace because we had misused our days of prosperity and peace; You allowed a bloody war to arise. You summoned our enemies for our chastisement; they had to draw their swords, slaughter us, lay the country waste, and fill us with terror and dread. Although we had deserved to be completely wiped out by this war, still in Your anger You remembered mercy. You brought about peace after all, and for that we return our glad and heartfelt thanks. At Your command the sword went back to its sheath, the refugees are returning, and we may again pass in and out of our gates quietly and without danger. Praise the Lord, O Jerusalem! Praise your God, O Zion! He strengthens the bars of your gates. He blesses your children within you. He makes peace in your borders.

What a blessed treasure peace is, and the whole country rejoices in it! Today You renew to us the promise: "You will dwell in your land securely. I will give peace in the land, and you shall lie down, and none shall make you afraid . . . and the sword shall not go through your land" (Leviticus 26:5–6). O Lord, make this peace to last during the time of our life; lift up Your face upon us and give us peace, as a glorious portion of that divine blessing that You have laid on Your people. Let our peace be like a stream of water that never diminishes, but wells up from its source and flows constantly. You alone maintain peace according to Your sure promise. Let righteousness and peace kiss one another, and righteousness look down from heaven.

Give us Your Holy Spirit, that we may not misuse this blessed peace in wasteful living, gluttony, and security, but for building ourselves up and walking in the fear of the Lord. Refresh the devastated land with Your blessing, and always regard us with thoughts of peace. At the end of our lives let us depart in peace and enter the home of peace. Amen.

HYMN

Now thank we all our God
   With hearts and hands and
voices,
Who wondrous things has done,
   In whom His world rejoices;
Who from our mothers' arms
   Has blest us on our way
With countless gifts of love
   And still is ours today.

Oh, may this bounteous God
   Through all our life be near us,
With ever joyful hearts
   And blessèd peace to cheer us
And keep us in His grace
   And guide us when perplexed
And free us from all ills
   In this world and the next!

All praise and thanks to God
　The Father now be given,
The Son, and Him who reigns
　With them in highest heaven,
The one eternal God,
　Whom earth and heav'n adore;
For thus it was, is now,
　And shall be evermore. LSB 895:1–3

BELIEVING CHRISTIANS PRAY TO GOD WHEN THEIR COUNTRY HAS BEEN VISITED WITH HARD TIMES AND FAMINES

EXHORTATION

Son of man, behold, I will break the supply of bread in Jeru-
salem. They shall eat bread by weight and with anxiety, and they
shall drink water by measure and in dismay. Ezekiel 4:16

As tame and wild animals are trained by means of hunger, so God, as a rule, puts a bit and bridle into the mouths of humans when they will not submit to Him. God seeks to attract them for a long time with blessings, but if they will not let His goodness lead them to repentance, He sends famine into their land, either by a failure of crops or by war, or by hard times and scarcity, or by withholding His blessing from the food, so that people eat and are not satisfied.

This chastisement is usually visited upon people when they esteem the Word of God lightly, and only think of high living (Isaiah 5:13); when they persecute godly people and the servants of God (Jeremiah 11:22); when they gladly hear the voice of false prophets (Jeremiah 14:15–16); when they are stiff-necked (Jeremiah 24:10); when they remain disobedient (Ezekiel 4:16); or when they practice violence toward their inferiors (2 Samuel 21:1–2). In the wake of famine comes poverty, distress, and starvation. When to such a physical famine there is an added spiritual hunger (Amos 8:11), the distress is unspeakable.

PRAYER

O righteous God, You render to everyone according to his works, and You allow wrath, tribulation, and anguish to come upon those who do evil. We come before Your most holy face, ashamed because we have sinned so grievously that You must force us to prayer and obedience by means of hunger. Oh, how abundantly You fed us in former years! We had bread in abundance; the earth brought forth the loveliest and best fruits. Like bands of love these gifts should have drawn us to You, the generous giver, and led us to repentance. But how shamefully were they misused for gluttony, high living, and excess, so that these very creatures had to groan because ungrateful people received them with ungrateful hands. Is it a wonder, then, that our fertile land bears nothing because of the sins of those dwelling in it? You chastise us with hard times, scarcity, and drought, so that the earth yields its fruits sparingly, and our country is oppressed with want.

O Lord, hear the cry of the poor who are begging for bread and cannot appease their hunger. Let Your heart be moved with the cries of the children, the wails of their parents, the distress that fills all homes in town and country. It seems that You have withdrawn Your blessing from our food: we eat, and are not satisfied; we take much food, and almost faint with hunger. And the cattle, the dumb creatures, are crying to their Creator for food.

O Lord, gracious and merciful, patient and abundant in goodness, have mercy on us. Return to us with Your blessing that You have withdrawn from us. Your rivers are full of water; visit the earth and water it. Let heaven hear the cry of the earth, and may You hear us from Your sanctuary. Let the famine cease. Return to us with Your grace. Feed the hungry. Gladden the poor. Bless our scant supply of bread, which is dealt out to us each day. We perceive now that we cannot live by bread alone, but chiefly by the Word of blessing that proceeds out of Your mouth and by which strength is put into our food. Let the fields soon be teaming again with fruits. Increase our little supply of meal like that of the widow of Zarephath (1 Kings 17:8–16), and let our small supply suffice for the support of many. Meanwhile let Your Word ever be our food, that we may derive nourishment from it. Your Word is the rejoicing of our hearts, our honey and honeycomb, and we will glorify and praise You for this mercy as long as we live. Amen.

HYMN

There is a time for ev'rything,
A time for all that life may bring:
A time to plant, a time to reap,
A time to laugh, a time to weep,
A time to heal, a time to slay,
A time to build where rubble lay,
A time to die, a time to mourn,
A time for joy and to be born,

A time to hold, then be alone,
A time to gather scattered stone,
A time to break, a time to mend,
A time to search and then to end,
A time to keep, then throw away,
A time to speak, then nothing say,
A time for war till hatreds cease,
A time for love, a time for peace.

Eternal Lord, Your wisdom sees
And fathoms all life's tragedies;
You know our grief, You hear our sighs—
In mercy, dry our tear-stained eyes.
From evil times, You bring great good;
Beneath the cross, we've safely stood.
Though dimly now life's path we trace,
One day we shall see face to face.

Before all time had yet begun,
You, Father, planned to give Your Son;
Lord Jesus Christ, with timeless grace,
You have redeemed our time-bound race;
O Holy Spirit, Paraclete,
Your timely work in us complete;
Blest Trinity, Your praise we sing—
There is a time for ev'rything! LSB 762:1–4

BELIEVING CHRISTIANS PRAY IN TIME OF WIDESPREAD SICKNESS

EXHORTATION

But if you will not obey the voice of the LORD your God or be careful to do all His commandments and His statutes that I command you today, then all these curses shall come upon you and overtake you. . . . The LORD will send on you curses, confusion, and frustration in all that you undertake to do, until you are destroyed and perish quickly on account of the evil of your deeds, because you have forsaken Me. The LORD will make the pestilence stick to you until he has consumed you off the land that you are entering to take possession of it. Deuteronomy 28:15, 20–21

When wrath, tribulation, and anguish come upon those that do evil (Romans 2:8–9), contagious diseases and pestilence must certainly be included in that anguish. To a large extent this plague comes when people put no faith in the word of warning and admonition (Numbers 14:12); when they serve God only outwardly and not with the heart (Jeremiah 14:12); when they even put God out of their minds entirely by their disobedience (Jeremiah 24:10; 27:9); when they despise the servants of God (Jeremiah 29:17); when the people become bold and unruly (Ezekiel 14:19); when fornication and murder are rampant (Ezekiel 33:26–27); when no admonition to repentance is any longer heeded (Amos 4:10); on account of adultery (Numbers 25:6–9); on account of blasphemy (2 Kings 19:35); on account of pride (2 Samuel 24:15); and also on account of other sins. Now, when God inflicts this chastisement, it is necessary that people repent because the Lord allows Himself to be entreated according to His mercy; hence David from among three plagues chose this one (2 Samuel 24:12–14) rather than the others.

PRAYER

O strong and mighty God, great is Your wrath against willful sinners who will not permit Your kindness to lead them to repentance. For a time You deal with people like a loving father, who seeks with much patience to draw back his disobedient children to himself, but then, when people willfully abuse Your grace, You manifest Yourself as a stern judge. We, too, are experiencing this now, O just God. We hear that in many places a contagious disease has appeared, devouring many thousands of people, so that death is a guest in many homes and there are not enough hands to bury the dead. We are consumed by Your anger, and by Your wrath we are troubled. Have we not strong reasons to fear that You will send this spreading contagion also into our borders and our city? O jealous God, we need not think that those on whom Your heavy rod is now descending are worse sinners than the rest; rather, we confess that we all deserve to perish like them. There is found among us security in our sinfulness, contempt of Your Holy Word, stubbornness, wastefulness, fornication, unrighteousness, worldliness, and pride. Yes, there is scarcely any fear of God in our land; the godly ceases and the faithful fail among the children of men. If You, O Lord, kept a record of iniquity, O Lord, who could stand?

O Lord, when You said, "Seek My face," my heart said to You, "Your face, Lord, do I seek" (Psalm 27:8). You have no pleasure in the death of the sinner, but that the sinner turn from his way and live. Therefore, we abhor ourselves and repent in dust and ashes. Do not look upon our countless sins; graciously pronounce us not guilty. Comfort us in our distress and remove all punishments from us. We have sinned with our ancestors; we have committed iniquity and done wickedly. Command the destroying angel who is wielding the sword of vengeance to cease, and say to him, "It is enough." Let us live, and we will glorify Your name. Although we do not deserve any mercy, we are in need of it. Although we are all children of death, You have promised the penitent that You would exercise mercy instead of justice toward them.

Oh, grant us Your grace and life, for Jesus' sake, our only mediator and advocate. Have mercy, have mercy upon us, O God of mercy! Be gracious to us; spare us, good Lord! Be gracious to us; help us, good Lord, our God! Have mercy on the poor and afflicted who have been seized with this violent pestilence, who must suffer hunger and grief, who are destitute of all nursing care, and forsaken by others. Lead them to the knowledge of Your grace in Christ, Your dear Son. Aid them with Your comfort and let Your Spirit witness to their spirit that they are God's children, though they have to die of this plague. O Lord, hear our prayer! Protect our country, and we shall say: The Lord has done great things for us. Yes, You can deliver all who come to You.

Since He is ours, We fear no powers, Not of earth nor sin nor death. He sees and blesses In worst distresses; He can change them with a breath. Wherefore the story Tell of His glory With hearts and voices; All heav'n rejoices In Him forever: Alleluia! We shout for gladness, Triumph o'er sadness, Love Him and praise Him, And still shall raise Him Glad hymns forever: Alleluia! Amen. *LSB 818:2*

HYMN

Evening and morning,
Sunset and dawning,
    Wealth, peace, and gladness,
    Comfort in sadness:
These are Thy works; all the glory
    be Thine!
Times without number,
Awake or in slumber,
    Thine eye observes us,
    From danger preserves us,
Causing Thy mercy upon us to shine.

Father, O hear me,
Pardon and spare me;
    Calm all my terrors,
    Blot out my errors
That by Thine eyes they may no more
    be scanned.
Order my goings,
Direct all my doings;
    As it may please Thee,
    Retain or release me;
All I commit to Thy fatherly hand.
    LSB 726:1–2

BELIEVING CHRISTIANS PRAY DURING A TIME OF THREAT BY FIRE

EXHORTATION

Behold, the Lord GOD was calling for a judgment by fire, and it devoured the great deep and was eating up the land. Then I said, "O Lord GOD, please cease! How can Jacob stand? He is so small!" The LORD relented concerning this; "This also shall not be," said the Lord GOD. Amos 7:4–6

From this passage we chiefly learn three things. In the first place: God always accomplishes something when He permits calamities to befall humanity, and especially when He permits a conflagration to start. Thus the prophet says: "The Lord God was calling for a judgment by fire." God summons fire and hurls it upon people directly when He flings His lightning and sets forests and houses on fire. Indirectly, however, He calls to the fire when He permits either the wicked to start it or carelessness to cause it.

It follows, then, that when Christians hear that a wildfire has broken out near their home, they say to themselves: This does not happen by blind chance, but the Lord has done it; for shall there be misfortune in the city and the Lord has not done it? They remember that they, too, are under the mighty hand of God, who can visit them also on this occasion. They bow before God and beg Him to comfort and protect them. Like children, they commit themselves to God's mercy, in firm assurance that all things must work together for those that love God.

Furthermore, we learn from the passage cited that God frequently uses fire to chastise and punish people. For the prophet says He called to the fire for a judgment; it was to devour a great deep and was already eating up a part. God punishes people's sins, and He does so not only because of His holiness, by which He reproves and hates sin, but also because of His righteousness, by which He fulfills the threats of His pun-

ishment and chastening that He has pronounced against the disobedient and wicked in His Word. Moreover, God really punishes people for
their sins, sometimes with individual, sometimes with general plagues.
He visits them with individual plagues when He lays crosses and sicknesses on them, withdraws His blessing from them, and lets them suffer
various kinds of distress. In such instances they have to realize and learn
by experience what it means to forsake the Lord and not to be afraid of
our God. But if this has no effect, He sometimes sends general plagues by
which He reveals His wrath against sinners. To this end He sometimes
employs fire also, and permits it to spread terror everywhere and to cause
great devastation.

In this way God punishes people chiefly for their contempt of preaching and His Word; for their ingratitude toward Him for the great and innumerable blessings they have received from Him, as is plainly shown by
the instance recorded in Numbers 11:1; for their persistent impenitence,
as can be seen from what happened to Sodom and Gomorrah according
to Genesis 19. Accordingly, Christians must beware of these sins with
exceptional care, lest they call down upon themselves and their brothers the fiery vengeance of God. And when they hear of a wildfire that
has broken out everywhere, they must regard it as a well-deserved, divine chastisement. They must remember their sins and seek to stay God's
chastening rod, lest it come down on them also. They must let the wildfire rouse them to repentance, to amendment of life, and to vowing and
rendering new obedience to God.

Finally, we see from the passage cited above that God can be moved
by earnest and eager prayer to dismiss His wrath and change it into mercy. The prophet says: "Then I said, 'O Lord God, please cease! How can
Jacob stand? He is so small!' The Lord relented concerning this; 'This also
shall not be,' said the Lord God." Thus, by the humble intercession of the
prophet for the people of God, God became graciously inclined toward
them and changed His thoughts of wrath to thoughts of peace, having
compassion on them and ceasing their punishment of fire. The prayer of
a righteous man has great power in its working. So believing Christians
must resort to prayer when a wildfire has broken out. They must commit
themselves and their possessions to the guardian care and protection of

God. They must faithfully pray both for those involved already in calamity and for those who are threatened by it. Believingly, fervently, and persistently, they are to sigh: O Lord, cease from Your avenging anger, for from whom are we to expect help but from You? And they will surely obtain mercy and find grace to help in time of need.

PRAYER

Lord, You are infinitely good and kind, but also terrifying when Your anger has been roused and when You reveal to mankind Your displeasure by Your judgments. Your gracious face, which I have beheld so often and in so many ways, is now hidden. I see now that You are angry. Who can stand before Your anger and shield himself from Your hot displeasure? From all sides I now hear confusion, cries, weeping, and wailing. My own heart faints; my strength has forsaken me; my soul is very much frightened. A wildfire has broken out, which could not have happened without Your will and permission.

I do not know what started this conflagration, but I know certainly that my sins and the sins of my brothers and sisters are the chief cause of it. These have come before You and put an end to Your patience with which You have borne with us for so long a time. At last You have been compelled to punish us, and to show that You are not a God who takes pleasure in wickedness, nor can evil dwell with You.

O yes, Lord, we are sinners; great sinners, one and all. We have deserved Your wrath. We do not conceal our iniquities. We confess that we have sinned against heaven and in Your sight, and that we are no longer worthy to be called Your children. We see now before us Your fiery indignation, and see that in a few moments You could destroy and demolish us all. But O Lord, we beg You not to do so. Cease from Your anger. In the midst of Your wrath, remember Your great mercy, mercy promised to those that seek Your face. However, do not remember our sins only, but also, yes, much more, the precious and all-sufficient atoning sacrifice of Your Son, our Savior Jesus Christ. Spare us for His sake, and do not reward us according to our works. Quench the fire of Your hot anger in the blood of the Lamb. O God Father, remember the death of Christ: behold His crimson wounds, the very payment and ransom for the sins of the whole world. This is our comfort at all times, and we hope in Your mercy. I, too, hope in it especially in the present distress and danger, and therefore turn to You, my only support and deliverer.

I commend to Your gracious charge and protection above all, my loved ones, my house, my goods, and all the gifts that Your hands have given. Keep the flames from spreading too far; let them be extinguished before they can reach my dwelling. Strengthen my faith, my trust, and my hope in Your goodness, lest I lose heart if the danger should come closer. Give me wisdom and understanding that I may conduct myself in such a way that will be to Your glory and my benefit. Let the whole calamity pass by happily in the end, and I will increasingly laud and praise Your name, telling what great things You have done for me.

O gracious God, have mercy on those who must now behold their homes and possessions wasted and consumed by the flames. Fill their hearts with courage and comfort to hope in You. Be their strong shield and mighty support in the great affliction that has come upon them, and graciously deliver them. Care also for those who are near the seat of danger. Command the fury of the flames to cease and not attack their dwellings. Speak the word only, and it will be done. Remember the precious promise You made to us when You said: "When you walk through fire you shall not be burned, and the flame shall not consume you. For I am the LORD your God, the Holy One of Israel, Your Savior" (Isaiah 43:2–3). Remember this promise and in Your great mercy bring it to pass.

Bless the good efforts being made even now to extinguish the fire, and let them succeed. Fill all who come to the aid of the suffering with true love, tender pity, and Your fear, that they may render their assistance and help honestly. And if evil persons mingle with them, intending to rob and to steal, touch their heart powerfully and cause them to turn away from their wicked purposes and not to grieve and injure the afflicted still more. Make a speedy end of our distress. Let order and quiet be restored in this place. Quench the smoldering flames and do not allow them to break out afresh.

However, grant also that we may be humbled and improved by this chastisement that You have decreed for us, and that we may be brought to fear Your wrath and no longer purposely act contrary to Your commandments. Help us to walk before You as long as we live in holiness and righteousness. Graciously hear this my prayer and the prayers of all other godly Christians, and send forth Your help, and we will praise and glorify You for this and all other benefits in time and afterwards in eternity.

Father, O hear me, Pardon and spare me; Calm all my terrors, Blot out my errors That by Thine eyes they may no more be scanned. Order my goings, Direct all my doings; As it may please Thee, Retain or release me; All I commit to Thy fatherly hand. Amen. *LSB 726:2*

HYMN

From depths of woe I cry to Thee,
In trial and tribulation;
Bend down Thy gracious ear to me,
Lord, hear my supplication.
If Thou rememb'rest ev'ry sin,
Who then could heaven ever win
Or stand before Thy presence?

Thy love and grace alone avail
To blot out my transgression;
The best and holiest deeds must fail
To break sin's dread oppression.
Before Thee none can boasting
stand,
But all must fear Thy strict de-
mand
And live alone by mercy.

Therefore my hope is in the Lord
And not in mine own merit;
It rests upon His faithful Word
To them of contrite spirit
That He is merciful and just;
This is my comfort and my trust.
His help I wait with patience.

And though it tarry through the
night
And till the morning waken,
My heart shall never doubt His
might
Nor count itself forsaken.
O Israel, trust in God your Lord.
Born of the Spirit and the Word,
Now wait for His appearing.

Though great our sins, yet greater
still
Is God's abundant favor;
His hand of mercy never will
Abandon us, nor waver.
Our shepherd good and true is He,
Who will at last His Israel free
From all their sin and sorrow.
LSB 607:1–5

BELIEVING CHRISTIANS PRAY WHEN THEY HAVE SUFFERED BY FIRE

EXHORTATION

The LORD gave, and the LORD has taken away; blessed be the name of the LORD. Job 1:21

What excellent words pious Job muttered as so many evil tidings reached him, touching his children and his earthly possessions. One of the messages he received was: "The fire of God fell from heaven and burned up the sheep and the servants and consumed them" (Job 1:16). Even this dreadful message did not terrify or unsettle him. Here is an excellent example to Christians who are reduced to similar conditions by a fire that has damaged their goods and property. Let them compare their conduct with the model conduct of godly and pious people and follow their example, just as Sirach exclaims: "Consider the ancient generations and see: who ever trusted in the Lord and was put to shame?" (Sirach 2:10 RSV); and also Paul, who writes: "Whatever was written in former days was written for our instruction, that through endurance and through the encouragement of the Scriptures we might have hope" (Romans 15:4).

And so, when Christians, by the inscrutable and righteous counsel of God, are visited by misfortune, so that they must forfeit and lose much of their property, they must compose themselves and strive to follow the example of Job. This godly man not only accepted with composure whatever the hand of God brought his way, but he also resigned himself trustingly to the will and guidance of God.

True Christians must do likewise and therefore observe the following duties: Their first duty is not to believe themselves forsaken by God, but to approach Him with childlike humility and call upon Him for other and renewed blessings. Their second duty is not to lose heart when they see before them a scantier supply than formerly, but to pray and labor more diligently, and at the same time believe firmly that God is able to restore to them abundantly what they have lost. Their third duty is to trust firmly in God, and to be assured that He has thousands of ways of repairing the damage they have suffered, and that He will certainly do this according to His great faithfulness after He has attained His loving purposes regarding them.

If Christians act in this way, they will definitely notice and experience that it is an easy thing for God to bless them and make them rich again, that He will remove their want and deal with them in such a way that in the end they will be forced to exclaim from a heart stirred to His praise: Blessed be the name of the Lord!

PRAYER

Lord God almighty, what a fearful thing it is to fall into Your hands! How unbearable is Your wrath when poured out on us! We have now experienced this, since You not only visited us with a fire but also have taken away from us a great portion of Your former blessings. We confess frankly that we have justly merited Your punishment for our sins. We confess our sins to You and do not hide our iniquity. We have not made faithful use of Your gifts as we should have. We have at times been unjust stewards. Perhaps we owe You more than ten thousand talents. No wonder, then, that You have thus chastised and punished us in Your righteous wrath. We have sinned so grievously! We have grossly insulted Your divine majesty! We prostrate ourselves before You and humbly beg Your mercy. We plead guilty and repent in dust and ashes. We seek Your face. Let us find grace before You for the sake of Jesus, our Lord! Incline Your ear and hear us in our pitiful weeping and wailing. Do not rebuke us in Your anger or chasten us in Your wrath, but rather be gracious to us, for we are weak. Heal us, O Lord, for our bones are troubled. Be merciful to us according to Your goodness; according to the multitude of Your tender mercies blot out our transgressions. Enter no further into judgment with Your servants, for in Your sight no man living can be justified.

Remember that we are dust and ashes. Show us a token of Your kindness. Comfort us again after You have smitten us so sorely. Heal us after wounding us so severely. Restore to us by Your blessing what the flames have devoured and reduced to ashes. Raise up compassionate and kind hearts for us that will lovingly assist and help us. Bless our calling, our labor, and the work of our hands. Yes, prosper our work for Your name's sake. Let goodness and mercy follow us all the days of our life, and let us never experience Your eternal wrath, which we have merited with our sins. Make us truly cautious, lest we be careless in handling fire and light and cause terror and injury to our fellow human beings.

Above all, though, make us truly pious. Grant that the cross and suffering that we have endured may lead us to You and keep us with You until our end. Give us strength to avoid sin and to walk before You in newness of life. Let us rightly use the new blessings that You bestow on us in such a way that we may be able to render a good account to You. Lead us at all times by Your Spirit into the land of uprightness, and graciously bring us at last into Your heavenly kingdom, that from the beginning You have prepared for those who love You. Amen.

No danger, thirst, or hunger, No pain or poverty, No earthly tyrant's anger Shall ever vanquish me. Though earth should break asunder, My fortress You shall be; No fire or sword or thunder Shall sever You from me. Amen.   *LSB 724:8*

HYMN

As rebels, Lord, who foolishly have wandered
*   Far from Your love—unfed, unclean, unclothed—*
Dare we recall Your wealth so rashly squandered,
*   Dare hope to glean that bounty which we loathed?*

Still we return, our contrite words rehearsing,
*   Speech, that within Your warm embrace soon dies;*
All of our guilt, our shame, our pain reversing
*   As tears of joy and welcome fill Your eyes.*

A feast of love for us You are preparing;
*   We who were lost, You give an honored place!*
"Come, eat; come, drink, and be no more despairing—
*   Here taste again the treasures of My grace."* *LSB 612:1–3*

BELIEVING CHRISTIANS THANK GOD AFTER SAFELY PASSING THROUGH A FIRE

EXHORTATION

Rejoice with those who rejoice, weep with those who weep.
Romans 12:15

This is an admonition that earnestly calls all Christians to sympathetic interest in everything that happens to their fellow human beings. It is an admonition that they should be mindful of at all times, especially when they see their sisters and brothers visited with fires and other calamities, and see them eating their bread with tears and mingling their drink with weeping. When they observe this, they must weep with them and share their sorrow as a sorrow that they experience with them, because they are members with them of one body. But when they see that their fellow human beings are recovering, and, after passing through their anxiety, are becoming joyful again, they must join them and raise their voices in songs of joy to the honor of Him who has so gloriously helped them and done all things well.

When a fire has started, but has soon been put out, Christians must, first of all, show sympathy to their neighbor by refusing to rejoice over the misfortune that has befallen him. They must not wish him any such thing, thinking: "That's what I like to see!" That is a proof of malice, meanness, and lack of love—none of which are options for Christians. They must rather reflect that the fire might just as well have started with them as with their neighbors; that it might have damaged them as well as others, and they must, accordingly, show the same interest in it as if it had happened to them, and must mourn and weep with a sorrowful heart.

Further, they must refrain from all uncharitable judgments; they must not pronounce anyone injured by the fire the greatest sinners and regard themselves as holier and better than others. They must not boldly declare that this misfortune that has befallen their neighbors is a just punishment of their wickedness, but rather put their hand on their mouth and say to themselves: "It is the Lord's doing; and who has ever been His counselor?"

Christians who have suffered no damage by the fire must show and prove to the fire-stricken their genuine sympathy in still other ways. They must return to the unfortunate persons anything they had held during the fire for safe-keeping, and not withhold the least thing. That would be stealing and would still more grieve those who are already suffering—and that would be inexcusable.

Finally, they must show their sympathy also in this way, that they contribute gladly, willingly, and liberally, according to their means, toward the relief of the sufferers, if the latter request it, just as they would wish their fellows to do for them in a similar case. Thus they weep with them that weep, and share their distress and affliction. In like manner Christians must rejoice with them that do rejoice. When they see that their injured brothers and sisters take heart again, that they lift up their voices to God and thank Him because in their distress He was the health of their countenance and their God, they must join them in spirit, praising and glorifying God, and must from the heart offer Him thanks for having relieved their fellows, just as they would give thanks for their own protection and safety. If Christians do this, they discharge a duty, and that brings nothing but favor and blessing. God is well pleased with them. He takes them under His protection. He will remember them in future troubles and deliver them. He will always let them taste and see that He is good.

PRAYER

O holy and righteous God, You have brought Your judgment upon us for our punishment, chastisement, and improvement. You have indeed shown us Your earnestness. But You have at the same time done great things for us, so that we are forced to confess: You are righteous, O Lord, and just in all Your doings. I am still trembling when I think of the cries, groans, wailing, and weeping that but a short while ago filled my ears on all sides. I am still unable to compose myself when I recall how many parents, children, infants, sick, and dying persons were in imminent danger of being devoured by the flames, how they cried to You in their distress, and how many thousand might have been rendered unhappy.

You have indeed permitted many people to lose all they had and become poor, but in Your anger You remembered mercy. You have commanded the conflagration to halt and not spread further. You have heard the sighs of the distressed and turned Your gracious countenance to us again, so that the violent flames have not consumed everything. What mercy and goodness! For this we give You praise and glory. However, we wish to praise and thank You especially for the great mercy that You have shown to the poor on this occasion.

I am not better than my brothers and sisters; I have deserved a similar punishment, but You have mercifully spared me. You have given me courage and comfort in the midst of trouble. You have kept the fire from my dwelling. You have left me and my loved ones, my goods and possessions, unscathed. Oh, how shall I ever praise You for this? Thousand, thousand thanks to You, my King, for Your mercy! "Oh, that I had a thousand voices To praise my God with thousand tongues! My heart, which in the Lord rejoices, Would then proclaim in grateful songs To all, wherever I might be, What great things God has done for me" (*LSB 811:1*). But because my ability is too feeble and poor to thank You, O God, as the goodness and favor which You have shown me require, accept my will for the deed and be pleased to accept my poor stammering.

Grant me at the same time ability and strength to consecrate my entire life to You, and to make a thank-offering to You, that I may diligently shun sin, zealously strive for holiness, unwavering cling to You, and faithfully serve You until my blessed end. Thus show me Your mercy for Jesus Christ's sake, and keep me in Your grace, that I may enjoy it here in time and hereafter in eternity.

However, I commend to Your special care those who have suffered by the fire which has now been extinguished. Raise them up with Your divine consolations, and make them see Your holy will. Give them patience in their affliction, and let them with true resignation cling to You and Your grace. Restore to them by Your blessing the losses they have suffered, and give the grace to perceive Your fatherly love, goodness, and faithfulness toward them, and to praise and glorify You without end in the age to come.

Lord, our God, be gracious and merciful to us in the days ahead. Take us daily into Your sheltering protection. Guard us against future danger by fire. Mercifully remember us at all times. Do good unto us in Your good pleasure for Your mercies' sake. Do good to us until the end of our days, and we shall offer You the fruit of our lips, as we are now doing, bending before You and saying:

O bless the Lord, my soul! Let all within me join And aid my tongue to bless His name Whose favors are divine. O bless the Lord, my soul! Nor let His mercies lie Forgotten in unthankfulness And without praises die! 'Tis He forgives thy sins; 'Tis He relieves thy pain; 'Tis He that heals thy sicknesses And makes thee young again. He crowns thy life with love When ransomed from the grave; He that redeemed my soul from hell Hath sov'reign pow'r to save. He fills the poor with good; He gives the suff'rers rest. The Lord hath judgments for the proud And justice for th' oppressed. His wondrous works and ways He made by Moses known, But sent the world His truth and grace By His beloved Son. Amen.

LSB 814:1–6

HYMN

From all that dwell below the skies
Let the Creator's praise arise;
*   Alleluia, alleluia!*
Let the Redeemer's name be sung
Through ev'ry land by ev'ry tongue.
*   Alleluia, alleluia!*
*   Alleluia, alleluia, alleluia!*

Eternal are Thy mercies, Lord;
Eternal truth attends Thy Word.
*   Alleluia, alleluia!*
Thy praise shall sound from shore to shore
Till suns shall rise and set no more.
*   Alleluia, alleluia!*
*   Alleluia, alleluia, alleluia!*

All praise to God the Father be,
All praise, eternal Son, to Thee.
*   Alleluia, alleluia!*

Whom with the Spirit we adore
Forever and forevermore:
Alleluia, alleluia!
Alleluia, alleluia, alleluia! LSB 816:1–3

BELIEVING CHRISTIANS PRAY TO GOD DURING A LONG BOUT OF WET WEATHER

EXHORTATION

For behold, I will bring a flood of waters upon the earth to destroy all flesh in which is the breath of life under heaven. Everything that is on the earth shall die. Genesis 6:17

Thus God long ago declared His mind to pious Noah, and revealed to him a severe judgment that He intended to send upon a sinful world. In this way God taught Noah, in the first place, that the coming flood was caused by God alone and depended on His wisdom and power, as He said: "I will bring a flood of waters upon the earth."

God reveals to Noah, furthermore, that He intends to do this in anger on account of man's sins. Finally, God remarks that He intends to use this flood for the punishment and destruction of sinners, for He says: "to destroy all flesh in which is the breath of life under heaven. Everything that is on the earth shall die." All this happened as foretold. The deluge came, the waters rose, all flesh perished, all that breathed and had not entered the ark with Noah died.

This is to us a convincing proof both of God's truthfulness, according to which He fulfills most accurately all His predictions, His threats as well as His promises, and of His justice, according to which He bears indeed with the transgressions of humanity for a long time and overlooks them, but punishes them when they will not turn from their sins and repent. And though God has promised that He will not again chastise the world with a universal flood and destroy people, though this fact is settled to all eternity, still, for the purpose of humbling and rousing the sinful to repentance, God at times sends floods, violent torrents of rain, and continuous wet weather, when the rain seems never to stop.

Now, when Christians observe these occurrences, they remember, first, that they come from God and are happening as part of His wise government. Accordingly, they commit themselves trustingly into His hand, in the firm confidence that God will do all things well.

In such visitations Christians reflect, furthermore, that God is angry with them because of their sins and disobedience. Accordingly, they examine themselves and seek to know their evil ways and living, to feel sorry for it, and in genuine repentance, to seek grace and forgiveness for the sake of Jesus Christ.

Finally, Christians reflect on such occasions that they could easily turn to their ruin. They are not indifferent, but they revolve in their minds what God might do to them. This leads them to perceive readily that, if the wet season would be drawn out too long, the ground would become too soft, the fruits of the field would rot, vegetation would be destroyed, food would be lacking for humans and animals, want, famine, hunger, sickness, and ultimately, universal distress would arise. This drives them to God: They commit themselves into His hand. They cry to Him and call on Him in their trouble. They beg Him to avert the punishment that threatens them. They seek with childlike confidence the help and deliverance they need in such days. If they do this, God will incline His heart toward them again, and will become as gracious to them as He was angry before. He will have compassion on them and grant them fruitful seasons and fill their hearts with food and gladness.

PRAYER

O God, glorious in power and majesty, You have laid the foundations of the earth and have created all that lives and moves and has being. We see with our eyes that You rule and order all things according to Your good pleasure. How soon You can change the face of the earth! How soon You can deprive it of its beauty and glory! How soon You can withdraw from us the goods and blessings that You had only recently given to us!

We experience this especially at this time, when You have opened the windows of heaven and caused the rain to fall without ceasing. Everything is sad and gloomy; the world appears downcast. The sun withholds its cheering light and warm rays. Our eyes and hearts feel oppressed because everywhere we behold dark and heavy clouds. The earth is covered with water, the grass and the fruits of the field are about to rot. The rivers are rising, and we are threatened with floods. The roads are becoming impassable, and make trade and commerce difficult. Who can tell what other damage and losses may still be caused by the calamity that has been visited on us?

O Lord, look upon our distress, and in Your mercy have compassion on us. You are plainly showing that You are angry with us. And we know full well that we have roused Your anger by our sins, by our disobedience, our unfaithfulness, and our obstinacy. Indeed, we are sinners, great sinners, and have fallen utterly short of Your glory. We have sinned against You and are not worthy to be called Your children. We have deserved, fully deserved, that You should take away Your blessings from us and make us feel Your displeasure instead. And so we confess our sins to You and do not hide our iniquities. We humble ourselves before You in true repentance, and we pray for Your mercy and grace.

Return to us with mercy after You have so keenly smitten and afflicted us. Remember us and bless us. Remember us for good. Remember that we are dust and ashes. Remember the perfect atonement of Jesus, and for His sake let mercy rule over us rather than justice. You have promised that while the earth remains, seedtime and harvest, summer and winter, cold and heat, day and night will not cease. You have promised to satisfy the desire of every living thing on earth. You have made the precious promise never again to destroy the earth or its inhabitants by a flood. Remember this promise now, and fulfill it for us, O God, You who are rich in grace and faithfulness! Clear the murky sky and cause the glorious sun to shine once again. Dry and warm the moist earth. Let everything grow again and ripen fully, so that in due season we may gather with joy our needful supply of earth's bounty. Grant us in the future weather that is seasonable for our crops. Guard us from hailstorms and tempests. Give us the early and latter rain in season, and let the cheering sun again refresh the earth now that You have watered it, that the grass may grow for the cattle and grain for the use of human beings.

However, let us also receive with gratitude the gifts You have so wonderfully preserved and bestowed on us, and let us never forget the great things You have done in our behalf. Soften our hard hearts by the goodness and the truth You have shown us, that we may sincerely mend our lives, shun intentional sins, follow after righteousness and godliness, and until our end walk before You in ways that please You. At last receive us by Your grace into Your eternal, heavenly kingdom, keeping us faithful to the end. Then we will render you more perfect thanks than we can show You in our present weakness for all the benefits that You have showered on us. Where sweetest hymns Your saints forever raise You, we, too, shall praise You!

Holy, holy, holy! Though the darkness hide Thee, Though the eye of sinful man Thy glory may not see, Only Thou art holy; there is none beside Thee, Perfect in pow'r, in love, and purity. Holy, holy, holy! Lord God Almighty! All Thy works shall praise Thy name in earth and sky and sea. Holy, holy, holy, merciful and mighty! God in three persons, blessed Trinity! Amen.

LSB 507:3–4

HYMN

Rejoice, my heart, be glad and sing,
A cheerful trust maintain;
For God, the source of ev'rything,
Your portion shall remain.

He is your treasure, He your joy,
Your life and light and Lord,
Your counselor when doubts annoy,
Your shield and great reward.

Why spend the day in blank despair,
In restless thought the night?
On your Creator cast your care;
He makes your burdens light.

Did not His love and truth and pow'r
Guard ev'ry childhood day?
And did He not in threat'ning hour
Turn dreaded ills away?

He only will with patience chide,
His rod falls gently down;
And all your sins He casts aside

In ocean depths to drown.

His wisdom never plans in vain
Nor falters nor mistakes.
All that His counsels may ordain
A blessèd ending makes.

Upon your lips, then, lay your hand,
And trust His guiding love;
Then like a rock your peace shall stand
Here and in heav'n above. LSB 737:1–7

BELIEVING CHRISTIANS PRAY TO GOD DURING CONTINUOUS HOT WEATHER AND DROUGHT

EXHORTATION

Elijah was a man with a nature like ours, and he prayed fervently that it might not rain, and for three years and six months it did not rain on the earth. Then he prayed again, and heaven gave rain, and the earth bore its fruit. James 5:17–18

The real aim of the holy apostle James in placing this example of the prophet Elijah before us was not at all to teach us that it had been at the option and power of this prophet to procure rain for the land or to withdraw it, but rather to show us that believing, sincere, and God-pleasing prayer has great power and can accomplish many things. By citing this instance, the apostle wishes to confirm and render unquestionable his previous statement: "the prayer of a righteous person has great power as it is working" (5:16).

We gather three truths from the incident that he has cited. First, that God alone is the dispenser of rain, that He alone has power to send us rain or to withhold it. It is reserved to His will alone to open the heavens or to keep them closed. Not only does this power belong to God, as the Lord of creation, the creator, preserver, and sustainer of the world, who

can do whatever He pleases and has everything under His control, but it
is also emphatically ascribed to Him alone in His Holy Word. For this is
what the Prophet Jeremiah writes: "Are there any among the false gods
of the nations that can bring rain? Or can the heavens give showers? Are
you not He, O LORD our God? We set our hope on You, for You do all
these things" (Jeremiah 14:22). It is God, then, who causes the rain to fall
or not upon the earth; He orders wet seasons and droughts. And so Elijah
turns to Him in prayer. Accordingly, when we see what is happening on
earth, we must at all times acknowledge and humbly revere His hand and
counsel in it all. Christians, then, must not ascribe the advent or absence
of rain to nature or fate, but to the Lord of creation. They recognize the
working and rule of God in this matter and entirely submit to it.

The other truth is this: it is a great mercy of God when He sends rain
in due season, but when He withholds it, this is severe punishment. Elijah's prayer to God relates to both of these acts. At first he prayed for the
cessation of rain, in order that the people might be punished for their
sins. Afterward, he prayed God to remove the punishment, to change
His wrath into mercy, and to refresh the parched land once more with
rain. And, indeed, it is a great mercy of God when He sends us rain. The
soil is made soft by it and fit to produce fruit. The seeds lying in the earth
are prepared for germination and made to sprout. Fields and forests are
invigorated. Humanity and beasts are refreshed. All nature becomes ani-
mated and is preserved in its glory. Hence, who would not acknowledge
that rain is a true blessing that God by His grace bestows on humanity? For this reason God even promises this blessing especially to those
who walk in His ways and observe His commandments and do them. He
expressly says: "And if you will indeed obey My commandments that I
command you today, to love the LORD your God, and to serve Him with
all your heart and with all your soul, He will give the rain for your land
in its season, the early rain and the later rain, that you may gather in
your grain and your wine and your oil. And He will give grass in your
fields for your livestock, and you shall eat and be full" (Deuteronomy
11:13–15).

However, as it is a great mercy of God when He sends the needed rain
for a land, so it is, on the other hand, a grievous and severe punishment

when He withholds rain and smites a land with drought and a season of hot weather. God permits this punishment to overtake people when they sin against Him and do not walk in His commandments. This punishment is as just as it is severe and sharp. How wretched and distressing everything looks when the rain fails and the heat and drought become oppressive! The earth cracks, and has no power to produce its plants. The meadows become like deserts. The trees decay and the fruit drops. The cattle thirst and people languish. Famine, want, sickness, and pests easily arise. In the midst of summer the entire land looks like it has been robed in a shroud. What a sad sight! What a keenly felt punishment! When we behold and feel it, we must not remain indifferent, but rather commune with our own heart, acknowledge our own transgressions, with a humble and penitent heart seek reconciliation with God through Jesus Christ, and in a contrite spirit call on Him to mitigate to us His just punishment and for turning it away altogether.

The third truth is this: sincere and God-pleasing prayer is the surest means of obtaining from God every blessing, also this favor, that He removes our punishment and refreshes and saturates the parched ground with blessed rain. The example of Elijah shows this. He was indeed a prophet of the Lord, but in other respects a man, a sinful mortal, powerless and feeble, as we are. He prayed, and God granted his request. He prayed in accordance with God's will and good pleasure, and he was heard. We can obtain good fortune in the same way. We can have the same blessing; for with God there is no respect of persons. He accepts whoever fears Him and does what is righteous. He hears the person who asks anything according to His will. Accordingly, when Christians see that God has extended His hand to punish them, when they see that He withholds the rain from them and visits them with a season of heat and drought, they must have recourse to prayer, and offer their prayer in such a manner that it must come before God and be a sweet smell to Him. They must pray, sincerely acknowledging their sins, seeking forgiveness of them by faith in Christ Jesus, banishing even the least doubt from their hearts while they pray, and never becoming slack, but persevere in prayer, until the desired help has been granted to them. Then they may rest assured that God will hear them and give them the desire of their heart.

Then they will soon behold the fulfillment of their request, for the Lord is near to all who call upon Him, to all who call upon Him in truth. He fulfills the desire of those who fear Him; He hears their cry and saves them!

PRAYER

O Lord our God, You are gracious and merciful, long-suffering and abundant in goodness and truth. Help us now! In great distress we come before You to beg Your mercy. Help us in this great affliction that has come upon us. Help us and graciously deliver us from it. You have threatened Your people of long ago that if they would not obey Your voice and live according to Your commandments and laws, You would make the heavens above them brass and the earth beneath their feet iron, give them dust and ashes instead of rain for their land, and punish them even to the point of destroying them from the earth. You are now beginning to fulfill this just and terrible threat also on us. For some time You have visited us with continuous hot weather and a drought that withers everything. For quite a while You have shut up the heavens against us and commanded the clouds either to fly past or to give us no rain. It seems as if the heaven above us had become brass and the earth beneath us iron. How sad and pitiable everything looks in the fields and meadows, on the mountains and in the valleys, in the fruit-gardens and vineyards—indeed, everywhere! The earth gapes and groans to be refreshed. People and animals pant from the great heat. The trees are drying up. The grass withers. Nowhere are fruits able to thrive and mature. The cattle lack fodder and our rivers, streams, and wells must finally become dry, and we shall have to suffer a famine of water. What sad results that will bring about!

O Lord, behold our distress and make an end of it. We must indeed acknowledge before Your holy countenance that we have fully merited such hard punishments with our persistent disobedience toward Your commandments, with our base ingratitude toward Your many blessings, and with our appalling misuse of the bounties You have showered on us. Yes, we are forced to confess that You would do us no wrong at all if You would afflict us with even more grievous punishments for our many transgressions. But, O Father of mercy, behold, we prostrate ourselves before You, crushed and humbled. Forgive our grievous sins and turn

Your gracious countenance toward us again. Have compassion on us and at least turn this severe affliction from us.

It is You who does so much good for us. You give rain from heaven and fruitful seasons. You fill our hearts with food and gladness. You water the hills from Your chambers; the earth is satisfied with the fruit of Your works. You cause grass to grow for the cattle and plants for man to cultivate, to bring forth food from the earth. And so the eyes of all look to You, and You give them their food at the proper time. You open Your hand and satisfy the desire of every living thing. Remember us now for Your name's sake and refresh us with an invigorating and penetrating rain. O almighty Creator and preserver of all things, open the windows of heaven, visit the earth again as it pants for Your bounty. Water the land that the fruits in our farms, orchards, and vineyards may ripen; that the plants in our fields may grow, and grass come up in our meadows, so that people and animals everywhere may again find their food and sustenance.

O God, though we have been disobedient children in the past, nevertheless we are Your children, reconciled to You by Christ. And so we humbly call upon You for His sake: graciously hear our sighing and prayers in this urgent and persistent need. Gladden every living thing with water from above. Protect our country and our homes also in the future from contagious diseases, famine, and other well-earned chastisements. Let the punishment we have now experienced serve for our improvement and our sincere conversion to You. To that end, let Your Spirit enter our hearts and make us entirely different people—people who faithfully walk in Your ways and observe Your commandments. Sanctify us wholly through Him, that our whole spirit, soul, and body may be preserved blameless until the coming of our Lord Jesus Christ. O Lord our God, we hope in Your goodness! Let us live before You and spread abroad Your praise. Hear our prayer, and we shall be heartily thankful for Your mercy, and shall highly exalt Your name as long as we live, here in time and hereafter in eternity. Hear us, dear Father, in heaven; for You alone are our God. Hear us according to Your faithfulness that never ends, according to which You have promised us comfort and help in every trouble. Hear us for Your own sake.

Abide with Your protection Among us, Lord, our strength, Lest world and Satan fell us And overcome at length. Abide, O faithful Savior, Among us with Your love; Grant steadfastness and help us To reach our home above. Amen. *LSB 919:5–6*

HYMN

Hear us, Father, when we pray,
Through Your Son and in Your Spirit.
By Your Spirit's Word convey
All that we through Christ inherit,
That as baptized heirs we may
Truly pray.

When we know not what to say
And our wounded souls are pleading,
May Your Spirit, night and day,
Groan within us interceding;
By His sighs, too deep for words,
We are heard.

Jesus, advocate on high,
Sacrificed on Calv'ry's altar,
Through Your priestly blood we cry:
Hear our prayers, though they may falter;
Place them on Your Father's throne
As Your own.

By Your Spirit now attend
To our prayers and supplications,
As like incense they ascend
To Your heav'nly habitations.
May their fragrance waft above,
God of love. LSB 773:1–4

FOR THE USE OF THE DYING AND THOSE ATTENDING THEM

Scripture Index